Aesthetic Approaches to Children's Literature

An Introduction

Maria Nikolajeva

The Scarecrow Press, Inc.
Lanham, Maryland • Toronto • Oxford
2005

SCARECROW PRESS, INC.

Published in the United States of America
by Scarecrow Press, Inc.
A wholly owned subsidary of
The Rowman & Littlefield Publishing Group, Inc.
4501 Forbes Boulevard, Suite 200, Lanham, Maryland 20706
www.scarecrowpress.com

PO Box 317
Oxford
OX2 9RU, UK

British Library Cataloguing in Publication Information Available

Library of Congress Cataloging-in-Publication Data

Nikolajeva, Maria.
    Aesthetic approaches to children's literature : an introduction / Maria
Nikolajeva.
        p.   cm.
    Includes bibliographical references and index.
    ISBN 0-8108-5426-0 (pbk. : alk. paper)
    1. Children's literature, American—History and criticism—Theory, etc.
2. Children's literature, English—History and criticism—Theory, etc.
3. Children—Books and reading—North America.   I. Title.
PS490.N55   2005
810.9′9282—dc22   2004024130

∞ ™ The paper used in this publication meets the minimum requirements of
American National Standard for Information Sciences—Permanence of Paper for
Printed Library Materials, ANSI/NISO Z39.48-1992. Manufactured in the United
States of America.

Contents

Preface

As college courses in children's literature become more established and numerous in the United States and elsewhere, spreading from undergraduate to graduate levels and frequently moving from departments of education to English and comparative literature, there is an intense need for textbooks that offer aesthetic rather than educational approaches to children's texts. While academic studies of children's literature have grown by leaps and bounds over the past fifteen to twenty years, producing many outstanding publications, there are currently very few textbooks attempting to bridge the gap between scholarly discussions and discussions of children's literature in college classrooms. The present textbook will hopefully fill this need. Unlike most of the existing textbooks in children's literature, it does not introduce a wide scope of children's books, arranging them by subject matter, genres and kinds, or the readers' age. This book is not about teaching literature to children, but about becoming critical adult readers of children's literature.

The book covers a number of contemporary literary theories, adjusting them to suit the specifics of children's literature. There are many general reference works and textbooks on critical theory; however, they are seldom appropriate for children's literature courses since they for obvious reasons ignore the specific properties that distinguish children's texts from general fiction. I have explored, in a number of scholarly studies, the particular aesthetics of children's fiction and the ways critical theory may be applied to children's texts. The present book is thus based on the results of my own research as well as the achievements of other scholars, and it contains original contributions to the scholarship of both children's literature and general literary theory since previous scholars in the general literary field have missed the profound implications that a study of children's texts brings to literary theory as a whole. At the same time, the book is based on twenty years of extensive classroom experience in teaching children's literature at all levels and in different countries. This experience shows that students gladly accept critical theory and the analytical tools it offers as long as they are presented in an accessible and meaningful way, that is, not theory for its own sake, but theory as support for the concrete study of literature.

Some contemporary theories, such as psychoanalytical and feminist theory, have been widely applied to children's texts, and there are several book publications in these fields. Other important theories, such as narrative theory and carnival theory, have been used only sporadically, and no book-length studies exist. Further, as every college teacher knows, it is virtually impossible to assign scholarly publications as required readings, since students will most likely lack the necessary framework and background knowledge such publications presuppose. The present textbook aims to be accessible to a college readership without prior specialized knowledge of literary theory.

It is my conviction that theories are only legitimate insofar as they open new dimensions of literary texts and insofar as they can be successfully translated into comprehensible and easy-to-use analytical tools. The purpose of this book is to provide students of children's literature with such a tool kit, while showing through concrete demonstration how each tool might best be used. This rationale dictates that, rather than organizing the chapters around unfamiliar theories, I organize them around familiar and easily recognized features of literary texts such as author, work, genre, theme, composition, setting, character, narration, style, medium, and reader. These aspects constitute the subject matter of the eleven main chapters of the book.

Each chapter includes short introductions to specific theoretical approaches, examples of their application to literary texts, a number of activities and exercises, and suggestions for further explorations. Each chapter has several subsections, arranged in increasing order of theoretical complexity. An instructor may thus decide whether to assign the whole chapter or a portion of it, and each individual student may choose to go beyond the assigned subsections to investigate more complex approaches to the topic or retreat to a more elementary level for repetition. A brief conclusion at the end of each chapter, "How to go further," contains suggestions for yet other theories and approaches. In this way, the book can be used in a variety of courses, from general survey and introductory undergraduate courses to more specific advanced graduate courses and seminars. This makes it radically different from most existing textbooks in its practical relevance.

The theoretical issues are illustrated by a limited selection of texts from the North American children's literature canon, that is, children's books frequently used in college courses in children's literature. These include *Little Women*; *The Wizard of Oz*; *Anne of Green Gables*; *The Secret Garden*; Laura Ingalls Wilder's *Little House* series; *Charlotte's Web*; Dr. Seuss's books; *Curious George*; *Where the Wild Things Are*; the *Ramona* books; *The*

Great Gilly Hopkins; *Roll of Thunder, Hear My Cry*; *The Planet of Junior Brown*; *The Giver*; *Holes*; and the *Harry Potter* books. The selection reflects the historical, thematic, ethnic, and gender-related diversity of children's fiction. One evident, and deliberate, omission is children's poetry, the reasons being manifold. First, there are very few theoretical studies of children's poetry to draw experience from; in the first place, there are no studies of children's poetry emphasizing its special aesthetics as opposed to general poetry. Second, poetry calls for rather specific analytical tools, so much different from the ones used in the examination of narrative prose that this area would need a separate textbook. While poetry, like fairy tales, is a given part of a textbook arranged by kinds and genres, it is in no way a self-evident component when theory is in the focus. By contrast, the part of children's poetry and verse that can be called narrative, such as Dr. Seuss's *The Cat in the Hat*, can be studied with the same tools as prose.

The reason for using a limited number of well-known texts is to ensure that both instructors and students either have previous knowledge of most of the texts discussed or can read them within a reasonable time, such as the duration of a college term. Since theories in the present book are introduced largely by demonstrating their use with specific literary texts, it is desirable that students be familiar with these texts. Yet it is equally important to avoid the limitations of centering all the theoretical argument around one single text (as some theoretical studies and textbooks do), as this significantly restricts the practical use of the textbook. Further, no single text can possibly provide examples of all the aspects of children's fiction, such as various genres, types of plot, character, narrative perspective, and so on. In summary, the choice of primary material is carefully balanced between comprehensiveness and the assignment limitations of a one-term course. Unlike most existing textbooks in children's literature that strive to introduce as many different children's books as possible, the purpose of this book is, with a minimal number of texts, to demonstrate some ways to read and discuss them. The idea is that when you have mastered the tools, you will be able to apply them to any text.

The argument in the individual chapters does not presuppose that the students have read all the children's books under discussion, even though it may facilitate the understanding of specific theories. Each theoretical stance is usually illustrated by a number of children's texts so that the students and the instructors have a sufficient freedom of choice. The instructors may themselves wish to decide what readings to assign and in what order. The title index provides guidance to the places where particular texts are discussed. For instance, *The Wizard of Oz* and the *Harry Potter* books are extensively discussed, with a number of analytical tools, in several chapters.

While the sheer number of theories and analytical methods may feel overwhelming at first glance, they are organized and presented in a way that stimulates a natural learning process. In discussing the various aspects of children's fiction, the book moves in the direction in which texts are created and mediated: starting with the author and the relationship between the author and the text, proceeding toward the different features of the text itself, and concluding with the relationship between the text and its readers. Since the chapters of the book follow each other logically and each subsequent chapter often makes use of the theoretical argument and terminology of the previous ones, it is advisable to study the chapters in the suggested order. It is, however, fully possible to use one chapter, or even subsection, at a time as a quick introduction to a particular theory or model or as a support for a deeper study of a particular text. Cross-references are provided to facilitate orientation. The instructors can also use the book more liberally, assigning chapters and sections in a different order to suit their syllabi. It should, however, be kept in mind that the sections within each chapter increase in sophistication.

Unlike many similar books, this one does not contain a glossary with brief definitions of terms and concepts. My experience as an instructor is that such definitions are seldom helpful once taken out of the context of the specific theoretical argument in which they are employed; they can on the contrary be confusing and misleading. Besides, quite a few terms and concepts, such as genre, are rather controversial, and providing a single glossary definition implies interrogating the very argument that the chapter on genre presents. Not least, a number of terms have different meaning in different theories, and a necessary multiple definition would prove confusing. The main thrust of this book is to make the students aware of the plurality of theories and analytical tools, which renders universal glossary definitions superfluous. Instead, a detailed subject index is offered, where readers can easily find reference to pages where the concepts are introduced and discussed.

The different exercises and activities provided in the chapters include the following:

Contemplate encourages the student to think and pose questions, often after browsing through a free selection of books. The task can be assigned by the instructor as homework, or it can be used at the beginning of the class to introduce a particular issue.

Let us explore implies that some questions will be posed and then examined in the chapter. These are the kind of questions an instructor might pose in class to initiate a discussion, so that the students are encouraged to provide their own responses before they read on and get the argument from the book. The exploration does not have to be actually pursued; rather it is a mental exercise to put the students in a critical state of mind. However, the instructors may assign these questions as homework, for an oral report or short weekly essay. It is also possible to ask similar questions about a different set of children's books, since it is the argument, not the concrete text, that is in the focus.

Exercise is an assignment in which the students are encouraged to test their understanding of the material without being given a solution. An exercise often sums up a section and provides questions stimulating the students' critical thinking. It should thus be viewed as an invitation to a mental exercise rather than an actual task to be performed. However, many of these assignments are also suitable for written essays, both short weekly reports and more substantial research papers. The instructors may suggest concrete examples of relevant texts to be used in such exercises, selecting them from their syllabi or from the students' previous reading. The purpose of an exercise is not to give the students more work to do, but to invite them to incorporate their previous knowledge into the relevant critical context.

Activity implies a visit to a library or to a virtual site. It can also be used as a mental exercise. The understanding of the material is not dependent on performing any particular activity; it is merely another way of stimulating analytical thinking. Some activities can be assigned for weekly oral or written reports or even take-home exam papers.

How to go further suggests directions that students might want to pursue within the relevant area. Any individual chapter can by no means be exhaustive in the particular area the chapter explores, and this short section provides some further theoretical issues relevant to the topic. Normally these will point to yet more profound and sophisticated tools of inquiry, also those hardly ever applied in children's literature research. The questions posed in this section may be discussed in class, assigned for advanced written essays, or merely viewed as a way to make the students aware of the scholarly approaches beyond the scope of the present book. At best, they will stimulate new research within yet unexplored spheres.

At the end of each chapter, an annotated bibliography of sources relevant to the chapter's particular subject is provided. There is also a general bibliography at the end of the book. Unlike the majority of recent textbooks in children's literature, I do not provide a list of electronic resources, partly because they are very easy to find anyway, partly because the addresses change often and become outdated even before a book may appear. This does not mean that I do not trust electronic resources; on the contrary, I view them as a valuable educational tool. Yet I believe that the implied audience of this book is sufficiently trained in Internet research.

Finally, the book is in no way exhaustive; for every aspect of the text, a few other approaches can be suggested. My intention is not to offer every possible kind of analytical tool, but to provide insight into the variety of available tools, showing that each tool opens a new dimension of the textual aspect under discussion.

In working on this book, I have naturally incorporated many ideas developed by my colleagues and presented in their textbooks, in the first place those by Perry Nodelman and Rebecca Lukens. I gladly acknowledge their priority in examining certain aspects of children's fiction that are also reflected in my book. Yet, most of the ideas in this book are based on my own teaching experience, and I would like to express my gratitude to all my past and present students for unknowingly serving as test cases.

I am indebted to Mary Galbraith for reviewing the first outline of this book, as well as for the stimulating discussions we had during my stay in San Diego, California, from 1999 to 2001. Many thanks to Michael Cadden and Lilian Rönnqvist for reading and commenting on some chapters. As usual, Carole Scott's careful and sensitive editing has proved indispensable.

I would also like to thank my husband, Staffan Skott, and my daughter, Julia Skott, for reading and commenting on significant portions of the book.

Introduction

Do We Need a Separate Aesthetics for Children's Literature?

One of the crucial questions in the field of children's literature studies, ever since it became a legitimate academic discipline, has been whether children's literature is different from any other kind of literature, what we normally call adult, or general, or mainstream literature. The issue that follows is equally fundamental for the way children's literature is studied. If it is part of, or basically identical with the mainstream, then we can easily import the analytical tools from general literary criticism to approach and assess it. If, however, children's literature is a specific phenomenon that, as many scholars claim, is, unlike "literature" at large, primarily an educational implement, then perhaps the employment of general literary theories will prove useless, and the study object calls for a theory of its own.

It is obvious, and is often argued, that children's literature is, or at least can be, both a form of art and an educational vehicle; yet the two opposed standpoints have always had their passionate advocates, and therefore the question is still relevant today. It is frequently referred to in children's literature criticism as the "literary-didactic split." Those few scholars who have ventured to reconcile the opposites have often come to conclusions that children's literature reflects the adult authors' nostalgic visions of childhood rather than a faithful depiction of it. In other words, children's authors tend to tell their readers what their childhood should be like, rather than what it is. This does not prevent children's literature from being art, but it presupposes a strong pedagogical thrust. Yet it would be preposterous to use the literary-didactic blend of children's literature as a criterion for distinguishing it from what we normally simply call "literature," but what in the context of children's literature we have to specify as "general, or adult literature." In fact, it is quite legitimate to state that all literature is "both," that is, both an art form and a didactic, or rather ideological, vehicle. In this respect, children's literature is not unique. Perhaps the ideological, or pedagogical, intention is often more explicit in children's literature, but it is a matter of grade, not of nature.

HISTORICAL PREREQUISITES

Let us begin with a brief look at the historical, social, and literary peculiarities of children's literature. Although stories have been used for education as well as entertainment of young people ever since the dawn of time, children's literature is a late phenomenon in human history. Children's literature as a separate category cannot exist before childhood is acknowledged as a special phase in a human being's life. This did not happen in our Western culture until the eighteenth century, with the Enlightenment and later the Romantic period, as many well-known studies have shown, such as Philippe Ariès's *Centuries of Childhood*, Peter Coveney's *The Image of Childhood*, or Lloyd de Mause's *The History of Childhood*. Thus, although stories have been used for educational purposes since ancient times, we cannot truly speak about the emergence of children's literature as a clearly separate category until the late eighteenth and early nineteenth centuries. This is not a universal view, as some scholars, such as Gillian Adams, claim that children's literature existed already in Mesopotamia, and definitely during the Middle Ages. This, however, is a matter of definition. If by children's literature we mean a substantial corpus of texts deliberately directed toward a particular audience, such literature cannot exist before the audience itself is acknowledged.

What is, then, the consequence of children's literature's having a considerably shorter history than the mainstream? Literature as such—that is, written narratives used for instruction or amusement or both—has in our Western culture a history of at least three thousand years if we start in the Middle East and Mediterranean areas, and longer still if we go further, to China and India. Western literature has undergone tremendous changes; it has shaped and reshaped its various genres; it has developed various ways of correlation to reality. One of the seminal works on the history of Western literature, *Mimesis* by the German-American philosopher Erich Auerbach, shows how different the perception of reality has been throughout history. Children's literature has had a much shorter time span to develop. Naturally, it could make use of the achievements of the mainstream, not least in the reflection of reality. Yet, historically, children's literature has always lagged behind the mainstream in the development of its artistic means. If Western mainstream literature entered its modern or modernistic phase at the turn of the twentieth century, children's literature is still in the process of discovering the modern and postmodern ways of portraying reality, including such artistic devices as genre eclecticism, intersubjectivity, heteroglossia, and metafiction.

SOCIAL FACTORS

Naturally, there are also other factors contributing to the specific ways in which children's literature has evolved. The most essential is its role in society. Children's literature has, undoubtedly, to a much greater extent been used for educational purposes. As already mentioned, some scholars would even claim that children's literature is, in its very essence, educational. Yet this is not wholly true. Mainstream literature has also been widely used for educational—or perhaps we should rather say ideological—purposes. Both the Christian church and the dictatorial regimes knew very well how to use literature to affect the masses. Children's literature has from start been used to educate and direct its audience. As we have seen, some scholars go so far as to deny children's literature a place in the literary system; they say children's literature can only be discussed and studied in an educational context. It would be disappointing to reduce the social role of children's literature to an educational tool, yet we cannot ignore this aspect altogether. Children's literature has without doubt been consciously and consistently used to educate and socialize its audience; its literary values have been acknowledged relatively recently, and still today these values are often perceived as secondary to educational values. At best, the educational aspect is declared to be part of children's literature aesthetics.

What are the consequences of the special social role of children's literature? How does this role affect the way children's literature is written? Some common prejudices about children's literature, maintained not only by its adversaries but even by its most ardent supporters, include the claims that children's literature is simple, action oriented rather than character oriented, optimistic and with happy endings, didactic, and repetitive. At first glance, most of us will certainly agree. However, taking a more thorough look at some renowned children's authors, we will notice that if we use these descriptions, none of them would fit into the definition of children's literature. When confronted with such writers, we must either admit that they do not write for children—which some of them have declared they do not, although their books are marketed as books for children—or redefine our concept of children's literature.

DECEITFUL SIMPLICITY

Let us merely explore the statement that children's literature is simple. It is challenging to define a "simple" narrative, but the different aspects of simplicity should involve both story (what is narrated) and discourse (how it is narrated). As far as story is concerned we may apply the following criteria: concrete and familiar subject matter; clear distinction between genres and text types (adventure story, family story, school story); one single, clearly delineated plot without digressions or secondary plots; chronological order of events; a limited number of characters who are easy to remember; "flat" characters, that is characters comprised basically of one typical feature who can easily be ascribed either the quality "good" or "evil"; closed characters, who are easy to understand from their doings and sayings; familiar settings, recognizable from the child's immediate surroundings, like nursery, home, school, playground, summer camp, and so on. As far as discourse is concerned, we can suggest as criteria for "simplicity" a distinct narrative voice; a fixed point of view; and preferably an authoritarian, didactic, extradiegetic narrator who can supply the young reader with comments, explanations, and exhortations without leaving anything unuttered or ambiguous, a narrator possessing greater knowledge and experience than both the characters and the readers. Complex temporal and spatial constructions are excluded. Naturally, the verisimilitude of the story, the reliability of the narrator, or the sufficiency of language as the artistic expressive means cannot be interrogated. Obviously, most of these criteria match conventional children's literature as well as larger portions of what is written and published as children's literature today. However, as we will see in the subsequent chapters, the repertory of contemporary children's fiction goes far beyond these restrictions.

In terms of content, certain subjects, characters, and settings are traditionally believed to be suitable for children. The abundance of animals and toys in children's books is especially striking. However, if we regard these figures as metaphorical representations of the weak and the oppressed, or as the children's projections of their own desires, we should not be misled by the outer form. The death of a pet in a children's book may just as well be a disguised depiction of the death of a close relative; the trials of a doll may be a camouflaged story of a child's suppressed fear of his own sexuality. Recently, first the adolescent novel and then literature for younger children burst the boundaries of earlier tabooed subjects by introducing such controversial themes as, for instance, homosexuality or incest. When dystopia becomes a prominent genre in children's fiction, with Lois Lowry's prize-winning *The Giver* as the most outstanding, but far from unique, example, it seems that the last genre limitation has been discarded. Children's literature, utopian or Arcadian by definition, has come to its own antithesis. Basically, there are no restrictions any longer as to what subjects can be treated in children's literature; the question is rather how they are treated.

CHILDREN'S LITERATURE AS COMMUNICATION

In this respect, the nature of communication between the author and the reader is decisive. The most elementary communicative model, to which we will be repeatedly returning throughout this book, looks like this: sender → message → receiver. The specific feature of communication between a children's writer and a young reader is that it is asymmetrical. A young reader's cognitive capacity, life experience, and linguistic skills are normally different from those of an adult writer (please observe that I say "different," not "less" or "inferior"). We will in due time put this situation under closer scrutiny and also discuss the possibility of the dual audience of children's literature, as developed in Barbara Wall's influential study *The Narrator's Voice*. At this point, however, it is sufficient to state that in its basic communicative function children's literature is somewhat different from general literature. Some scholars claim therefore that children's literature is always adapted to the needs of its audience, presenting *adaptation* as the most characteristic feature of children's literature, involving subject matter as well as form. It can be argued that all literature and art is inevitably adapted to its audience, and if adaptation is more prominent in children's literature than in the mainstream, it does not make adaptation a distinctive feature of children's literature; the difference is quantitative rather than qualitative. Yet, the asymmetry between the writer and the reader in the case of children's literature certainly affects the way children's novels are written, in terms of style, theme, plot, narrative perspective, and many other textual aspects.

CHILDREN'S LITERATURE AND POWER

There is yet another aspect in the characteristic of children's literature that, unlike the literary-didactic controversy, has only recently been noticed by some critics. It is power, featured in the subtitle of Roberta Trites's excellent study, *Disturbing the Universe: Power and Repression in Adolescent Literature*. Yet while Trites emphasizes power as a trait and motif inherent in young adult fiction, it can be argued that it is in some way or other present in all children's literature, which, perhaps not unexpectedly, makes it conspicuously similar to other literatures dealing with powerless societal groups: women's literature, indigenous literature, or gay literature. In each case, the main thrust of the literary work is the examination of power positions, the affirmation or interrogation of the existing order of power. The "discovery" of each of these suppressed groups has led to the emergence of a critical theory: feminist theory, postcolonial theory, and queer theory. Specific as they are, these theories have much in common as they interrogate the power position and what especially queer theory calls "norm" and "normativity." There is a term that successfully encompasses all these theories and that can also be applied to children's literature research: *heterology* (from Greek *heteros*, other, different; and *logos*, word, law, study, theory), the inquiry into imbalance, inequality, and asymmetry between different social groups. In the case of children's literature, we are dealing with the imbalance, inequality, and asymmetry between children and adults the way it is presented and assessed in children's books, books intended for the young audience.

Modern children's literature, let us say the post-WWII Western children's literature, has cautiously started subverting its own oppressive function. It can describe situations in which the established power structures are interrogated. If we translate the favorite concept of queer theory, heteronormativity, to the conditions of children's literature, we can speak about adult normativity. The adults have unlimited power in our society, as compared to children, which is regarded as norm, in real life as well as in literature. Queer studies test how we can exchange an established pattern, in our case, adult normativity, for another one and examine what happens if we depart from child in power as norm and the powerless child as deviation. Queer theory tries to demonstrate, firstly, that norms are often arbitrary, and secondly, and perhaps more important, that the whole argument about "norms" and "deviations" gives the norm priority over deviation, and thus more authority and power. Queer theory does not strive to replace one norm by another, but claims that all conditions are equally normal.

It is been repeatedly pointed out that some children's writers "take the child's part." In fact, taking the child's part, lending out a voice to the silenced child and similar metaphors of power have been used to emphasize the author's unique position in writing for children. However, an adult author can no better wholly take the child's part than a white author can wholly take a black character's part or a male author wholly take a female character's part, and so on, as heterological studies make us aware.

In her insightful book *Don't Tell the Grownups*, Alison Lurie claims that all children's literature is subversive by definition. It would be more reasonable to say that children's literature can indeed be subversive against adult normativity, but considerably more often it confirms rather than interrogates it.

THE AESTHETICS OF
CHILDREN'S LITERATURE

All these historical, social, communicative, and power-related factors together have contributed to the particular aesthetics of children's literature.

The word "aesthetics" (from Greek *aesthesis*, sensation, perception), originally indicating the way a piece of art evokes a sense of beauty, means a set of artistic features characterizing a specific phenomenon in the field of art. Children's literature does share a number of features with the mainstream. For instance, it reflects, albeit indirectly, our own reality; it conveys ideological values; it has strong potential to affect the mind; and it also appeals to our emotions. Yet in some essential ways children's literature is different from the mainstream because of its historical and social context, because of its strong educational affiliation, and because of its implied audience. It is not necessarily simpler or artistically inferior to the mainstream, as some scholars maintain; it is different. If we accept this statement, we must also accept that children's literature does have an aesthetics of its own, and if so, we must study this specific aesthetics in order to understand how children's literature functions and how it affects its readers. It does not mean that in our approach to children's literature we must adopt a strict essentialist position, that is, claim that the phenomenon under discussion has certain essential traits. In doing so, we would then need to delve into the questions of what literature is, and what a child is, and so on. Even though some critics do engage in such discussions, they seldom yield any results worthy of note. To avoid the fallacy of essentialism, we should view children's literature as one of the many kinds of literature, yet attempt to point out its specific features.

One of the best illustrations of the need for a separate aesthetics is the question of genre. More than half of the genres discussed in general criticism are irrelevant for children's literature, while many genres prominent in children's literature, such as fantasy, seldom get the attention of general critics. Further cases can be gathered from the various aspects of inquiry. In discussion of narrative perspective, general scholars are confined for their examples of a naive point of view to Henry James's *What Maisie Knew*, while in children's literature this narrative perspective is the rule rather than the exception. In exemplifying the approximation to the totally unreliable narrator, most critics resort to Benjy in *The Sound and the Fury*, while any child first-person narrator in children's fiction will serve as an example. The intersubjective construction of characters, for instance in the novels by Virginia Woolf, has been pinpointed as the foremost achievement of modernism, while a parallel phenomenon, the collective protagonist, is more or less the token of conventional children's fiction. In his theoretically framed study of Proust, *Narrative Discourse*, Gérard Genette claims that the iterative frequency is, if not unique to Proust, at least extremely unusual, while most traditional children's fiction makes wide use of this narrative device. In fact, general critics' understanding of some of the functions and principles of literature would be considerably amplified if they knew something about children's fiction.

In this book, we will be looking at the different aspects of children's litera-

ture—such as genre, theme, composition, and characterization—from different points of view: historical, social and communicative, but in the first place
aesthetic, that is, focusing on the question of the specifics of children's literature as opposed to the mainstream. We will also investigate how we can use
the tools offered by a number of contemporary literary theories in order to
address the issues raised. These tools and analytical models are by no means
exhaustive, but they will provide a broad enough spectrum for addressing a
wide scope of aesthetical questions in children's fiction. The primary purpose of the book is not to present critical theory in a systematic way, but to
select the analytical tools that each theory can offer us.

REFERENCES

In this section, only sources that directly discuss the fundamental nature of children's
literature are listed. All specific issues will be treated in the subsequent chapters.

Adams, Gillian. "The First Children's Literature: The Case of Sumer." *Children's
Literature* 14 (1986): 1–30.
———. "Medieval Children's Literature: Its Possibility and Actuality." *Children's
Literature* 26 (1998): 1–24.
Ariès, Philippe. *Centuries of Childhood: A Social History of Family Life*. New York:
Vintage-Random House, 1962.
Auerbach, Erich. *Mimesis: The Representation of Reality in Western Literature*. 4th
ed. Princeton, NJ: Princeton University Press, 1974.
Carpenter, Humphrey. *Secret Gardens. The Golden Age of Children's Literature*.
London: Unwin Hyman, 1985.
Clark, Beverly Lyon. *Kiddie Lit: The Cultural Construction of Children's Literature
in America*. Baltimore: The Johns Hopkins University Press, 2003.
Coveney, Peter. *The Image of Childhood: The Individual and Society: A Study of the
Theme in English Literature*. Harmondsworth: Penguin, 1967.
Dusinberre, Juliet. *Alice to the Lighthouse: Children's Books and Radical Experi-
ments in Art*. London: Macmillan, 1987.
Genette, Gérard. *Narrative Discourse: An Essay in Method*. Ithaca, NY: Cornell Uni-
versity Press, 1980.
Hollindale, Peter. *Signs of Childness in Children's Books*. Stroud, UK: Thimble Press,
1997.
Hunt, Peter. "Childist Criticism: The Subculture of the Child, the Book and the
Critic." *Signal* 43 (1984): 42–59.
———. "Questions of Method and Methods of Questioning: Childist Criticism in
Action." *Signal* 45 (1984): 180–200.
———. *Criticism, Theory and Children's Literature*. London: Blackwell, 1991. Chap.
1, "Criticism and Children's Literature"; chap. 2, "The Situation of Children's
Literature"; chap. 3, "Defining Children's Literature."
———. "The Decline and Decline of the Children's Book? The Problems of Adults

Reading Children's Books and What Can Be Done about Them." Pp. 1–14 in *Children's Literature and Contemporary Theory*, edited by Michael Stone. Wollongong, Australia: University of Wollongong Press, 1991.

Inglis, Fred. *The Promise of Happiness: The Value and Meaning in Children's Fiction*. Cambridge: Cambridge University Press, 1981.

Lesnik-Oberstein, Karín. *Children's Literature: Criticism and the Fictional Child*. Oxford: Clarendon, 1994.

———. "Defining Children's Literature and Childhood." Pp. 17–31 in *International Companion Encyclopedia of Children's Literature*, edited by Peter Hunt. London: Routledge, 1996. Also as "Essentials: What is Children's Literature? What is Childhood?" Pp. 14–29 in *Understanding Children's Literature*, edited by Peter Hunt. London: Routledge, 1999.

———. "Childhood and Textuality: Culture, History, Literature." Pp. 1–28 in *Children in Culture: Approaches to Childhood*, edited by Karín Lesnik-Oberstein. London: Macmillan, 1998.

———, ed. *Children's Literature: New Approaches*. London: Palgrave Macmillan, 2004.

Lurie, Alison. *Don't Tell the Grownups. Subversive Children's Literature*. Boston: Little, Brown, 1990.

de Mause, Lloyd, ed. *The History of Childhood*. New York: Harper & Row, 1974.

McGillis, Roderick. *The Nimble Reader: Literary Theory and Children's Literature*. New York: Twayne, 1996. Chap. 1, "Beginnings."

Natov, Roni. *The Poetics of Childhood*. New York: Routledge, 2003.

Nikolajeva, Maria. *Children's Literature Comes of Age: Towards a New Aesthetic*. New York: Garland, 1996.

———. "Exit Children's Literature?" *The Lion and the Unicorn* 22, no. 2 (1998): 221–236.

———. *From Mythic to Linear: Time in Children's Literature*. Lanham, MD: Scarecrow, 2000.

———. "Growing up: The Dilemma of Children's Literature." Pp. 111–136 in *Children's Literature as Communication*, edited by Roger D. Sell. Amsterdam: John Benjamins, 2002.

Nodelman, Perry. "Progressive Utopia, or How to Grow Up without Growing Up." Pp. 146–154 in *Proceedings of the 6th Annual Conference of ChLA*, edited by Priscilla A. Ord. Villanova, PA: Villanova University Press, 1980. Also pp. 74–82 in *Only Connect*, edited by Sheila Egoff et al., 3rd ed. Toronto: Oxford University Press, 1996.

———. "Children's Literature as Women's Writing." *Children's Literature Association Quarterly* 13, no. 1 (1988): 31–34.

———. *The Pleasures of Children's Literature*. New York: Longman, 1992. 2nd ed. 1996.

———. "Fear of Children's Literature: What's Left (or Right) After Theory?" Pp. 3–14 in *Reflections of Change*, edited by Sandra L. Beckett. Westport, CT: Greenwood, 1997.

———. "Pleasure and Genre: Speculations on the Characteristics of Children's Fiction." *Children's Literature* 28 (2000): 1–14.

Paul, Lissa. "Enigma Variations: What Feminist Criticism Knows about Children's Literature." Pp. 148–166 in *Children's Literature: The Development of Criticism*, edited by Peter Hunt. London: Routledge & Kegan Paul, 1990.

———. *Reading Otherways*. Stroud, UK: Thimble Press, 1998.

Rose, Jacqueline. *The Case of Peter Pan, or The Impossibility of Children's Fiction*. London: Macmillan, 1984.

Sell, Roger D., ed. *Children's Literature as Communication*. Amsterdam: John Benjamins, 2002.

Shavit, Zohar. "The Ambivalent Status of Texts: The Case of Children's Literature." *Poetics Today* 173 (1980): 75–86.

———. *Poetics of Children's Literature*. Athens, GA: University of Georgia Press, 1986.

———. "The Double Attribution of Texts for Children and How It Affects Writing for Children. Pp. 83–99 in *Transcending Boundaries: Writing for a Dual Audience of Children and Adults*, edited by Sandra L. Beckett. New York: Garland, 1999.

Steig, Michael. "Never Going Home: Reflections on Reading, Adulthood and the Possibility of Children's Literature." *Children's Literature Association Quarterly* 18, no. 1 (1993): 36–39.

Stephens, John. *Language and Ideology in Children's Fiction*. London: Longman, 1992.

Thacker, Debora Cogan, and Jean Webb. *Introducing Children's Literature. From Romanticism to Poststructuralism*. London: Routledge, 2002.

Trites, Roberta Seelinger. *Disturbing the Universe: Power and Repression in Adolescent Literature*. Iowa City: University of Iowa Press, 2000.

Wall, Barbara. *The Narrator's Voice: The Dilemma of Children's Fiction*. London: Macmillan, 1991.

Watson, Victor. "The Possibilities of Children's Fiction." Pp. 11–24 in *After Alice*, edited by Morag Styles, Eve Bearne, and Victor Watson. London: Cassell, 1992.

Weinreich, Torben. *Children's Literature: Art or Pedagogy?* Roskilde, Denmark: Roskilde University Press, 2000.

Zipes, Jack. *Sticks and Stones: The Troublesome Success of Children's Literature from Slovenly Peter to Harry Potter*. New York: Routledge, 2001.

Zornado, John. *Inventing the Child: Culture, Ideology, and the Rise of Childhood*. New York: Garland, 2000.

1

The Aesthetic of the Author

We will begin our exploration of literary texts written for, marketed for, and read by young people by looking at the creator—or, in communication terms, the sender. It would seem that the author is the key figure in the communicative process: no author, no book. The interest in authors is, however, a relatively recent phenomenon, emerging during the Romantic period with its focus on individual expression and on the work of art as a reflection of the author's ideas. In earlier times, the work of art was believed to be a reflection of some aspect of external reality. Contemporary criticism has, driven by various premises, interrogated the role of the author, sometimes going so far as to declare "the death of the author" in favor of the autonomous existence of the literary text. The validity of "author's intention" has undergone special scrutiny. The perception of the role and importance of authors has thus varied considerably according to the literary theory employed, and in children's literature the role of the author may be considered different from that in mainstream literature. For one thing, due to the overall didactic purpose of children's literature, children's fiction may by definition be viewed as more intentional than general fiction, and critics of children's literature may be more inclined to investigate the intentions of children's writers. On the other hand, the "intentional fallacy"—a New Criticism claim that it is not the artist's fulfilled or failed intention we evaluate but the work of art as such—is naturally as relevant for children's fiction as for any other art form.

CONTEMPLATE

Write down the titles of ten books you liked when you were a child (if you don't remember the titles, just write down an event, a character, or some other detail as a reminder). Try to remember the names of the authors. How many could you remember? Are the authors' names important to your memories of the books?

All stories have an origin, even though for many stories, such as myths and folktales, we do not know the exact origin. With few exceptions, the authors of children's novels are known and announced on the covers. Sometimes there will be some information about authors inside the books, on the back cover or the flap: where they live, what other books they have written, what awards they have received, and so on. Such information is called a *paratext* (para = "side"); it is not part of the novel and therefore not mandatory. A different edition of the same book does not have to carry the same information, or indeed any information about the author at all. In many cases therefore we will have no other information about the author than the name.

As adults, especially if we are critics and scholars of literature, we may be interested to know something about the authors of the books we are reading or working with. Young readers normally pay little attention to authors' names. In a library, they will ask for *Babar* or *Animorphs* or *Anne of Green Gables*, not for books by Jean de Brunhoff, K. A. Applegate, or L. M. Montgomery. The *Harry Potter* books are a very good illustration of this trend, since even teachers, librarians, and scholars tend to refer to Harry Potter and not to J. K. Rowling. Does this mean that authors are less important for children's fiction than they are for general fiction?

Another interesting aspect concerning children's authors is that their relationship to their readers is asymmetrical. All other kinds of literature are written by adults for adults. Children's literature is written—with very few exceptions—by adults for children, who have less life experience and therefore different reference frames, and whose vocabulary and other linguistic skills are generally less developed. What are the implications of this unequal power position? Can adult writers at all communicate with their young readers? Some critics seriously doubt it.

In this chapter we will take a closer look at some of these questions and see how different literary theories describe the relationship between authors and their texts.

THE PERSON BEHIND THE BOOK

Biography means literally "life description." In a biographical approach to literature, the author is the focus of attention. However, literary biographies can be of different kinds, from pure life story to literary criticism in the form of "life and letters," perhaps the oldest form of literary study. There is no radical difference between the biography of a writer and that of a musician, politician, or movie star. In a pure biography or autobiography, the focus is on actual life, and if the subject happens to be a writer, the books, plays, or poems written by this person are mentioned as facts of her or his life. A biography does not normally contain any detailed discussion of the works as such, though it may possibly mention how they were received by their contemporaries. By contrast, a "life-and-letters" study treats the literary texts in close connection with biographical facts, even sometimes explaining texts in terms of events from the writer's life.

Literary biography for children is not a prominent genre. There are books about popular authors written for young readers, but they are not as common as biographies of famous historical figures. The reason may be that lives of authors are not always exciting enough to make a good story for children. As adults, we do not necessarily read an author's biography for excitement, but probably because we are interested in authors, whether or not their lives contain extraordinary events. Literary biographies of children's authors written for adults may have different purposes. Primarily, they serve as background information for adult mediators, as a way to promote reading.

What Do We Want to Know?

LET US EXPLORE

Suppose you were to prepare a short talk in a classroom or a library for a group of young readers about a children's writer whose book or books they are going to read. What facts about the writer would you include and why?

The first thing we perhaps want to know about authors is whether they are still alive, and if not, when they lived. Why is this essential? We need to put the work we are discussing into a relevant historical context. We cannot accuse L. M. Montgomery of not allowing Anne Shirley to become a fully emancipated woman because it would be impossible at the time the books were written. We cannot accuse Mark Twain of letting his characters use words perceived as offensive today, because these words were part of the everyday idiom during Twain's lifetime. It would be very strange if street urchins in a small Southern town in the 1840s used the politically correct language of our own time. By contrast, we can judge the *Harry Potter* books from our own sociohistorical perspective, because J. K. Rowling is our contemporary.

Knowing the authors' life dates, we can also decide whether they are writing from their own life experience or not. Some writers choose contemporary settings for their books, describing something they have experienced as adults. Others go back to their own childhood, while yet others prefer to go beyond their own life span. Does it matter? In many cases, it does. We usually put higher demands on authenticity if we know that the subject matter of a literary work is based on the author's experience. Some recent debates on Holocaust fiction have brought forward the claims that only eyewitnesses are entitled to write about this topic. We can certainly understand such claims, but what about other subjects? No living author today has firsthand experience of the Civil War—does it mean that it is impossible to write about the Civil War? Yet we certainly have different expectations from a novel about the Civil War written during or immediately after it, and a novel written on the same subject in the twenty-first century. This is just one example of why authors' life dates can be of consequence.

We may also be interested in where the author lived. Mark Twain describes in *The Adventures of Tom Sawyer* the small town of Hannibal on the Mississippi River that he knew very well, although he called it something else in the novel. L. M. Montgomery writes in *Anne of Green Gables* about Prince Edward Island where she grew up, and many events of Anne Shirley's life are taken from the author's own childhood and adolescence. Knowing that the author of *The Lion, the Witch and the Wardrobe* is British certainly explains some details in the book that a young reader in the United States may wonder about. For instance, in the beginning of the book, the four children are sent away from London because of the air raids. Young American readers may not be familiar with this part of European history. As adult mediators, we may want to point this out for them.

Are we interested in whether the author is a man or a woman? In most cases, we can guess the author's gender from the name, but occasionally the name will not reveal the gender (is S. E. Hinton male or female?), or else a female writer can use a male pseudonym (occasionally the other way round). Note that J. K. Rowling has deliberately chosen to use initials rather than her full name, Joanne, apparently to avoid being immediately identified as a female (although who does not know her today?). Does this imply that male writers have higher status? Writing children's literature has at times been considered a female profession and therefore enjoyed lower prestige than "real" writing. Yet does it matter for our understanding and appreciation of a book whether the author is male or female? We will come back to this question later on.

Are we interested in knowing whether the author was married or had children and perhaps grandchildren? Are the books based on close observation of the author's own children? Were the stories perhaps told to a particular child before they became a book? Some great children's books were indeed first told to a child in the author's vicinity (not necessarily her or his own child): *Alice in Wonderland*, *Winnie-the-Pooh*, or *Pippi Longstocking*. Yet just as many great books have no connection whatsoever with any real children. We may be fascinated to know that some of the children's classics were written by cheerless hermits or prudish old maids who had no experience of living with children and only their own childhood memories to rely on.

What else may be essential to know about the authors' lives in order to understand the work? Did they have a happy, harmonious childhood, or did they experience painful confrontations with their parents? Were they rich or poor; did they have to work hard for their basic necessities, or did they enjoy a leisurely, wealthy existence? Many children's books focus on upper-class and middle-class children, which naturally is the consequence of their authors' social origins. The authors' political or religious beliefs can also be reflected in their texts.

The Validity of Biography

We must remember that biographical facts do not necessarily have to be true: sometimes they are part of the mythmaking surrounding an author. Media have made much fuss about J. K. Rowling's being a poor single mother and writing the first *Harry Potter* book in a coffee shop, the only warm place she could find. This may or may not be true, but, in the first place, is this fact relevant for our understanding of the book?

There exist several biographies of famous authors, especially authors from the nineteenth century. A biography written long after the author's death may be based on new facts (for instance, when a diary or correspondence of the author has been disclosed); or it may reflect a reevaluation of the author, including the changing attitudes toward gender and ethnicity. For instance, all the existing biographies of Louisa M. Alcott present her from different perspectives and thus offer different points of departure for the study of her texts. Two recent biographies of Lewis Carroll have portrayed him in two radically different manners, both strongly deviant from the standard view proposed in a biography written in 1899 by his nephew. One of these paints Carroll as a pedophile, based on his ostensibly pathological interest for little girls. The other biography, going back to Carroll's unpublished diaries, points out that the "little girls" in question were in fact around twenty-five years old, and that they used to visit Carroll unchaperoned, which in the eyes of his contemporaries was highly immoral. Apparently, the myth of the author's interest for "little girls" was deliberately created by his family to hide what they regarded as inappropriate, while children were considered pure and innocent and therefore suitable as a cover. For us today, pedophilia is certainly a worse offense. This is a good example of how facts about an author can be interpreted differently. Our understanding of *Alice in Wonderland* can be affected by our understanding of the author's views on children.

EXERCISE 1

Find and read a biography of one of your favorite children's authors (you may be amazed to find out that there is no biography of your very favorite author!). Alternatively, find and study a web page dedicated to your favorite author. Consider the following questions:

- What is the main purpose of this biography? Is the primary focus on the author's life, or are the literary works discussed in connection with biographical facts?
- Which facts about the author's life were familiar to you, and which were not?
- Did the new facts you learned about the author make you understand his or her works better? In what way?
- If you were to give a talk to young readers about this author, what facts would you select as indispensable? Why?

EXERCISE 2

Read and compare two biographies of the same author or compare two Web page presentations. Note the differences in approach and in interpretations of biographical facts. Try to account for them in terms of the time when they were written, the biographer's aims, or the presumed audience.

What Matters—and Why?

Let us now go back to the question of authors and young readers. If young readers do not care much about who wrote the books they are reading, why would authors' lives matter at all?

LET US EXPLORE

- Do we get a better understanding of Hans Christian Andersen's fairy tales knowing that during his whole life he was lonely and unhappy, often hopelessly in love and rejected by those he loved?
- Does it help us to know that the characters of *Little Women* were modeled on Louisa M. Alcott's family?
- Is it essential to know that C. S. Lewis was a devoted Christian?

When we say "does it help" or "is it essential to know," we do not mean that all knowledge is useful, or that we may be fascinated by a person as such, apart from his or her books; but the questions are put in a very pragmatic sense: how do certain facts of an author's life illuminate literary texts? Or even more drastic: does our lack of knowledge of the author's life impede our understanding of the texts? Let us try to address each of these questions.

Many readers find Andersen's fairy tales dark and dismal. It is especially true about people who have first seen the Disney movie of *The Little Mermaid* and then read the original story. Most of Andersen's fairy tales are radically unlike traditional folktales, as they lack happy endings, the trademark of true folktales. The little match girl freezes to death; the little tin soldier is thrown into the oven and melts. *The Little Mermaid* is the best example though. She, who has sacrificed everything and endured so much to win the love of the prince, does not live happily ever after with her beloved. Why did Andersen choose these sorrowful endings for his fairy tales, so sorrowful that the Disney Studios felt compelled to change the ending completely to adapt the story to a contemporary American audience? Turning to Andersen's biography, we may see the origins of his dark worldview. Born in a poor family, Andersen's foremost dream was to become successful in society, and he would stop at nothing to achieve his goal. During his long life (1805–1875), he mixed with nobility and royalty but apparently had an inferiority complex because of his ancestry, which he tried carefully to conceal (he never went back to visit his sick and alcoholic mother). He was extremely ugly and was repeatedly rejected by the women (and the young men) with whom he was infatuated. Many of his fairy tales, including *The Little Mermaid*, depict a person of low origin in love with somebody of higher rank: the tin soldier and the pretty ballerina; the top and the morocco ball who considers herself more aristocratic; and of course the little mermaid and the prince, who is fond of her as a nice child but would never dream of choosing her as a bride. Being rejected by someone he loved was presumably Andersen's recurrent experience of human relationships. Obviously, we get a better understanding of his fairy tales if we are familiar with this fact.

Louisa M. Alcott used herself and her family as models for *Little Women*. Quite a few facts of the author's biography can easily be traced in her writing, including her father's philosophical and pedagogical ideas, which are especially reflected in the sequels where Jo starts a school. The untimely death of Beth March is also based on a true fact. With the knowledge of Alcott's life, we get a better insight into some essential aspects of *Little Women*, not least the character of Professor Bhaer, the fatherly figure whom Jo marries. Further, in the figure of Jo, Alcott describes her own career as a writer and the hardships she had to go through. This does not mean, however, that Jo March is identical with Louisa M. Alcott, or that all the events described in

Little Women and sequels have really taken place, although many of them do indeed have a connection with the author's life.

Concerning C. S. Lewis, often when it is pointed out for the students that *The Lion, the Witch and the Wardrobe* has explicit biblical allusions, the reaction is, "You are just making it up; there may be some parallels, but the author certainly did not mean it." Knowing that C. S. Lewis not only was a devoted Christian, but quite intentionally put the Christian message into his children's books, we can ask whether their message does indeed reach the readers, that is, whether the intention was successful. We can also quite legitimately ask whether our understanding of the Narnia Chronicles is seriously impeded if we do not possess information about C. S. Lewis's Christianity. If a teacher decides to read *The Lion, the Witch and the Wardrobe* in the classroom, is it desirable to tell the students about the Christian context? Many American schools are sensitive about religious matters. And if the information does not add anything to the aesthetic appreciation of the novel, why bother?

EXERCISE

After the discussion above, go back to the biography of your favorite author and consider whether any facts that you learned from it are absolutely indispensable to understand his or her writing.

THE AUTHOR ON THE ANALYST'S COUCH

A number of contemporary literary biographies use an explicit psychoanalytical approach to their subject matter. Psychoanalysis is, however, not a literary theory, but a method of clinical therapy. It is therefore essential to distinguish between clinical psychoanalysis and a psychoanalytical approach to literary texts. Sigmund Freud, the founder of clinical psychoanalysis, as well as his followers, used literary texts to illustrate some of their statements and methods. The Oedipus complex is perhaps the most famous of Freud's concepts; it has its origin in the story found in the tragedy by the ancient Greek author Sophocles, *King Oedipus*, the protagonist of which unknowingly kills his father and marries his mother. Freud utilized this story to discuss young males' traumatic relationship with their parents. He was not interested in whether Sophocles had experienced a similar situation, nor in the way the readers perceived Oedipus's predicament. He just drew parallels between this famous story and the condition of some of his patients.

The direction of literary criticism that finds inspiration in Freud's, Carl Gustav Jung's, and their disciples' clinical theories, and which will henceforth in this book be referred to as psychoanalysis, has developed along several diverse lines. One possibility is to examine how readers are affected by the story and how their reaction to stories reveals their own conditions. This method is widely employed in bibliotherapy, where books and stories are used to help patients to come to terms with their mental disturbances. Further, the characters' actions can be analyzed in terms of their psychological development. We will consider this interpretative model when we discuss literary character in chapter 7. In this section, we are interested in the ways we can discuss the writer's relationship to the text within the premises of psychoanalytical theory. Since classic psychoanalysis views the origin of mental disturbances in the conflict between our sexual desires and societal restrictions, literature is seen as a sanctioned channel for expressing the authors' forbidden, suppressed desires.

Literature as Confession

There are two directions in author-oriented literary psychoanalysis, depending on whether the author or the text is the primary focus of attention. For instance, C. G. Jung's follower Marie-Louise von Franz has written an exciting study about Antoine de Saint-Exupéry, the author of *The Little Prince*, in which she uses the novel to explain the author's psychological traumas. She is thus using the literary text exactly as a practicing analyst would use a patient's stories and dreams, in which his suppressed desires are revealed.

Let us return to Hans Christian Andersen and see how a psychoanalytically oriented critic would use a text to explain the author. One of the well-known fairy tales that ends happily is *The Ugly Duckling*. The poor duckling is mocked and humiliated because he is so ugly, but he finally turns into a beautiful swan. On closer examination, what does this story say? It has been usually interpreted as follows: after many hardships, patience and perseverance will be rewarded. But if we stop to think about it, the ugly duckling has turned into a swan only because he was hatched from a swan's egg. If he had been a real duckling, he would have grown into a duck. What does Andersen mean by his tale? Some biographers believe that Andersen was not the son of a washerwoman and a cobbler, but the illegitimate child of a nobleman, perhaps even the king of Denmark. There is no direct evidence for this, but the indications are strong. Perhaps *The Ugly Duckling* is the author's way of saying, "I have achieved fame and wealth only because I am in fact of noble birth."

Another possibility is that Andersen himself believed that he was of noble birth, even if it was not true. In this case, Andersen was suffering from an obsession, a psychotic condition, traces of which we see in his fairy tale. This is an example of a speculative biographical approach. It would perhaps be unwise to apply it as a consistent critical method, but it does illustrate the possibility of using literary works to illuminate the author's life. However, this approach has little to do with the study of literature. If the focus of psychoanalysis is on the author, then the literary text is used merely as any narrative the patient may tell to the analyst.

Life Reflected in Letters

On the other hand, if a psychoanalytically oriented scholar is primarily interested in the text itself, facts of the author's life are used to explain some features of the text. Several critics have discussed James M. Barrie, the author of *Peter Pan*, in terms of his sexual immaturity. Although he was married, there are strong indications that the marriage was never consummated; in any case, Barrie's aversion for sex is well documented, as is his fascination with very young boys. The character of Peter Pan, seen in psychoanalytical terms as a projection of the author's psychological disturbance, reflects in this interpretation the author's wishful thinking about the possibility of remaining young and sexually innocent forever. (It is necessary to point out that those familiar with *Peter Pan* only through the Disney movie will naturally not find much of the original's psychological charge in it.) Viewed in this light, the text indeed reveals a great deal about its author's psyche.

The reluctance to grow up, interpreted as the author's suppressed fear of sexuality, can be named the Peter Pan complex and makes for an interesting comparison with the Oedipus complex. The Oedipus complex—not as a clinical condition, but as a literary pattern—appears in adult as well as in children's fiction. The Peter Pan complex seems to be inherent to children's fiction, since it is connected with the central motif and dilemma of all children's fiction: growing up. In Barrie's case, the image of a child who never grows up was also connected to an event of his childhood: his brother died in a skating accident at the age of thirteen. In the family's memory, he remained forever young.

Most psychoanalytically oriented critics, who have investigated children's authors' lives and the ways in which they have shaped the authors' works, have focused on childhood traumas, often the loss of parents or siblings. This may feel a bit reductive. According to her biographers and her own accounts, Astrid Lindgren, the author of *Pippi Longstocking*, had a very happy childhood. Looking only at her own childhood, it is impossible to find the origins of the numerous portraits of orphans and abandoned children in her books. It helps, however, to know that when she was very young and unmarried, Astrid gave birth to a son whom she was forced to give away for adoption. Perhaps her concerns about this child (whom she took back as soon as she could afford it) resulted in the poignant depiction of longing and abandonment.

Other biographical facts that may have left tangible traces in an author's writing are participation in wars and other dramatic events, or immigration and readjustment in a new country.

EXERCISE

Go back to the biography of your favorite author and consider whether any facts of the author's life can be interpreted psychoanalytically as they are reflected in the books. Not many books allow a fruitful psychoanalytical interpretation, and you may find out that your author had no visible traumas that can be traced in his or her writing.

WHAT DOES IT MEAN "TO WRITE LIKE A WOMAN"?

We have already briefly considered the question regarding the significance of the author's gender for our understanding of the text. We will now take the question further and discuss whether the author's gender, as well as ethnicity and some other biographical facts, have an impact on the writing as such. To do so, we will make use of feminist and postcolonial theories.

Just as psychoanalytical literary methods should not be confused with clinical psychoanalysis, feminist literary theory should not be confused with feminism as an ideology or a political movement. Feminist literary theory borrows some basic concepts from feminist ideology and modifies them for application to literary texts. Henceforth in this book, feminist theory will only refer to its expression in literary criticism. Like psychoanalysis, feminist theory covers several study objects. It can be reader oriented, investigating whether men and women read and interpret literary texts differently; it can be mimetically oriented, examining how actual gender patterns in reality are reflected in literary texts; it can also be text oriented, that is, focusing on the portrayal of men and women, boys and girls, in the texts. Further, it can be author oriented, and this is what we will explore in this section.

Some of the questions a feminist critic interested in the relationship between the writers and their writing would raise are: Do men and women write differently? If so, what exactly is the difference? Do men and women choose different genres and styles? Can a man write like a woman? Can a woman write like a man? Some of the French feminist critics, notably Hélène Cixous, have tried to define *écriture feminine*, "women's writing," in terms of style and other features, and the direction of the Anglo-Saxon feminist criticism sometimes labeled as "gynocritics" has pursued the same goal.

EXERCISE

Choose two children's novels or picture books involving somewhat similar subject matter, one written by a male, the other by a female writer. Study them carefully and try to answer the following questions:

- Is there any difference at all in the way the two novels are written? Can the difference be accounted for by the author's gender?
- If you did not know, would you be able to guess which author was male and which was female? What criteria would you use in your guesswork: plot, language and style, the gender of the main character, the narrative point of view?

Does Gender Matter?

The first and perhaps easiest observation we can make is the correlation between the authors' and the protagonists' gender. It would be natural to assume that children's writers find inspiration in the memories of their own childhood and therefore choose same-gender protagonists, which enables them to draw on their own experiences. This is true about such books as *The Adventures of Tom Sawyer* or *Holes*, written by male authors about male protagonists, and about *Little Women, Anne of Green Gables, Little House in the Big Woods*, the *Ramona* books, *Harriet the Spy*, and *Walk Two Moons*, written by female authors about female protagonists. It is not true about *The Wizard of Oz* (male author, female protagonist), *The Outsiders, The Planet of Junior Brown, The Giver*, or the *Harry Potter* books (female authors, male protagonist). From the latter selection, it would seem that female writers more often choose male protagonists than the other way round. Moreover, there are quite a few female writers who have successfully written about both genders. For instance, Katherine Paterson has a male protagonist in *Bridge to Terabithia*, but a female protagonist in *The Great Gilly Hopkins*. A hasty conclusion would be that "feminine writing" includes the cross-gender choice of protagonist.

Let us, however, look at these books more carefully. Some of them are plot oriented and mainly describe the external flow of events. This is the case of *The Wizard of Oz*, in which a male writer has chosen a female protagonist, but does not enter her inner world. By contrast, *The Outsiders, The Planet of Junior Brown, The Giver*, and *Bridge to Terabithia* depict the deepest and most secret corners of the different-gender protagonists' minds. *The Outsiders* also uses a male narrative voice. Does this mean that "feminine writing" tends to be character oriented and introspective even when a male protagonist is portrayed? In fact, there are very few successful introspective portraits of female protagonists created by male writers. The heroines of *The Island of the Blue Dolphins* and *The True Confessions of Charlotte Doyle* are examples of male authors using the female first-person perspective. On the other hand, there are plenty of examples of female writers keeping to the external representation, irrespective of the protagonist's gender, such as Frances Hodgson Burnett who has somewhat comparable characters in *Little Lord Fauntleroy* (male), *The Little Princess* (female), and *The Secret Garden* (male and female). Beverly Cleary uses third-person perspective in the *Ramona* books, and self-reflexive diary form in *Dear Mr. Henshaw*, which has a male protagonist. Even though some of Harry Potter's thoughts may be revealed to us, the *Harry Potter* novels are primarily plot oriented. Maurice Sendak has described complex internal worlds of a young boy in *Where the Wild Things Are* and of a young girl in *Outside Over There*. What is the difference in his two stories? Perhaps Max's emotions are more aggressive, resulting in the depiction of monsters, while Ida's feelings are those of longing and anxiety, taking the shape of faceless, almost amorphous goblins. Are the female emotions more difficult for a male writer/illustrator to portray so that they appear more vague in the text?

Gender, Language, and Power

Looking at the genres and themes of the above-mentioned books, we cannot establish that masculine and feminine writing is significantly distinct. Concerning style and language, we may make use of the idea of *genderlect* (a relatively new concept suggested by feminist criticism and coined in analogy with dialect), denoting the differentiated idiom of men and women. A genderlect reflects our abstract ideas of how men and women talk. Some rather loose criteria are, for instance, that men are reasonable, while women are imaginative; that masculine language is ordered and structured, while feminine language is impulsive and fragmentary; or that women use more figurative speech. So far there have been no consistent studies of genderlects in children's fiction and very little in general fiction, so it is too early to come up with any statements. But surely the thought is worth pursuing.

Summing up this discussion, our aesthetic explorations of the problem have an affirmative answer to the questions: Can a woman write like a man? Can a man write like a woman? Obviously, male and female writers can choose similar topics, write within the same genres, use protagonists of the same as well as of the opposite gender, use both male and female narrative voices, and so on. Even though many writers do write within the "gender-bound" norms, there does not seem to be any natural, biological reason why men and women should write differently. After a meticulous examination of a variety of aspects, we would most probably decide that the *Harry Potter* books are masculine texts.

Among the many ways of handling the question of authors' gender, we might consider the power position, the socially constructed gender, which has little to do with the biological gender of the authors. Women in our Western society have since time immemorial been the weaker, the oppressed group—something that feminist ideology has made us aware of. Without going into detail, let us remember that until the twentieth century, women were not allowed to vote or have property, they had no access to higher education or to most of the professions, and so on. Even though in most Western countries today women enjoy equal rights with men, at least legally, still women's actual status in society is lower than men's. Writing from this oppressed position, women have to make their voices heard; therefore they have to employ certain strategies in their writing. For instance, Louisa M. Alcott could not say in plain words that women should have the same rights as men; yet her opinion reaches across to the readers through a number of minor details in her writing. This is what we mean by saying that women's writing is—or can be—subversive. It questions the existing societal norms without necessarily going openly into social or political debates. Feminist criticism has suggested the concept of *palimpsest* to denote the subversive strategy of women's writing within patriarchal society. A palimpsest is a term from archival research, meaning a bit of papyrus or parchment from which the original script has been erased and a new script written instead. A modern scientist can reconstruct the erased, hidden text, which occasionally proves more interesting than the text written on top of it. In feminist theory, palimpsest denotes a text that has a different, hidden message below the superficial plot, often a message about women's liberation through creativity. Is this a typically feminine way of writing? In a way yes, since there is usually no need for most men in our society to disguise their messages or to write from defensive positions. Among possible strategies for subversive writing is the choice of genre. Fantasy and science fiction are two genres that allow writers to play with gender and eradicate the existing gender inequalities.

Writing from a Minority Viewpoint

The question of the impact of the author's gender on writing can naturally be extended to other essential biographical facts. Postcolonial and queer theories have posed questions about writing similar to those presented by feminist critics. Can white authors write like black authors? Can white authors write like Native American authors? Can Anglo-Saxon African authors write like Zulu or Swahili authors? Can Gentile authors write like Jewish authors, especially when writing about the Holocaust? Can heterosexual authors write like homosexual authors? Radical postcolonial critics claim that "the oppressors" cannot, and should not, try to express the concerns of "the oppressed." This is a very sensitive issue, since many talented white authors are sincerely willing to lend their voices to minority groups. But will their voices always sound a bit false?

EXERCISE 1

Choose a children's novel or a picture book written by an African-American or a Native American author, and another novel or picture book written by a white author, describing African-Americans or Native Americans. Study them carefully and compare the way topics, characters, and settings are described. If you did not know, would you be able to guess which book was written by which author?

Virginia Hamilton and Mildred Taylor are two excellent African-American children's authors who deliberately and consistently choose African-American topics, characters, and settings in their novels. In *Roll of Thunder, Hear My Cry*, Taylor not only makes racial segregation the main conflict of her plot, but comments on it, through her narrator, in many details: black and white children go to different schools, and so on. Virginia Hamilton paints a bright picture of the urban black community in *The Planet of Junior Brown*. The fact that the characters are black is not in any way emphasized in the novel, but the settings and the life conditions of the characters make it clear. These are examples of authors who utilize the authority of their own ethnicity to be subversive.

To conclude the discussion of the relationship between authors and texts, let us connect it to the overall issue of the essence of children's literature. Children's authors are in a peculiar way in the same position as male authors writing about women, or white authors writing about ethnic minorities, or heterosexual authors writing about gays. Even though all children's authors once were children, still the parallel is obvious. Some of the arguments used by feminist and postcolonial theories can be summed up as follows. "Lending a voice" to an oppressed minority is undesirable, because the author is writing from a superior power position and cannot adopt the minority's subjectivity. On the other hand, it can be positive, as the author is lending a voice to a silenced group. Yet, it is still undesirable, because lending a voice is always usurping the voice. Further, the activity can be viewed as self-indulgent and motivated by self-justification. Not least, it is impossible, because the authors cannot use their own experience in their writing. The counter-argument to this last stance is that it is possible for a talented author to adopt an Other subjectivity.

The most radical advocates of feminist and postcolonial theories claim that only the oppressed and silenced groups should write their own discourse. This may be plausible about female, black, Jewish, or gay writers—but what about children? Can they write their own discourse in a way that adults would listen? Within childhood culture studies, examinations of children's own stories, oral and written, have become prominent. Shall we let children write their own literature?

Further, if, for instance, white authors writing about native characters can be viewed as self-justification, is writing children's literature self-justification for adults? Drawing this to the extreme, we can say that adults have two reasons for writing for children. They may want to give children the illusion that childhood is a nice, benevolent place to be; to keep them innocent as long as possible. This is a dubious purpose, since the image of an idyllic childhood is, not least in our day, a blatant lie. Another incentive for writers may be to offer themselves a nostalgic sense of lost childhood, therapy for the frustration of having grown up, for unfulfilled dreams and lost hopes. This is clearly self-deceit, self-delusion.

How can we circumvent this? What are the authors' intentions with children's books? Is children's literature for children? Books like *Winnie-the-Pooh*, *Peter Pan*, and many others have been questioned as children's books, among other things, on the basis of their authors' intentions. On the other hand, nice, sweet, mind-numbing, purposeless children's books about bunnies, kittens, and happy children in happy homes have never been praised by critics. Feminist and postcolonial theories draw our attention to the question of power in the relationship between the writer and the reader, and to the way the writer's authority can either enhance the existing power positions or interrogate them. Alison Lurie has in her book *Don't Tell the Grownups: Subversive Children's Literature* discussed a number of children's novels that she believes question adult authority and present an affirmative picture of childhood. Even though we might not agree with Lurie in all her assessments, the concept of subversive children's literature can still be extremely useful. We will return to it repeatedly in later chapters.

EXERCISE 2

Choose a children's novel or picture book and consider it from the point of view of the author's authority in terms of gender, ethnicity, class or social group, and so on. Try to pose as many questions as possible along the lines of the argument in this section. Contemplate how these questions have increased your understanding of children's literature.

HOW TO GO FURTHER

From this chapter, it should be clear that the scope of questions concerning the relationships between the author and the text in children's

literature is large and varying. Yet anyone setting out to conduct author-oriented studies today will meet with considerable resistance.
Poststructural theories of literature, as represented by Jacques Derrida,
Paul de Man, and Michel Foucault, have strongly interrogated the role
of the author in the existence and functioning of art. Not least Foucault's essay "What is an Author?" has brought this seemingly self-
evident question into the limelight. The author's subjectivity and the
complicated relationship between the author's consciousness and the
text created out of the authorial intention is the cornerstone of these
theories that draw heavily on philosophy and psychoanalysis. Even
though, as this chapter has shown, the role of children's authors is in
some respects considerably different from their counterparts in the
mainstream, quite a few poststructuralist ideas can be successfully applied. Some directions within childhood studies, focusing on the author, the expression of the author's and society's views on childhood,
and the author's own childhood experiences, seem especially fruitful
and promising.

REFERENCES

General

Abrams, M. H. *The Mirror and the Lamp: Romantic Theory and Critical Tradition.*
Oxford: Oxford University Press, 1953. Discusses the expressive theories of literature emerging during Romanticism and ascribing authors a considerably stronger
position than previously accepted.

Barthes, Roland. "The Death of the Author." Pp. 142–148 in his *Image—Music—
Text.* London: Fontana, 1977. Also pp. 166–172 in *Modern Criticism and Theory:
A Reader*, edited by David Lodge. London: Longman, 1988.

Burke, Sean, ed. *Authorship: From Plato to the Postmodern.* Edinburgh: Edinburgh
University Press, 1995. This anthology presents a variety of theories about the
role of the author.

De Man, Paul. "The Resistance to Theory." Pp. 354–370 in *Modern Criticism and
Theory: A Reader*, edited by David Lodge. London: Longman, 1988.

Epstein, William, ed. *Considering the Subject: Essays in the Postmodern Theory and
Practice of Biography and Biographical Criticism.* West Lafayette, IN: Purdue
University Press, 1991.

Foucault, Michel. "What is an Author?" Pp. 196–210 in *Modern Criticism and Theory: A Reader*, edited by David Lodge. London: Longman, 1988.

Galbraight, Mary. "Agony in the Kindergarten: Indelible German Images in American Picture Books." Pp. 124–43 in *Text, Culture and National Identity in Children's Literature*, edited by Jean Webb. Helsinki: Nordinfo, 2000.

———. "What Must I Give Up in Order to Grow Up? The Great War and Childhood Survival in Transatlantic Children's Books." *The Lion and the Unicorn* 24,

no. 3 (2000): 337–59. Mary Galbraith argues in her essays for a new biographical approach to children's literature, based on tracing the authors' childhood experiences as expressed in their texts.

Golden, Joanne M. *The Narrative Symbol in Childhood Literature: Exploration in the Construction of Text*. Berlin: Mouton, 1990. Chap. 5, "Agents: Author and Reader."

Lowe, Virginia. "'Stop! You Didn't Read Who Wrote It!': The Concept of the Author." *Children's Literature in Education* 22, no. 2 (1991): 79–88.

Lurie, Alison. *Don't Tell the Grownups: Subversive Children's Literature*. Boston: Little, Brown, 1990.

Wimsatt, William K. *The Verbal Icon: Studies in the Meaning of Poetry*. Lexington, KY: University of Kentucky Press, 1954. This central work of New Criticism contains two major essays written in collaboration with Monroe C. Beardsley, "The Intentional Fallacy" and "The Affective Fallacy," both dealing with the position of the author.

Biographical Studies of Children's Literature

There are of course hundreds of biographies of children's authors. This is a brief selection illustrating the different approaches discussed in this chapter. For more author biographies consult the general bibliography at the end of the book.

Andronik, Catherine M. *Kindred Spirit: A Biography of L. M. Montgomery, Creator of Anne of Green Gables*. New York: Atheneum, 1996. An illustrated biography geared toward young readers.

Bedell, Madelon. *The Alcotts: Biography of a Family*. New York: Charles N. Potter, 1980.

Birkin, Andrew. *J. M. Barrie and The Lost Boys*. London: Constable, 1979. The biography is focused on the author's pathological interest for little boys.

Christopher, Joe R. *C. S. Lewis*. Boston: Twayne, 1987.

Cohen, Morton N. *Lewis Carroll: A Biography*. New York: Knopf, 1995. This biography presents Carroll as a depraved pedophile.

Collingwood, Stuart Dodgson. *The Life and Letters of Lewis Carroll (Rev. C. L. Dodgson)*. New York: The Century, 1899. This early biography written by Carroll's nephew carefully omits anything that might seem offensive to his contemporaries.

Coren, Michael. *The Man who Created Narnia: The Story of C. S. Lewis*. Grand Rapids, MI: Eerdman, 1996.

Dunbar, Janet. *J M Barrie: The Man Behind the Image*. London: Collins, 1970.

Elbert, Sarah. *A Hunger for Home: Louisa M. Alcott and Little Women*. Philadelphia: Temple University Press, 1984.

Green, Roger Lancelyn. *C. S. Lewis*. London: Bodley Head, 1957.

Grønbech, Bo. *Hans Christian Andersen*. New York: Twayne, 1980.

Hurwitz, Johanna. *Astrid Lindgren: Storyteller to the World*. New York: Viking Penguin, 1989. A biography of the famous Swedish children's author, written for young readers.

Leach, Karoline. *In the Shadow of the Dreamchild: A New Understanding of Lewis Carroll.* London: Peter Owen, 1999. This biography, based on Carroll's unpublished diaries, strongly questions his earlier image as a man mainly interested in little girls.

MacDonald, Ruth K. *Louisa M. Alcott.* Boston: Twayne, 1983.

Meigs, Cornelia. *Invincible Louisa: The Story of the Author of Little Women.* Boston: Little, Brown, 1933. A biography for children.

Milne, Christopher. *The Enchanted Places.* London: Methuen, 1974. A very personal biography of A. A. Milne, written by his son. The main purpose of the book seems to be to disperse the image of Christopher Robin, the figure of the Pooh books, loosely based on Christopher Milne.

Saxton, Martha. *Louisa May: A Modern Biography.* New York: Avon, 1978. This is a biography that presents the author in a radically different light as compared to the previous publications.

Stern, Madeleine B. *Louisa May Alcott.* Norman: University of Oklahoma Press, 1950.

Wilson, Andrew Norman. *C. S. Lewis: A Biography.* London: Collins, 1990.

Wullschläger, Jackie. *Hans Christian Andersen: The Life of a Storyteller.* New York: Knopf, 2001. This biography is considerably more open about some facts about Andersen's life, such as his alleged homosexuality.

Psychoanalytical Author-Oriented Studies

Franz, Marie Loiuse von. *Puer Aeternus: A Psychological Study of the Adult Struggle with the Paradise of Childhood.* 2nd ed. Santa Monica: Sigo, 1981.

Kelley-Lainé, Kathleen. *Peter Pan: The Story of Lost Childhood.* Shaftesbury: Element, 1997.

Rose, Jacqueline. *The Case of Peter Pan, or The Impossibility of Children's Fiction.* London: Macmillan, 1984.

Wullschläger, Jackie. *Inventing Wonderland: The Lives and Fantasies of Lewis Carroll, Edward Lear, J. M. Barrie, Kenneth Grahame and A. A. Milne.* London: Methuen, 1995.

Feminist Studies

Åhmansson, Gabriella. *A Life and its Mirrors. A Feminist Reading of L. M. Montgomery's Fiction.* Uppsala: Acta Universitatis Upsaliensis, 1991.

Alberghene, Janice M., and Beverly Lyon Clark, eds. *Little Women and the Feminist Imagination: Criticism, Controversy, Personal Essays.* New York: Garland, 1998.

Attebery, Brian. *Strategies of Fantasy.* Bloomington: Indiana University Press, 1992. The study discusses female authors who use the fantasy form to convey feminist messages.

Eagleton, Mary, ed. *Feminist Literary Theory: A Reader.* Oxford: Basil Blackwell, 1986. Contains, among other things, the essay by Joyce Carol Oates, "Is There a Female Voice?"

Gilbert, Sandra M., and Susan Gubar. *The Madwoman in the Attic: The Woman Writer and the Nineteenth-Century Literary Imagination*. New Haven: Yale University Press, 1977.

———. *No Man's Land: The Place of the Woman Writer in the Twentieth Century*. New Haven: Yale University Press, 1988.

Russ, Joanna. *To Write Like a Woman: Essays in Feminism and Science Fiction*. Bloomington: Indiana University Press, 1995.

Showalter, Elaine. *A Literature of Their Own: British Women Novelists from Brontë to Lessing*. London: Virago, 1982.

———. "Feminist Criticism in the Wilderness." Pp. 243–279 in her *The New Feminist Criticism: Essays on Women, Literature, and Theory*. London: Virago, 1986. Also pp. 330–353 in *Modern Criticism and Theory: A Reader*, edited by David Lodge. London: Longman, 1988. One of the most influential essays on the strategies of women's writing.

———. *Sister's Choice: Tradition and Change in American Women's Writing*. Oxford: Clarendon Press, 1991. Includes a chapter on *Little Women*.

Spender, Dale. *Man Made Language*. 2nd ed. London: Pandora, 1998.

Woolf, Virginia. *A Room of One's Own* (1929). San Diego: Harcourt Brace Jovanovich, 1989.

2

The Aesthetic of the Work

In this chapter we will be looking at a literary work as a whole, and discussing various theories about how we can understand and interpret a piece of literature. We will also ask some probing questions about the relationship between literary texts.

INTERPRETING THE SIGNS

Literature is a form of communication. A message (a literary text) is sent by one agency (a writer) to be received by another agency (a reader): sender → message → receiver. In order to send the message, the sender makes use of a set of signs. In literature, the signs—on the most primitive level—are the letters of the alphabet from which the sender constructs words and sentences. In other forms of communication, other signs are used. For instance, Native Americans used smoke from fires to communicate. In order to be able to receive the message, the receiver must know what the sign indicates. If you do not know the implication of two or three puffs of smoke, the message is wasted on you. If you cannot read, the written message has no meaning. The communication is thus dependent, first, on a shared background, or context, and second, on the codes shared by the sender and the receiver:

$$\text{context}$$
$$\text{sender} \rightarrow \text{message} \rightarrow \text{receiver}$$
$$\text{code}$$

The theory about communication with signs is called *semiotics* (from Greek *semeion*, sign). It explains how different types of signs can convey messages.

A sign is thus something that stands for something else. Every sign consists of two parts: the signifier and the signified. The signifier is the form of the sign, for instance a puff of smoke or a word. The signified is the content, or meaning, of the sign, for instance the message "Danger" conveyed by two puffs of smoke, or the image of the animal conveyed by the word "cat." (See fig. 2-1.)

Depending on the relationship between the signifier and the signified, signs can be iconic or conventional.[1] Iconic, or representational, signs are those in which the signifier and the signified are related by common qualities, that is, where the sign is a direct representation of its signified. A picture of a printer on a computer's command menu is an icon, which is a direct representation of the actual object it signifies. In most cases, we do not need special knowledge to understand a simple icon. (See fig. 2-2a.)

Conventional signs have no direct relation with their signified. The word "print" in a menu only conveys a meaning if we possess the code, that is, know what the letters stand for, can put letters together to produce words, and understand what the words represent. Conventional signs are based on a convention, an agreement between the bearers of a particular language, both natural languages and others, such as gestures, dress code, or emblems. For anyone outside the given community, conventional signs do not carry any meaning, or at best the meaning is ambivalent. (See fig. 2-2b.)

In explaining signs on a very basic level, semioticians like to use traffic signals to illustrate the various types of signs. We know that a red light means stop, yellow means be alert, green means go. Yet, we only associate these meanings with the colors because some people in the 1920s agreed on this—this is a convention (agreement); thus traffic lights are conventional signs.

If you see the signs shown in figure 2-2c on two adjacent doors, you would most probably choose the correct door. These are iconic signs, representing the two genders schematically (even though many women nowadays wear long pants). However, if you are traveling in a foreign country and see

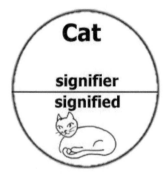

Figure 2.1   A sign consists of two parts.

two doors marked H and N, you may be at a loss (tip: watch people come out!). The letters stand for Finnish *"Herrat"* ("Gentlemen") and *"Naiset"* ("Ladies"), and of course you have no chance of guessing if you do not know the convention. Yet, a seemingly iconic sign may be conventional in a second degree.

Suppose the two doors have the signs shown in figure 2-2d. You might figure out that one of them represents men and the other women, but which is which? In the particular country where I encountered these signs, the sun turned out to be male and the moon female. But in many cultures, it is the other way round. The concepts of the sun and moon, connected with the iconic signs, are thus conventional, culturally dependent signs to denote gender.

Iconic signs can also have a grammar, albeit simple. An X or a diagonal line, as shown in figure 2-2e, usually means a negation. A crossed-over picture of a cigarette means it is forbidden to smoke. A crossed-over picture on a door of a walking man means that the entrance is forbidden. This is a universal iconic sign that does not need special knowledge to be understood. By contrast, conventional (verbal) signs such as "No smoking," "Nicht rauchen," "Rökning förbjuden," "Nie palic," and so on, have a meaning only if you know the language.

In our everyday life, we frequently communicate through different forms of signs. We need to know the conventions in order to understand conventional signs. We also have to be aware of the fact that some "universally" conventional signs can in other cultures mean something different or even the opposite, like nodding for "no."

CONTEMPLATE

When you walk or drive around your community, note the occurrence of iconic and conventional signs: road signs, advertisements, shop signs and boards, and so on. Observe yourself and people around you: what kind of signs are they displaying, explicit and implicit? A cross or a star of David signifies religious community, as do certain clothes, such as the headdress some Muslim women wear. Many people nowadays announce their sexual orientation by wearing specific signs. Tattoos are popular among young people today, while they earlier often were (and in some cultures still are) associated with the world of crime. Naturally, expensive brand clothes, watches, and jewelry signify wealth.

Now you may ask, what does it all have to do with children's literature?

Humpty Dumpty, the Great Semiotician

Literature uses language to communicate, and language consists of conventional signs. It means that before we can understand a work of literature,

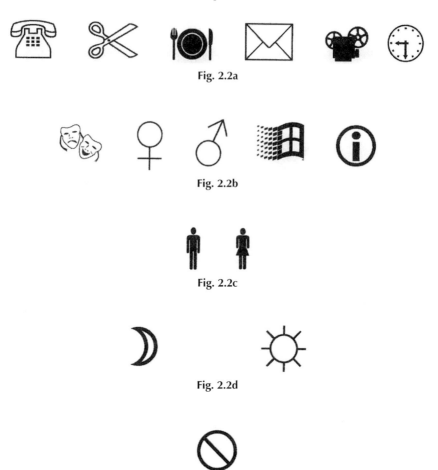

Fig. 2.2a

Fig. 2.2b

Fig. 2.2c

Fig. 2.2d

Fig. 2.2e

we need to be trained in a number of conventions. On the most basic level, we must know how to read, how to make sense of the letters, words, and sentences. Fiction is, however, more complex than, for instance, everyday language, since it also involves figurative speech and other features and artistic devices which need special knowledge to be understood. Early semioticians made a great point of distinguishing between the everyday language and the poetic, or artistic, language used in fiction. Even if this distinction is more complicated and less pronounced than some semiotic studies make it, the language of fiction certainly demands a knowledge of and training in certain codes. Semiotics explains how messages can be encoded in literary texts by writers and how they can subsequently be decoded by readers.

In Lewis Carroll's classic children's book *Through the Looking Glass*, Alice meets Humpty Dumpty, a figure from a nursery rhyme:

> Humpty Dumpty sat on a wall,
> Humpty Dumpty had a great fall . . .

The word "Humpty Dumpty" does not have a meaning in English (at least it did not have a meaning before Carroll's novel was published): it is a signifier without the signified. When Alice sees a large egg with eyes and a nose and mouth, she somehow recognizes the figure: "she saw clearly that it was HUMPTY DUMPTY himself." The writer thus supplies a signified to a previously empty verbal sign. Chapter 6 in the novel, where this encounter takes place, provides a splendid lesson in semiotics. In a much-quoted conversation between Alice and Humpty Dumpty we learn the following:

> "When *I* use a word," Humpty Dumpty said, in rather a scornful tone, "it means just what I choose it to mean—neither more nor less."
> "The question is," said Alice, "whether you *can* make words mean so many different things."
> "The question is," said Humpty Dumpty, "which is to be master—that's all." (196; italics in the original)

What Humpty Dumpty is saying illustrates the arbitrary nature of verbal signs. Like Humpty Dumpty, a writer puts meaning into words, and the reader has to share the code in order to understand them. Impressed by Humpty Dumpty's cleverness, Alice asks him to explain the meaning of a poem she has learned behind the looking glass:

> 'Twas brillig, and the slithy toves
>   Did gyre and gimble in the wabe:
> All mimsy were the borogoves,
>   And the mome raths outgrabe.

Most of the words of the poem are empty signs, signifiers without a signified. We have no idea what the words mean. However, we can still make some sense out of the poem since it follows correct syntax. It is reminiscent of the famous sentence used in linguistics (originally by Noam Chomsky) to demonstrate the difference between some essential functions of language: "Green colorless ideas sleep furiously." Grammatically, this sentence is correct, while logically it is impossible. In Carroll's poem, we can see that "brillig" is an adverb; "slithy," "mimsy," and "mome" are adjectives; "toves," "wabe," "borogoves," and "raths" are nouns, some of them used in the plural; and "gyre," "gimble," and "outgrabe" are verbs, the latter in the past tense. In explaining the poem to Alice, Humpty Dumpty supplies content for the signs: "'*Brillig*' means four o'clock in the afternoon—the time when you begin *broiling* things for dinner . . . '*slithy*' means 'lithe and slimy' . . . '*toves*' are something like badgers—they're something like lizards—and they're something like corkscrews. . . . To '*gyre*' is to go round and round like a gyroscope. To '*gimble*' is to make holes like a gimlet. And '*the wabe*' is the grass-plot round a sun-dial. . . . It's called '*wabe*' you know, because it goes a long way before it, and a long way behind it— . . . '*mimsy*' is 'flimsy and miserable'. . . . And a '*borogove*' is a thin shabby-looking bird with its feathers sticking out all around—something like a live mop . . . a '*rath*' is a sort of green pig: but '*mome*' I'm not certain about. I think it's short for 'from home'—meaning that they'd lost their way . . . '*outgribing*' is something between bellowing and whistling, with a kind of sneeze in the middle. . . ." (198f; italics in the original). Of course the poem is still rather absurd after the explanations; yet Humpty Dumpty demonstrates clearly how the relationship between the signifier and the signified is created. (See fig. 2-3.)

Pooh, Pippi, and Other Linguists

In *Winnie-the-Pooh*, several words lack the signified, for instance the Heffalump (whom the illustrator makes look rather like an ordinary elephant),

Fig. 2-3 John Tenniel's illustration from *Through the Looking Glass*.

woozles and wizzles, or the Spotted and Herbaceous Backson, who are not illustrated. In the woozle-hunt chapter, Pooh is wondering whether he and Piglet are following two Grandfathers, and what a Grandfather might look like. This is a complete reversal of notions where a word that is completely normal for the reader is for the character as meaningless as "woozle" is for the reader. The writer thus draws the reader's attention to the arbitrary nature of language. "Grandfather" is an empty signifier for Pooh, since there is no referent for it in his world.

In Dr. Seuss's books, we also meet a number of nonsensical words, which the author provides with a signified, often by means of illustration. Thus rather than explaining what a Grinch looks like, he gives us a visual portrait. In *Dr. Seuss's ABC* a number of strange creatures are featured: a duck-dog, a Fiffer-feffer-feff, an Icabod, a quacker-oo, and a Zizzer-Zazzer-Zuzz. Likewise, in *Marvin K. Mooney, Will You Please Go Now!*, the nonexistent names of various means of transportation are visualized: a Zike-Bike, a Crunk-Car, a Zumble-Zay, and a Bumble-Boat. *Green Eggs and Ham* is based on the incongruity between a linguistically correct expression and the absence of its correspondence in the perceptible world. In a picture, the logically impossible green eggs and ham can easily be depicted. In *The Cat in the Hat* Seuss does something different. The naughty cat carries in a big red box, announcing that it contains two things. The word "thing" is in this case a so-called linguistic shifter, that is, an expression the content of which can only be determined by the situation ("a thing" can denote almost anything, although perhaps most often an inanimate object). However, on the next page, the word acquires a concrete and tangible signified, as it refers to two living creatures. The word "thing" ceases to be a shifter and becomes a regular signifier, while the signified, Thing One and Thing Two, are portrayed in the picture, thus visualizing the concretized abstraction. Something similar occurs in *Horton Hears a Who*, where the interrogative pronoun "who" (a shifter) is turned into a signifier with a specific signified.

Pippi Longstocking "invents" a new word one day, "spink," and of course as she shares her discovery with her friends, they wonder what the word means. Pippi, however, has invented a signifier without a signified, and, as she says, "The only thing I know is that it doesn't mean vacuum cleaner" (*Pippi in the South Seas*, 31). Pippi then tries to find a referent, a signified that would suit the arbitrarily created signifier (acting, as Pippi usually does, contrary to the normal course of events). She tries to buy some spink in a store, goes to a doctor and complains of acute spink, and so on, finally deciding that the name matches a tiny bug she sees on the path.

These rather unusual children's books (sometimes labeled as "nonsense") illustrate some extreme cases of discrepancy between the signifier and the signified, in which the arbitrariness of language is brought to our attention. However, in every literary text, we have to decode the signs (that is, identify the relationship between the signifier and the signified) before we can grasp the meaning. In most cases, we do this automatically, but if this automatic decoding for some reason fails, the message will be misinterpreted. For instance, in *Winnie-the-Pooh*, Pooh does not know the meaning of the difficult words Owl is using, such as "Customary Procedure," so he tries to find the closest possible signified, making it into "Crustimony Proseedcake." Similarly, on hearing the word "ambush," Pooh interprets it as a kind of "bush," like a gorse bush. It is of course not accidental that Pooh, who represents a very young child, does not know the meaning of abstract notions and instead chooses a signified he perceives as concrete and tangible, even though the signifier may not exist. In fact, we become familiar with the perceptible world long before we master the language to describe it. In *Ramona the Pest*, on Ramona's first day in kindergarten her teacher says to her: "Sit here for the present" (17). Ramona misinterprets the abstract phrase, meaning "for now" or "for the time being," and expects a gift from the teacher for sitting still. She is greatly disappointed when she does not get any present and thinks that "[w]ords were so puzzling. *Present* should mean a present" (27; italics in the original).

We will learn more about the use of language in children's fiction in chapter 9. We will also be going back to semiotic interpretations of the different textual elements throughout this book. So far, let us just be aware of the way signs work in the literary texts we are reading. Since literature communicates through language, and since linguistic signs, as we have agreed, are primarily conventional, as readers we have to be successively introduced to the various conventions in order to master the decoding process. That is what happens when a child moves from easy readers toward more complex narratives.

ABC books and picture dictionaries present the most elementary relationship between the signifier and the signified. The picture of an apple and the word "apple" create an immediate connection between the object and the sign, that is, the word (even though the picture in itself is a sign too). A novel is an extremely complex conventional sign, or rather it consists of a large number of complex conventional signs on various levels: besides language, one encounters plot construction, characterization, narrative perspective, underlying ideology, intertextual links, and so on. In order to understand the signified behind this complex signifier we must possess the key to all the encoded messages on every level. Although it is infinitely more problematical to understand a novel than to understand the connection between an apple and the word "apple," the basic task is the same: to investigate the relationship between the sign and the phenomenon it stands for.

EXERCISE

Choose a variety of children's books, including a picture dictionary, a picture storybook, a novel, and an information book. Study the books carefully and consider the relationship between the signifier and the signified in them. Here are some questions to assist you:

- Is the book communicating primarily with iconic or conventional signs?
- Are the iconic signs used in the book simple and easy to understand or complex and demanding special knowledge?
- Are the conventional signs (that is, words) simple in the sense that they have tangible, easily recognizable signifieds?
- What special codes do we need to decode and understand the message of the book? For instance, does the book contain any indication of its genre (such as the initial formula, "Once upon a time . . . ," for a fairy tale)?
- What, if any, is the difference in communication between an information book and a novel?

FROM THE WHOLE TO DETAILS—AND BACK

From the previous section it should be clear that we cannot make sense of a literary text without interpreting it. The theory about interpretation of texts is called *hermeneutics*. The word alludes to the name of the Greek god Hermes who was the messenger between gods. Hermeneutics thus emphasizes that a message needs someone to carry it, someone to explicate, to elucidate, to interpret. A hermeneutic analysis involves pointing out and explaining how what we read or otherwise perceive embodies a meaning.

The main premise of hermeneutics is that in extracting a meaning from a piece of art we alternate between the whole and the details. For instance, when we look at a painting, we can start by perceiving it as a whole, noting the general composition, theme, color scheme, and so on. Provided that we are interested enough in learning more about the painting, we may then study the details, for instance each depicted object, figure, or shape; the foreground and the background; the particulars of hues and saturation; the individual brushstrokes (or other technique); and so on. However, if we stop at this stage, our perception of the work will be fragmentary. Therefore we must go back to studying the whole, this time with a better preconception, since we know more about the constituent parts of the whole. (See fig. 2-4.)

In studying a literary text, we also usually begin with the whole: the storyline, the central characters, and their role in the story. When reading for pleasure, we often stop at that. Working with the text professionally, as critics or teachers, we will most probably go on to study the details: composition, characterization, narrative perspective, style, and underlying messages.

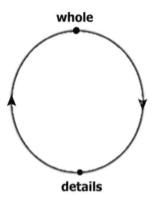

Fig. 2-4   The hermeneutic circle.

We may go still further into particulars, for instance, and only examine metaphors, or only concentrate on direct speech, or only investigate how female characters are portrayed. Such a detailed study is, however, only fruitful if we afterward go back to the whole, and hopefully we will then have a better understanding of the text. Many famous texts, such as Shakespeare's plays, have been studied in minute detail, with books, articles, and dissertations written perhaps about just one tiny aspect of one single play. These detailed studies contribute to our general understanding of Shakespeare.

As anyone who has ever read books to a child knows, young children frequently want to hear the same story over and over again, until they seemingly know it by heart and cannot get anything new from it. Apparently, the deeper understanding of the meaning is achieved by first getting the gist of the story, concentrating more on the details on second reading, incorporating details into the whole on the third, and so on. As adults, we presumptuously believe that we have "understood" a book after having read it once. Yet if we take the effort to reread a book, we clearly notice details that escaped our attention the first time. When no longer held in suspense following the storyline, we can focus on such aspects as characterization, composition (for instance, foreshadowing), point of view, and so on.

The hermeneutic circle is an eternal course. Obviously, the more complex the work, the more room there is for searching deeper into its various layers; yet the hermeneutic approach in itself presupposes the never ending process of interpretation. Surely, this presents a problem. If each rereading, each shift from the whole to details and back, leads us further into the meaning of a literary text, this implies that we can never reach its ultimate meaning. This, however, is a metaphysical observation. In practice, we are satisfied by following the hermeneutic circle two or three times, making sure (1) that we have not missed any essential details, and (2) that we have reassembled the details into a meaningful whole. After all, it is the overall impression of a literary work that affects the reader. As critics, we may for the time being be interested in a particular feature of the text we are analyzing, let us say, characterization; however, this study is only relevant in connection with a more comprehensive view of the work. Thus, hermeneutics brings to our attention the importance of the relationship between the general and the particular, which can also be applied in a broader sense.

EXERCISE

Choose a picture storybook that you have not read before and read it as you would have read it together with a child. On this first reading, you will most likely pay attention to the storyline: what happens? Who does what? How does it go? You will probably look at the pictures briefly, but mainly you will concentrate on the words.

Now read the story again, this time paying attention to the details, words as well as pictures. Spend as long as you can studying each page, even if there are just a few words on it. There are sure to be details in the pictures that you have missed during the first reading. You may also have missed some elements of the text. What is the language like? Are there any unusual words in the story? Is the language everyday or poetic? Are there any interesting narrative devices used in the story, such as repetition or contrast? Who is telling the story? Are the words and the pictures telling exactly the same story, or do they contradict each other in some way?

Now reread the story for the third time. Has it changed after you have studied the details?

Students, even college students, often complain that analyzing texts destroys the joys of reading. It is, of course, easy to kill the lust for reading by boring analyses; yet the hermeneutic approach shows us that by studying details we have a better understanding of the whole—and, it can be added, also a greater aesthetic appreciation of the whole.

All the World Is a Theme

A direction of criticism drawing on the ideas of hermeneutics is thematic criticism, developed primarily in France. The method of analysis involves identifying a theme in the works of a particular writer, or sometimes even more broadly, within a literary school or epoch. *Theme* is in this theory something different than in traditional criticism; it is rather a recurrent pattern, image, concept, or even character found in all or most of the relevant

works. The hermeneutic process in this approach is characterized by studying every particular work and then viewing them all together as one whole.
This broader context will presumably help us see each individual work in a
new light.

Many children's writers have recurrent patterns, or trademarks, in their
works. Lloyd Alexander has a cat and a musician in every book. Patricia
MacLachlan often includes an object connected with looking and seeing:
binoculars or a camera. These recurrent patterns help us see works by a certain author in a broader context, see connections between them. In Lloyd
Alexander's case, it may be more the question of self-amusement: he loves
cats and music. In MacLachlan's case, "seeing beyond the surface" (a phrase
used in her novel *Unclaimed Treasures*) is the overall theme of her writing.

EXERCISE

Choose an author who has written several books with which you are
familiar. These should be separate books, not a series, nor a book with
several sequels. Dr. Seuss would be a good example. Reread the books
carefully and see whether there are any recurrent themes, types of
character, or images that reappear in all of them or at least most of
them. Contemplate how the recognition of these recurrent elements
has contributed to your understanding of each individual work.

The obvious drawback of this approach is that you have to be familiar with
all, or at least most of the novels by a particular writer in order to be able to
see the recurrent patterns. You cannot study an isolated text. However, texts
never exist in isolation, which brings us to the next question, that of the relationship between texts, or intertextuality.

TEXTUAL CROSSROADS

Literary texts do not appear in a vacuum. Literature in our Western society
has been written for several thousand years, and literature written specifically for children has existed for at least two hundred years. Thousands of
children's books are published every year. Writers have usually read books
by other writers or are at least aware of them. In the case of children's writers, they are most likely to have read the major children's classics, but they
have probably also read mainstream literature. Whether conscious about this
or not, writers are affected by what they read and even by what they have
not read but only heard about. Literature is also disseminated through other

channels, such as film and television. When we read a book, we are often struck by its similarities to others we know.

LET US EXPLORE

Compare *The Lion, the Witch and the Wardrobe* and *Harry Potter and the Sorcerer's Stone*. Try to see as many similarities as possible: events, settings, characters, symbols, messages. Now try to find the ways in which the two novels are different. What is the nature of the difference?

The direction of literary criticism that studies various types of connection between authors, texts, and literatures is called comparative. In comparing two literary works, we pursue the goal of identifying their similarities and dissimilarities as well as providing possible reasons for those. Some straightforward reasons for similarity can be the following:

- the two texts are written by the same author (*Bridge to Terabithia* and *The Great Gilly Hopkins* show considerable similarities in the depiction of an underprivileged child);
- the two texts are written within the same genre (*The Wizard of Oz* and *The Lion, the Witch and the Wardrobe* are both fantasy novels);
- the two texts are written more or less at the same time (*Slake's Limbo* and *The Planet of Junior Brown* are both published in the 1970s when children's novels were often focused on social issues).

Imitation or Creativity?

A further reason, frequently employed in comparative studies, is the assumption that a writer has been influenced by another, earlier writer. Since the first *Harry Potter* book appeared almost forty years later than *The Lion*, it is natural to see the influence of the older book on the later one (although if you read *Harry Potter* first you may believe that C. S. Lewis has borrowed all his ideas from J. K. Rowling). The question of literary influence has, however, been under serious debate during the last twenty years. Harold Bloom discusses in his widely known study *The Anxiety of Influence* a pattern of literary evolution in which every writer has a model, The Great Literary Father, from whose influence he (writers are by definition male in Bloom's theory) must liberate himself. A true writer will, according to Bloom, achieve at least some degree of freedom from the model, by both absorbing and transforming his strength. Thus, for Bloom, literary activity basically implies a rewriting—or in Bloom's terms, creative *misreading*—of a previously existing text. Yet the anxiety of not being able to compete with the Master is an inevitable part of the creative process. The indisputable Literary Father for Bloom is Shakespeare; thus the task of a literary critic is, on the most primitive level, to compare the writer under scrutiny with Shakespeare and state the degree to which he achieves the stature of the Master: knee high or waist high.

Some critics of children's literature take Bloom as a starting point, suggesting that in the case of children's literature, the "anxiety of influence" is not an issue. Some dismiss the whole idea by stating that authors of children's books seem to be less anxious than mainstream writers. It is true, they say, that children's novels belonging to the same genre are sometimes so similar that you may wonder whether you are confronted with imitation. Still we should stop feeling the need to make excuses for children's books because similarity and repetitiveness are part of children's literature aesthetics. While in contemporary mainstream novels we look for fresh and innovative themes and narrative devices, children's literature is by definition marked by "sameness"; it is all "variations of the same theme." While the call to stop being anxious on behalf of children's writers is appealing, still the question of origin and influence needs clarification.

CONTEMPLATE

Visit a library or a bookstore (perhaps an electronic one) and browse through the shelves in the children's department marked "classics." Try to see whether there is one single book or author that you would perceive as The Classic.

Children's literature lacks an unequivocal Great Master, as Shakespeare is (at least in the English language) for general literature. Many North American scholars choose *Charlotte's Web* as a yardstick for their discussion of children's literature; however, this novel is not used for comparison with all other children's novels. It may be considered a typical children's novel or a typical American children's novel, but it is not the ultimate masterpiece that all subsequent children's writers are trying to surpass. Yet it is not completely erroneous to view *The Lion, the Witch and the Wardrobe* as a model for subsequent fantasy writers. Not only is it a widely popular book, read and enjoyed by many generations of young readers, it is a book pointed out in many textbooks in children's literature as a typical fantasy novel. But it is precarious if not wrong to ascribe this novel an influence on the *Harry Potter* books, which it may or may not have exercised. From the interviews with J. K. Rowling, it is apparent that she is a well-read individual, well acquainted with children's literature classics. She has in fact especially emphasized the

importance of the Narnia books for her own writing. The question of influence and inspiration sources is in this case justified.

Quite a few fantasy writers have acknowledged their debt to Edith Nesbit;
Mark Twain's *The Adventures of Tom Sawyer* is admittedly the master text
of boys' fiction, just as *Little Women* is the master text of domestic fiction;
and *Where the Wild Things Are* is central to any general discussion of picture
books. We can undoubtedly single out certain books as especially influential.
Many children's authors, however, have promptly denied having read books
that critics have identified as their possible models. An interesting example
is C. S. Lewis himself. In *The Lion, the Witch and the Wardrobe*, when the
faun asks Lucy where she comes from, she says, rather confused, that she
has come through the wardrobe in the spare room. The faun misinterprets
her words, thinking that she comes from "the far land of Spare Oom where
eternal summer reigns around the bright city of War Drobe" (17). One
would judge this to be a very original idea. Yet, in a short story by Edith
Nesbit, "The Aunt and Amabel," written forty years prior to Lewis's Narnia
books, a railway station on the way to a magic realm is called BIGWARD-
ROBEINSPAREROOM. The borrowing then would seem obvious, yet
Lewis vehemently denied any influence from Nesbit in the Narnia Chronicles. The wardrobe in a spare room may be a coincidence, or Lewis may have
indeed read Nesbit's story and forgotten it. We are not getting any closer to
our understanding of the text, whether we accept the influence or deny it.

Literary Texts in a Dialogue

It is here that the concept of intertextuality can help us to unveil the dimensions of children's texts that traditional comparison cannot. In intertextual analysis, we do not any longer simply state that two or more texts are
similar, or that one text originates from another, but try to examine the ways
in which the later text develops motifs, patterns, or ideas from its predeces-
sors. Intertextual studies show that children's literature is more complex
than earlier believed; they also suggest a new look at genres and individual
authorships.

The intertextual method has its origins in the works of the Russian critic
Mikhail Bakhtin, introduced in the West by Julia Kristeva. Bakhtin does not
himself use the term "intertextuality"; instead he speaks of "dialogics." It
means that literature and art are created in a continuous conversation ("dialogue") between creators, where every new piece of art or literature is a new
line in the conversation. The meaning of the text is thus revealed for the
reader or researcher only against the background of previous texts, in a clash
between them and the present text. Obviously it is not a question of literary
influence, as in the traditional comparatism. As we have already seen, two
texts juxtaposed in a comparative analysis appear in a causal relation to each

other, and the assumption is that one author has been influenced by reading
another author, as J. K. Rowling acknowledges that she has been influenced
by Edith Nesbit or C. S. Lewis. Two texts in an intertextual analysis are equal
and are not necessarily supposed to have any direct connection. According
to the advocates of intertextuality, no artistic texts can be produced without
a confrontation between texts. Intertextuality is dynamic since every line in
the dialogue of texts does not only look back at previous texts (retrospective
intertextuality) but forward toward new, yet unwritten texts (prospective intertextuality). Intertextuality does not see literature as a static system of
completed texts, but as a movement, where the creation of a text is the crucial
moment.

   While comparatists are bound by evidence and proof, that is, literary or
nonliterary sources, intertextual scholars build their argumentation on the
codes present within the text. If we should engage ourselves in a serious comparative analysis of the *Harry Potter* books and the Narnia Chronicles, we
would not only be obliged to find proof that Rowling has read Lewis (which
she apparently has done), but also investigate exactly how she has been influenced. In an intertextual analysis we would not simply state that some
patterns in the two texts are similar, but try to see what the later writer
makes of the pattern from the previous text, what transformation the pattern
has undergone, and possibly why. J. K. Rowling is without doubt indebted
to many earlier writers, yet she has developed and transformed all the borrowed ideas, images, settings, plots, and characters in a most creative way.
We must give up the idea of one author's "borrowing" from another, but
instead become intent on hidden echoes and latent links.

   The notion of dialogics emphasizes the intention of writers and their active role in the act of writing (yet without "the anxiety of influence"), their
active responses to previous texts, as well as readers' making connections beyond authors' intentions. Intertextuality thus also presupposes the reader's
active participation in the decoding of text. Unlike traditional comparative
studies, intertextuality has proceeded from the examination of individual
loans to what a critic has called "an anonymous rush of voices." Naturally,
such tasks are quite demanding, since many of the hidden echoes in texts are
inaccessible, but on the other hand, intertextual studies can yield exciting
results. We can often reach dimensions of texts overseen by other approaches. For instance, studies of children's books with adult fiction as intertexts can reveal the nature of children's literature and give a better insight
into writers' intentions. Studies of particular authors, who have sometimes
been accused of epigonism (inferior imitation), help to reevaluate them and
see the creative treatment of other authors' ideas. Intertextual studies of separate motifs can help us understand the writers' intentions and messages,
their individual style. Intertextual studies within an authorship can lead to
more adequate interpretations of "difficult," many-dimensional texts.

Furthermore, intertextual links are often more evident in children's texts than in mainstream literature. John Stephens, who has a chapter on intertextuality in his study *Language and Ideology in Children's Fiction*, suggests that "literature written for children is also radically intertextual because it has no special discourse of its own" but rather "exists at the intersection of a number of other discourses" (86). One could perhaps protest against the assertion that children's literature lacks a discourse of its own, but it seems reasonable that contemporary children's literature has found inspiration in various discourses, literary as well as extraliterary. Intertextuality is very much a question of play and even playfulness, which makes children's literature a natural playground. Stephens discusses some interesting cases of intertextuality in poetry, fractured fairy tales, fantasy, and other literary texts. In our striving to free children's literature research from purely educational applications, such approaches seem both exciting and fruitful. It is also gratifying to view children's literature in a broader context—for instance, within the context of childhood, popular literature, general literary experience, myth, or culture—precisely at the crossroads of different discourses. We will, however, in the following pages focus on more specific, literary aspects of intertextuality, that is, on the links of literary texts to other literary texts.

Anagrams and Contaminations

There are several types of intertextual connections we can find in literary texts. They can be roughly divided into two major groups, labeled as *anagram* and *contamination*. An anagram is a coded message in which letters have changed place. By sorting out the order of the letters, it is possible to reconstruct the original message. The simplest case of anagram is interchanging letters in a word ("Amira" instead of "Maria"), or just writing backward. *Harry Potter and the Sorcerer's Stone* features the magic mirror of Erised, which, read backward, spells out its true nature. In intertextual analysis, the concept of anagram is used for texts in which we can easily identify the intertext by rearranging the constituent elements or merely by connecting each element to a similar element in another text. The term "contamination" is self-explanatory. In a contaminated text, elements of many other texts appear throughout, and it is not always possible to determine exactly where they come from.

If we decide that the text under scrutiny (let us call it "A-text") is an anagram of another text ("B-text"), we will examine A-text's direct relationship to B-text in terms of parallels in plot, character gallery, imagery, and so on. B-text is in this relationship called a *hypotext* ("hypo" = underneath), while A-text, receiving its inspiration from B-text, is called a *hypertext*[2] ("hyper" = above). Gérard Genette, who has elaborated the hypertextual model, sets two criteria on the connection between hypertext and hypotext. First, the connection should be extensive: not just a number of coincidences, but a whole pattern of correspondence. Second, it should be somewhat explicit: there must be some indication in the hypertext that points to the hypotext. Neither criterion permits mere speculation on the part of the reader or critic. Genette's example, which also appears in many other studies on intertextuality, is James Joyce's *Ulysses* with Homer's *Odyssey* as hypotext. (See fig. 2-5.)

Overt and Covert Dialogues

Children's literature abounds in hypotexts. For instance, Michel Tournier's *Friday and Robinson* is a modern version of Defoe's *Robinson Crusoe*. Tournier's book is a deliberate and conscious reply to Defoe, in which Tournier interrogates the ideology of the classic novel. Defoe's book is a hypotext, while *Friday and Robinson* is a hypertext. In examining the intertextual links between these two, we go beyond the surface of the hypertext to see how the later writer has used the hypotext to express his own ideas. We can even say that Tournier's text is a parody or pastiche (nonsatirical parody) based on Defoe; to enjoy the book fully we need to know what is being parodied. Parody is in fact a form of intertextuality, although by no means are all anagrams parodies. In *Little Women*, the March girls pattern their behavior in accordance with *The Pilgrim's Progress*, a seventeenth-century Christian allegory by John Bunyan, which was popular with many families at the time Alcott wrote her novel. Bunyan's book is explicitly mentioned in the first chapter which bears the title "Playing Pilgrims." Several subsequent chapters have titles alluding to Bunyan: "Beth Finds the Palace Beautiful,"

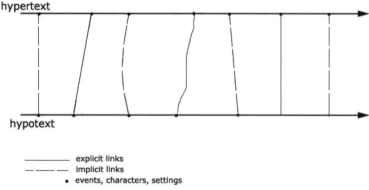

Fig. 2-5   Hypertext and hypotext.

"Amy's Valley of Humiliation," "Jo Meets Apollyon," and "Meg Goes to Vanity Fair." The chapter titles remind the reader of the girls' self-imposed burdens. Intertextuality is thus used to offer the readers an interpretative strategy.

The hypotext does not, however, have to be explicitly mentioned in the hypertext. The Bible is an obvious hypotext for C. S. Lewis's Narnia Chronicles, in which world history is described from Creation in *The Magician's Nephew* to the Apocalypse in *The Last Battle*. *The Lion, the Witch and the Wardrobe* contains the story of the Passions of Christ, his sacrificial death and resurrection. Philip Pullman's trilogy *His Dark Materials* has John Milton's *Paradise Lost* as hypotext. This fact is mentioned in the afterward to *The Amber Spyglass* (and of course extensively discussed by children's literature critics), but it is unlikely that many young readers will see the parallel. *Park's Quest* by Katherine Paterson has the medieval Parcifal legend as a hypotext, and many images from the legend, including the Holy Grail, appear in the novel. In all these cases, there is some indication in the hypertext that, at least for an observant and informed reader, points toward the hypotext. Thus Genette's criteria for hypertextuality are fulfilled.

Turning to a discussion of contamination, we can start with the simplest and most obvious cases: the appearance of direct quotations from, and allusions and references to, other texts. For instance, in *Ramona the Pest*, the teacher reads *Mike Mulligan and His Steam Shovel* in the classroom. We should, of course, not only state that another text is mentioned but try to account for this. It does not seem that the writer has any special intention with her intertext; it could have been any other famous children's book, since it does not provide any additional support for interpretation. For all we know, it may just be one of the writer's favorite books, and thus merely a funny detail. In the beginning of *The Magician's Nephew*, it is mentioned that the story takes place in the time when "Mr. Sherlock Holmes was still living in Baker Street and the Bastables were looking for treasure in the Lewisham Road" (9). The titles of the books are not mentioned, but both point firmly toward the beginning of the twentieth century. The function of the hypotext is to provide the temporal anchoring of the hypertext. Yet while *The Adventures of Sherlock Holmes* is a universally known classic, you have to be familiar with British children's literature to identify the Bastables as the characters from Edith Nesbit's adventure stories *The Treasure Seekers* and its sequels.

In *Daddy-Long-Legs*, the poor orphan Jerusha Abbot laments to her anonymous correspondent that she had never read "*Mother Goose* or *David Copperfield* or *Ivanhoe* or *Cinderella* or *Bluebeard* or *Robinson Crusoe* or *Jane Eyre* or *Alice in Wonderland* or a word of Rudyard Kipling" (29). Since Jerusha is now being educated to become a respectable young lady, the purpose of this enumeration is obviously to provide the young, presumably female, readers with a list of indispensable works of world literature. Characteristically, the two fairy tales mentioned are radically different examples for a young lady: *Cinderella* a model of rewarded patience, *Bluebeard* a cautionary tale of disobedience. The protagonist of *Jacob Have I Loved* mentions Shakespeare, Walter Scott, Dickens, and Fenimore Cooper as examples of her reading. The choice of authors emphasizes the romantic dreams of the young girl isolated on an island without any eligible objects for romance. The purpose of allusion is thus different from that in *Daddy-Long-Legs*.

From the examples above we see that children's novels can allude to other children's books as well as to adult novels. Apart from the Parcifal hypotext, another intertext in *Park's Quest* is Joseph Conrad's *Heart of Darkness*, which most probably only works on the adult level. We may certainly wonder what the writer's purpose was in mentioning this book. The young protagonist finds out that it was one of his deceased father's favorite books and tries to read it, but he is much too young to appreciate it. For an adult reader, the intertext indicates what kind of person Park's father might have been; besides, it connects to the quest theme of the novel.

Allusions can also be implicit rather than explicit. In *The Adventures of Tom Sawyer*, Tom plays Robin Hood with his friends, and he also seems to have read plenty of stories about pirates and robbers. Although no titles are mentioned, Tom's reading most probably consists of the "penny dreadfuls," cheap popular editions his aunt would have in her home. It is illuminating that although Tom hates school, he is obviously a skillful and ardent reader (in our day, he would have obtained his knowledge of stories from movies and television). The Narnia Chronicles are contaminated by stories other than the Bible, mostly classical, Norse and Celtic myths, but also Arabian Nights. While some scholars are skeptical of the mixture of Christian and pagan imagery in the novels, others see it as a deliberate and successful artistic device.

Pippi Longstocking contains implicit allusions to *Anne of Green Gables*. Like Anne, Pippi has red hair, but, unlike Anne, Pippi does not suffer from her red hair or her freckles. Pippi is everything that Anne is not allowed to be; that is, *Pippi Longstocking* is a direct intertextual reply to *Anne of Green Gables*, in which the author makes mock of the educational views expressed by Anne's surroundings. In particular the phrase "Children should be seen but not heard" is brilliantly parodied by Pippi.

Varieties of Intertextuality

A more subtle form of contamination is the appearance of titles, subtitles, and chapter titles alluding to other texts. Since these elements are called paratexts, this type of links is referred to as *paratextuality*. For instance, the title *Jacob Have I Loved* is a Bible quotation. It also appears within the novel and offers an interpretative strategy. The protagonist, Louise, applies the quotation "Jacob have I loved, but Esau have I hated" (Romans 9:13) to herself and blames all her misfortunes on the fact that she is the unloved twin, cursed by God. The title of Pullman's trilogy, *His Dark Materials*, alludes to a line from *Paradise Lost*: "Unless the almighty maker them ordain/His dark materials to create more worlds. . . ." The excerpt from the poem is printed in the first novel of the trilogy, *The Golden Compass*, as an epigraph, and it serves as a guideline for interpretation. *Park's Quest* involves an indirect paratextual connection, as the protagonist's name alludes to Parcifal, the hero of the Arthurian cycle. The word "quest" in the title amplifies the link by referring to Parcifal's search for the Holy Grail. However, as with Pullman's book, the title points to the main hypotext of the novel.

Yet another form of intertextuality may be the appearance of the narrator's or a character's comments about the narrative, such as, "this story is just like a fairy tale." In Patricia MacLachlan's *Unclaimed Treasures*, the protagonist says, "It was like a short story, that summer. . . . A short story with a beginning, a middle and an end" (1). Also such comments prompt a certain interpretation. Since the comments are of a metafictive nature (metafiction implies the indication of fiction being a literary construct; fiction about fiction; "meta" = over, beyond), this type is referred to as *metatextuality*.

Further, we can consider a text's relationship to a broader category, for instance to a genre. It is different from an anagram, because we cannot definitely say which hypotext our text is alluding to, but we are certain that the text is playing with, say, fairy-tale patterns, as in *Ella Enchanted*. The underlying story is called archetext ("arche" = old, ancient), and the allusion is thus *archetextual*.

Finally, *intratextuality* is used to denote writers' links to their own texts, such as self-quotations and self-allusions, recurrent patterns and symbols. One of the simplest cases of intratextuality occurs in *The Adventures of Huckleberry Finn* that begins, "You don't know about me, without you have read a book by the name of *The Adventures of Tom Sawyer*" (1). This is of course also a metafictive comment, since the narrator is aware of himself as a character in a book.

As we see, intertextuality may work on a macrotextual as well as a microtextual level. On the macrotextual level, we view the text as a whole, while on the mictotextual level we investigate particular details. In accordance with the hermeneutic model, these two processes can successfully complement each other.

Gérard Genette also includes in the concept of intertextuality all kinds of textual transformations, such as translation, versification, abridgement, and so on. We will consider these cases in chapter 10.

LET US EXPLORE

Try to identify as many different types of intertextual links in *Bridge to Terabithia* as you can. Contemplate why these links are used.

In the case of *Bridge to Terabithia*, we can see it as an anagram of *The Lion, the Witch and the Wardrobe*, while the text is also contaminated by allusions to other texts. Katherine Paterson's novels have been praised for their poignant realism, but she has herself stated that they have traditional heroic myths as archetexts (she does not use the term, though), and that her characters are each in some way a reincarnation of the traditional mythical hero. In *Bridge to Terabithia*, Paterson offers Jess and the readers Narnia Chronicles as a matrix for interpretation. Functionally, there is no difference between Narnia and Terabithia; both are sacred places where the hero is taken to be initiated. The passage into this sacred realm, represented in the Narnia Chronicles by the wardrobe, among other things, is in Paterson's novel just as clearly marked and just as dramatic, when Jess and Leslie have to swing over a river by a rope.

Among the many possible intertexts, the Narnia Chronicles are the most evident. Young readers are presumably expected to be familiar with Narnia, which poses an interesting question of authorial control. By alluding to C. S. Lewis, Paterson provides the readers with an interpretative strategy. However, this excludes readers who for some reason may have no knowledge of Narnia, for instance because of a different cultural background, or—like Jess—because of being culturally deprived. For these readers, the intertext will simply not work, since they will be as ignorant as Jess about the implication of Leslie's stories. It is doubtful, however, that Paterson is aware of this possibility since allusions to Narnia seem to be a conscious part in the construction of her text. Leslie's stories, being rather an interpretative guideline for the readers, acquire for Jess a pronounced character of spiritual guidance initiating the novice into a mystery. Since we have already stated that the Bible is a hypotext for the Narnia Chronicles, it is also a hypo-hypotext (still one layer deeper down) for *Bridge to Terabithia*. The Bible, or more precisely, the Passion story, is also directly alluded to, as it turns out that Leslie is not familiar with it. Yet in most cases it is Leslie who introduces Jess to the world of literature. Some of the books she retells for him or gives him to read are explicitly mentioned in the text; the Narnia Chronicles is just one example. *Hamlet* and *Moby Dick* are two more allusions; both have, like *The Lion, the Witch and the Wardrobe* and the New Testament, death as one of the central themes, which foreshadows Leslie's death and Jess's coping with it later in the novel. The link to Christ's sacrificial death suggests an interpretation of Leslie as a savior figure, sacrificing herself to save others. The irreversibility of death underscores the discrepancy between myth and reality.

Other books are only indirectly alluded to. For instance, in chapter 6, Jess is reading one of the books Leslie has equipped him with, describing the adventures of the assistant pig keeper. This may seem an insignificant detail, but it has several connotations. The unusual title of assistant pig keeper belongs to Taran, the protagonist of Lloyd Alexander's Prydain Chronicles. By mentioning these books, Paterson pays homage to one of the most outstanding American children's writers. She expects her readers to recognize the allusion and share the joy of reading with Jess. But the choice of allusion itself is not accidental. The Prydain Chronicles is a fantasy series, in some ways similar to the Narnia Chronicles: heroic quest novels, involving a struggle between good and evil. The allusion emphasizes the nature of the imaginative games that Jess and Leslie are playing in their secret realm. Further, the Prydain Chronicles features a strong-willed, intelligent, and independent female character, Princess Eilonwy, whose role against Taran may be seen as a parallel to Leslie's role against Jess. Finally, the allusion indirectly characterizes both Leslie herself, by her reading preferences, and her parents, who apparently encourage her reading of imaginative fantasy. Thus the covert allusion to Alexander provides an informed reader with an additional interpretative strategy.

Limitations

Some of the problems in connection with an intertextual approach to literature arise from the demands put on the reader. Do we have to recognize every single allusion in order to appreciate the text? What if we are not familiar with the Bible—can we still appreciate Lewis? Or if we are not familiar with Lewis—can we still appreciate Paterson? Apparently we can, even though assessing intertextuality will amplify our understanding of the text and perhaps even our aesthetical appreciation. Few readers today, especially young readers, are familiar with *Pilgrim's Progress*, which does not prevent *Little Women* from being read and enjoyed. The intentional intertextuality addressed to the writer's contemporaries is lost on today's readers and has instead become a confusing element.

Yet the evident limitation of an intertextual approach lies in its being rather subjective, as it often needs erudition and encyclopedic knowledge. The result of an intertextual interpretation will thus depend highly on the critic's personal background. We may overintrepret, finding meanings unintended by the authors. What we perceive as an intertextual link may in fact be a "commonplace," such as the frequent recurrent images of Romanticism: roses, gardens, or the innocent child. Furthermore, two texts that seemingly appear in an intertextual relationship may have a common source in a third text, for instance a myth. Although it is likely that C. S. Lewis found inspiration for the figure of the White Witch in Hans Christian Andersen's Snow Queen, both images may have a deeper archetypal origin.

Another problem lies in the complexity of intertextual links and the obvious difference in the reference frames of young and adult readers. Will children and adults make the same intertextual connections? Several intertexts have already been pointed out that would be transparent for an educated adult reader, but beyond the grasp of a child. On the other hand, some intertexts directly connected with childhood culture may be lost on adult readers. We will return to the question of dual readership in chapter 11.

Finally, like many other aspects of children's fiction, intertextuality should be regarded as a means of reader manipulation. By using myths, fairy tales, and literary works as hypotexts and by alluding to other literary pieces, authors exercise control over readers' interpretation. We have seen that Katherine Paterson prompts a mythical reading by employing hypotexts in *Bridge to Terabithia* and *Park's Quest,* and that Louisa M. Alcott amplifies the didacticism of her novel by alluding to *The Pilgrim's Progress.* Even though the readers may not recognize the intertexts, they are still affected by the intertextual links appearing in the books they are reading. Whether we view such manipulation as desirable or not is another question.

EXERCISE

Try to identify as many different types of intertextual links in the *Harry Potter* books as you can. They are extremely rich in intertextuality, so you should not have any problems. Start with general features and proceed to examine individual allusions and quotations. You may also choose some other children's book discussed above. Consider whether the knowledge of intertextuality has contributed to a better understanding of the text. Contemplate which of the intertextual links you have identified lie within the grasp of a young reader. What is the author's intention for using the intertext?

HOW TO GO FURTHER

In the study of text, interpretation and the relationships between texts are of utmost importance. Poststructural theory that basically denies literary texts any connection with external reality, including their creators, naturally focuses very much on the text itself and on the way meaning can possibly be extracted from it. The theoretical works of Michael Riffaterre, Jacques Derrida, Paul De Man, Michel Foucault, and some other contemporary critics open new vistas for research. So far few of these theories have been applied to children's literature, for several reasons. Because of its strong educational bias, children's literature criticism has been resistant toward most theories that deny intentionality, mimetic connections, and reader appeal in literary texts. Proponents of poststructuralism, on the other hand, seldom have any knowledge of or interest in children's texts, dismissing them as too simple and unworthy of serious study. Yet it is impossible and unwise to reject an analytical tool before testing it. Future research may show that some of these theories can indeed throw new light on the essence of children's literature. Michel Foucault's *The Archeology of Knowledge* seems to be an especially promising point of departure, while the concept of the text as *bricolage*, appearing in Derrida (reminiscent of a more common "montage" or even "collage"), can prove useful in discussing recent children's novels, heavily influenced by other media.

Deconstruction, originating in the works of Derrida, is perhaps the most radical contemporary theory concerning interpretation. Many critics have wondered whether deconstruction indeed implies a new direction of inquiry or merely a vogue term (as his "grammatology" seems to be merely a new word for semiotics), since Derrida's position is somewhat obscure, and the term itself has been used to denote a number of different phenomena. The central concept of the theory posits logocentrism as opposed to différance (which is a coinage combining "difference" and "deferment"). The model interrogates the presence of one given meaning in a text governed by an extrinsic law ("logos") in favor of viewing meaning as constantly deferred (that is, postponed, or suspended) by further and different interpretations. A deconstructional analysis is thus aimed at discovering the breaches or cracks in the text where new meanings can be detected. Some reevaluations of classic children's novels have at least partially leaned on this model.

NOTES

1. Conventional signs are sometimes called symbols. It is advisable not to use the term in this meaning, to avoid confusing it with its more traditional usage, as a figure of speech.

2. This term was established long before HTML.

REFERENCES

Semiotics

Barthes, Roland. *Elements of Semiology*. London: Cape, 1967.
Chomsky, Noam. *Syntactic Structures*. The Hague: Mouton, 1957.

Culler, Jonathan. *The Pursuit of Signs: Semiotics, Literature, Deconstruction.* Ithaca, NY: Cornell University Press, 1983.

Eagleton, Terry. *Literary Theory: An Introduction.* Oxford: Blackwell, 1983. Chap. 3, "Structuralism and Semiotics"; chap. 4, "Poststructuralism."

Eco, Umberto. *A Theory of Semiotics.* Bloomington: Indiana University Press, 1976.

Fordyce, Rachel, and Carla Marello, eds. *Semiotics and Linguistics in Alice's Worlds.* Berlin: de Gruyter, 1994.

Jakobson, Roman. "Lingustics and Poetics." Pp. 32–57 in *Modern Criticism and Theory: A Reader,* edited by David Lodge. London: Longman, 1988. The seminal work on semiotic communication.

Lotman, Yuri. *Semiotics of Cinema.* Ann Arbor, MI: University of Michigan Press, 1976. Despite the title, the study is extremely valuable for literary analysis.

———. *Analysis of the Poetic Text.* Ann Arbor, MI: University of Michigan Press, 1976.

———. *The Structure of the Artistic Text.* Ann Arbor, MI: University of Michigan Press, 1977.

Morris, Charles. *Writings on the General Theory of Signs.* The Hague: Mouton, 1971.

Saussure, Ferdinand de. *Course in General Linguistics,* edited by Charles Bally. New York: McGraw-Hill, 1966. The fundamental work about language as a system of signs.

———. "The Object of Study," "Nature of the Linguistic Sign." Pp. 2–14 in *Modern Criticism and Theory: A Reader,* edited by David Lodge. London: Longman, 1988. Two chapters from the above-mentioned work that offer a good introduction into the subject.

Scholes, Robert. *Semiotics and Interpretation.* New Haven: Yale University Press, 1982.

Stephens, John. *Reading the Signs: Sense and Significance in Written Texts.* Kenthurst: Kangaroo, 1992.

Hermeneutics and Interpretation

Derrida, Jacques. *Of Grammatology.* Baltimore: The Johns Hopkins University Press, 1976.

———. *Writing and Difference.* London: Routledge, 1978.

———. "Structure, Sign and Play in the Discourse of the Human Sciences." Pp. 107–123 in *Modern Criticism and Theory. A Reader* edited by David Lodge. London: Longman, 1988. A good start to get acquainted with Derrida's writings.

Eagleton, Terry. *Literary Theory: An Introduction.* Oxford: Blackwell, 1983. Chap. 2, "Phenomenology, Hermeneutics, Reception Theory."

Foucault, Michel. *The Archeology of Knowledge.* London: Tavistock, 1972.

Gadamer, Hans-Georg. *Truth and Method.* London: Sheed & Ward, 1989.

Hirsch, E. D. *Validity in Interpretation.* New Haven: Yale University Press, 1967.

———. *The Aims of Interpretation.* Chicago: University of Chicago Press, 1976.

Hoy, David. *The Critical Circle: Literature, History, and Philosophical Hermeneutics.* Berkeley, CA: University of California Press, 1978.

Jauss, Hans Robert. *Aesthetic Experience and Literary Hermeneutics.* Minneapolis: University of Minnesota Press, 1982.

Juhl, Peter D. *Interpretation: An Essay in the Philosophy of Literary Criticism.* Princeton, NJ: Princeton University Press, 1986.

Ricoeur, Paul. *The Conflict of Interpretations: Essays in Hermeneutics.* Evanston: Northwestern University Press, 1974.

———. *Interpretation Theory: Discourse and the Surplus of Meaning.* Fort Worth, TX: Texas Christian University Press, 1976.

———. *The Rule of Metaphor: Multi-disciplinary Studies of the Creation of Meaning in Language.* London: Routledge & Kegan Paul, 1978.

———. *Hermeneutics and the Human Sciences: Essays on Language, Action and Interpretation.* Cambridge: Cambridge University Press, 1981.

———. *A Ricoeur Reader: Reflection and Imagination.* Edited by Mario J. Valdés. New York: Harvester Wheatsheaf, 1991.

Spanos, William V., ed. *Martin Heidegger and the Question of Literature: Towards a Postmodern Literary Hermeneutics.* Bloomington: Indiana University Press, 1979.

Thompson, John B. *Critical Hermeneutics: A Study in the Thought of Paul Ricoeur and Jürgen Habermas.* Cambridge: Cambridge University Press, 1981.

von Wright, Georg Henrik. *Explaining and Understanding.* Ithaca, NY: Cornell University Press, 1971.

Intertextual Theory and Some Applications in Children's Literature Research

Åhmansson, Gabriella. "Mayflowers Grow in Sweden Too: L. M. Montgomery, Astrid Lindgren and the Swedish Literary Consciousness." Pp. 14–22 in *Harvesting Thistles: The Textual Garden of L. M. Montgomery*, edited by Mary Rubio. Guelph: Canadian Children's Press, 1994.

Allen, Graham. *Intertextuality.* London: Routledge, 2000.

Bakhtin, Mikhail. *The Dialogic Imagination.* Austin: University of Texas Press, 1981. A collection of essays presenting Bakhtin's most important ideas on the dialogical nature of literature.

Bergsten, Staffan. *Mary Poppins and Myth.* Stockholm: Almqvist & Wiksell International, 1978. An intertextual study of Pamela Travers's classic.

Bloom, Harold. *The Anxiety of Influence: A Theory of Poetry.* New York: Oxford University Press, 1973.

———. *A Map of Misreading.* Oxford: Oxford University Press, 1975.

Chaston, Joel D. "The Other Deaths in Bridge to Terabithia." *Children's Literature Association Quarterly* 16, no. 4 (1991–92): 238–241. An analysis of intertexts in Katherine Paterson's novel.

Clayton, Jay, and Eric Rothstein. *Influence and Intertextuality in Literary History.* Madison, WI: University of Wisconsin Press, 1991.

Colbert, David. *The Magical Worlds of Harry Potter: A Treasury of Myths, Legends, and Fascinating Facts.* Wrightsville Beach, NC: Lumina Press, 2001. Although far from scholarly, this study presents a vast collection of mythical intertexts overtly or covertly present in the *Harry Potter* novels.

Dusinberre, Juliet. *Alice to the Lighthouse: Children's Books and Radical Experiments in Art.* London: Macmillan, 1987.

Franson, J. Karl. "From Vanity Fair to Emerald City: Baum's Debt to Bunyan." *Children's Literature* 23 (1995): 91–114.

Genette, Gérard. *The Architext: An Introduction.* Berkeley, CA: University of California Press, 1992.

———. *Palimpsests: Literature in the Second Degree.* Lincoln, NE: University of Nebraska Press, 1997.

Kristeva, Julia. "Word, Dialogue and Novel." Pp. 34–61 in *The Kristeva Reader,* edited by Toril Moi. London: Basil Blackwell, 1986. In this essay, Kristeva introduced Mikhail Bakhtin's ideas in the West.

Jones, Amanda Rogers. "The Narnian Schism: Reading the Christian Subtext as Other in the Children's Stories of C. S. Lewis." *Children's Literature Association Quarterly* 29, nos. 1–2 (2004): 45–61.

Nikolajeva, Maria. *Children's Literature Comes of Age: Towards a New Aesthetic.* New York: Garland, 1996. Chap. 6, "Intertextuality in Children's Literature."

Nodelman, Perry. "Interpretation and the Apparent Sameness of Children's Literature." *Studies in the Literary Imagination* 18, no. 2 (1985): 5–20. Without employing the intertextual method as such, Nodelman compares a number of novels based on a similar motif, time travel.

Smedman, M. Sarah. "When Literary Works Meet: Allusion in the Novels of Katherine Paterson." *International Conference of the Children's Literature Association* 16 (1989): 59–66.

Stephens, John. *Language and Ideology in Children's Fiction.* London: Longman, 1992. Chap. 3, "Not by Words Alone: Language, Intertextuality, Society."

Stephens, John, and Robyn McCallum. *Retelling Stories, Framing Culture: Traditional Story and Metanarratives in Children's Literature.* New York: Garland, 1998. A study of folklore intertexts in contemporary children's fiction.

Todorov, Tsvetan. *Mikhail Bakhtin: The Dialogical Principle.* Manchester: Manchester University Press, 1984. An excellent introduction into Bakhtin's theory of dialogical discourse.

Wilkie, Christine. "Intertextuality." Pp. 131–137 in *International Companion Encyclopedia of Children's Literature,* edited by Peter Hunt. London: Routledge, 1996. Also pp. 130–137 in *Understanding Children's Literature,* edited by Peter Hunt. London: Routledge, 1999.

Worton, Michael, and Judith Still. *Intertextuality: Theories and Practices.* Manchester: Manchester University Press, 1990.

3

The Aesthetic of the Genre

There is no room here to go deeply into genre theory. And it would not be advisable to consult a dictionary of literary terms for a definition of this concept. There is no agreement among scholars as to how to define a genre, nor what genres there are, still less genres of children's literature. For our purpose, it is sufficient to accept that genres are categories into which we sort literary texts according to certain principles. In this chapter, we will take a close look at some ways of approaching the various categories of children's literature, as well as some ideas about the concept of genre as such.

It may help to know that the word "genre" comes from Latin *genus*, meaning "race" or "kind." Incidentally, "gender" has the same origin.

LABELING

LET US EXPLORE

Visit a library (or a website with recommendations on children's books) or look at your own bookshelf and choose at random ten or twelve children's books. Study them carefully and try to find a common denominator: how would you define children's literature based on these books?

Quite a few scholars of children's literature view their subject as a separate genre. According to our working definition of genre, we should be able to identify recurrent elements that characterize children's literature. Proponents of the view of children's literature as a homogeneous genre come up with statements that children's literature is simple, action oriented, optimistic, repetitive, and didactic. Although these features match some children's texts, they certainly do not match all of them. Even a picture book containing very few words, such as *Where the Wild Things Are*, is far from simple; *Anne of Green Gables* or *Little House in the Big Woods* is certainly not action oriented; *Slake's Limbo* or *The Giver* is anything but optimistic; *Alice in Wonderland* is perhaps more original than most mainstream novels; and nobody can accuse *Bridge to Terabithia* or *The Great Gilly Hopkins* of being didactic. If we are willing to include these books in the scope of children's fiction, we must apparently redefine the genre. Or, better still, we must admit that children's literature is not a uniform genre, but a broader category, incorporating a wide variety of different genres, some of which are action oriented, optimistic, and didactic, while others are not. An interesting question that follows from this is of course whether the genres of children's literature are different from those in the mainstream.

A Historical Look

By the time children's literature emerged, adult literature had already existed as an established literary system for many centuries. The traditional division since antiquity of literature into epic, lyric, and drama was from the beginning irrelevant to children's literature, and with rare exceptions, even today poetry and especially drama for children are marginal phenomena. While we cannot imagine our Western literary canon without Shakespeare, we do not, in the same way, have any canonized drama for children. As compared to children's novels, the amount and status of poetry for children are negligible.

Moreover, many prose genres discussed in general studies of literature, such as courtesy novel, fabliaux, sacred myth, epic, legend, allegory, confession, or satire, are not relevant for children's fiction. With very few exceptions, such as Roald Dahl's books, children's literature does not employ the grotesque. According to conventional genre definitions, all children's literature can be labeled as bildungsroman, a story about a young person's maturation. This obviously will not help us in our endeavor to describe the variety of children's texts. The nature of children's literature presupposes a different approach to genres, even though we can of course borrow some concepts and terms from general criticism.

When we speak about children's literature, we usually mean prose narratives, corresponding to the novel in the mainstream. Yet the novel is again too broad a category to be used for children's books. We must distinguish between contemporary everyday stories and historical novels, for one thing. We can further discern such categories as school stories, with a subcategory "boarding-school story" (actualized in the *Harry Potter* books), sports stories, horse and pony stories, or career stories (for instance, about young aspiring dancers, actors, or singers). All these kinds of stories have their own specific features. Possibly, some categories applicable to pulp fiction could also be useful for children's literature: romance, crime novel, adventure, thriller, Gothic novel, science fiction. These categories will, however, still not cover all the variety of children's texts, and definitely not pinpoint their significance within children's literature. Fantasy is one of the most prominent genres in children's fiction, which, unlike its counterpart in the mainstream, enjoys a high status. Animal and toy stories are more or less unique to children's literature. There is also such a specific group of texts as picturebooks. There seem to be more questions than answers.

How to Define Genres

In the first place, we still do not know exactly how we can differentiate one genre from another. In chapter 2, we discussed hermeneutic analysis. The concept of the hermeneutic circle can also be applied to the study of genres. We start an investigation of a genre (even if we view children's literature as a homogeneous genre) by defining the genre, that is, taking a view of it as a whole ("Children's literature is simple and optimistic . . ."). Then, we can illustrate our definition with a number of existing texts. Most likely, we will find that not all the texts match our definition. We will have to adjust the definition, and thus our general view of the genre, according to the details. As we add new texts to our study, our understanding of the genre will get broader and deeper, while our understanding of the particular work will be enhanced by our general picture of the genre. We may, for instance, state that some texts are unmixed from the generic point of view, that is, typical for the genre, while others may be a blending of different genres.

We often hear that some children's books are representative of, even epitomes of, their genres. *The Lion, the Witch and the Wardrobe* is frequently used as an example of fantasy; *The Adventures of Tom Sawyer* is a master text of naughty-boy fiction; and *Anne of Green Gables* is a typical girls' novel. In illustrating genres with these texts, we ascribe the texts features that we find indispensable for this particular genre.

CONTEMPLATE

- What makes *The Lion, the Witch and the Wardrobe* a fantasy novel?
- What makes *Tom Sawyer* a naughty-boy story?
- What makes *Anne of Green Gables* a girls' novel?
- What makes *Where the Wild Things Are* a picture book?
- What makes a *Nancy Drew* novel a mystery?

Try to identify as many indicators as you can. Note that we are not examining whether *The Lion, the Witch and the Wardrobe* is a good fantasy novel or whether *Anne of Green Gables* is of higher literary quality than *Nancy Drew*. We want to understand how we classify literary texts.

LET US EXPLORE

Books for boys and books for girls are labels frequently used to describe two clearly separate story types. What are the features that distinguish a boys' novel from a girls' novel? We can use *The Adventures of Tom Sawyer* as an example of a boys' book, and *Anne of Green Gables* as an example of a girls' book, but you may also choose your own examples. You may end up with something like this:

Boys' books	Girls' books
Male protagonist	Female protagonist
Outdoor setting	Indoor setting
Home = prison	Home = security
Adults negative	Adults positive
Episodic plot	Progressive plot
Action oriented	Character oriented
Static character	Dynamic character
External focalization	Internal focalization

We have thus identified what features we associate with each of the genres. When we encounter a new book, we can use these generic features to classify the book. For instance, we can state that *Little Women* has most of the traits of the girls' novel. One exception is that the first half of the novel presents an episodic plot: each chapter is more or less a self-contained story. Yet we cannot trust the protagonist criterion only: in the *Nancy Drew* novels, the protagonist is a girl, but all the other generic features will be similar to boys' books. Perhaps the labels of boys' books and girls' books are not very adequate after all? The protagonist's gender (as well as the implied readers' gender) is not as important as the other features. Therefore we should perhaps speak about the adventure story and the domestic story rather than about boys' and girls' stories. It is more common for adventure stories to have boy protagonists (and therefore perhaps appeal more to male readers), but it is not an absolute rule, as the example of *Nancy Drew* clearly shows. Mystery novels can have both girl (Nancy Drew) and boy (the Hardy boys) protagonists. Fantasy novels can have girls (*The Wizard of Oz*) and boys (*Harry Potter*) in the main roles.

Children's Literature Genres

Let us now take a closer look at some genre categories frequently used in textbooks in children's literature and discuss how these categories are defined, if they are defined at all. We will also try to determine whether any of these categories are typical for children's literature. We will not go through all the genres and subgenres of children's fiction; but hopefully the discussion will prove sufficient to continue with further explorations.

Folktales, Fairy Tales, and Myths

Most textbooks on children's literature start with folktales (sometimes also called traditional stories). However, folktales are strictly speaking not children's literature, even if they have at times been used as part of children's reading. Folktales existed and were told long before childhood was perceived as a category. Folktales were never created for an audience of children. Rather folktales were a makeshift solution at a time when there appeared to be no special literature for young readers. Thus the common label "folklore for children" is strictly speaking a contradiction in terms. The fact that folktales were part of this solution does not mean that they became children's literature. Most oral folktales are not suitable for children because they often contain violence and child abuse. Moreover, they are sometimes obscene and amoral, contradicting the ideals of proper upbringing.

Myths are sacred stories that, unlike folktales, are based on belief (that is, for the bearer of a particular culture, the content of the myth is true). When myths are retold for the entertainment of young readers today, they have lost both their sacred meaning and their connection with belief, which basically means that they have become fairy tales, narratives with supernatural elements.

What generic features do we associate with fairy tales? The opening "Once upon a time" is an immediate token of the genre, telling us that the story takes place in an indefinite past. Many fairy tales, but far from all, contain magic: magical helpers, objects, transformations, and so on. They always have a clear moral and a happy ending. Thus on the whole we recognize fairy tales on the basis of their recurrent formulas (such as "lived happily ever after"), as well as their set of characters and events.

Fantasy

In many textbooks, fairy tales and fantasy for children are treated together, as stories dealing with magic and the supernatural. Sometimes it is hard to draw a definite boundary between these genres; yet there is a significant difference. One element that we immediately recognize as characteristic of the fantasy genre is the presence of magic, or any other form of the supernatural, in an otherwise realistic world. This presence may be manifest in the form of magical beings, objects, or events; it may be unfolded into a whole universe or reduced to just one tiny element of magic. Thus, fantasy may be roughly defined as a narrative combining the presence of the primary and the secondary world, that is, our own real world and some other magical or fantastic imagined world.

Alice in Wonderland; *The Wizard of Oz*; *The Lion, the Witch and the Wardrobe*; and *Harry Potter and the Sorcerer's Stone* are good examples of fantasy that also demonstrate its variety. The story starts in an ordinary world, whereupon the protagonist is in some way carried away to another world, has adventures, performs a task, and in most cases is transported back into the real world. This safe homecoming is necessary to give the child readers security about their own reality. What makes these four novels different from each other is the way the magic world is connected with the real world, the way it is described, and even the purpose of sending the character into the other world. Otherwise, there are many elements in fantasy that we also find in adventure stories, for instance quest, mystery, and the struggle between good and evil.

Animal and Toy Stories

Animal and toy stories have often been presented as two genres specific to children's literature, and indeed there are not many mainstream books of this kind. It must be the Romantic belief in the child's unity with nature that has contributed to the vast number of animal and nature stories for children, while toys have been perceived as an indispensable part of a child's universe. Animal and toy stories are occasionally treated as subgenres of fantasy, or else singled out as separate categories. Both categories are, however, highly heterogeneous. Some animal stories describe animals in their natural surroundings with their natural behavior. Another large group of children's stories makes use of anthropomorphic animals, sometimes wearing clothes and always with a human mind.

Toy stories are another "unique" kind of children's literature. We should probably distinguish between toys existing in a world of their own and toys in contact with a child protagonist. Toys coming alive may for a child act as substitutes for missing friends, siblings, or even parents. Miniature people stories and personified object stories can also be seen as variations on the toy theme.

Let us, however, not be deceived by the superficial form. Both toys and animals in children's texts must be seen as representations of children. When writers present their characters disguised as animals or toys, it is merely a narrative device, which has little to do with genre. There are few similarities between *The Jungle Book*, *Spotty*, *Babar*, and *Peter Rabbit* besides their describing animals; on the contrary, each of them can be related to other books without animals: for instance, *The Jungle Book* to Robinsonnade, *Spotty* to books about multiethnic issues, the first *Babar* book to a sentimental story about an orphan who is taken care of by a nice rich lady, and *Peter Rabbit* to the naughty-boy books. Both toy stories and animal stories can be an adventure, a mystery, a love story, a family story, or a bildungsroman. An animal or toy that can communicate with a child protagonist is a disguised human friend. We need to apply other criteria than the presence of animals or toys to determine the genre of these stories.

Animal stories are sometimes treated together with fables. Fables are satirical or moral stories using animal shape to portray human vices and shortcomings. This genre, known already in ancient time, has nothing to do with children's literature, and if some fables have been incorporated in children's reading, it was just as much a makeshift solution as folktales.

Humor and Nonsense

Many textbooks on children's literature discern humor and nonsense as separate genres. Viewed more closely, however, humorous and nonsensical elements can be found in any kind of children's literature, prose as well as poetry, from picturebooks to young adult novels, and from straight realism to the wildest fantasy. Books as diverse as *Alice in Wonderland, Winnie-the-Pooh, The Cat in the Hat*, and *Pippi Longstocking* have been treated together as humor. It is perhaps more appropriate to suggest considering humor and nonsense as narrative and linguistic elements of texts rather than generic features. We will discuss nonsense as a stylistic device in chapter 9.

Historical Fiction

On the simplest level, the historical novel would fall under the category of realism. Yet there is a difference between novels set in easily recognizable milieus for young readers and novels deliberately detached from its readers through setting them far back in history. For a young reader, a distant historical epoch and an imaginary world may function in a comparable way. Therefore a historical novel, especially with an adventurous tone, may have more in common with fantasy than with an everyday realistic story. Fantasy novels utilizing time travel may share with "straight" historical fiction the purpose of presenting history in an engaging way. Normally, we put high demands for authenticity on a novel if we know that it is based on real events. When Jane Yolen uses a time-shift device to describe the Holocaust in *The Devil's Arithmetic*, it undermines the authenticity of the events, since readers normally connect time travel with fantasy.

Everyday Realism

Realism is one of the most ambiguous and controversial concepts in literary criticism, used to denote a variety of concepts, including styles, genres,
literary schools, and so on. In the context of children's literature, the term
realism is often used to describe any text devoid of magical or other supernatural elements. Thus, most formulaic fiction is, generally speaking, realistic. However, we usually reserve the term "realistic novel" for narratives set
in everyday surroundings and involving some form of everyday conflict, or
issue. The concept of the issue novel has been offered by critics as a category
of books distinct from both purely formulaic fiction and from other types
of stories without supernatural components, such as school stories, career
stories, naughty-boy stories, and so on. A more subtle concept, borrowed
from general criticism, is that of the psychological novel, focused on the
inner world and psychological development of the protagonist. However, it
is frequently next to impossible to differentiate between realistic genres, and
it is not necessarily desirable; we must, however, be aware of the presence of
these various elements in the texts.

Formulaic Fiction

Formulaic stories are narratives that follow a recurrent pattern—
formula—dictated by the mode: for instance, adventure novel, crime novel,
and romance. Adventure is probably the most popular form of children's
formulaic fiction, including such subgenres as mystery, horror, treasure
seeking, pirate story, and Robinsonnade. Unlike the psychological realistic
novel, formulaic fiction is action oriented, repetitive, and predictable. It is,
however, wrong to say that formulaic fiction is "bad" literature or "worse"
than the psychological novel; it is simply different and based on different
premises.

Multicultural Books

Many textbooks in children's literature identify this category among other
genres. Multicultural books is a useful notion for teachers and librarians who
need to find books featuring specific ethnic groups. From the literary point
of view, as a generic category, the term is irrelevant, since any genre can contain multicultural elements.

Young Adult Novel

If we do not view genres with regard to their readers but only with regard
to their intrinsic features, the young adult novel is neither a narrative aimed
at the upper-teen audience nor need it have a character of that age, although
in practice at least the second requirement is most often met. The young

adult novel (or teenage novel, or adolescent novel) is a genre depicting the character's marginal situation between childhood and adulthood, when there is no way back, but the inevitability of the final step into adult life has not yet been accepted. Although most children's novels, including formulaic fiction, depict the maturation of the hero, it is the marginality, the hesitation, and sometimes the inability of the hero to take the final step that characterizes the young adult novel. One of the best criteria to distinguish a young adult novel from a children's novel is the role of the parental figures. In children's novels, parents or guardians are comfortably removed to give the protagonist the freedom to explore the world. In a young adult novel, at least one parental figure has to be reintroduced, to allow a parental revolt, which is an indispensable step in maturation.

Picturebooks

In most textbooks on children's literature, picturebooks are treated as a genre.

CONTEMPLATE

Visit a library or a website and browse through fifteen to twenty randomly chosen picturebooks. According to our definition of a genre, do these books belong to the same genre? Can you find the common denominators that will allow you to put all these books into the same generic category? Try to find strong arguments both for and against picturebooks being a genre.

You have most probably discovered a variety of genres within your selection: traditional fairy tale (*Cinderella, Snow White, Hansel and Gretel*), modern fractured fairy tale (*The Paper Bag Princess*), fantasy (*Where the Wild Things Are*), naughty-boy story (*Curious George*), issue story (*Spotty*), family story (*Bread and Jam for Frances*), romance (*Little Blue and Little Yellow*), animal story (*The Very Hungry Caterpillar*), toy story (*Corduroy*), quest story (*Millions of Cats*), and so on. Can we speak about picturebooks being a separate genre? Is it not more reasonable to relate the genres we discover in picturebooks to the ones we have discovered in novels? Yet picturebooks are without doubt a very special kind of children's book. We will explore their specific characteristics in chapter 10.

Some Concluding Remarks

It is essential to understand that the concept of genre is merely a tool, an abstract category used to discuss texts. In other words, we cannot put labels on books and definitely claim that a particular book belongs to a particular genre. The same text can be ascribed different generic features, depending on the critic's specific attitude and preference. *The Lion, the Witch and the Wardrobe* can be categorized as fairy tale, fantasy, adventure, allegory, and so on; it is even occasionally treated as science fiction. This does not mean of course that genre categories are completely arbitrary, only that genres are not absolute categories determined once and for all. Contemporary literary criticism has developed a broader view of genres, which is especially relevant in our times when so many literary texts deliberately cross genre boundaries and also often use a mixture of genres. A genre is no longer conceived as a closed, self-contained unit, like a filing cabinet where texts can be neatly placed. Genre borderlines are fluent and dynamic; they change whenever new texts appear that do not really fit into the established categories; and, the most important aspect, we no longer say that texts belong to genres, but participate in them. The implication is that every text can participate in more than one genre, although most often features from just one genre will dominate.

At this stage we are perhaps more confused about the concept of genre than we were at the beginning of this chapter. Yet the purpose of the chapter is not to provide an easy-to-use system of filing cabinets, but to make ourselves aware of the richness and variety of children's fiction. It should be clear by now that children's literature is not a homogeneous genre. Yet there are no simple and consistent ways of classifying literary texts. How you treat genres and what you define as a separate genre depends on your purpose. If you are interested in the structure of the story, the difference between the adventure (going away) and the domestic story (staying at home) will be decisive, and you may combine the pirate story, Wild West story, and fantasy in the same category, while girls' novels and toy stories will fall into the other one. If you are interested in the presence or absence of magic, you will put *Cinderella*, *The Wizard of Oz*, and *Where the Wild Things Are* into the one category, and *Tom Sawyer*, *Anne of Green Gables*, and *Slake's Limbo* into the other. And if you are interested in examining the Robinsonnade, with survival as its central theme, you may end up discussing *Robinson Crusoe*, *The Adventures of Huckleberry Finn*, *Slake's Limbo*, *Hatchet*, and *Homecoming*. Genres are not defined once and for all. The same text may be classified in different ways.

Still, we do need some classification principles for various purposes. The most important thing to remember is that we must decide for ourselves what features we find indispensable for any particular genre.

EXERCISE

Try to arrange generic features into two columns, as we did with boys' and girls' books.

- What is the difference between fairy tales and fantasy?
- What are the common features of fairy tales and fantasy?

- What are the common features of fantasy and adventure?
- What is the difference between fantasy and adventure?
- What is the difference between fantasy and horror?
- What is the difference between fantasy and a historical novel?
- What are the common features of fantasy and a historical novel?

And so on. Figure 3-1 depicts one of the possible ways of exploration. Continue checking your understanding by asking yourself some of the following:

- What generic features are common to *The Lion, the Witch and the Wardrobe* and *The Wizard of Oz*?
- What generic features are common to *The Wizard of Oz* and *The Adventures of Tom Sawyer*?
- What generic features are common to *The Wizard of Oz* and *Anne of Green Gables*?
- What generic features are common to *The Lion, the Witch and the Wardrobe* and the *Harry Potter* books?
- What generic features are common to *Harry Potter* and *The Cat in the Hat*?

ACTIVITIES

- Visit your local library and examine how children's books are categorized. Do the labels on the shelves correspond to the genres we have discussed in this chapter? Find out where some of the books mentioned in this chapter are placed. Is there any difference in the approach? Why?
- Visit your local bookstore and make the same investigation.
- Visit Amazon.com and/or some other Internet bookstore and examine the categories used for children's books.
- Browse through a couple of textbooks in children's literature (see suggestions below) and note how the textbook authors categorize children's books.

LITERATURE AS DISPLACEMENT OF MYTH

There are several other ways to look at genres. The Canadian critic Northrop Frye views all literature as a displacement of myth, that is, consecutive deviations from the fixed and rigid structures we find in mythic narratives. Examples of displaced myth can be found in most children's stories. One of the

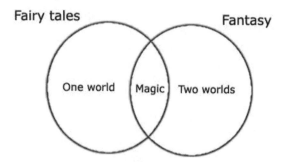

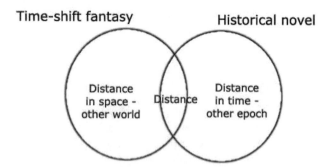

Fig. 3-1   Defining genres.

most universal myths, the myth of origin, appears in numerous children's novels depicting foundlings and orphans who eventually find their real parents. Thus, in *Little Lord Fauntleroy*, a poor boy in the United States discovers that he is in fact heir to a wealthy English lord. In *The Great Gilly Hopkins*, the myth is further displaced: Gilly does find her own mother, but the discovery brings disappointment rather than triumph.

For Frye, the difference between myth and literature lies in the fact that myth is based on belief: for the bearers of this particular culture, the events depicted in the mythic narrative are true; they have really happened. According to Frye, as soon as belief ceases, we are no longer dealing with myth, but with literature. For instance, the difference between myth and fairy tale is that the recipients of fairy tales are not supposed to believe in them. To assure this, storytellers insert special formulas in their stories, such as "Once upon a time, in a week of seven Fridays. . . ."

Stages of Displacement

Frye discerns five stages in the displacement of myth, including myth itself:

1. Myth: presents characters as being superior to both humans and the laws of nature (gods).
2. Romance: presents characters as being partially superior, idealized humans who are superior to other humans, but inferior to gods (semi-gods).
3. High mimetic narrative: presents humans who are superior to others, but not to the laws of nature or the power of Fate (heroes).
4. Low mimetic narrative: presents humans who are neither superior nor inferior to others.
5. Ironic narrative: presents characters who are inferior to other characters, and who are powerless when confronted with events around them.

Myth as such is absent from the history of Western children's literature. Since children's literature emerges long after Western civilization had lost its traditional mythical belief, this stage is not represented in children's fiction. Most of the classic myths, such as the Greek, Celtic, Native American, or African, are in the Western world retold for children who have no direct belief in them—myth has been displaced and instead functions as romance, as fairy tales. In fairy tales and fantasy, characters are empowered in a way that makes them superior to other human beings. They are endowed with magical agents enabling them to be transported in space, perform heroic deeds, and gain fortunes. Magic challenges the laws of nature; yet there are always forces that are more powerful than the protagonists, for instance good and evil wizards.

Adventure stories usually present characters and situations that are not impossible, but highly improbable. The young heroes always happen to be at the right place at the right time; they are extremely brave, clever, and skillful; they are certainly superior to their peers. Yet, there are no supernatural elements in the story: the characters are just exceptionally lucky. Historical novels also allow high mimetic representation, since the characters are placed in extraordinary situations where they can show heroism and other honorable qualities.

Most of the stories of everyday realism are low mimetic. The characters are neither superior nor inferior to other people, and the events are credible. While in high mimetic stories the readers are expected to look up to the characters as examples of bravery, virtue, or intelligence, low mimetic characters are ordinary children without any special qualities: not particularly bright or brave or lucky. In contrast, ironic characters are in some way inferior to their surroundings and to other people, not only the adults, but also their peers, including the readers. They can be inexperienced and inept; they can have some particular feature that makes them inferior in their peers' eyes, for instance obesity; or they can be outsiders for some reason. Unlike fairy-tale heroes, who may start as poor and oppressed, these characters are not empowered at the end of the story. At best, they remain the same; at worst they perish, incapable of coping with surrounding reality.

We can illustrate the notion of an ironic mode with an episode from *Ramona the Pest*. On her first day of school, Ramona has to learn "a puzzling song about 'the dawnzer lee light,' which Ramona did not understand because she did not know what a dawnzer was. 'Oh, say, can you see by the dawnzer lee light,' sang Miss Binney, and Ramona decided that a dawnzer was another word for a lamp." Apparently, the character's confusion is based on her ignorance and naiveté. The readers are supposed to recognize the words, which gives them a feeling of superiority. However, if for some reason they do not, the situation leaves them as helpless and puzzled as Ramona.

Children's authors may help their readers recognize irony through comments from other characters. For instance, when Pooh and Piglet in chapter 3 of *Winnie-the-Pooh* are hunting Woozles and Wizzles, walking four times around a grove following their own footsteps, the author lets Christopher Robin explain this blunder to Pooh, in case the readers have not realized it by then. *Winnie-the-Pooh* is an ironic narrative because the reader, together with Christopher Robin, is consistently allowed to be more intelligent than most of the toy characters.

EXERCISE

Illustrate each of Frye's categories with two or three children's texts. Here are some questions and considerations to assist you:

- Are the characters presented as superior or inferior or neither to their surroundings and to the reader? You must also remember that a children's novel has a child as an implied reader, so that the protagonist might be inferior to you as an adult reader, but equal to the child reader.
- Are the characters empowered at the beginning of the story? If they are, the story is most likely a romance or a high mimetic narrative.
- Are the characters assisted by any supernatural agent? If they are, the story is most likely a romance. Or do the characters possess supernatural powers themselves (e.g., Harry Potter)? If so, is there a power that is superior to them?
- Are the characters disempowered at the end of the story? Are they stripped of their supernatural qualities, do they lose their magical agent, do they wake up from a dream? How does this affect the overall mode of the story? For instance, if the magical adventure has been a dream, we can suggest that the story is in actual fact low mimetic.

The peculiarity (and perhaps weakness) of Frye's model is that his categories can be applied synchronically as well as diachronically. In other words, the five stages on the one hand reflect the historical development of world (= Western) literature; on the other the various modes of representation coexist within any given period. Applying the historical approach, we may state that fairy tales (romance) and didactic stories of virtue and heroism (high mimetic) were more common in earlier children's fiction, while today we are more likely to encounter low mimetic and ironic narratives. Yet, even today we can certainly find examples of all modes (except perhaps myth) being written and published for children.

Further, Frye's categories can even coexist within one and the same text, depending on how we interpret it. Let us, for instance, see how we can categorize *The Lion, the Witch and the Wardrobe* on the different levels of displacement. In order to view the story as myth, we must believe that it has actually happened to our forefathers and is happening all over again so that the story reiterates this eternal event. This certainly feels rather far-fetched. We are much more likely to read the novel as a romance, based on suspended disbelief. The characters are idealized, and they have access to magical agency. Instead of mythical connotations, we can say that this fantasy reflects the child's wish for superiority. Yet we can also apply an ironic reading, suggesting that the story only takes place in the children's imagination.

EXERCISE

Try to interpret some other texts in the same manner, for instance *The Wizard of Oz* or a *Harry Potter* novel. It may also be a greater challenge to see the different levels of displacement in books such as *Bridge to Terabithia* or *Slake's Limbo*.

Limitations

One serious argument we can bring forward against the mythic theory of genres is that the five categories (or rather four, since myth as such does not appear within children's fiction) are insufficient to describe all the variations we find in contemporary texts for children. Indeed, we will have to put both fairy tales and fantasy in the category of romance, while almost all the types of adventure stories, including mystery and crime, will constitute high mimetic modes since the characters of these stories are in an unconvincing way superior not only to their peers, but also to adults. At the same time, most of the realistic stories would go into the categories of low mimetic and ironic. If we now try to correlate Frye's categories and the genres of children's fiction we discussed in the previous section, we may end up with something like this:

- Romance: fairy tales, fantasy, horror
- High mimetic: adventure, mystery, crime, historical novel, pony story, sports story, career story
- Low mimetic: school story, domestic story, animal story, toy story
- Ironic: contemporary psychological novel, young adult novel

Naturally some types of stories can appear on different levels. For instance, a horror story may have supernatural elements (romance) or provide a rational explanation (high mimetic); a horse, sports, or career story may show the protagonist as exceptionally competent (high mimetic) or average (low mimetic). Many historical novels written for children today are low mimetic rather than high mimetic, as they focus on everyday life rather than great battles and other dramatic events. The difference between low mimetic and ironic modes is often a matter of interpretation. Young readers may, for instance, miss the irony in *Winnie-the-Pooh* and read it as low mimetic.

As we see, this model does not provide us with too precise a tool for generic classification. Yet, it does give us insight into the different degrees of credibility we connect with different genres. We are not surprised that Nancy Drew can drive cars and fly airplanes, or that she is smarter than any adult around her, as well as exceptionally good at golf, because we know that we are reading a high mimetic narrative. We would not accept Ramona's being as dexterous, because of different genre expectations. We are not surprised when Tom Sawyer finds a treasure and becomes rich, but when Stanley in *Holes* finds a treasure, we may feel that our initial genre expectations have been betrayed.

Comic and Tragic, Romantic and Ironic

Frye also gives us some additional instruments for categorization. He considers different modes of representation within two continuums: between comedy and tragedy, and between the romantic and the ironic. To make his argument more palpable, Frye connects the modes to seasons, which can be roughly represented in figure 3-2. The top half-circle represents the romantic world, an idealized, innocent, almost fairy-tale-like world that we so often find in traditional children's fiction. The bottom half-circle represents the ironic or satirical reflection of the romantic world, the world of realism devoid of any romantic ideals. Frye himself compares this circle with the Wheel of Fortune appearing in medieval paintings of the Last Judgment. Depending on the direction of the movement in the story, Frye places the different modes—in a way corresponding to genres—along the circle, which can be represented as in figure 3-3.

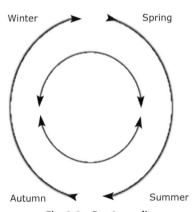

Fig. 3-2   Frye's modi.

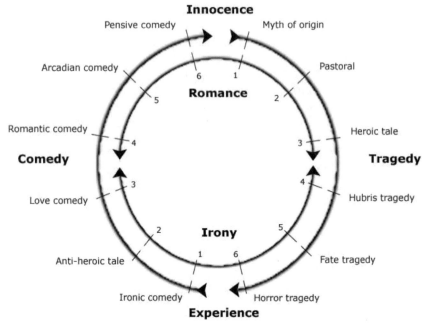

Fig. 3-3   Frye's genres.

Comedy and tragedy signify the movement between these two worlds, upward or downward, toward a happy or tragic ending. The tragic, downward movement takes the characters from innocence toward experience, from stability, through error or false step (*hamartia* in Greek), toward catastrophe. The comic, upward movement goes from threat toward a happy ending when the characters live happily ever after. It would seem that children's fiction with its special premises would, first, mainly exist within the upper part of the circle, the romantic, innocent world; and second, chiefly present an upward movement, toward happy endings. Yet, the variety of contemporary children's novels provides enough examples to fit all of Frye's modes.

The mythic theory of genres has as its objective not a simple, superficial classification of stories, but a more profound examination of the various ways of representing reality. From the examples above, it should be clear that with this theory we do not make any distinction between "realistic" and "nonrealistic" narratives, but treat all stories as equally representing the various aspects of human existence. This attitude does more justice to children's fiction, especially since we seldom draw rigid barriers between fantasy and realism in the mainstream, and should not do so in children's literature either.

EXERCISE

Study Frye's cycle and try to illustrate each category with a children's novel. You may find that some categories are easier to exemplify than others. Yet you have to remember that the difference between Arcadian comedy and pensive comedy is vague and ultimately a matter of interpretation. This activity is a mental exercise rather than a quiz where a correct answer can be provided. You must consider the following:

- Does the story exist and move within the romantic or the ironic world? In other words, is the fictive world of the novel safe and secure, or is something threatening it?
- Do the characters remain more or less in the state of initial innocence, or are they taken, albeit tentatively, toward experience and maturity?
- Are the characters brought back to the state of security and innocence, or are they left in the ironic world?

HOW TO GO FURTHER

One of the most controversial issues in genre theory is the definition of realism. As should be clear by now, the question of realism in children's literature is more intricate than merely indicating the absence of supernatural elements. In structural theory, originating from linguistics, the difference is made between metaphoric and metonymic modes, the former based on similarity, the latter on contiguity. According to this view, the literature of Romanticism is largely metaphoric, while the realistic novel is metonymic. Some children's literature scholars, for instance John Stephens, have adopted this theory, claiming that the difference between fantasy and realism is indeed decisive. We have, however, seen that in mythic theory all literature is basically metaphoric, and the same can be said about most directions of psychoanalytical theory. The approach to genres will thus highly depend on the general approach to literature. Besides, it can be maintained that in children's literature, metaphoric and metonymic modes work differently for sophisticated and unsophisticated readers; the latter being more likely to interpret literature metonymically. Yet it is by all means fruitful to investigate genres from a linguistic point of view, as John Stephens does in *Language and Ideology in Children's Fiction*.

Essential to remember in genre studies is that many general theories of genre are more or less irrelevant for children's literature since they discuss genres that do not exist in children's fiction. Thus the numerous theoretical studies of genres in ancient and medieval literature (for instance, Mikhail Bakhtin's "The Problem of Speech Genres" or Gérard Genette's *The Architext*) hardly offer anything directly applicable for a children's literature scholar to draw upon, yet for someone deeply interested in the question they certainly should not be neglected. Any comprehensive and consistent theory of genres in children's fiction has not been proposed yet.

REFERENCES

General

Bakhtin, Mikhail. "The Problem of Speech Genres." Pp. 60–102 in his *Speech Genres & Other Late Essays*. Austin: University of Texas Press, 1986.

Fowler, Alastair. *Kinds of Literature: An Introduction to the Theory of Genres*. Cambridge, MA, Harvard University Press, 1982.

Frye, Northrop. *Anatomy of Criticism: Four Essays*. Princeton, NJ: Princeton University Press, 1957.

———. *Fables of Identity: Studies in Poetic Mythology*. New York: Harcourt, Brace & World, 1963.

———. *The Secular Scripture: A Study of the Structure of Romance*. Cambridge, MA: Harvard University Press, 1976.

Genette, Gérard. *The Architext: An Introduction*. Berkeley, CA: University of California Press, 1992.

Hume, Kathryn. *Fantasy and Mimesis: Responses to Reality in Western Literature*. New York: Methuen, 1984.

Jakobson, Roman. "On Realism in Art." Pp. 82–87 in *Readings in Russian Poetics: Formalist and Structuralist Views*, edited by Ladislav Matejka and Krystyna Pomorska. Cambridge, MA: MIT Press, 1971.

———. "The Metaphoric and Metonymic Poles." Pp. 57–61 in *Modern Criticism and Theory: A Reader*, edited by David Lodge. London: Longman, 1988.

Lodge, David. *The Modes of Modern Writing: Metaphor, Metonymy, and the Typology of Modern Literature*. London: Arnold, 1977.

Stephens, John. *Language and Ideology in Children's Fiction*. London: Longman, 1992. Chap. 7, "Words of Power: Fantasy and Realism as Linguistically Constituted Modes."

Todorov, Tzvetan. *Genres in Discourse*. Cambridge: Cambridge University Press, 1990.

Textbooks and Surveys Discussing a Variety of Genres in Children's Literature (A Selection)

Cullinan, Bernice E. *Literature and the Child*. San Diego, Harcourt Brace Jovanovich, 1981. Includes chapters on picture books, folklore, fantasy, science fiction, poetry and verse, realistic fiction, historical fiction, biography, nonfiction, and books for multicultural understanding.

Hillman, Judith. *Discovering Children's Literature.* 2nd ed. Upper Saddle River, NJ: Merrill, 1999. Includes chapters on folklore, picture books, poetry, fantasy, contemporary realism, historical realism, biography, and nonfiction.

Hunt, Peter, ed. *International Companion Encyclopedia of Children's Literature.* London: Routledge, 1996. Part 2, "Types and Genres," contains a large number of essays on genres and types of children's fiction.

Lukens, Rebecca J. *A Critical Handbook of Children's Literature.* 4th ed. New York: HarperCollins, 1990. Chap. 2, "Genre in Children's Literature"; chap. 10, "From Rhyme to Poetry"; chap. 11, "Picture Books"; chap. 12, "Nonfiction."

Lynch-Brown, Carol, and Carl M. Tomlinson. *Essentials of Children's Literature.* Boston: Allyn and Bacon, 1993. Includes chapters on poetry, picture books, traditional literature, modern fantasy, realistic fiction, historical fiction, nonfiction, and multicultural and international literature.

Nodelman, Perry, and Mavis Reimer. *The Pleasures of Children's Literature.* 3rd ed. Boston: Allyn and Bacon, 2003. Chap. 11, "Poetry"; chap. 12, "Picture Books"; chap. 13, "Fairy Tales and Myths." As compared to the first edition of the book, the chapter on fiction and subgenres of fiction (toy stories, "children with problems," and time fantasies) has been deleted.

Norton, Donna E. *Through the Eyes of a Child: An Introduction to Children's Literature.* 5th ed. Upper Saddle River, NJ: Merrill, 1999. Includes chapters on picture books, traditional literature, modern fantasy, poetry, contemporary realistic fiction, historical fiction, multicultural literature, and nonfiction.

Stoodt-Hill, Barbara D., and Linda B. Amspaugh-Corson. *Children's Literature: Discovery for a Lifetime.* 2nd ed. Upper Saddle River, NJ: Merrill, 2001. Includes chapters on picture books, poetry, traditional literature and modern fantasy, contemporary realistic fiction, historical fiction, biography and nonfiction, and "literature for children with real-life challenges."

Sutherland, Zena, and May Hill Arbuthnot. *Children and Books.* 8th revised ed. New York: HarperCollins, 1991. Includes chapters on folktales, fables, myths and epics, modern fantasy, poetry, modern fiction, historical fiction, biography, and informational books.

Tunnell, Michael O., and James S. Jacobs. *Children's Literature Briefly.* 2nd edition. Upper Saddle River, NJ: Merrill, 2000. Includes chapters on traditional fantasy, modern fantasy, contemporary realistic fiction, historical fiction, biography, information books, picture books, poetry, multicultural and international books, and "controversial books."

Books Dealing with Specific Genres

Fairy Tales

Bettelheim, Bruno. *The Uses of Enchantment: The Meaning and Importance of Fairy Tales.* New York: Knopf, 1976.

Bottigheimer, Ruth. *Grimm's Bad Girls and Bold Boys: The Moral and Social Vision of the Tales.* New Haven: Yale University Press, 1987.

Cooper, J. C. *Fairy Tales: Allegories of Inner Life.* Wellingborough: The Aquarian Press, 1983.

Lüthi, Max. *The Fairytale as Art Form and Portrait of Man.* Bloomington: Indiana University Press, 1984.

Tatar, Maria. *Off With Their Heads! Fairy Tales and the Culture of Childhood.* Princeton, NJ: Princeton University Press, 1992.

Warner, Marina. *From the Beast to the Blonde: On Fairy Tales and Their Tellers.* New York: Farrar, Straus and Giroux, 1994.

Zipes, Jack. *Breaking the Magic Spell: Radical Theories of Folk and Fairy Tales.* Austin: University of Texas Press, 1979.

———. *Fairy Tales and the Art of Subversion.* New York: Wildman, 1983.

———. *When Dreams Came True: Classical Fairy Tales and Their Tradition.* New York: Routledge, 1999. This book also treats some works usually classified as fantasy, such as *Pinocchio* and *The Wizard of Oz.*

Fantasy

Attebery, Brian. *The Fantasy Tradition in American Literature: From Irwing to Le Guin.* Bloomington: Indiana University Press, 1980.

Egoff, Sheila. *Worlds Within: Children's Fantasy from the Middle Ages to Today.* Chicago: American Library Association, 1988.

Hunt, Peter, and Millicent Lenz. *Alternative Worlds in Fantasy Fiction.* London: Continuum, 2001. Focuses on Ursula Le Guin, Terry Pratchett, and Philip Pullman.

Jackson, Rosemary. *Fantasy: The Literature of Subversion.* New York: Methuen, 1981.

Lochhead, Marion. *The Renaissance of Wonder in Children's Literature.* Edinburgh: Canongate, 1977.

Manlove, C. N. *Modern Fantasy: Five Studies.* Cambridge: Cambridge University Press, 1975.

Molson, Francis J. *Children's Fantasy.* San Bernardino: Borgo, 1989.

Nikolajeva, Maria. *The Magic Code: The Use of Magical Patterns in Fantasy for Children.* Stockholm: Almqvist & Wiksell International, 1988.

Sale, Roger. *Fairy Tales and After.* Cambridge: Cambridge University Press, 1978.

Sammonds, Martha C. *"A Better Country": The Worlds of Religious Fantasy and Science Fiction.* New York: Greenwood, 1988.

Smith, Karen Patricia. *The Fabulous Realm: A Literary-Historical Approach to British Fantasy, 1780–1990.* Metuchen, NJ: Scarecrow, 1993.

Swinfen, Ann. *In Defence of Fantasy: A Study of the Genre in English and American Literature since 1945.* London: Rutledge & Kegan Paul, 1984.

Todorov, Tzvetan. *The Fantastic: A Structural Approach to a Literary Genre.* Cleveland: The Press of Case Western Reserve University, 1973.

Westfall, Gary, and George Edgar Slusser. *Nursery Realms: Children in the Worlds of Science Fiction, Fantasy, and Horror.* Athens, GA: University of Georgia Press, 1999.

Animal and Toy Stories

Blount, Margaret J. *Animal Land: The Creatures of Children's Fiction.* New York: Morrow 1974.

Kuznets, Lois. *When Toys Come Alive: Narratives of Animation, Metamorphosis and Development.* New Haven: Yale University Press, 1994.

Adventure

Fisher, Margery. *The Bright Face of Danger: An Exploration of the Adventure Story.* London: Hodder & Stoughton, 1986.

Phillips, Richard. *Mapping Men and Empire: A Geography of Adventure.* London: Routledge, 1997.

Domestic Fiction/Girls' Novel

Cadogan, Mary, and Patricia Craig. *You're a Brick, Angela! The Girls' Story 1839–1985.* London: Gollanz, 1986.

Foster, Shirley, and Judy Simons. *What Katy Read: Feminist Re-readings of "Classic" Stories for Girls.* London: Macmillan, 1995.

Tucker, Nicholas, and Nikki Gamble. *Family Fictions.* London: Continuum, 2001.

School Story

Quigly, Isabel. *The Heirs of Tom Brown: The English School Story.* London: Chatto & Windus, 1982.

Mystery and Horror

Dyer, Carolyn Stewart, and Nancy Tillman Romalov, eds. *Rediscovering Nancy Drew.* Iowa City: University of Iowa Press, 1995.

Gavin, Adrienne, and Christopher Routledge. *Mystery in Children's Literature: From the Rational to the Supernatural.* Basingstoke: Palgrave, 2001.

Inness, Sherrie A., ed. *Nancy Drew and Company: Culture, Gender, and Girls' Series.* Bowling Green, OH: Bowling Green State University Popular Press, 1997.

Kies, Cosette. *Young Adult Horror Fiction.* New York: Twayne, 1992.

Reynolds, Kimberley, Geraldine Brennan, and Kevin McCarron. *Frightening Fiction.* London: Continuum, 2001.

Rudd, David. *Enid Blyton and the Mystery of Children's Literature.* New York: St. Martin's Press, 2000.

Westfall, Gary, and George Edgar Slusser. *Nursery Realms: Children in the Worlds of Science Fiction, Fantasy, and Horror.* Athens, GA: University of Georgia Press, 1999.

Young Adult Fiction

Cart, Michael. *From Romance to Realism: 50 Years of Growth and Change in Young Adult Literature.* New York: HarperCollins, 1996.

Nilsen, Alleen Pace, and Kenneth L. Donelson. *Literature for Today's Young Adults.* 6th ed. New York: Longman, 2001.
Trites, Roberta Seelinger. *Disturbing the Universe: Power and Repression in Adolescent Literature.* Iowa City: University of Iowa Press, 2000.

Picture Books

Bader, Barbara. *American Picturebooks: From Noah's Ark to the Beast Within.* New York: Macmillan, 1976.
Doonan, Jane. *Looking at Pictures in Picture Books.* Stroud: Thimble Press, 1993.
Nikolajeva, Maria, and Carole Scott. *How Picturebooks Work.* New York: Garland, 2001.
Nodelman, Perry. *Words About Pictures: The Narrative Art of Children's Picture Books.* Athens, GA: The University of Georgia Press, 1988.
Stewig, John Warren. *Looking at Picture Books.* Fort Atkinson, WI: Highsmith Press, 1995.

Mythic Theory

McGillis, Roderick. *The Nimble Reader: Literary Theory and Children's Literature.* New York: Twayne, 1996. Chap. 3, "The Totality of Literature: Myth and Archetype."
Nikolajeva, Maria. *From Mythic to Linear: Time in Children's Literature.* Lanham, MD: Scarecrow, 2000. This study proposes a radically new generic classification of children's novels, based on the degree of accomplishment of the protagonist's maturation process.
Nilsen, Don L. F. "Northrop Frye Meets Tweedledum and Tweedldee: Adolescent Literature as Comedy, Romance, Tragedy, and Irony." *Journal of Evolutionary Psychology* 19, nos. 1–2 (1998): 10–20.
Roxburgh, Stephen D. "'Our First World': Form and Meaning in The Secret Garden." *Children's Literature in Education* 10, no. 3 (1979): 120–130.
Wilson, Raymond. "Slake's Limbo: A Myth-Critical Approach." *Children's Literature in Education* 18, no. 4 (1987): 219–226.
Wolf, Virginia L. "Paradise Lost? The Displacement of Myth in Children's Novels." *Studies in the Literary Imagination* 18, no. 2 (1985): 47–64.
———. "The Cycle of Seasons: Without and Within Time." *Children's Literature Association Quarterly* 10, no. 4 (1986): 192–196.

4

The Aesthetic of the Content

The distinction between content (what the story is about) and form (how the story is told) is one of the most basic in literary criticism. It would seem that that question of how to define the content of a literary work is unequivocal and cannot raise any controversies. The content is what the book is about, and there can seemingly be no doubts concerning what a book is about. Yet there are a variety of approaches to what exactly makes the content of literature. In this chapter, we will explore some ways of dealing with themes, motifs, values, and other content-related elements of the text.

LITERATURE AS A MIRROR

One of the most established concepts of literature, going back to Aristotle, is that literature—and art in general—is a direct reflection of reality. Aristotle used the word *mimesis*, which means imitation, or reflection, to denote the relationship between literature and reality. The approaches based on this premise are called mimetic. The objective of a mimetic literary analysis is to investigate exactly how reality is depicted in a concrete text, or in the oeuvre of a particular writer, or in a specific genre, or during a specific epoch.

Portraying Society

There are a number of analytical models based on mimetic approaches: Marxism, New Historicism, and the mimetically oriented directions of feminist and postcolonial theories. All these models investigate, from slightly different premises, how social structures are represented in literature, as well as how texts reflect the time and society within which they were produced. Sociohistorical studies of fairy tales provide good examples. By comparing versions of the same tale, we can draw conclusions about the views on child-hood and other social values during the time the tales were told or written. In Charles Perrault's version of *Little Red Riding Hood*, the wolf gobbles up the girl, and that is the end. The moral that young female readers of the tale should learn was not to trust strangers, or, on a more subtle psychological level, to be cautious about their sexual desires (in this version, Little Red ends up in bed with the wild beast). In the Brothers Grimm's version, a hunter comes along to save Red. A civilized male is thus more acceptable than the wild wolf, and the female is portrayed as helpless and submissive. In contemporary feminist versions, Red saves herself and sometimes shoots the wolf, sometimes marries him, or even, as a cartoon strip suggests, "successfully reintroduces him into his natural habitat." In fairy tales such as *Hansel and Gretel* we clearly see a reflection of the common practice of abandoning children in times of famine, a habit that we today perceive as barbarian. Fairy tales about young girls, such as *Beauty and the Beast* or *The Frog Prince*, reflect the practice of arranged marriages, and so on.

Mimetic approaches are perhaps the most common in studies of children's literature. Such studies investigate the ways society and particular social groups (boys, girls, disabled people, immigrants, blacks, gays) are represented in children's novels, nonfiction, and picture books. Many of these studies focus on the values expressed in the books. We assess the social values of a text as progressive if they interrogate the present social structure and call for social improvement. For instance, *The Adventures of Huckleberry Finn* explicitly questions the institute of slavery, and *Little Women* implicitly questions the inferior status of women in society (women are not admitted to higher education, they have no right to vote, and many occupations are closed to them). We judge the social content of a book as conservative if the text seems to be comfortable with the social structure it presents. For instance, the Narnia books seem to be content with the gender stereotypes, ethnic inequality, and power structures they portray. In formulaic fiction, the depiction of society is usually conservative, and the values emphasized are physical appearance, wealth, and high social status (for instance, which school you go to). Finally, we may pronounce the text reactionary if it supports social structures that belong to the past. Thus, a book written today that explicitly or implicitly defends slavery would be considered reactionary. For most people, books denying the Holocaust or representing the perpetrators in a favorable light are considered reactionary.

Family and School

In children's fiction, two social institutions are of paramount importance: family and school. Family is in fact the first social structure a child experiences, and parents (or parental substitutes) are the first authority a child meets and interrogates. For obvious reasons, parents play a more prominent part in children's fiction than in mainstream literature. Children are dependent on their parents, physically and emotionally, and part of growing up involves liberation from parental protection. Folktales most often present family as a firm authority. Sons must obey their fathers' orders and accept the unfair distribution of inheritance (*Puss in Boots*), while daughters must live with the fathers' choice of husband (*Beauty and the Beast, The Frog Prince*). We can from these stories draw clear conclusions about the child/parent relationship at the time the stories were told or written. In children's novels, parents have generally retained the traditional folktale roles, even though the relationships are substantially more psychologically complex. However, the scope and function of parental figures varies between kinds and genres of children's fiction, and it has also changed over time. In her insightful study *Disturbing the Universe*, Roberta Seelinger Trites investigates parental authority in children's and adolescent novels, also pointing out the necessity of revolt against parents in a young person's maturation process. It is therefore essential that we do not judge absent or insensitive parental figures from the mimetic point of view alone. Assessing the *Harry Potter* books, for instance, we may be amazed at how irresponsible Dumbledore is when he places the infant Harry in the care of his relatives where he knows Harry will be neglected and humiliated. It may seem equally careless to let Harry and his friends roam free at night on the dangerous grounds of Hogwarts, instead of locking them in the dorms and thus protecting them from danger. From the mimetic point of view, the actions of Dumbledore and other "positive" parental figures in the *Harry Potter* books are illogical, yet they are essential for the plot (what would the story be if Harry obediently stayed in his bed?) as well as for character development. In order to initiate a physical, emotional, and spiritual growth in the character, children's authors have to remove the parents, either permanently, by death (Harry Potter's parents), or temporarily, in the form of physical or emotional absence. While in reality parents or guardians are the most important figures in a child's life, in fiction, parents seldom play any significant role in the child character's development. If they do, they have a negative role, denying the child physical and spiritual freedom and thus preventing independence and growth. The use of a parent substitute may make the liberation process less offensive (in the same manner that a wicked stepmother is less offensive than a wicked mother). We see this once again reflected clearly in Harry Potter's foster family.

Further, there is a difference in the presentation of parents in various genres. In classical boys' and adventure stories, parents often hinder adventure. They restrict the protagonist's freedom, demand that he comes home for meals, has decent clothes, and washes his hands. Aunt Polly in *Tom Sawyer* is a good example. Other adults are seldom models for the male protagonist; rather they are presented as hypocrites who create rules, set limits, and make demands. In this respect, rebellious teenage fiction has inherited the secondary character gallery from boys' books. In classic girls' novels, adults are commonly models and idols. The March girls adore their mother and their absent father. Laura in the *Little House* series has full trust in her parents and loves them without reservation. The teacher Miss Stacy is a paragon for Anne Shirley. Contemporary psychological novels often depict a harmonious relationship with at least one adult, although not necessarily a parent. In many contemporary children's novels, parents are a problem: they fail to understand the child's needs, that is, they are emotionally absent.

EXERCISE

Consider the role of parents or parent substitutes in some children's novels, for instance *Little Women, Tom Sawyer, Anne of Green Gables, Little House in the Big Woods, Curious George, Sylvester and the Magic Pebble, Where the Wild Things Are, Ramona the Brave, Holes,* or the *Harry Potter* books. Remember that "evil" or absent parents may be a necessary element of the plot, so we should not treat them exclusively mimetically, for instance concluding that Max's mother does not love him.

School is yet another social institution that plays a prominent role in a child's everyday life. Given its importance, it is amazing what a marginal role school occupies in children's stories. School as setting is not uncommon, especially in the school stories from *Tom Brown's Schooldays* to *Harry Potter*. Various relationships within school are also inevitable: conflicts and friendships with teachers and peers, academic and athletic competition, and so on. The *Ramona* books are a very good illustration of this. Very seldom do we meet any elaborate description of actual schoolwork. A lesson may be used to introduce an issue, such as democracy, gender, ecology, or birth control. It may also be used for humorous purposes, like the chapter "Pippi Goes to School" in *Pippi Longstocking*. School stories seldom depict lessons, but rather mischief, recreation, and sports. In fact, the tradition of portraying school in children's fiction is remarkable, from the point of view of the messages conveyed to readers. School is an inevitable evil in *The Adventures of Tom Sawyer*, an arena for "slow suffering" (42) that children are meant to escape as much as possible. When confronted with the prospect of being adopted by Wendy's mother, Peter Pan's first question is, "Would you send me to school?" Upon getting an affirmative reply, he retorts, "I don't want to go to school and learn solemn things" (181). School is often presented as the opposite of freedom, integrity, and imagination. *Ramona* books may seem to contradict this statement; on a closer look, they focus on pranks and mischief rather than learning. School can also be used as an allegory of society, for instance in *The Chocolate War.*

Assessing Mimetic Representation

LET US EXPLORE

Contemplate the way society is presented in some of the following books: *The Secret Garden*; *Babar*; *Curious George*; *The Lion, the Witch and the Wardrobe*; *Charlie and the Chocolate Factory*; *The Outsiders*; *Roll of Thunder, Hear My Cry*; *The Giver*; *Harry Potter and the Sorcerer's Stone*; and *Holes*. Use the questions below as support for your argument:

- Does the depiction of society take a prominent place in the story? Is it integral, that is, essential for our understanding of the story? Is the depiction explicit or implicit?
- Are any social institutions ever mentioned, such as government, law, school, or church? What attitudes toward these institutions does the text present, explicitly or implicitly?
- How are power structures reflected in the story? Who has power and authority and why? Is the power hierarchy ever interrogated?
- Is any higher authority presented or mentioned in the story? It can be a deity, royalty, a political figure, or an authoritative adult. Is this authority ever interrogated? By whom and how?
- Are there any laws and rules presented, explicitly or implicitly? Are these rules absolute, that is, pertaining to all the members of the society, or do they only apply to the oppressed members?
- What values are important? Money, noble origin, age, gender, ethnicity, education. . . ? Are conflicting values represented?
- Does the society endorse conformity or diversity?

Let us consider just a few examples of possible ways to address these questions.

In *The Lion, the Witch and the Wardrobe*, we meet a preindustrial, rural society ruled by an evil usurper. At the end of the novel, the four children are crowned kings and queens and shown as just and wise rulers. In the sequels, we see Narnia ruled by a long dynasty of benevolent kings, every now and then challenged by various evil opponents. Narnia is a strictly hierarchic society. For one thing, as explained in *The Magician's Nephew*, some animals are bestowed with human intelligence and can talk, while others are referred to as "dumb." It is a crime to kill a talking animal, but there are no rules about killing dumb beasts. Translating this circumstance into human conditions, we are struck by the horrible inequality. For years, European conquerors referred to the native people of Africa, Asia, Australia, and America as "dumb," denying them human qualities and feelings. The Narnian society is thus copied from the British Empire. It is also based on a firm and unquestioning belief in higher authority, The Emperor Behind the Sea, and his corporeal representation, Aslan. Whether or not we draw direct parallels to the Christian doctrine, we can state that the laws and rules of Narnia, even those we find sensible and morally acceptable, are imposed from above. When the White Witch in *The Lion, the Witch and the Wardrobe* is defeated, Aslan proclaims the four children, Peter, Susan, Edmund, and Lucy, kings and queens of Narnia. They accept this without question, although a more democratic way would have been to let the Narnians elect their own ruler. A similar event is described in *The Magician's Nephew*, when a London cabby and his fiancée are crowned by Aslan to rule over Narnia. A ruler from a "higher" civilization is thus unquestionably acceptable in Narnia.

Similarly, we can clearly identify that society in the *Harry Potter* books is based on authority and regulations. Although the wizards believe themselves to be morally superior to Muggles, that is, the ordinary people, the wizard world meticulously imitates the real world, with its laws and rules, government, banking, penitentiary system, and not least, education. In fact, the *Harry Potter* books offer a magnificent cross-section of contemporary Western society, with its bureaucracy, struggle for power, and—more relevant than ever—international terrorism. It is gratifying to perform a genuinely Marxist analysis of *Harry Potter*, with questions such as, Who owns the production means (magic)? and, How do the mighty exploit the masses? In *Harry Potter and the Goblet of Fire*, Hermione gets involved in the movement for house elves' rights. The issue is not pursued particularly far, but among the many statements we meet in this book is the one affirming that elves genuinely like to be slaves. Even though the statement may be ironic, there is a danger that the irony will be lost on many young readers, and the social structure reflected in the book appears rather reactionary. It can be compared to the critical responses to the depiction of Oompa-Loompas in *Charlie and the Chocolate Factory*: oppressed workers deprived of any legal rights, who, in addition, are regularly doped with chocolate to keep them content. Since in books such as the *Harry Potter* novels or *Charlie and the Chocolate Factory* the presentation of society is far from the primary focus of our attention, young readers are likely to overlook the covert ideology.

The Giver presents a seemingly harmonious and just society: everybody has a job; all children receive the same education; nobody is hungry, homeless, or deprived; and all decisions are made collegially. The family structure is ideal: two parents, two children, a boy and a girl, all carefully matched. Gender stereotyping is avoided: the mother is a lawyer, while the father is a nurse. On closer examination, the novel depicts a totalitarian regime driven to the extreme. The citizens are brainwashed, complete conformity of thought and behavior is imposed, and the tiniest dissent is punished by death, euphemistically named "release." In this novel, the reader is supposed to discover the true nature of the depicted society together with the protagonist. Further, even though many of the most repulsive practices of this society may seem alien to us, it is not hard to draw parallels to such phenomena as the "one-child policy" in China or the persecution of political dissidents in Latin America. Language as a means of ideological manipulation is also a well-known fact. Thus the world of *The Giver* is in fact an amplified picture of all the negative features of our own society.

Holes depicts several important aspects of society. First, Stanley is falsely accused for a crime he has not committed. It is implied that if his family could afford a good lawyer, he would not have been found guilty. In the end, this implication is confirmed, as Stanley indeed gets legal help to avoid the correctional institution. The institution itself, Green Lake Camp, presents the society in miniature. The Warden has absolute power, while the counselors implement the rules. They in their turn have absolute power over the boys; for instance, they can punish Stanley by denying him drinking water. There is a hierarchy among the boys, as well as mechanisms for exploitation. Stanley teaches Zero to read in exchange for Zero digging his holes for him. On the other hand, X-Ray, the leader, can make other boys work for him by the mere power of his authority. The work, digging holes, is completely meaningless for the purpose it supposedly achieves: "If you take a bad boy and make him dig a hole every day in the hot sun, it will turn him into a good boy. That was what some people thought." The author is of course mocking the penitentiary system. Yet there is an economic design behind it, since the Warden is hoping to find the treasure. When Stanley does find the treasure, he is immediately elevated to a higher social status, including the economic power to engage a lawyer and move to a "better" neighborhood.

The Outsiders is a ruthful depiction of open class conflicts in society. The questions of class affiliation and class loyalty are explored. Such explicit social conflicts are more likely to be found in young adult novels—not because social issues do not exist for younger children, but mainly because the child may not be aware of them. Further, a strong social issue is more likely to be found in a text written from the point of view of the oppressed group, for instance in *Roll of Thunder, Hear My Cry*, where segregation is given the central place and is quite explicit. Black and white children go to different schools, black children have to stay away from school for most of the year because they are needed in the fields and in the household, and open confrontations between black and white communities are frequent. By contrast, in a book written from the upper- or middle-class perspective, such as *The Secret Garden*, the issue of race is downplayed. Mary comes from India, where native servants were not treated as human beings. The issue is brought forward as Mary learns that she cannot treat the servants in her uncle's English home the way she treated servants in India. The social differences are presented, but not interrogated. Moreover, Mary also becomes aware of the difference in social status between herself and others: she has as much money as she may need, while both the servant girl Martha and her brother Dickon must work hard to earn their living.

Curious George is the story of a happy little monkey who is by force taken out of his familiar surroundings and introduced into a society where he does not know the rules, yet is expected to obey them. The story does not tell us whether he has been separated from his biological parents, yet it does say that George was initially happy where he was. The Man in the yellow hat commits himself to being a surrogate parent for George, who of course represents the child. It would be natural to expect that the Man would show affection toward his foster child and make him happy and comfortable. Instead, the Man catches George by cunning, takes him away from the world he is used to ("George was sad," the text informs us, and the pictures confirm this by showing George's facial expression), takes him on board a big ship—a dangerous and unfamiliar place for a little child, and after a short talk dismisses him by saying, "Now run along and play, but don't get into trouble." How would a little child know how not to get into trouble in this situation? The text says that "it is easy for little monkeys to forget," but should not the adult have some responsibility for the child he has so casually adopted? Over and over again George is forced into situations he is incapable of handling, and each time he is abandoned by the adult, culminating in his being shut in prison. This may be perceived as a humorous detail, but think what it is telling us about the relationship between the adult and the child. After George, thanks to his ingenuity, has escaped from the prison and gotten involved in a number of further pranks, he is put in the Zoo, with the text self-righteously stating, "What a nice place for George to live!" Rather than taking care of the child he has so lightheartedly withdrawn from his natural environment, the adult places him in an institution, acting on the conviction that he is pursuing the child's best interests. This plot can be easily "translated" into the situation of, for instance, a Native American child taken away from his or her tribe and placed in a home, with the motivation, "What a nice place for you to live!" Because the child, George, is disguised as a monkey we may believe that the society and the social values we meet in this book are of no relevance; yet they definitely are, and we must learn to identify and assess them.

In the first *Babar* book, a little elephant whose mother is killed by a human hunter is adopted by an old lady and has to adjust to her ways of living. Babar's acquisition of human manners and behavior involves wearing clothes, living indoors, sleeping in a bed, eating at a table, and using tools and machines. When in *The Travels of Babar* the former savage is stripped of these tokens of civilization and treated as a dumb beast, he feels deeply humiliated. Upon returning to the jungle (which luckily coincides with the old elephant king's death) Babar brings civilization with him. In *Babar the King* we witness how in order to build a city for his subjects, Babar must cut down the jungle (some of the editions omit the actual picture where this act is shown, since today we perceive it as ecological crime), the result being a boring, regular settlement with identical huts and two monstrous public buildings: a Bureau of Industry and an Amusement Hall. School is among the top priorities, alongside a number of other social institutions. The movement of the *Babar* books propagates the development of the character from "savage" to "civilized," which, especially in the light of contemporary post-colonial theory, can be perceived as offensive.

As seen from this discussion, on closer examination the depiction of society in some children's books is far from what we would normally called "progressive." Many critics suggest banning such books, either by literally removing them from libraries or by avoiding using them in classrooms or in leisure reading with children. Most people who believe in freedom of speech are against censorship in any form. How are we then to deal with books that may have many other merits, but present conservative or reactionary views of society and power? To begin with, we must be aware of these views. Then we can try to decide how we can teach children to recognize them.

EXERCISE

Analyze the way society is depicted in some other children's books, for instance *Little Women, The Adventures of Tom Sawyer, The Wizard of Oz, Winnie-the-Pooh, Little House in the Big Woods, Charlotte's Web, Sylvester and the Magic Pebble, The Great Gilly Hopkins,* or *The Planet of Junior Brown.* Use the questions from the previous assignment as guidelines.

Themes and Motifs

One of the most common tools in mimetic studies of children's literature is the examination of motifs and issues. A motif is a textual element—an event, character, or object—recurring in many works of literature. Friendship, love, quest, journey, struggle, and revenge are examples of literary motifs. We can distinguish between primary, or leading, motifs and secondary, or subsidiary, motifs; primary motifs can also be defined as the theme of the book, its most persuasive abstract claim or doctrine. Thus, the theme of *The Adventures of Huckleberry Finn* is, as one critic has put it, "freedom and integrity," while some motifs involved in the book are running away, pursuit and escape, friendship and loyalty, and death. Themes and motifs can be explicit (open and clear) and implicit (understood). The explicit theme of *The Wizard of Oz* is magical adventure, the implicit theme a quest for self-discovery. Some motifs are genre bound; for instance transportation into a magical world and time displacement are two motifs associated with fantasy. By contrast, quest and struggle between good and evil may appear in fantasy as well as in other genres, for instance adventure.

Quest is by far the most common motif in children's literature, especially if we treat it broadly, not limiting it to the search for objects or persons, but also including the quest for identity. Quests are common in folktales where the hero leaves home in order to search for treasure, a kidnapped princess, or simply fortune. We see the motif most clearly in genres closely related to folktales, primarily heroic fantasy. In contemporary psychological novels, quests are predominantly of a symbolic nature, which may be emphasized by the title, such as *Park's Quest*. In adventure stories, there are many examples of searching for treasure, *Treasure Island* being the best known.

Journey is another fundamental pattern in children's fiction, even found in picture books for very young children. We find a variety of journeys in fantasy novels, for instance *The Wizard of Oz*. In mimetically oriented narratives, the most famous example is perhaps Huckleberry Finn's journey on the raft down the Mississippi, but journey is also the dominant motif of *Homecoming*. Running away, pursuit, and escape are auxiliary motifs associated with journey as well as quest. Survival in threatening surroundings is the central motif of the Robinsonnade, having its origin in *Robinson Crusoe*. It is also found in an episode in *Tom Sawyer*. If we consider the motif of survival as such and not the setting, it is also present in *Slake's Limbo*. The motif of mystery is associated with crime novels. Friendship is a common motif, which is, however, treated differently in books for boys and books for girls. Friendship between boys often means having adventures together (*Tom Sawyer*), while friendship between girls implies feelings, sharing secrets, and so on (*Anne of Green Gables*). Love, jealousy, and rivalry are common in books for teenagers. The treachery of adults toward the child has become a recurrent motif of the contemporary realistic novel, although it has also been successfully explored in fantasy.

Death as a motif in children's fiction has been subjected to a profound change during the last two hundred years. In nineteenth-century children's books it was very common, and a book could depict the main character's death as well as that of parents, grandparents, siblings, or close friends. It is easy to explain by social factors: child mortality was high, so many children in a family would die in infancy; several generations lived together, and to see an old relative die was part of a child's everyday life. Because of strong Christian values in Western children's literature, death was not perceived as a tragedy. In Western countries after the Second World War, urbanization and higher standards of living made death into something alien and therefore dangerous. Most old people die in hospitals, child mortality is low, and death has become a phenomenon that children normally do not meet in their everyday life. During a certain period, death was not considered a suitable motif for children's books. When it returns in many Western countries during the '60s and '70s, it has a strongly negative charge, as something threatening. A child's encounter with death and thoughts about death become a central motif in many contemporary books for children, for instance *Bridge to Terabithia*.

The motifs of realistic everyday stories are sometimes called issues. We can discern issues such as physical or mental disability, sibling rivalry, divorce, stepparents, adoption, ethnic identity, bullying, drug abuse, sex, war, violence, and so on. Sometimes, the label of an issue novel, or problem novel, is used if the issue clearly dominates over the personality of the characters and also when the narrative has an overtly didactic tone. Most children's books have one or more of these issues, but they can be presented in a more sophisticated way. For instance, *Bridge to Terabithia* is often recommended as a good book to discuss the issue of death. The author has been rather critical about this evaluation, saying that the book is not "about death," but about friendship, child/adult relationship, and other human matters. It is naturally fully legitimate to use fiction in a classroom situation as a basis for discussion of certain issues; yet children's books should not be viewed as pamphlets from social services, valuable simply for presenting issues.

The reason why certain motifs are more widespread in children's fiction than in the mainstream is most probably the characters' (and the readers') age. Journeys, both real and imaginary, discoveries, the search for identity, and survival on one's own without adults' assistance are all important components in a young person's psychological development. Insight about death is necessary for a young person to be able to go further and become adult. On the other hand, some motifs that are more prominent in adult literature, such as marriage and adultery, professional career, parenthood, and old age, are unusual in children's fiction, although they can of course be present as secondary motifs.

EXERCISE

Identify the most prominent motifs in some of the following novels: *The Secret Garden*; *Charlotte's Web*; *The Outsiders*; *Harriet the Spy*; *Roll of Thunder, Hear My Cry*; *The Great Gilly Hopkins*; *Walk Two Moons*; or *Holes*. Examine how these motifs are introduced and developed in the story and how they support the theme of the novel. What are the most common motifs you have discovered in these texts? Which of the motifs would you characterize as issues? Contemplate the advantages and disadvantages of mimetic approaches to children's literature.

LITERATURE AS AN INNER JOURNEY

Psychoanalytical theories of literature do not view literary works as a reflection of any tangible, objective reality, but as a reflection of an individual's internal world. In discussing authors (chapter 1), we stated that author-oriented psychoanalysis sets out to find traces of authors' childhood traumas in the way stories are told. Text-oriented psychoanalysis is focused on the way the text itself is formed.

Process of Individuation: A Quest in Three Phases

The main thesis is that literature depicts the psychological development of an individual, a complex process that in Jungian theory is called the process of individuation, the process of becoming an independent, whole, and integral individual. Let us remember that psychoanalysis is a clinical therapeutic method. The process of individuation is an attempt to describe what happens to an individual moving from childhood toward maturity and what can go wrong during this development, causing psychic disturbances. According to C. G. Jung and his followers, patients can speed up their individuation and bring it back to normal by use of imagination, stories, dreams, and nightmares. As in all directions of psychoanalysis, the unconscious plays an important role. The process of individuation is propelled by the interaction of the conscious and the unconscious.

Applying this model to literature, we examine how the psychological process described by Jungian theory is reflected in texts. We thus assume that a text presents some character's, usually the protagonist's, process of individuation. According to Jungians, this process has three stages. The first is the unconscious stage, a state of natural and perfect innocence in childhood, when the individual is happily unaware of the troubles and dangers of the outer world. We seldom see depictions of this stage in mainstream fiction, for several reasons. First, the characters of mainstream novels are habitually adults who have already passed this initial stage. Of course, there are novels partly or wholly devoted to childhood, such as *Oliver Twist* or *What Maisie Knew*. Yet even in these childhood narratives, the child is confronted with events that perturb happiness. Oliver is exposed to many dark sides of life,

and Maisie struggles to understand the strange world of adults. The innocence of childhood is often brought to an abrupt and violent end in the mainstream. Second, the complete harmony of the initial stage does not allow for
any of the serious conflicts necessary to construct a story. Indeed, if nothing
disturbs the perfect balance, nothing can "happen," which is a prerequisite
for a story. Yet in many children's books, we see attempts to create a sense
of complete idyll, for instance *The Secret Garden*, *Winnie-the-Pooh*, or *Little
House in the Big Woods*.

The second stage of the process of individuation is the conscious stage,
when the individual becomes aware of his faults and the faults of the surrounding world. This is the stage of unrest, anguish, and disintegration of
personality. This is where most literary characters stand at the beginning of
the story: something has destroyed the initial harmony. The individual has
two choices from this point. He may try to return to the first stage, where
he was happy and seemingly whole. This is, however, a false strategy. Initial
harmony, being a static, unchanged condition, can never be satisfactory for
an individual who seeks true perfection and integrity. Going back to the unconscious after having reached the conscious stage merely means suppressing
the awareness of disharmony. This is, according to Jung, the origin of many
mental disturbances: instead of handling the problems, the patient flees from
them. The problems, however, remain unresolved, and the true wholeness of
the individual, which is the goal of individuation, can never be attained.

Instead of regressing to the first stage, the individual should go further
to the third stage, which integrates the conscious and the unconscious, thus
achieving a happy reconciliation, a balance, a harmony. Whenever this stage
is not reached in literature we as readers experience frustration—in plain
words, we prefer happy endings. However, in children's literature we most
often see the process unaccomplished, or merely in an intermediate stage, a
temporary reconciliation, because a child is not a fully developed individual
yet. The very basic description of the process of individuation in myth and
fairy tale takes the form of descent to hell (symbolic death), trials, ascent,
and resurrection.

Archetypes: Images of the Unconscious

During the process of individuation, each person is confronted with a
number of symbolic figures, called in Jungian analysis *archetypes* ("arche"
= old, ancient; "typos" = image). Archetypes are recurrent images in stories that have particular functions in individuation. Anima (literally meaning
"soul") is the archetype representing subconscious creative powers, the positive female aspects of the male's psyche. Leslie in *Bridge to Terabithia* is a
good example of the Anima archetype. The correspondence for a female
character is Animus (that is, this archetype must be necessarily represented

by a figure of the opposite gender). For instance, Call is Louise's Animus in
Jacob Have I Loved. In contrast, the Shadow is the expression of primitive,
animal feelings and instincts. In literature it is often symbolized by doubles,
mirror reflections, and other similar images. The pretty twin sister is Louise's Shadow. Voldemort is Harry Potter's Shadow. The Wise Old Man (for
a male character) or the Progenitrix (for a female character) is the spiritual
principle, a guide. Dumbledore is an example of such a spiritual leader in
Harry Potter's individuation. The Self is the archetype representing reconciliation, the union of the conscious and the subconscious, the final goal of the
process. It is often symbolized by the image of a perfect circle, sometimes
with a center. Jungian critics refer to this image as mandala, which is an ancient Oriental symbol of harmony. The well-known sign of yin and yang
is another variant. There are many other archetypes encountered in Jungian
interpretations, but the four mentioned are the most central. (See fig. 4-1.)

The goal of individuation is thus to meet and acknowledge the hidden part
of one's psyche, to integrate both the positive and the negative sides into the
Self and create a balance between them, that is Anima/Animus, the Shadow,
and the guide—the figures that in literary texts can appear as concrete people, but in the analysis are interpreted as constituents of the individuating

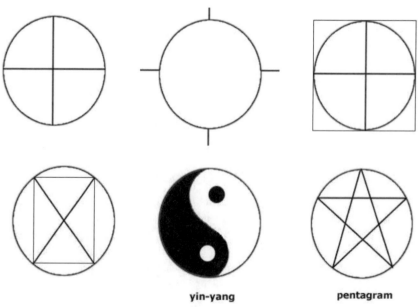

                              yin-yang   pentagram
                    Fig. 4-1   Forms of mandalas.

person's inner world. Individuation is a painful process, taking the person through trials and agony. These may seem negative, but in the end they lead to something positive, to self-fulfillment.

It is essential to remember that Jungian analysis views literary texts as a reflection of an individual's internal processes. It means that archetypal figures in stories are in fact projections of the protagonist's inner qualities rather than people existing in an external reality. That is, in her individuation, Louise ascribes Call, Caroline, and other people in her surroundings the qualities she finds inside herself. What these people are really like is beyond the interest of a Jungian critic.

External Pictures of Internal Reality

Fairy tales are among the favorite objects of Jungian analysis, since the process of individuation is very transparent in them. The evil that the hero meets in these narratives is in Jungian interpretation not an external factor, but a part of the protagonist's psyche. Marie-Louise von Franz, one of Jung's disciples, has written several excellent studies of fairy tales with Jungian tools. Two popular texts for Jungians are Dante's *Divina Commedia* and Lewis Carroll's *Alice in Wonderland*, both complex, dreamlike narratives involving journeys that can easily be translated into a quest for the inner self. Indeed, Jungian analysis has been primarily performed on stories with supernatural elements, that by their very structure prompt a symbolic rather than mimetic interpretation. Let us, for instance, see how we can interpret *The Wizard of Oz* in terms of individuation. At the beginning of the story, Dorothy lives in a happy state of innocence and ignorance. Her life is hardly exciting, but since this is the only life she knows, she does not long for anything else. On arrival in the land of Oz, Dorothy feels lost and disoriented. She has now entered the second stage, when she becomes conscious of her own imperfection. Characteristically, her split self is tangibly represented by her three companions, who also have the function of her Animus. Dorothy lacks—or at least thinks she lacks—some of the basic human qualities: brain, heart, and courage. The archetypes she meets during her journey include the good witches (Progenitrices) and the bad witches (Shadows). Dorothy's trials in the land of Oz get her to know and understand herself, to realize that she is in fact a whole and integral individual. The realization is described symbolically through her companions' receiving the objects of their desires. After that, Dorothy can return home, because she can now reconcile the newly gained consciousness with the initial happiness of childhood. Home as the central point of her life is the symbol of the Self.

In applying the Jungian model, we treat events and characters as symbols, that is, images representing something else. For instance, such elements as caves, castles, or forests are symbols for the individual's inner landscape at the second stage: unfamiliar and dangerous places where it is easy to get lost. Jungian interpretations lean heavily on symbols, ascribing them a variety of meanings. It would, however, be wrong to believe that only fairy tales and fantasy are suitable material for psychoanalytical investigation. It is, on the contrary, more challenging and gratifying to identify the process of individuation in texts that would normally invite mimetic readings. For instance, *The Secret Garden* does not contain any magic; the setting and the events are fully credible. Yet Mary's exploration of the hidden and the forbidden spaces, the many rooms of the mansion, as well as the garden itself, can be interpreted as her self-discovery, leading to moral and spiritual improvement. In fact, gardens in Jungian analysis symbolize wholeness and harmony.

Holes does not contain any direct supernatural events either. Yet in the beginning of the novel we clearly see the protagonist in a state of mind that a Jungian would describe as split. Stanley is exiled from his normal surroundings to an unfamiliar and desolate place and exposed to vile and humiliating treatment, far from the idyllic innocence of childhood. Stanley's life at Camp Green Lake is very similar to a descent into hell (the camp lies in the South; and the South with its heat and drought is one of the many symbolic representations of hell). He suffers physically and mentally, he is made to perform meaningless tasks as a punishment for his sins, but eventually he is resurrected, presumably as a morally and spiritually better individual. To support the interpretation of Stanley's trials as a process of individuation, a parallel, more explicitly mythical story is added.

EXERCISE

Apply the Jungian model to some children's books, for instance *The Secret Garden*; *The Lion, the Witch and the Wardrobe*; *Where the Wild Things Are*; *Bridge to Terabithia*; *Jacob Have I Loved*; *Slake's Limbo*; *Holes*; *Walk Two Moons*; *The Planet of Junior Brown*; or *Harry Potter and the Sorcerer's Stone*. Start by deciding at which stage you first meet the protagonist and proceed to investigate when in the story a transition to a different stage occurs and what activates this transition. Identify the archetypes appearing in the text. Pay attention to the resolution of the story: does the character regress to the first stage or go on, albeit tentatively, toward the third one. Contemplate whether you have discovered another dimension of the text by applying the psychoanalytical approach.

LITERATURE AS TIME-OUT

Yet another nonmimetic way of looking at literature is viewing it as a symbolic representation of a socially liberating process, a subversive, that is, disguised, interrogation of authorities. We find some tools for such analysis in carnival theory, elaborated by the Russian philosopher and critic Mikhail Bakhtin. The essence of the medieval carnival (a short period of grotesque festivities and excesses preceding Lent), Bakhtin points out, was the temporary reversal of the established order when all societal power structures changed places. The fool was crowned king, while kings and bishops were dethroned and denigrated. Carnival was sanctioned by the authorities who therefore had control over it. Moreover, the temporary nature of carnival presupposed the restoration of the initial order. Yet, as Bakhtin sees it, carnival had a subversive effect, since it showed that social hierarchies were not unquestionable. Bakhtin applies the concept of carnival to literature, viewing it as a narrative device used to describe reality in a distorting mirror, in a state of temporary deviation from the existing order, as well as total freedom from societal restrictions.

Carnival theory is highly relevant for children's literature. Children in our society are oppressed and powerless, having no economic resources of their own, no voice in political and social decisions, and are subject to a large number of laws and rules which the adults expect them to obey without interrogation. Yet, paradoxically enough, children are allowed, in fiction written for their enlightenment and enjoyment *by adults*, to become strong, brave, rich, powerful, and independent—on certain conditions and for a limited time. The most important condition is the physical dislocation and the removal, temporary or permanent, of parental protection, allowing the child protagonist to have the freedom to explore the world and test the boundaries of independence. The child may be placed in a number of extraordinary situations, such as war or revolution; exotic, faraway settings; temporary isolation on a desert island; extreme danger; and so on. All these conditions empower the fictional child, and even though the protagonist is most frequently brought back to the security of home and parental supervision, the narratives have a subversive effect, showing that the rules imposed on the child by the adults are in fact arbitrary. Fantasy is another common carnivalesque device, as an ordinary child is empowered through transportation to a magical realm, through the possession of a magical agent (object or helper), and through the acquisition of a set of heroic traits or magical force, impossible or at least improbable within the existing order of things (what we normally call the "real world.") Carnival, reversing the existing order, elevates the fictional child to a position superior to adults. Yet, the inevitable reestablishment of order in the end of a carnivalesque children's story brings the characters down to levels at which they are only slightly more powerful than their environment, equal to it, or inferior to it.

Versions of Carnival

LET US EXPLORE

Consider in what way the character is empowered in some children's books, for instance *The Wizard of Oz*; *The Lion, the Witch and the Wardrobe*; *Where the Wild Things Are*; *Harry Potter*; *Tom Sawyer*; *Homecoming*; *The Cat in the Hat*; and *The True Confessions of Charlotte Doyle*. Is the character disempowered in the end? If yes, how and why? How does the temporary empowerment affect the character?

There are several ways in which a fictive child can be empowered. In *The Wizard of Oz*, Dorothy finds herself in a foreign country where she performs deeds impossible in her everyday life in Kansas. She can show herself clever, caring, and brave, but in the end she is sent back to Kansas, and we never learn whether she can use her newly gained insights. *The Lion, the Witch and the Wardrobe* presents a still stronger empowerment of ordinary children, literally transforming them into heroes. While Dorothy's victories over the two wicked witches are accidental, Peter is supposed to participate in a real battle, including intentional killing. Further, unlike Dorothy, who is never considered as a possible ruler of the Emerald City, Peter and his siblings are literally crowned in the end, thus occupying the highest possible position in the medieval world of Narnia. Yet their enthronement is temporary: after many happy years of rule in Narnia, they are brought back to their own world, regress into their child shapes, and are apparently stripped not only of the power, but also of the wisdom they gained during their time-out in Narnia. Max in *Where the Wild Things Are* is also crowned as "the most wild of all" and "king of all wild things." In the end, he is brought back to the world where his mother has the power of providing or denying him food. Max has mastered the monsters (his own aggressions), but as a child, he is still at his mother's will. In the last picture, he has not only lost his crown, but is losing his wolf suit, which was the initial device of his empowerment (becoming a wild thing). Carnival theory enables us to see how power reversal works and decide whether return to order cancels the time-out or has some subversive effect. It would seem that Harry Potter is empowered permanently, since he is an omnipotent wizard. Yet Harry's power has its limitations. First, although he is born a wizard and has some inherent force, he still has to learn the true uses of magic, that is, to steer and control his power. So far, the adults at Hogwarts have more power than Harry. Second, Harry is repeatedly sent back to the magicless world of Muggles, where he is not allowed to use his power. Even though he occasionally breaks the rules to take revenge on his nasty cousin Dudley, creating a truly carnivalesque chaos, these are merely small deviations from the order in which Harry is oppressed and can any time be locked in his little room under the staircase.

Tom Sawyer is empowered in a different manner. First, like many children's literature heroes, he is incredibly lucky to be an orphan (almost a sacrilege to state from a mimetic point of view, but a necessary condition for carnival) and to have an almost unrestricted freedom of movement. Running away from home is a carnivalesque strategy applicable in nonfantastic narratives. In *Tom Sawyer*, the characters are empowered by finding a treasure that immediately gives them a considerably higher social status. While running away is an innocent prank in *Tom Sawyer*, in *Homecoming*, the children are empowered by the necessity to take care of themselves when left without adult assistance. Adult society is all the time after them, attempting to restrain their freedom and independence by putting them into proper social care. They are finally disempowered by coming under their grandmother's protection. Yet the adventure has definitely taught them that they can cope on their own, and they will not let anyone make choices for them.

In *The Cat in the Hat*, chaos enters everyday order, all rules are eliminated, and everything is turned upside down. This is carnival in its purest form: wild, uncontrolled, and nonsensical. The cat can be interpreted as the child's imagination that comes unbound when the adult leaves the scene; however, as soon as the mother is within reach, the cat and the results of his hilarious games are eliminated. Yet this approved and channeled rebellion has a liberating effect.

Finally, *The True Confessions of Charlotte Doyle* is an excellent example of how a girl can be empowered through cross-dressing. Stranded as the only passenger on a transatlantic ship with a morally dubious captain and crew, and having involuntarily caused a man's death, Charlotte sheds her female clothes as well as her well-bred manners and joins the crew to make up for the ill she has brought about. The fact that Charlotte finds men's clothes "surprisingly comfortable," to use her own words, is illuminating. Although the text does not mention it, we may assume that she is subject to the torture of Western female clothing in the 1830s: stays, tight shoes, and so on. Putting on practical, loose-fitting sailor's clothes, she is symbolically confronted with gender inequality and is prepared to take the first step toward liberation. In adopting an androgynous image, Charlotte also finally performs the symbolic action many of her literary sisters have done before her: she cuts off her hair. Upon arrival to Providence, Charlotte, who has managed the hard trial of being a deck hand under an inhuman captain, must once again change her identity by means of clothes, discovering this time how confining her usual female outfit feels after weeks of freedom. However, the inner change in Charlotte is so profound that it cannot be camouflaged merely by a change of clothes. Having experienced freedom and independence, she cannot accept the oppression her father imposes on her. Since she has kept her men's clothes as a reminder of her new self, she can easily slip back into this role. Unlike a number of female cross-dressing characters, for instance Jo March, who are forced back into the prescribed female roles, Charlotte is once again empowered in this vivid open ending.

From the examples discussed we can see that children's writers use different strategies in empowering and disempowering their child characters, but that the basic mechanism is the same: empowerment is allowed on certain conditions, and it is almost without exceptions temporary. The temporary nature of carnival is thus its most essential feature.

Carnival theory has not been applied to children's literature on a wide scale yet. However, it has great potential, since it allows us to examine power positions between children and adults in texts as well as in society without necessarily tying them to ideology, as is often the case with feminist and postcolonial studies.

EXERCISE

Try to apply carnival theory to some of the following stories: *Little Women, The Secret Garden, Curious George, Charlie and the Chocolate Factory, And To Think That I Saw It on Mulberry Street, Charlotte's Web, Ramona the Brave, Slake's Limbo, The Giver, The Paper Bag Princess,* or *The Great Gilly Hopkins.* Contemplate whether the theory has opened some new dimensions in the text.

HOW TO GO FURTHER

Whether we view literature as a reflection of reality, a rite of passage, or a symbolic time-out, childhood is the primary content of all children's books. Childhood studies is a relatively new direction of inquiry, emerging on the crossroads of literary criticism, psychology, social anthropology, and education. Some studies within this area, such as *Children's Literature: Criticism and the Fictional Child*, by Karín Lesnik-Oberstein; *Inventing the Child: Culture, Ideology, and the Rise of Childhood*, by John Zornado; or *The Poetics of Childhood*, by Roni Natov, focus on the discrepancy between the depiction and construction of a fictional child and the actual, sociohistorical conditions of childhood. Childhood studies investigate the content of children's literature from a broader sociohistorical perspective than traditional mimetic studies, taking into consideration new achievements in a number of adjacent disciplines including neurobiology. The direction has not yet developed any specific analytical toolkit, and there are many questions and controversies among scholars. The risk with this interdisciplinary approach is that literature as such is obscured by the purely historical, social, or psychological issues, but it is definitely worth a closer examination for anyone who is interested in a more profound study of themes and motifs of children's fiction.

Another direction that may prove fruitful is applying the ideas of Michel Foucault, which has been done on a very modest scale as yet.

REFERENCES

General

Brannigan, John. *New Historicism and Cultural Materialism*. New York: St. Martin's Press, 1998.

Booth, Wayne C. *The Company We Keep: An Ethics of Fiction*. Berkeley, CA: University of California Press, 1988.

Foucault, Michel. *Discipline and Punish: The Birth of the Prison*. New York: Random House, 1979.

———. *The Essential Foucault*. Edited by Paul Rabinow and Nicholas Rose. New York: New Press, 2003.

Hollindale, Peter. "Ideology and the Children's Book." *Signal* 55 (1988): 3–22.

Hunt, Peter. *Criticism, Theory and Children's Literature*. London: Blackwell, 1991. Chap. 8, "Politics, Ideology, and Children's Literature."

Jameson, Fredric. *The Political Unconscious: Narrative as a Socially Symbolic Art*. London: Methuen, 1981.

The Lion and the Unicorn 14, no. 1 (1990): a special issue on politics and ideology.

Lukens, Rebecca J. *A Critical Handbook of Children's Literature*. 4th ed. New York: HarperCollins, 1990. Chap. 5, "Theme."

Mackey, Margaret. "Ramona the Chronotope: The Young Reader and the Social Theories of Narrative." *Children's Literature in Education* 21, no. 3 (1990): 179–187.

McGillis, Roderick. *The Nimble Reader: Literary Theory and Children's Literature*. New York: Twayne, 1996. Chap. 4, "Journey to the Interior"; chap. 5, "Politics and Critical Practice."

Nodelman, Perry, and Mavis Reimer. *The Pleasures of Children's Literature*. 3rd ed. Boston: Allyn and Bacon, 2003. Chap. 8, "Literature and Ideology."

Sarland, Charles. "Ideology." Pp. 41–57 in *International Companion Encyclopedia of Children's Literature*, edited by Peter Hunt. London: Routledge, 1996.

Williams, Raymond. *Marxism and Literature*. Oxford: Oxford University Press, 1977.

Mimetic Studies of Children's Literature (A Selection)

ARIEL 28, no. 1 (1997): special issue on children's literature and postcolonial theory.

Avery, Gillian, and Kimberley Reynolds, eds. *Representations of Childhood Death.* New York: St. Martin's Press, 2000.

Bosmajian, Hamida. *Sparing the Child: Children's Literature About Nazism and the Holocaust.* New York: Garland, 2001.

Bottigheimer, Ruth. *Grimm's Bad Girls and Bold Boys: The Moral and Social Vision of the Tales.* New Haven: Yale University Press, 1987.

Butts, Dennis, ed. *Stories and Society: Children's Literature in its Social Context.* London: Macmillan, 1992.

Cart, Michael. *Gay and Lesbian Fiction for Young Adults.* Lanham, MD: Scarecrow, 2004.

Clyde, Laurel A. *Out of the Closet and into the Classroom: Homosexuality in Books for Young People.* Melbourne: ALIA Thorpe, 1992.

Cummins, June. "The Resisting Monkey: 'Curious George,' Slave Captivity, and the Postcolonial Condition." *ARIEL* 28, no. 1 (1997): 69–83.

Cunningham, Hugh. *The Children of the Poor: Representation of Childhood since the Seventeenth Century.* Oxford: Blackwell, 1991.

Dixon, Bob. *Catching Them Young.* London: Pluto Press, 1977. Vol. 1, "Sex, Race and Class in Children's Fiction"; vol. 2, "Political Ideas in Children's Fiction."

Fraser, James H., ed. *Society and Children's Literature.* Boston: Godine, 1978.

Gannon, Susan R., and Ruth Anne Thompson, eds. *Cross-Culturalism in Children's Literature.* West Lafayette, IN: Children's Literature Association, 1989.

Johnson, Dianne. *Telling Tales: The Pedagogy and the Promise of Afro-American Literature for Children.* Westport, CT: Greenwood, 1990.

Keith, Lois. *Take Up Thy Bed and Walk: Death, Disability, and Cure in Classic Fiction for Girls.* New York: Routledge, 2002.

Khorana, Meena. *Africa in Literature for Children and Young Adults: An Annotated Bibliography of English-language Books.* Westport, CT: Greenwood, 1994.

Kokkola, Lydia. *Representing the Holocaust in Children's Literature.* New York: Routledge, 2003.

Kutzer, Daphne M. *Empire's Children: Empire and Imperialism in Classic British Children's Books.* New York: Garland, 2000.

Latham, Don. "Discipline and Its Discontents: A Foucauldian Reading of *The Giver.*" *Children's Literature* 32 (2004): 134–151.

Lathey, Gillian. *The Impossible Legacy: Identity and Purpose in Autobiographical Children's Literature Set in the Third Reich and the Second World War.* Bern: Lang, 1999.

Leeson, Robert. *Children's Books and Class Society: Past and Present.* London: Writers and Readers Publishing Cooperative, 1977.

The Lion and the Unicorn 17, no. 2 (1993): a special issue on theories of class in children's literature.

Logan, Mawuena Kossi. *Narrating Africa: George Henty and the Fiction of Empire.* New York: Garland, 1999.

MacCann, Donnarae. *White Supremacy in Children's Literature: Characterizations of African Americans, 1830–1900.* New York: Garland, 1998.

MacLeod, Anne Scott. *American Childhood: Essays on Children's Literature of the Nineteenth and Twentieth Century.* Athens, GA: University of Georgia Press, 1994.

Malarté-Feldman, Claire-Lise, and Jack Yeager. "Babar and the French Connection: Teaching the Politics of Superiority and Exclusion." Pp. 69–77 in *Critical Perspectives on Postcolonial African Children's and Young Adult Literature*, edited by Meena Khorana. Westport, CT: Greenwood, 1998.

McCoy Lowery, Ruth. *Immigrants in Children's Literature.* New York: Peter Lang, 2000.

McGillis, Roderick, ed. *Voices of the Other: Children's Literature and the Postcolonial Context.* New York: Garland, 1999.

Myers, Mitzi. "Missed Opportunities and Critical Malpractice: New Historicism and Children's Literature." *Children's Literature Association Quarterly* 13, no. 1 (1988): 41–43.

Nikolajeva, Maria. "'A Dream of Complete Idleness': The Depiction of Labor in Children's Literature." *The Lion and the Unicorn* 26, no. 3 (2002): 305–321.

O'Dell, Felicity Ann. *Socialization Through Literature: The Soviet Example.* Cambridge: Cambridge University Press, 1978.

O'Sullivan, Emer. *Friend or Foe? The Image of Germany and the Germans in British Children's Fiction from 1870 to the Present.* Tübingen: Narr, 1990.

Robinson, Debra. *Portraying Persons with Disabilities: An Annotated Bibliography of Fiction for Children and Teenagers.* New Providence, NJ: Bowker, 1992.

Rudman, Masha Kabakow. *Children's Literature: An Issues Approach.* 3rd ed. White Plains, NY: Longman, 1995.

Slapin, Beverly, and Dora Seale. *Through Indian Eyes: Native Experience in Books for Children.* Philadelphia: New Society, 1992.

Watkins, Tony. "History, Culture, and Children's Literature." Pp. 32–40 in *International Companion Encyclopedia of Children's Literature*, edited by Peter Hunt. London: Routledge, 1996. Also pp. 30–38 in *Understanding Children's Literature*, edited by Peter Hunt. London: Routledge, 1999.

Zipes, Jack. *Breaking the Magic Spell: Radical Theories of Folk and Fairy Tales.* Austin: University of Texas Press, 1979.

———. *Fairy Tales and the Art of Subversion.* New York: Wildman, 1983.

———. *Happily Ever After: Fairy Tales, Children and the Culture Industry.* New York: Routledge, 1997. See especially chap. 2, "The Rationalization of Abandonment and Abuse in Fairy Tales."

Jungian Studies

Bloomingdale, Judith. "Alice as Anima: The Image of the Woman in Carroll's Classic." Pp. 378–390 in *Aspects of Alice*, edited by Robert Phillips. New York: The Vanguard Press, 1971.

Franz, Marie-Louise von. "The Process of Individuation." Pp. 160–229 in *Man and His Symbols*, edited by C. G. Jung. London: Aldus, 1964.

———. *Interpretation of Fairy Tales.* Zürich: Spring, 1970.

———. *Problems of the Feminine in Fairytales.* Zürich: Spring, 1972.

———. *Shadow and Evil in Fairy Tales.* Zürich: Spring, 1974.

Jung, C. G., ed. *Man and His Symbols.* London: Aldus, 1964. A collection of essays by Jung and his disciples.

Nikolajeva, Maria. *From Mythic to Linear: Time in Children's Literature.* Lanham, MD: Scarecrow, 2000. The study does not employ Jungian theory consistently, but it gathers inspiration from certain Jungian ideas, such as the process of individuation.

Segal, Robert A., ed. *Jung on Mythology.* Princeton, NJ: Princeton University Press, 1998. This annotated anthology offers a quick orientation in Jung's statements on myth and psychology.

Sigman, Joseph. "The Diamond in the Ashes: A Jungian Reading of the 'Princess' Books." Pp. 183–194 in *For the Childlike: George MacDonald's Fantasies for Children,* edited by Roderick McGillis. Methuchen, NJ: Scarecrow, 1992.

Veglahn, Nancy. "Images of Evil: Male and Female Monsters in Heroic Fantasy." *Children's Literature* 15 (1987): 106–119.

Carnival Theory

Bakhtin, Mikhail. *Rabelais and His World.* Cambridge, MA: MIT Press, 1968.

Chaston, Joel D. "Baum, Bakhtin, and Broadway: A Centennial Look at the Carnival of Oz." *The Lion and the Unicorn* 25, no. 1 (2001): 128–149.

Elick, Catherine L. "Animal Carnivals: A Bakhtinian Reading of C. S. Lewis's *The Magician's Nephew* and P. L. Travers's *Mary Poppins.*" *Style* 35, no. 3 (2001): 454–471.

Morson, Gary Saul, and Caryl Emerson. *Mikhail Bakhtin: Creation of a Prosaics.* Stanford: Stanford University Press, 1990. A good comprehensive introduction into Bakhtin's theories of literature.

Nikolajeva, Maria. *Children's Literature Comes of Age: Towards a New Aesthetic.* New York: Garland, 1996. Chap. 4, "From Epic to Polyphony."

Russell, David L. "Pippi Longstocking and the Subversive Affirmation of Comedy." *Children's Literature in Education* 31, no. 3 (2000): 167–177.

Stephens, John. *Language and Ideology in Children's Fiction.* London: Longman, 1992. Chap. 4, "Ideology, Carnival and Interrogative Texts."

Childhood Studies

Christensen, Nina. "Fictive Childhoods: On the Relationship between Childhood Studies and Children's Literature." *Tidsskrift for børne- & ungdomsklultur* 46 (2003): 107–122.

Coats, Karen S. "Keepin' It Plural: Children's Studies in the Academy." *Children's Literature Association Quarterly* 26, no. 3 (2001): 140–150.

Coveney, Peter. *The Image of Childhood: The Individual and Society: A Study of the Theme in English Literature.* Harmondsworth: Penguin, 1967.

Flynn, Richard. "The Intersection of Children's Literature and Childhood Studies." *Children's Literature Association Quarterly* 22, no. 3 (1997): 143–146.

Galbraight, Mary. "Hear My Cry: A Manifesto for an Emancipatory Childhood Studies Approach to Children's Literature." *The Lion and the Unicorn* 25, no. 2 (2001): 187–208.

Kincaid, James. *Child-Loving: The Erotic Child and Victorian Culture.* New York: Routledge, 1992.

Lesnik-Oberstein, Karín. *Children's Literature: Criticism and the Fictional Child.* Oxford: Clarendon, 1994.

Lesnik-Oberstein, Karín, ed. *Childhood in Culture: Approaches to Childhood.* New York: Macmillan, 1998.

The Lion and the Unicorn 25, no. 2 (2001): a special issue on childhood studies.

de Mause, Lloyd, ed. *The History of Childhood.* New York: Harper & Row, 1974.

McGavran, James Holt, ed. *Romanticism and Children's Literature in the Nineteenth-Century England.* Athens, GA: University of Georgia Press, 1991.

———. *Literature and the Child: Romantic Continuations, Postmodern Contestations.* Iowa City: University of Iowa Press, 1999.

Natov, Roni. *The Poetics of Childhood.* New York: Routledge, 2003.

Nodelman, Perry, and Mavis Reimer. *The Pleasures of Children's Literature.* 3rd ed. Boston: Allyn and Bacon, 2003. Chap. 5, "Common Assumptions about Childhood."

Travisano, Thomas. "Of Dialectic and Divided Consciousness: Intersection between Children's Literature and Childhood Studies." *Children's Literature* 28 (2000): 22–29.

Warner, Marina. *Six Myths of Our Time.* New York: Vintage, 1994. Chap. 3, "Little Angels, Little Monsters: Keeping Childhood Innocent."

Zornado, John. *Inventing the Child: Culture, Ideology, and the Rise of Childhood.* New York: Garland, 2000.

5

The Aesthetic of Composition

In a story, the material is organized in an artistic way. We sometimes say that a certain story has poor composition, meaning that it is incoherent and hard to follow, that there is no logic in the events. In this chapter, we will be exploring various approaches to the ways stories are constructed.

BEGINNING, MIDDLE, AND END

LET US EXPLORE

Let us choose five very different stories—*Puss in Boots*, *The Adventure of Tom Sawyer*, *The Wizard of Oz*, *Anne of Green Gables*, and *Where the Wild Things Are*—and see whether we can find some common elements in their composition. You may add as many other stories as you wish to this list, the more the better.

The first element we find in the beginning of each of these stories is that the protagonist leaves home. There are different reasons for this. The miller's youngest son is forced to go and seek his fortune, Tom is mischievous and likes adventure, Dorothy is involuntarily removed from home, Anne comes from an orphanage to what will become her new home, and Max escapes into the world of imagination. In each case, the change in the protagonist's situation brings about a complication. Puss's master must win the princess, Tom meets with all kinds of dangers, Dorothy is set on several perilous journeys, Anne must adapt to her new surroundings, and Max has to tame the monsters. The complications reach their highest point eventually, and a resolution follows. In some of the stories, protagonists return to their initial home; in others they establish a new home of their own. This sequence of events in a story, "what is happening," is called a plot. In constructing a plot, the author makes a selection of significant events, ignoring others that do not contribute to plot development (for instance, what the protagonist had for breakfast). A good plot consists of a tension between lack and the liquidation of it, between wish and fulfillment. In other words, the engine of the plot is a conflict.

Conflicts: Building Blocks of a Plot

There are several types of conflict that comprise the basis for a plot. Person-against-person conflict is probably the most common in children's novels, since it originates from traditional literature, myths, and folktales. The protagonist meets his adversary in some sort of combat (Dorothy meets the Witch of the West, Tom Sawyer meets Injun Joe, and so on). This conflict is presumably easiest for a young reader to understand, since this is the type of confrontation children encounter in their everyday surroundings, with adults and peers. In a person-against-society conflict, the character meets social conventions that prevent him from reaching the goal or compel him to make a moral choice (Pippi Longstocking's ways are a revolt against the existing rules; Wilbur in *Charlotte's Web* must find a way to survive in a society in which it is habitual to turn pigs into ham and sausage). In a person-against-nature conflict the character is confronted with natural elements in a struggle for his survival, as is Robinson Crusoe. All Robinsonnades and many other adventure stories have this type of conflict. Finally, in a person-against-self conflict, probably the most sophisticated, an inner struggle is depicted. In most books, several conflicts are combined. Further, the conflicts may look different at the different levels of the text. In *The Wizard of Oz* we find conflict of the "person-against-person" type on the surface: Dorothy is struggling against the wicked witch. On a more symbolic level, she is on a quest for self-discovery, shown through her companions, who learn that they already possess the qualities they seek.

EXERCISE

Identify the central conflict in some children's stories, for instance *Cinderella*; *Little Women*; *The Adventures of Tom Sawyer*; *Anne of Green Gables*; *Babar*; *Curious George*; *Ramona the Pest*; *Where the Wild Things Are*; *Sylvester and the Magic Pebble*; *Roll of Thunder, Hear My Cry*; *Hatchet*; *The Giver*; and *The Great Gilly Hopkins*. Try to see whether the conflict can be viewed on different levels.

Master Plot

The most traditional narrative plots are to be found in oral stories, and these have been adopted by children's fiction. The typical plot in children's literature, which we may call a basic plot or a master plot, follows this pattern: home → departure from home → adventure → homecoming. Home provides safety, but the character must depart from home, since nothing exciting ever happens there. Being away is exciting, but also dangerous, so the characters must return home, often after they have found a treasure or gained knowledge and maturity.

A classic adult novel frequently follows the character from birth to death—a biographical plot. For obvious reasons, such a plot would not work in children's fiction. Yet, most plots in children's fiction are indeed constructed in the traditional manner, with a beginning, middle, and end, as prescribed by Aristotle. We will therefore start by taking a closer look at such a plot. Normally, a plot is constructed according to the following pattern. First, we have an *exposition* where characters and setting are introduced. For instance, the first pages of *The Wizard of Oz* present Dorothy, her Uncle Henry and Aunt Em, as well as their house and the surrounding prairies. Then follow *complications*: Dorothy is carried away by the cyclone. The events accumulate in a *rising action*, with constantly increasing dangers: Dorothy meets her three companions, experiences a number of hardships on the road to the Emerald City, reaches the Wizard, and is send to kill the Witch of the West. Some devices to build up the rising action are, for instance, suspense, cliffhanger, and foreshadowing. *Suspense* is a state that makes the reader go on reading, a curiosity about what happens next. Contrary to common belief, suspense is a characteristic not confined to crime and adventure novels, although it is more prominent in these genres. In *The Wizard of Oz*, the suspense is first maintained by curiosity about whether Dorothy and her friends will reach the Emerald City and whether the Wizard will grant their wishes; later whether Dorothy will defeat the Witch and how. Throughout the book, the reader is kept in suspense as to how Dorothy will get home. A *cliffhanger* is an exciting chapter ending that prevents the reader from putting the book aside (or, if the child is read aloud to, ensuring that the child will ask for more the day after), for instance when the Lion falls asleep in the poppy field, or when the Wizard goes away in the balloon and Dorothy is left behind. *Foreshadowing* is a device used to counterbalance suspense without destroying it. It consists of small clues spread throughout the story to indicate the final outcome or a temporary twist. In *The Wizard of Oz*, Dorothy's safe homecoming is foreshadowed by the silver slippers.

The peak and turning point of the plot is called the *climax*. The climax is closely related to the conflict and its solution. Dorothy's melting the Witch is the climax of the book, something that the whole story has been moving toward. Afterward follows the *resolution, a falling action*. For Dorothy, still another adventure remains, but the most exiting episode is already passed. Resolution, at least in classic Aristotelian poetics, does not imply the solution of the conflict; it is merely the part of the plot following the climax. The final pages of *The Lion, the Witch and the Wardrobe*, describing the children's happy rule as the kings and queens of Narnia after the climax of the victory over the Witch, offer a good example, as the various deeds of the characters are presented. Resolution should therefore not be confused with *dénouement*, when the fate of the character is known, the initial order restored, and the narrative brought to *closure*. In *The Wizard of Oz*, the three companions receive what they have been looking for, and Dorothy is eventually sent back home. In *The Lion, the Witch and the Wardrobe*, the four royal rulers find the passage back to their own world and become children again. (See fig. 5-1.)

The Happy Ending

It is necessary to distinguish between structural closure (a satisfactory roundup of the plot) and psychological closure, bringing the protagonist's personal conflicts into balance. Normally, in a children's story these coincide. When Pinocchio is turned into a human boy, the plot, involving his achieving this transformation, is concluded, and the protagonist's conflicts with the external enemies as well as with his own self are solved. Peter Pan's victory over Hook is synchronized with Wendy's accomplished quest for self and her readiness to go home. However, there may be a discrepancy between the structural and psychological closure. For instance, the arrival in their grandmother's house is a natural way to finish the Tillerman children's journey in *Homecoming*; however, it does not solve the main conflict of the

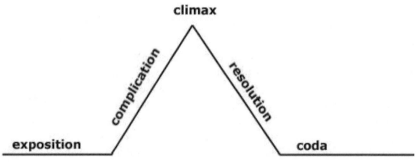

Fig. 5-1   Plot construction.

story, does not bring back the children's mother, and does not necessarily promise an easy and happy future for the characters. The superficial plot is concluded; the "human" plot is left open-ended. The ironic title adds to the ambiguity of the ending. Such closure can be called dissonant.

The consonant closure, or happy ending—which in most cases presupposes a combination of structural and psychological closure—is something that many adults immediately associate with children's literature, and that many scholars and teachers put forward as an essential requirement in a good children's book. Folktales always have a happy ending, expressed by the *coda* "lived happily ever after." Since children's fiction borrows many of its structures from folktales, most traditional children's books have a happy ending, at least superficially: Dorothy returns home, the White Witch is eliminated, the treasure is found, and so on. In contemporary novels for children, we notice a deviation from the obligatory happy ending, on a structural as well as a psychological level. Instead of closure, implying rounding off the plot, a happy reunion of the protagonist and his object of quest (often a kidnapped friend, pet, sibling, or parent), the victory over the antagonist, and so on, we see a new opening, *aperture*.

Unlike a structural open ending, aperture does not in the first place imply the possibility of further events (providing an opportunity for a sequel), but an indeterminacy concerning both what has actually happened and what might still happen. Aperture is thus an ending that allows an infinite bifurcation of interpretations. Aperture in fact precludes a sequel, since depending on the bifurcation we choose, the course of further events would be radically different. We could therefore reserve the terms "closed ending" and "open ending" for denoting structural settlement of the plot, while "closure" and "aperture" would describe the psychological completion of the character at the end of the narrative. Closure presents the character as fully depicted, leaving no questions about his qualities. Aperture allows us to contemplate further.

Let us illustrate the concept of aperture with *The Giver*. In the end of the novel, Jonas has escaped from his community with his baby brother Gabriel, and we see him struggling through the hostile snowy landscape toward an unknown destination. There are several indications in the final chapter that Jonas is dying of exposure and that the vision of a sledge on the slope and the sounds of Christmas carols are his death-agony hallucinations. Since the word Elsewhere has been used in the novel as a euphemism for death, Jonas's heading for and reaching Elsewhere can be interpreted as his dying. Yet, we may also decide that Jonas survives and reaches Elsewhere which actually exists outside his community. However, this Elsewhere may either prove just as cruel as his own community, or it may be different. If it is another totalitarian society, Jonas may either be killed or extradited to his own community. If it is a free world, he and Gabriel may be accepted, adopted into a nice and loving family, and live happily ever after. But he may equally be rejected as an alien and a spy from an antagonistic world. If he is rejected, he either dies or returns to his own community . . . and so on. This bifurcational argument may seem a fruitless speculation, but we can deliberately stretch the text to illustrate the point. Thus aperture leaves it for the reader to decide what happens, sometimes even what has actually happened and what conclusions the character must draw. Aperture stimulates the readers' imagination in a way traditional closure can never do. In any case, aperture seems a more natural ending for a children's novel, because child characters are always left halfway in their maturation; they are by definition not fully developed as individuals. (See fig. 5-2.)

The happy ending is one of the foremost criteria in the conventional definitions of children's literature, as well as one of the most common prejudices about it. However, the notion of the happy ending depends on the cultural and historical context. In the sentimental and moral nineteenth-century stories for children written in the Western world, the death of the main character was a happy ending: the child was united with God and thus was rewarded for his earthly sufferings, for instance in Andersen's fairy tale *The Little Match Girl*. Today we do not view a child's death as a happy ending. Endings are also genre dependent. In a love story, the reunion of the hero and heroine is a happy ending. In many Westerns, the hero rides away from the heroine toward the setting sun—an opening rather than closure. If a character in a contemporary existential novel suddenly marries a film star, inherits a million dollars from an unknown aunt, and finds himself heir to a newly deceased count, we will certainly view this as a serious style deviation, or more likely a parody; however, such things happen daily in soap operas.

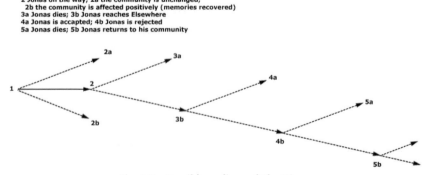

1 Jonas leaves his community
2 Jonas on the way; 2a the community is unchanged;
  2b the community is affected positively (memories recovered)
3a Jonas dies; 3b Jonas reaches Elsewhere
4a Jonas is accapted; 4b Jonas is rejected
5a Jonas dies; 5b Jonas returns to his community

Fig. 5-2   Possible endings of *The Giver*.

In Disney's version of *The Little Mermaid*, the tragic ending of the original was changed into a happy ending, apparently to adjust to the unsophisticated young American audience used to action and suspense but obviously untrained to appreciate introspection.

Going Up or Down?

In Aristotelian poetics, a distinction is made between comic and tragic plots, or plots with upward and downward movement. In a comic plot, a character disempowered and oppressed in the beginning gains power and riches in the end. In a tragic plot, a character in power is brought down, by either fate or his own actions, for instance Oedipus or King Lear. Traditionally, children's literature only makes use of comic plots; yet we have already seen that this is not always the case, especially in contemporary children's fiction.

EXERCISE

Consider the endings in some of the following stories: *Cinderella, Snow White, Beauty and the Beast, Little Women, The Secret Garden, Anne of Green Gables, Little House in the Big Woods, Charlotte's Web, Curious George, Sylvester and the Magic Pebble, Charlie and the Chocolate Factory, Ramona the Brave, Bridge to Terabithia, The Great Gilly Hopkins, Hatchet, Slake's Limbo, Holes,* a Nancy Drew novel, and a Sweet Valley novel. Examine them in terms of upward and downward plot movement, structural and psychological conclusion, open and closed endings, closure and aperture.

Progressive and Episodic Plots

The type of plot developing from complications through the climax toward a closure is called progressive, or epic. There are two kinds of epic plots: romantic and moral. The romantic plot develops from desire toward fulfillment (as in *The Wizard of Oz*). The moral plot evolves from imperfection toward improvement (as in *Harriet the Spy*). Sometimes it is hard to separate the two kinds, and often it is a matter of interpretation. We can say that *The Adventures of Tom Sawyer* presents a romantic plot, in which he finds a treasure and wins the favors of his princess, Becky. On the other hand, Tom shows higher moral qualities toward the end of the novel, when he abandons the childish oath to Huck Finn and witnesses against Injun Joe in court.

EXERCISE

Analyze plot elements in some of the following children's stories: *The Tale of Peter Rabbit*; *Charlotte's Web*; *Charlie and the Chocolate Factory*; *Roll of Thunder, Hear My Cry*; a Nancy Drew novel; or *Harry Potter and the Sorcerer's Stone*. Pay special attention to the amplifying elements: suspense, cliffhangers, and foreshadowing. Determine whether the plots are romantic or moral.

Now try to analyze the plots of *Little Women*, *Little House in the Big Woods*, *Winnie-the-Pooh*, or *Ramona the Brave*. You may notice that they are different from the progressive plot we have discussed.

In children's books, usually for young children, there occur other types of plots. In an episodic plot, single events or short episodes are linked together by common characters, settings, or themes (a more poetic term is "string-of-pearls plot"). Within each episode, however, we can often distinguish the master plot: home → away → homecoming; complication → climax → resolution. *Little House* books and *Pippi Longstocking* have episodic plots. The separate episodes can be read in an arbitrary order without our understanding of the story being affected. We may perhaps want to know something about the characters' background, which is given in the first chapter, but it is not essential.

Episodic and progressive plots can be combined within one and the same narrative, for instance *The Adventures of Tom Sawyer*. Tom's pranks, running away from home, romance with Becky, and so on are single episodes. In each one Tom leaves home, has adventures, and returns home. Each episode in itself has the structure home → away → home, and they are arranged in concentric circles, taking the protagonist further and further away from home, into more and more dangerous realms. There are, however, at least two progressive plots that hold the book together. The first one involves conflict with Injun Joe and the murder accusation of Muff Potter. The second one, connected with the first, involves the treasure hunt. The two plots are interwoven, but they develop at a different pace, reach climaxes at different points, and have different closures. Both make use of suspense and cliffhangers, for instance when Tom and Becky get lost in a cave.

In *Little Women*, the first fourteen chapters are separate episodes, each featuring one of the four March girls as the protagonist. The order of these events is arbitrary; they have no connection to each other in terms of composition. Beginning with chapter 15, in which the mother has to leave home, and the girls are left to care for themselves, the plot turns into a progressive one, presenting a development through complications (the father's illness) toward closure (the father's return home). Unlike *Tom Sawyer*, where the episodic and the progressive plots are intertwined, in *Little Women*, they follow each other successively.

Yet another example of combined episodic and progressive plots is the *Ramona* series. Ramona obviously does grow up physically as she moves from kindergarten to third grade. However, each chapter is more or less a self-contained adventure or prank. Within each book, the episodes can change place, and even episodes from different books in the series can be read out of order, because the connection between them is thematic rather than temporal or causal.

Some Other Plot Structures

Cumulative plot is a pattern where a new character or event is added in every subsequent episode. For small children this is an excellent device to help them remember the characters. In *Winnie-the-Pooh*, a new character with its special features is introduced in every chapter: first Pooh and Christopher Robin; in the second chapter we meet Rabbit, then Piglet, next Eeyore and Owl, and so on. All of them partake in a feast in the final chapter. It is possible that the order of appearance was suggested by the order in which the boy—both the fictive character and the real Christopher Robin—received his toys; further it represents a little child's successive discovery of the surrounding world. Episodic and cumulative plots are uncommon in adult novels. We must therefore consider them as specific devices in children's literature aesthetics.

Embedded plot, on the contrary, is a common pattern in the mainstream, for instance in such classics as *The Canterbury Tales* and the *Decameron*. In some early children's adaptations of *Robinson Crusoe* frames were added where a father told the story of Robinson to his children. In children's literature, *Winnie-the-Pooh* has an embedded plot: in the outer frame, a little boy is listening to his father's bedtime stories; in the inner frame, a number of episodes, held together by setting and characters, take place. The outer plot is, however, barely discernible and not really essential. We learn very little about the characters in the outer frame, the father and the son. Some overtly postmodern children's novels have intricate embedded plots ("Chinese box plots"). Another type of plot, encountered mostly in postmodern fiction, is called *mise-en-abyme* (literally, "throw into the abyss"), or mirror-plot: a duplication of the plot in a separate subplot within it, potentially to infinity, like images in a facing mirror reflecting one another and disappearing into invisibility. These plots are very unusual in children's literature, but we should not neglect the possibility. (See fig. 5-3.)

It is otherwise common for children's books to have one, clearly delineated plot. It is sometimes believed that children cannot remember or follow more than one plot line. This of course depends on the readers' age. Books

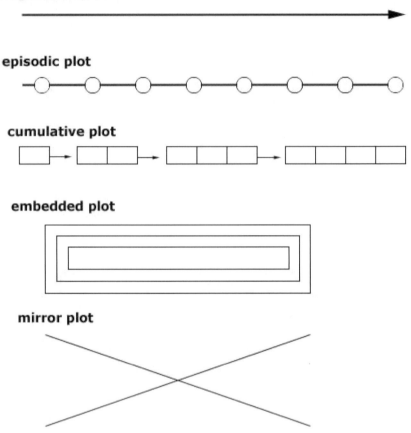

Fig. 5-3   Plot types.

for younger children often have one plot. Books for older children can have one primary plot and one or several auxiliary plots. One reason why Tolkien's *Lord of the Rings* trilogy is often treated as an adult book, unlike *The Hobbit*, may be the many parallel plots when the Fellowship of the Ring split up. We have already seen how single episodes are combined with a progressive plot in *Tom Sawyer*. In the *Harry Potter* novels, there are several plots intertwined. The primary plot, which presumably will be fully developed and brought to closure in the seventh book, involves the struggle between good and evil, between Harry and Voldemort. In each book, there is a separate plot, most often dealing with a mystery or, as in book four, a contest. In all the books, there are auxiliary plots supporting the main plot. For instance, Harry's achievements in Quidditch and his ongoing competition with Draco Malfoy can be singled out as separate plots. Harry's secret infatuation with a classmate is an auxiliary plot: will he win her attention or not? Some contemporary children's and juvenile novels have multiple plots, which is not the same as parallel ones. Multiple plots may be related by their theme, setting, or occasionally character, but they have no direct connection. Instead, they support and reflect each other, in a dialogical manner. *Holes* contains two plots: one dealing with Stanley's trials in the juvenile detention camp, the other describing the adventures of his forefather many years prior. The two plots are of course connected through the protagonists, since they are related; the events also happen in the same place; furthermore, the forefather's actions in the past turn out to affect Stanley's fate in the present.

A GRAMMAR OF STORIES

In discussing plots, plot elements, and types of conflict in a narrative we have already fashioned a number of working tools for describing composition, how stories are made. Yet, the conventional description of a plot (exposition → complication → climax → resolution → closure) is obviously too general, since all plots in all books ever written can be described in this manner. We need more precise instruments to investigate the building blocks of stories in greater detail. We can find some of these instruments in Formalist and Structuralist theories that are often inspired by linguistics and the way the grammar of a natural language is described. Two basic parts of grammar are morphology (classification of the constituent elements) and syntax (the rules for combining these elements). We will now investigate the morphology and syntax of a story.

Plot Agents

LET US EXPLORE

Consider the composition of some of the following stories: *Little Red Riding Hood; Puss in Boots; Cinderella; The Wizard of Oz; The Tale of Peter Rabbit; The Lion, the Witch and the Wardrobe;* and *Harry Potter and the Sorcerer's Stone.* Try to identify all the elements that these stories have in common.

The first thing we may notice is that these stories have a similar set of characters. In all of them, we have a *hero*. Let us agree that in the grammar of stories, gender is not essential. The term "hero" will apply both to the female protagonists, Red, Cinderella, or Dorothy, and to the male characters, such as Peter Rabbit or Harry Potter. It is also merely a label and has nothing to do with the heroic features of the character. Dealing with composition, we are not interested in the psychological qualities of the characters or the deeper messages of the text; we are just discussing the way the story is built. A hero is thus a figure who has a certain role in the text, a certain function. The hero is the central figure in the story, the one to whom the story is happening.

All the stories also have an *antagonist*, a villain, who is trying to injure the hero and against whom the hero struggles: the wolf, the ogre, the evil stepmother, Mr. McGregor, the Witch of the West, the White Witch, and Voldemort. Most of the stories also have the figure of a *helper*: the hunter who kills the wolf; Puss who assists his master; Cinderella's fairy godmother; Dorothy's faithful companions the Scarecrow, the Tin Woodman, and the Lion; the beavers and other creatures of Narnia; and Harry's friends Ron and Hermione. In some stories, there is a figure who sends the hero on a quest. For instance, Little Red's mother sends her to take a basket of food to the grandmother. The Witch of the North sends Dorothy to see the Wizard. This *sender* (or *dispatcher*) initiates the story, sets it in motion. Another role we may find in some stories is that of a *giver* (or *donor*): somebody who provides the hero with a magical agent. Father Christmas gives Peter a sword, Susan a bow and arrows, and Lucy a magic potion. Harry gets his superbroom from an unknown benefactor, and later also a magical map and an invisibility cloak. Sometimes, the three roles, helper, sender, and giver, can be combined in the same figure in the story: the fairy godmother sends Cinderella to the ball; gives her pretty clothes, a carriage, and a pair of glass slippers; and thus helps her to win over the antagonist. In considering the grammar of stories, we are looking for the functions of characters, not their actual image.

Naturally, in every story there is a certain goal, the *object of the quest*. In many folktales, the hero's goal is marrying a princess, for instance in *Puss in Boots*. Therefore this role is sometimes called a *princess*. But of course Cinderella's quest object is not a princess, but a prince. Just as the hero is merely a label, not necessarily a figure of male gender, the princess in the grammar of stories is not necessarily a female of royal blood. For instance, Harry's quest object is the magical stone. Dorothy wants to go home to Kansas, and the children in *The Lion, the Witch and the Wardrobe* strive to set Narnia free.

Finally, some stories present a figure who comes with false claims, trying to harm the hero and usurp his position. Cinderella's sisters try hard to win the prince's attention and even resort to dirty tricks to squeeze on the slipper. But they are finally exposed and punished. This role is called *the false hero*: someone who fails in the task where the hero succeeds. We can perhaps say that Edmund is the false hero since he acts contrary to what is expected from a real hero. He is, however, reformed and forgiven in the end.

We have now identified the seven roles that can appear in stories: hero, false hero, villain, sender, giver, helper, and quest object (princess). We have done exactly what the Russian folklore scholar Vladimir Propp did in his famous study *Morphology of the Folktale*. Of course, Propp examined several hundred tales, and we have just looked at a few; yet we have been able to identify the same roles that Propp described in his book.

The Actions

Propp's next step was to see what function each figure had in the stories and generally what recurrent events constituted a story. After a thorough examination of his material, Propp came up with the following conclusions:

1. The characters' functions (that is, actions, or patterns of behavior) in every story are identical, irrespective of exactly which concrete figure performs them and how.
2. The number of functions (that is, recurrent actions) in a story is limited.
3. The sequence of functions (that is, the order of their appearance in the story) is constant.

Propp identified thirty-one functions in the Russian folktales he examined. Some of his followers tried to make the system more compact by combining two or more functions into one. It does not matter exactly how many recurrent patterns we find in stories; what matters is that they indeed appear regularly in every story and can be classified (morphology), and that we can define certain rules for how they can be connected to each other (syntax). The most essential functions are the following: prohibition, violation of prohibition, injury or lack, departure, trial, provision of a magical agent, struggle, victory, pursuit, rescue, difficult task, solution, punishment of the villain, and reward of the hero. As can easily be seen, many functions appear in pairs: struggle—victory, pursuit—rescue, task—solution. Naturally, these functions can only appear in this particular order: victory cannot come before struggle. But also generally the order is fixed. Neither struggle nor tasks can appear before the hero has departed from home, and the villain cannot be punished before the injury is done.

Not every story will necessarily have all functions, and some sequences can be duplicated in a story, whereupon a character's role can change. For instance, in *The Wizard of Oz*, the first sequence takes Dorothy and her friends to the Emerald City. At this point, the goal is to find the Wizard, so he is the quest object. Then the Wizard assigns them a new task, that is, he now acts as a sender, and the goal is to kill the Witch. Yet Dorothy's primary objective is to return home.

Some of Propp's followers have attempted to reduce his model to a very basic scheme, as illustrated in figure 5-4.

This model is called the actantial model, and the agents in this model are called *actants*, they perform actions. This concept helps us to distinguish between the concrete figure in a plot (an actor) and the role or function of the actor. The collective hero may consist of several actors, but is one and the same actant. The four children in *The Lion, the Witch and the Wardrobe* have the same function in the plot, so together they are one actant. Dorothy's three companions have the same function in the plot, thus they are also one actant. The actantial model describes the very fundamental structure of every story, but unlike the conventional description of the plot, it emphasizes the relationships between the agents and the actions they perform in the story. Yet another schematic presentation is based on the choices between action and nonaction, or realization or nonrealization of a potential. For instance, when the children decide that they will stay in Narnia and assist in the struggle against the White Witch, they realize a potential in a choice. Had they chosen to return home, the outcome would have been different. Text analysis according to this model implies identifying the points in the text where choices are made and investigating the consequences of each choice. (See fig. 5-5.)

Limitations and Applications

Now we may ask whether we can without further consideration apply models that have been designed for the investigation of folktales to other kinds of stories. In his study *The Hero with a Thousand Faces*, Joseph Campbell has suggested a model for describing the structure of myth. The recurrent patterns Campbell has found in many myths from all over the world include the following: leaving home, receiving a message about the special task, acquiring help, crossing a threshold, trials, meeting the Goddess, atonement with the father, triumph and reward, and return home. That is, Campbell has, independent of Propp, identified a similar basic story structure: both a limited number of recurrent actions, and the particular order of their appearance. Of course, myths and folktales are by definition stories with very rigid structure. Yet the structural analysis has been successfully applied

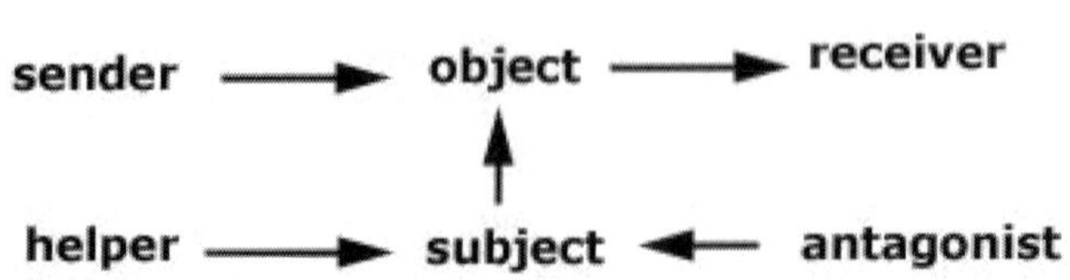

Fig. 5-4   Actantial model.

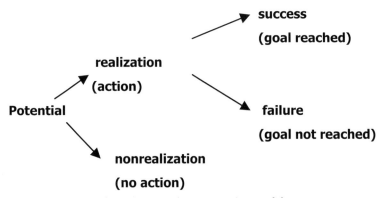

Fig. 5-5   Narrative progression model.

to a number of genres with fixed structure, in the first place formulaic fiction (crime novels, mystery, adventure, horror, and romance). A famous essay by Umberto Eco applies Propp's model to the James Bond novels. A structural approach presented by John G. Cawelti in his book *Adventure, Mystery and Romance: Formula Stories as Art and Popular Culture* singles out four roles in a detective story: the victim, the criminal, the detective, and those threatened by the crime but incapable of solving it. These roles correspond to Propp's characters of princess, villain, hero, and false hero. They can also be pressed into the actantial model.

In contrast, formal approaches are seldom applied to contemporary psychological novels, where critics as well as readers are normally more interested in characters than in actions. Structural models are more suitable for plot-oriented than for character-oriented stories. When some critics claim that functional or actantial theory is "inadequate," they presumably mean that it is inadequate for analyzing complex character-oriented narratives. When a children's critic quite correctly questions the value of applying Propp's model to *The Outsiders*, it is not the matter of deficient theory as such, but of choosing the wrong implement for the task. The vast majority of children's books are plot oriented. This does not only include fairy tales and formulaic fiction, but also novels of quality, such as *The Wizard of Oz* and *The Lion, the Witch and the Wardrobe*.

Peter Neumeyer has successfully applied Propp's model to *The Tale of Peter Rabbit*. This is a relatively simple tale with few characters and a clearly delineated plot. The tension between prohibition (Peter is not supposed to go to McGregor's garden) and violation is the main engine. Peter is pursued by his opponent and escapes, encouraged, if not directly helped, by some other characters. Unlike the traditional folktale hero, he is not rewarded, but on the contrary punished for misbehavior, yet in fact he triumphs over his opponent by having survived. We could go through the story step by step, as Neumeyer has done, identifying Propp's functions in more detail.

Let us, however, try to apply the same tools to *The Wizard of Oz*, a longer and more complex story. We have already stated that Dorothy is the hero (disregarding gender) and that the Witch of the West is her chief antagonist. We have defined the Scarecrow, the Tin Woodman, and the Lion as Dorothy's helpers. Yet we could also suggest a different role distribution. Although Dorothy and her three companions have different wishes, they are on the same quest and therefore can be perceived as one actant. Then the role of helpers will be reserved for the Queen of the field mice and some other secondary figures. Exact casting is a matter of interpretation; there is no one single correct way of doing it.

The very first function in Propp's model is *absence*. The hero must be removed from home and parental protection to start on his quest. For instance, in *Puss in Boots* and *Cinderella*, the parent dies; in *Peter Rabbit*, the mother goes out; and in *The Lion, the Witch and the Wardrobe*, the children are sent away from home. Dorothy is blown away by the cyclone. Unlike Peter, she is not directly *forbidden* to leave home, but in a way she does *violate* the prohibition by failing to hide in the cellar. The two following pairs of functions in Propp's model are *reconnaissance—delivery* and *deceit—complicity*. They are not present in the first part of *The Wizard of Oz*, but very prominent in *The Lion, the Witch and the Wardrobe*: the faun spies on Lucy in order to deliver her to the Witch, while the Witch deceives Edmund by means of the enchanted food, and he lets himself be deceived. *The Wizard of Oz*, in contrast, moves directly to the next function, *injury or lack*. Dorothy is not exactly injured, but she wants to go back to Kansas, and this lack becomes the foremost engine of the plot. The sender, the Witch of the North, *mediates* the goal to Dorothy: she has to go to the Emerald City, and Dorothy *reacts* to the sender's message by deciding to take the journey. She *departs* on her quest immediately, after she has been *provided with a magical agent*, the silver shoes, which will eventually take her home, even though she will not know it for a long while. Like in *Cinderella*, it is the sender who gives Dorothy the shoes, so the Witch of the North also performs the role of the giver.

In accordance with the folktale's magical number, three, Dorothy meets her three companions, and the function of *trial* is repeated threefold. In folktales, the hero usually meets the giver/helper and has to *respond* in the right way in order to receive help. Dorothy saves the Scarecrow and the Tin Woodman and promises them the fulfillment of their wishes. She does not exactly save the Lion, but makes him realize his shortcoming. Together the hero and the helpers (or the multiple hero, if you prefer) *journey* toward their goal. Since this sequence of the story is patterned as a quest rather than a struggle, and there so far is no pronounced antagonist, there follow a number of *tasks* and hardships (crossing precipices, the river, and the poppy field), with successful *solution*; and the travelers are also *pursued* by the Kalidahs, successfully *escaping* them, whereupon the initial goal is achieved. In a simple single-sequence plot, Dorothy would be immediately sent back to Kansas, getting her *reward*. However, a new sequence of functions is introduced, as the Wizard sends Dorothy on another quest. This time, there is a clear antagonist and a clear *injury*: the Witch of the West is evil and has enslaved the Winkies. Dorothy *departs* again, and this time the antagonist *spies* on her with her sharp eye, and also uses *deceit*—the assistance of Winged Monkeys—to conquer her. Eventually Dorothy engages in an open *combat* with the antagonist and *wins*. The lack is *eliminated*: the Winkies are now free. In the process, she acquires a new *magical agent*, the Golden Cap. This action can also be viewed as *branding*, receiving a mark, by which the hero will be *recognized* at arrival (she is previously recognized by her silver shoes and the mark of the good witch's kiss on her forehead). In a classic folktale plot, a false hero would *claim* that he had killed the witch, Dorothy would then produce the Cap to prove her right, and the false hero would be *exposed* and *punished* (cf. Cinderella's sisters). As it is, the role of the false hero is in a way taken on by the Wizard himself, since he has claimed to be able to grant the companions' wishes. He is duly exposed, but not punished. Moreover, he is, after all, able to give the Scarecrow, the Tin Woodman, and the Lion the objects of their desires.

Again, the plot could have stopped here, either in a folktale manner, by Dorothy's becoming the queen of the Emerald City (instead, the Scarecrow is *enthroned*), or in a more appropriate way, by her going back home. The author, however, adds still another complication and thus a new sequence. A new *lack* is introduced: Dorothy's means of getting back home disappears (interestingly enough, she repeats the same mistake as at the beginning of the story, running away to look for Toto in a decisive moment, thus *violating* the order to stay inside the basket of the balloon). A new sender, the soldier, sets the companions on yet another journey, to seek Glinda, with new dangers, successfully overcome. Then Dorothy's wish is finally granted, and her three companions are duly rewarded by becoming rulers of their respective realms. While Dorothy, on returning to Kansas, is stripped of her magical power (of which she was happily ignorant), the Scarecrow, the Tin Woodman, and the Lion are *transformed* and *empowered*.

In the analysis above, the actions corresponding to Propp's functions are italicized. Most of the thirty-one functions appear in some way in *The Wizard of Oz*, and they also appear more or less in the same order that Propp discovered in folktales. L. Frank Baum deliberately followed the pattern of folktales; indeed, he referred to his book as a "modern fairy tale." We have examined the basic structure of the story: who does what and for which purpose. What we naturally miss completely is the vivid de-

piction of settings, humor, and characterization. But this is not the intention of structural analysis.

EXERCISE

Try to examine another text, for instance *The Lion, the Witch and the
Wardrobe* or *Harry Potter*, in the same manner. Start by distributing
the roles—you may find several options. In *The Lion, the Witch and
the Wardrobe*, the most natural way is to treat the four children as a
collective hero, one actant. But what if we read the story with Aslan as
the hero? Then apparently the children must be given a different role.

Go through the story and try to identify as many functions as you
can. Remember that sequences of functions can be duplicated and intertwined. Note which actant performs which actions—it will help you
to further decide on the roles. Since these stories are not folktales, but
literary texts, the model might not work perfectly, but it will still help
you to see more clearly how the story is constructed.

Binary Opposites

In applying the functional model, we have examined the stories chronologically, the way they are told. We have divided the story into smaller pieces
chained to each other. Such significance-bearing pieces of text are called syntagms, and the type of formal analysis identifying syntagms is called syntag-
matic. Another way of investigating story structures is extracting elements
from the text and arranging them in groups or categories, called paradigms—
from which comes paradigmatic analysis. The purpose of studying paradigms is primarily opposing them to each other—in so-called binary
opposites. Roderick McGillis has done this for *Charlotte's Web*. We can try
to determine some essential opposites at work in *The Wizard of Oz*. The
most important opposition, which governs the plot, is that between home
and away. Let us take it as our point of departure and tie other binaries to
it:

home	away
Kansas	Oz
boring	eventful
color	less colorful
nonmagical	magical
human	witch
human	man-made (Scarecrow, Woodman)
female	male

young	old
good	evil
powerless	powerful
naive, honest	cunning (the Wizard)

and so on.

We can then arrange all the events and actions of the story around the tension between these opposites. For instance, the assets and disadvantages of being made of flesh are constantly emphasized: Dorothy has to eat, drink, and sleep, while the Scarecrow and the Woodman do not, but on the other hand, she has brains and a heart. Thus we discover some fundamental structural features of the story, and we have gone slightly deeper into its meaning, but of course we have completely lost the chronological order of events that we examined with Propp's model.

EXERCISE

Try to set up binary opposites for *The Lion, the Witch and the Wardrobe* or *Harry Potter*. In the former, the primary tension is obviously between good and evil. In the latter, you may want to start with the opposition between the wizard world and the Muggle world.

How can the formal and structural theories help us assess children's stories? For one thing, we can state that all stories do indeed have some common compositional traits, both in their set of characters and in their sequence of actions. Further, we can observe how much children's books have inherited their composition from traditional narratives, that is, myths and folktales. We can also note exactly how children's books deviate from folktale structures (for instance, through final disempowerment of the hero), how they gradually become more complex and start focusing more on character than on plot. The basic structure of a story is a skeleton that holds it together. In order to have the diversity of stories we can discover in contemporary children's literature, we also need skin, flesh, blood, and nervous system. These are, for instance, setting, characterization, style, and ideology. While the basic structure of the story may remain the same, by varying the setting, the characters, and other elements, storytellers end up with texts as diverse as *Cinderella*, *Peter Rabbit*, and *Harry Potter*. Yet it can be useful to start with the structure as the most fundamental element of the text.

WHAT MAKES A STORY?

Contemporary narrative theory develops still more accurate tools for analyzing the way stories are constructed, proceeding from surface structures to deeper ones. The study object of narrative theory is not the narrative as such, but narrativity, the set of properties characterizing narrative.

Temporality and Causality

The classical argument used in narratology to illustrate the concept of narrativity goes as follows. Consider the text: "The king died." Is this a story? Not really. This is a single event. A single event cannot constitute a story. How about: "The king died. The queen died." Is this a story? No, even though there are two events, there is still no story because there is no connection between the events. Let us go further: "The king died. Then the queen died." Something very essential has been added: temporality. We can now see at least some, however vague, connection between the events: one has happened before the other. However, we need a much stronger connection to make it a real story, for instance, "The king died. Then the queen died of grief." Now we have a cause-and-effect connection between the events, besides the temporal connection. A minimal story thus contains either two states and an event between them, or two events in a temporal and causal relationship. Causality and temporality are the two most essential elements of narrativity.

In real life, we do not necessarily see events around us in a cause-and-effect relationship. In literature, we expect that if an event or an action is depicted it must be important for the plot. That is, we place a higher demand on causality and intentionality in fiction than in real life. Therefore the way events and actions are combined in children's fiction is of overall importance. Let us consider the following options:

1. An event/action follows another event/action (very weak causality). Example: Pippi Longstocking moves into her new house. *Then* Tommy and Annika make her acquaintance.
2. An event/action makes another event/reaction possible (stronger causality). Example: Anne Shirley moves to Avonlea *because* Matthew and Marilla need someone to help them in the household.
3. An event/action directly causes another event/reaction (very strong causality). Example: Curious George is mischievous and is *therefore* put into prison.
4. An event/action is arranged so that it will cause another event/action (intention). Example: The White Witch enchants Edmund with Turkish Delight *in order to* prevent Aslan from taking power in Narnia.

Naturally, when reading novels, we do not consciously make all these causal connections; however, in the long run they certainly help us to understand the interconnection of events. We have already explored the concept of foreshadowing: events that anticipate other events. In backshadowing, an event described later in the narrative helps us understand something that has happened earlier. In sideshadowing, a parallel event—a "might-have-been"—casts a light on an event.

Story and Discourse

Narrative theory explores the elements of narrativity that go far beyond the surface structures examined by structuralist approaches. In fact, it makes a prompt distinction between surface structures and deep structures. Most scholars describe this distinction in terms of story and discourse. Story refers to the content of the narrative: what happens; who does what, where, when, how, and why. Its constituents are events (actions and happenings), agents (characters who perform actions and participate in happenings), and setting (time and place of events). Except for setting, we have already discussed the components of the story and some ways of analyzing them.

Discourse refers to the way the events are organized in the narrative. For instance, are they revealed to the reader in the same order they happened? Is the story told by an omniscient, omnipresent narrator, or is it refracted through the eyes and mind of a character? Are all the events told to the reader or is something omitted? In a crime novel it would be improper to tell the reader who the murderer is. Finally, although we have discussed the function of characters in the plot, we have yet to examine how we get to know them and how they can be interpreted, from the social, ideological, and psychological viewpoints. The main constituents of discourse are thus temporality, perspective, and characterization.

Aspects of the Narrative

Narrative theory offers us a number of valuable tools for assessing narrativity. We will return to characterization and perspective in subsequent chapters, so here we will just take a brief look at temporal structure. The most essential difference between story and discourse is that while events in a story take place in a certain order and have certain causal relations, writers can choose to present them in a different manner, for instance start the narrative at the end, go back to the same events several times, or sum up certain events and elaborate on others. The temporal structures reveal to us how the text is constructed. The components of temporality are *order* (in which events are narrated in relation to the story), *duration* (how narrative time relates to story time), and *frequency* (how many times an event is narrated in relation to how many times it happens in the story). In other words, temporality involves the relation between story and discourse, between the time of the story and the (pseudo)time of the discourse.

Most classical children's novels present events chronologically. This structure is considered suitable for children, because especially very young children may have problems reconstructing the actual flow of events unless they are rendered chronologically. It is also believed that children need very clear causal relations in a narrative. However, often there are deviations from the chronological order, called *anachronies*. Anachrony means that the normal order of events in a story is distorted; the narrative moves to some other point in the story, either before or after the "present" where the story happens to be. There are two types of anachronies: the one moving the narrative to a point before the "now" of the primary story is called *analepsis* (other terms are flashback, switchback, and retrospection); the one moving it to point after the "now" is called *prolepsis* (flashforward, anticipation). Prolepses in children's literature may take the form of "as we soon shall see" or "As I learned already the next day . . . ," in which the reader is encouraged to pay attention to a certain event that may turn out to be important later. Analepses, which take the narrative to a time before the primary story, are used to provide background to characters and events, as well as to create suspense (for instance, when the narrative starts with a murder and then goes back to tell about the circumstances which have led to this murder).

Anachronies can be of different reach and extent; they can be external and internal, simple and embedded, and all these aspects add to the variety of discursive structures. Very few children's books feature extremely complicated order, but we should still have appropriate tools to analyze it.

EXERCISE

Examine the temporal patterns of *Walk Two Moons*. "Rewrite" the story in the order the events really happened. What is the earliest event mentioned? How long a time does the story take, from the earliest mentioned event to the moment Sal is telling her story? How are the temporal shifts marked? What are the reach and extent of the anachronies? How does the complex temporality affect our perception of the story?

The concept of duration is used to describe the relationship between time span in story and time span in discourse. Duration is an important narrative element, since it denotes the rhythm, or tempo, of the text. The five duration patterns are scene (story time = discourse time), summary (discourse time shorter than story time), ellipsis (discourse time is zero), pause (story time is zero), and stretch (discourse time longer than story time). Together with order, these aspects contribute to the variety of composition. Assessing these features can also help us see some developments in children's literature. In early children's fiction, it was more common to have summaries, especially in girls' books that often have a large time span, up to several years. Modern children's novels usually have a much shorter time span, sometimes just a few days or even hours, and therefore there are fewer summaries and more detailed scenes. According to many narratologists, this observation is true about fiction in general: the abstraction of classical literature (summary) is contrasted to the expressivity of modern literature (scene). The dominance of scene over summary can be regarded as a quality criterion.

EXERCISE

Anne of Green Gables is a very good text for studying duration. Read the novel carefully and examine how the tempo is varied. Does it speed up or slow down as the novel progresses? You may roughly count the number of pages devoted to each year that Anne spends at Avonlea. How do you account for this change in speed?

Some other books you may want to analyze in terms of duration are, for instance, *The Secret Garden, The Island of the Blue Dolphins, Bridge to Terabithia*, and *Holes*. Note the appearance of ellipses and summaries. What events are rendered as scenes, and what are summed up or omitted? Are there any descriptive pauses? Are there any stretches? How does the variation in tempo affect our appreciation of the novel?

Frequency denotes the relationship between the number of times an event takes place in the story and how many times it is rendered in the narrative. The singulative frequency (one event in a story is narrated once) is the most common. We assume, unless otherwise stated, that a narrated event has only happened once in a story. The repetitive mode (one event in a story is narrated several times) is common, for instance, in crime novels, where several witnesses each tell their version of the same event. The iterative mode (the narrative renders only once something that has taken place several times) is probably the most interesting narrative phenomenon to discuss in connection with children's fiction. General narratology regards the iterative as an extremely rare device, used, for instance, by Marcel Proust. However, the iterative seems to be a very common device in children's fiction, acquiring a special significance, since the iterative reflects a child's perception of time as cyclical, nonlinear, where recurrent events and routines—Christmas, summer holidays, birthdays—emphasize the eternal cycle rather than the linear flow of time. The ending of *The House at Pooh Corner* evokes a sense of eternity by stressing the recurrent action: "Wherever they go, and whatever happens to them on the way, in that enchanted place on top of the Forest a little boy and his Bear will always be playing." The ending of the third *Pippi* volume has the same significance: "She will always be there."

It is not only the global perception of time that makes children's writers use the iterative. A child's life is apparently—or is perceived by the child to be—more regular and regulated than an adult's life; therefore recurrent patterns are of greater significance, which is reflected in the stories. The iterative does not describe an event that is happening or has happened, but an event that happens all over again. Some languages have special grammatical tenses for this phenomenon. Otherwise, the iterative can be indicated by such words as "often," "sometimes," "several times," "every Sunday," "during summers," and so on.

EXERCISE 1

Identify and analyze the iterative passages in, for instance, *The Secret Garden, Little House in the Big Woods,* or *Bridge to Terabithia*. Contemplate for which purpose iterative frequency is used in these novels.

EXERCISE 2

Try to make a more or less complete temporal analysis of a children's novel of your choice, including order, duration, and frequency. Contemplate how the study of temporality has contributed to your understanding of the text.

HOW TO GO FURTHER

It would seem that the structure of stories has been studied thoroughly, both with conventional methods, outlined in the beginning of this chapter, and with the assistance of more advanced theories. It would perhaps further appear that with the emergence of postmodern literature, plots as textual elements have more or less lost their significance and thus their interest for a scholar of literature. Yet studies such as Peter Brooks's *Reading for the Plot* and some others clearly show that plots have survived poststructural denigration and also that there are many exciting methods left for discussing the structure of literary works. Brooks combines a structural approach with a psychoanalytical one and thus goes beyond the plot surface to investigate the interdependence of plot and intention, and not least, the way characters function in the plot. The weakness of early structural studies was that they examined text composition as such, without connection to other text components. By expanding the study of narrative to such elements as temporality and perspective we can considerably increase our understanding of the ways literary texts are made. The three volumes of Paul Ricoeur's *Time and Narrative* open especially some new horizons. These aspects may be of little value when we are dealing with simple, straightforward narratives of traditional children's literature, but indispensable as soon as we set off to explore more complex, contemporary children's novels with multiple plots and narrative levels. Further, by combining purely narratological studies with other theories and methods we may disclose the mutual dependence of form and content, which structuralism and narratology traditionally neglect. From the examination of structural elements we can proceed to posing questions of exactly how narrative elements work as bearers of psychological qualities, social values, and ideology.

REFERENCES

General Studies

Forster, E. M. *Aspects of the Novel* (1927). San Diego: Harcourt, Brace, 1985. Chap. 5, "The Plot," contains a discussion around the example, "The king died and then the queen died," and so on (p. 86).

Golden, Joanne M. *The Narrative Symbol in Childhood Literature: Exploration in the Construction of Text*. Berlin: Mouton, 1990. Chap. 2, "Act: Plot."

Lukens, Rebecca J. *A Critical Handbook of Children's Literature*. 4th ed. New York: HarperCollins, 1990. Chap. 4, "Plot."

McQuillan, Martin, ed. *The Narrative Reader*. London: Routledge, 2000. This anthology contains short excerpts from all the major texts on composition, structure, and narrative, from Plato and Aristotle to our day.

Nodelman, Perry. "Text as Teacher: The Beginning of Charlotte's Web." *Children's Literature* 13 (1985): 109–127.

Formal and Structural Approaches

Barthes, Roland. "Introduction to the Structural Analysis of Narratives." Pp. 79–124 in his *Image—Music—Text*. London: Fontana, 1977. Also pp. 45–60 in *Narratology*, edited by Susana Onega and José Angel García Landa. London: Longman, 1996.

Bremond, Claude. "The Logics of Narrative Possibilities." Pp. 61–75 in *Narratology*, edited by Susana Onega and José Angel García Landa. London: Longman, 1996. Develops Propp's model in order to unify and simplify some of his functions, resulting in the "potential—realization" schema.

Campbell, Joseph. *The Hero with a Thousand Faces*. New York: Pantheon, 1949.

Cawelti, John G. *Adventure, Mystery and Romance: Formula Stories as Art and Popular Culture*. Chicago: University of Chicago Press, 1976.

Culler, Jonathan. *Structuralist Poetics: Structuralism, Linguistics and the Study of Literature*. London: Routledge, 1975.

Eagleton, Terry. *Literary Theory: An Introduction*. Oxford: Blackwell, 1983. Chap. 3, "Structuralism and Semiotics."

Eco, Umberto. *The Role of the Reader*. Bloomington: Indiana University Press, 1979. Chap. 6, "Narrative Structures in Fleming," contains a structural analysis of the James Bond novels.

Greimas, Algirdas Julien. *Structural Semantics: An Attempt at a Method*. Lincoln, NE: University of Nebraska Press, 1983. Introduces the actantial model.

Lévi-Strauss, Claude. "The Structural Study of Myth." Pp. 202–228 in his *Structural Anthropology*. Garden City, NY: Anchor Books, 1967.

———. *The Raw and the Cooked: Introduction to a Science of Mythology*. Chicago: University of Chicago Press, 1983. In this study, Lévi-Strauss works with binary opposites to define the basic structures of human culture.

Lotman, Yuri. *Analysis of the Poetic Text*. Ann Arbor, MI: University of Michigan Press, 1976.

———. *The Structure of the Artistic Text*. Ann Arbor, MI: University of Michigan Press, 1977.

Matejka, Ladislav, and Krystyna Pomorska, eds. *Readings in Russian Poetics: Formalist and Structuralist Views*. Cambridge, MA: MIT Press, 1971. Contains excerpts from the central works of Russian theory.

McGillis, Roderick. *The Nimble Reader: Literary Theory and Children's Literature*. New York: Twayne, 1996. Chap. 2, "The Science of Literature: Formalism and New Criticism"; chap. 6, "Constructivist Reading: The Structuralist Activity."

Medvedev, P. N., and Mikhail Bakhtin. *The Formal Method in Literary Scholarship*. Baltimore: The Johns Hopkins University Press, 1978.

Nikolajeva, Maria. "How Fantasy is Made: Patterns and Structures in *The Neverending Story* by Michael Ende." *Marvels and Tales* 4, no. 1 (1990): 34–41. An example of a Proppian analysis of a fantasy novel.

———. "Stages of Transformation: Folklore Elements in Children's Novels." *Canadian Children's Literature* 73 (1994): 48–54. The essay shows how composition of traditional stories is modified in contemporary novels for children.

Neumeyer, Peter. "A Structural Approach to the Study of Literature for Children." *Elementary English* 44, no. 8 (1977): 883–887. A Proppian analysis of *The Tale of Peter Rabbit*.

Prince, Gerald. *A Grammar of Stories*. The Hague: Mouton, 1973.

Propp, Vladimir. *Morphology of the Folktale*. Austin: University of Texas Press, 1968.

Rodari, Gianni. *The Grammar of Fantasy: An Introduction in the Art of Inventing Stories*. New York: Teachers and Writers Collaborative, 1996. The Italian children's writer Gianni Rodari proposes many exciting methods of teaching children to appreciate and tell stories, using Vladimir Propp's structural model.

Scholes, Robert. *Structuralism in Literature: An Introduction*. New Haven: Yale University Press, 1974.

Narratological Approaches

Bal, Mieke. *Narratology: Introduction to the Theory of Narrative*. 2nd ed. Toronto: University of Toronto Press, 1997. Part 2, chaps. 2–4, "Sequential Ordering, Rhythm, Frequency"; part 3, chap. 2, "Events"; part 3, chap. 4, "Time."

Brooks, Peter. *Reading for the Plot: Design and Intention in Narrative.* Cambridge, MA: Harvard University Press, 1984.

Chatman, Seymour. *Story and Discourse: Narrative Structure in Fiction and Film.* Ithaca, NY: Cornell University Press, 1978. Chap. 2, "Story: Events."

Children's Literature Association Quarterly 15, no. 2 (1990): a special issue on narrative theory.

Cobley, Paul. *Narrative.* London: Routledge, 2001. A good historical overview of the development of narrative forms.

Genette, Gérard. *Narrative Discourse: An Essay in Method.* Ithaca, NY: Cornell University Press, 1980. Chaps. 1–3, "Order," "Duration," and "Frequency."

———. *Narrative Discourse Revisited.* Ithaca, NY: Cornell University Press, 1988. Chaps. 4–6, "Order," "Speed," and "Frequency."

Hunt, Peter. "Narrative Theory and Children's Literature." *Children's Literature Association Quarterly* 9, no. 4 (1984–85): 191–194.

———. "Necessary Misreadings: Directions in Narrative Theory for Children's Literature." *Studies in the Literary Imagination* 18, no. 2 (1985): 107–121.

Kermode, Frank. *The Sense of an Ending: Studies in the Theory of Fiction.* London: Oxford University Press, 1968.

Martin, Wallace. *Recent Theories of Narrative.* Ithaca, NY: Cornell University Press, 1986.

Prince, Gerald. *Narratology: The Form and Functioning of Narrative.* Berlin: Mouton, 1982.

Ricoeur, Paul. *Time and Narrative.* Vols. 1–3. Chicago: University of Chicago Press, 1984–88.

Rimmon-Kenan, Shlomith. *Narrative Fiction: Contemporary Poetics.* London: Routledge, 1983. Chap. 2, "Story: Events"; chap. 4, "Text: Time."

Rushdy, Ashraf H. A. "The Miracle of the Web: Community, Desire, and Narrativity in Charlotte's Web." *The Lion and the Unicorn* 15 (1991): 35–60.

Scholes, Robert, and Robert Kellogg. *The Nature of Narrative.* London: Oxford University Press, 1966.

Studies in the Literary Imagination 18, no. 2 (1985): special issue on narrative theory and children's literature.

Todorov, Tzvetan. *The Poetics of Prose.* Ithaca, NY: Cornell University Press, 1977.

Uspensky, Boris. *A Poetics of Composition: The Structure of the Artistic Text and Typology of a Compositional Form.* Berkeley, CA: University of California Press, 1973.

6

The Aesthetic of the Scene

TIME AND PLACE

The time and place of the events depicted in a story are called setting. It is essential to bear in mind that by "time" we here mean the actual time when the events happen, not the duration and other temporal components of the narrative, which have already been treated in the previous chapter.

LET US EXPLORE

Consider the setting in some children's novels, for instance *Little Women, The Adventures of Tom Sawyer, The Wizard of Oz, Anne of Green Gables, Winnie-the-Pooh, Little House in the Big Woods, Curious George, Charlotte's Web, The Cat in the Hat, Slake's Limbo, The Planet of Junior Brown, Bridge to Terabithia, Jacob Have I Loved,* and *Harry Potter and the Sorcerer's Stone.* Pay attention to both components of the setting, the time and the place. Are they important? In what way? Is the description of setting extensive? How does the setting contribute to our understanding of the story?

First of all, setting can be integral—that is, essential and indispensable for the story—or backdrop—that is, merely a background for an action that basically can take place anywhere and anytime. Integral settings are especially significant in certain types of stories, while in others the setting may be of less importance. For instance, a historical novel, whether written from realistic premises or employing the time-shift device, demands a somewhat authentic setting to be credible. A story about Australian Aborigines or Native Americans demands an authentic setting with correct details. Naturally, a writer cannot take the liberty of placing the Golden Gate Bridge in New York or the Empire State Building in Chicago: once a setting has been established, the authenticity of details should be followed. On the other hand, if the setting is "a small town in the Midwest" no specific details of setting are required. Moreover, even if a concrete place is mentioned, it does not necessarily make the setting integral. *Harriet the Spy* takes place in New York, but there is nothing in the story that could not have happened in any other big city or even a smaller city. Next, a writer may elaborate on the setting, giving us many details, which can either be self-sufficient or enhance our understanding of the story; it is, however, equally possible that the setting is barely mentioned at all or merely implied.

Where and When?

Little Women is set in a little town during the Civil War. Let us contemplate why the time and place are important for the story. The atmosphere of a little town creates both a sense of security and of restriction. Especially on hearing Laurie's stories about Europe, the March sisters feel the provinciality of their own existence, and when Jo in the sequel goes to live in New York, the change in the setting is decisive. The initial setting is far away from the dangers of war, yet definitely in its shadow. The father is away at the front, and the mother has to go away when he gets sick, leaving the daughters to cope on their own. War has also brought about the sense of poverty, even though the March family is far from being really poor, as they see clearly when confronted with genuine misery. The lifestyle reflects the time of the events, but the March parents' progressive views on women and education emphasize the overall tone of the novel, which is easy to miss unless we see it in the correct context.

The Adventures of Tom Sawyer is set in the 1840s in a small town on the Mississippi River, modeled on the author's hometown of Hannibal. It could of course have been a different small town, but the way the society is described, it has to be a Southern state, and the time is long before the abolition of slavery. While slavery is not an important issue in this novel, it is central in *The Adventures of Huckleberry Finn*, which has a similar setting. *Anne of Green Gables* presents a very concrete place, and from some indications we can also conclude that the time of action is around 1900. Yet, this concreteness is at the same time somewhat indeterminable: Avonlea could have been a different place, in Canada as well as somewhere in New England, without the story's being considerably affected. The time could be easily stretched both backward and forward, since the most essential token of time is the inferior position of women, which was still true in rural North America in the 1920s. The setting of *Anne of Green Gables* is thus more universal and less integral than in *Little Women* or *Tom Sawyer*.

The Wizard of Oz starts in Kansas and moves on to a fantasy realm "beyond the great desert." The contrast between the bleak landscape of Kansas and the brightly colored world of Oz is part of the binary structure of the story, discussed in chapter 5. The time of action is indeterminable. Presumably, Baum described his own time, but the story does not feel outdated when we read it today, not least because most of it takes place in the timeless land of Oz. The *Harry Potter* books are also based on two contrasting settings: the ordinary and boring London and the exciting and dangerous Hogwarts. The time of action is deliberately indeterminable, devoid of any specific identifiable tokens of time, apparently to make the stories last. This makes the *Harry Potter* books different from the Narnia Chronicles, firmly anchored in a concrete historical period in the ordinary world. *Curious George* presents a completely different contrast of two settings: one is "wilderness," the other "civilization," while the change of setting supposedly indicates the character's positive development from savage to civilized. The ordinary world is thus positive, while the "other" world is negative, something to be left behind.

The most prominent feature of the setting in *Winnie-the-Pooh* is its stasis. It is a never ending idyll, which cannot be connected to any concrete reality: a perfect image of childhood paradise. Time does not exist, the characters do not get older, and even though some seasonal changes occur, they do not indicate any flow of time. A somewhat similar setting beyond space and time is presented in *Charlotte's Web*: a rural idyll without any notable tokens of time. Yet while the Hundred Acre Wood is of course integral to the plot, being the essential part of the thematic tension, *Charlotte's Web* could take place more or less anywhere and anytime, not least with its focus on the eternal question of life and death.

Little House in the Big Woods presents a different kind of idyll. The time is specified as "Once upon a time, sixty years ago . . . ," an almost fairy-tale temporal indication, especially if we take into consideration that for a young reader, sixty years is equal with eternity. If we do want a concrete historical anchoring, it is the 1870s, and the place is the dangerous and exciting frontier. Despite this, the protagonist's life is safe and secure, because the setting is secluded, and the protagonist is happily unaware of the outside dangers. The setting is integral and minutely described, since the details of everyday existence are in a manner the story itself. In contrast, the setting in *The Cat in the Hat* is of the backdrop type. It is not essential for the story where and when it happens. The events take place indoors, and it could be anywhere. The nature of events gives no indication whatsoever about the time of action: the story is timeless.

Bridge to Terabithia utilizes the archetypal rural idyll of children's fiction, but deconstructs and strongly interrogates it. Growing up in a small village, Jess is deprived of the opportunities offered by big cities. Although he lives within a short driving distance from Washington, D.C., with its abundance of museums and other cultural events, he never visits them until he is taken on a trip by his teacher. Rural life is far from idyllic in the novel, since Jess's family must work hard to make ends meet, and young as he is, Jess must contribute to this work. Further, Leslie's parents have brought her from her usual urban surroundings to the countryside because they have suddenly come to an insight about simple rural life. Leslie gets bullied in school and is profoundly unhappy, until she befriends Jess. In the end, the move to the country turns out to have caused her death. The exact time of the story is not indicated, but the reference to the hippie movement and the mention of the Vietnam War, as well as Leslie's parents' radical ideas, serve as time tokens.

The setting of *Jacob Have I Loved* is another example of quasi-idyll. A peaceful island may seem to be an adequate space for a happy childhood. The action, however, takes place during World War II, and the dark shadow of the war hovers over the inhabitants of Rass. Louise, the protagonist and narrator, has, like Jess, to work hard to contribute to the family's meager budget. She hates the island with its limited possibilities and dreams about leaving it as soon as possible. The contrast between the restrictive childhood home and the open landscape of the mainland enhances the theme of the book.

Slake's Limbo and *The Planet of Junior Brown* are both set in New York, and the setting is absolutely indispensable for the stories. It is unfriendly and even threatening toward the characters, and the image of happy childhood is subverted. The time of action is indeterminable, but corresponds to the time the books were written. It could, however, be stretched well into the 1990s.

As seen from the examples discussed, the settings of children's novels know practically no limitations. They can be domestic or exotic, indoors or outdoors, rural or urban, isolated or open, authentic or imaginary. A setting can remain the same throughout the novel or change dramatically. A novel can be set in a middle-class home, a boarding school, a desert island, the New York subway, on a ship crossing the Atlantic (*The True Confessions of Charlotte Doyle*) or in a Nazi concentration camp (*The Devil's Arithmetic*). In each case, if the setting is integral, it contributes to our understanding of the story.

Writer's Time and Story Time

In terms of time, it is important to distinguish between contemporary, historical, retrospective, and futuristic settings. All these terms refer to the relationship between the writer's time and the time of the depicted events. A novel is thus contemporary if it describes more or less the historical period when it was written, as do *Bridge to Terabithia*, *Slake's Limbo*, and *The*

Planet of Junior Brown. A retrospective novel deals with the epoch of the writer's childhood: the writer describes events in retrospect, for instance *Little House in the Big Woods* and *Jacob Have I Loved.* A historical novel describes the past beyond the writer's personal experience, while a futuristic novel, as the term itself suggests, is projected into the future. Why is such distinction necessary? We may today read *Little Women* and *The Adventures of Tom Sawyer* as historical, but they were not written as historical: *Little Women* depicts the writer's contemporary time, while *Tom Sawyer* goes back to Mark Twain's own childhood and adolescence. In assessing the novels, it is important to bear this in mind. A novel written in the late twentieth century, but depicting the same time as *Tom Sawyer* or *Little Women* would be historical, for instance *Lyddie.* We have different expectations from a historical novel than we do from a contemporary novel. The historical perspective must therefore be related to the writer and not to the reader. A novel with a futuristic setting may as time goes by seem to depict the past. The best example is Orwell's *1984,* which was futuristic when it was published in 1948, but which today depicts a year that is already in the past for us. This, however, should not affect our understanding of the futuristic, dystopian nature of the story. There are few futuristic novels for children in which a concrete year is mentioned. For instance, we do not know whether *The Giver* takes place twenty or two hundred years in the future. What is important, however, is that the setting is futuristic in relation to the time when the novel was written.

Finally, there is still another possibility for a setting, contrafactual, that is, a setting that contradicts the actual flow of history. It can be, for instance, a setting in which World War II has never happened. Contrafactual settings have become increasingly popular in postmodern mainstream literature, while they are so far infrequent in children's fiction, obviously for didactic reasons. An adult reader is supposed to be familiar with the actual historical facts and therefore to recognize the setting as contrafactual. A young reader may fail to understand this and perhaps get a wrong impression about history. Some postmodern fantasy novels for young readers present a series of parallel settings representing a variety of contrafacts. In Diana Wynne Jones's novel *A Tale of Time City,* it is mentioned in passing that, in the parallel world from which the protagonist comes, World War II starts at Christmas 1938. An informed reader will immediately take the hint that this parallel world is not the same as our own. A reader without pertinent knowledge may miss the clue and may even believe that this is a true fact. In Philip Pullman's trilogy *His Dark Materials,* some historical facts contradicting history as we know it also help us identify the depicted setting as parallel to our own world: Reformation has not happened, the Pope has his seat in Geneva, and the United States is called New Denmark. The author, however, never comments on the setting. In contrast, in Joan Aiken's contrafactual series, published in the 1960s, beginning with *The Wolves of Willoughby Chase*, young readers are given some assistance in identifying the setting: "The action of this book takes place in a period of English history that never happened—shortly after the accession to the throne of Good King James III in 1832. At this time, the Channel Tunnel from Dover to Calais having been recently completed, a great many wolves, driven by severe winters, had migrated through the tunnel from Europe and Russia to the British Isles." Ironically, at the time the novels were published, the Chunnel was still in the planning stages. The series has been treated in critical studies as fantasy, but the setting is contrafactual rather than fantastic. The same can be said about pseudohistorical novels, such as Lloyd Alexander's Westmark or Vesper series. They have a vague historical atmosphere, and the place is either indeterminably Central European or half mythic, such as Illyria or Eldorado. Since there are no magical events in the novels, they cannot be classified as fantasy. Although such specific forms of setting are unusual in children's novels, we should not neglect them, since they contribute significantly to our interpretation of the texts.

EXERCISE

Choose a children's novel and try to transpose its plot and characters into a different setting. Contemplate whether this change affects our perception of the story and in what way.

The Function of Setting

Setting in a children's novel can have a variety of functions and serve different purposes. At the simplest level, as already shown, it states the place and time of action. For many successful stories, a correct and careful description of setting is necessary, which may also serve educational purposes. Details of setting can, in other words, offer information about places and historical epochs that goes beyond the young readers' experience. It does not necessarily mean that these details become obtrusive; in the best books, the practical knowledge is hidden in the background and does not disturb the plot. There are many ways in which a writer can create a credible setting. Mentioning the year and place, as in *Lyddie*, is the simplest. Historical atmosphere can be created by interior and exterior descriptions, clothes, food, transportation, people's ways and habits, and not least the nature of human relationships, including the relationships between children and adults. A sense of place can similarly be enhanced by concrete details. In *Homecoming* and *Walk Two Moons* it is possible to follow the characters' journeys on an ordinary map. This creates a sense of authenticity that contributes to our interpretation of the novels.

Setting has, however, other functions in a story besides describing the scene as such. It can contribute to and clarify the conflict, especially in plots that take the characters from their familiar surroundings, which happens both in fantasy and in everyday stories. At the beginning of *The Lion, the Witch and the Wardrobe*, set during the Second World War, four children are evacuated from London to a house in the country, which creates a point of departure for their adventures. The war in the background accentuates the universal character of their struggle against evil in Narnia. Also the children's immediate surrounding, the old house, is important, with its endless rows of rooms filled with strange objects and paintings. The setting prepares the children—and the reader—for the adventures to come; the objects they see—knights' armor, a harp (the old storytellers' attribute), old books—lead one's thoughts to fairy tales; it is not specified what the paintings show, but it is easy to think that there are scenes which can stimulate imagination. If we interpret the children's adventures in Narnia as make-believe, there is enough in the house to inspire their fancy. It is easy to overlook the setting in the ordinary world, because naturally the Narnia setting is more exotic and therefore more exciting; however, if we are interested in how narratives work, we should not ignore the careful buildup of the setting in the beginning of the novel. In fact, quite a few children's novels start with a radical change of setting when the protagonist is sent away from the familiar surrounding to the unfamiliar, often to an old country house. The setting shifts accentuate the contrast between home and away, city and countryside, nature and culture, security and danger.

In person-against-nature plots, setting is the antagonist of the character. The motif of survival, typical of all kinds of Robinsonnades, demands that the protagonist be exposed to some hostile surrounding, which can be a desert island (*Hatchet*) as well as a big city (*Slake's Limbo*). The prerequisite is of course that there is no easy escape from the threatening setting, and often also that the exposure is involuntary. By placing the character in an "extreme" setting, which can vary from war to a slightly deviating situation in a relative's home, a writer can initiate and amplify a maturation process, which would be less plausible in a normal setting. A good example is *The True Confessions of Charlotte Doyle*, in which the female protagonist, a thirteen-year-old upper-class girl fresh from "Barrington School for Better Girls," is placed on a ship crossing the Atlantic from England to the United States in the 1830s. Her self-discovery, not least her overtly androgynous behavior, would not be possible in her usual setting. Thus setting can function as a catalyst for character evolution.

Setting can illuminate the character, for instance whether the characters are portrayed primarily indoors or outdoors, whether they prefer home and safety or dangerous places away from home. We see clearly that Tom Sawyer is unhappy at home, in school, or in church, while he feels free and safe in the open. Anne Shirley is more of an indoor character, although this is because of societal expectations rather than because of her own disposition. Besides, she has a strong sense of natural beauty, which makes her radically different from her rational and down-to-earth foster parents. Characters portrayed against idyllic rural landscapes, such as Mary Lennox, are perceived differently from characters who act within urban, menacing environments. Although the character in *Slake's Limbo* feels confident and safe in the New York subway, this setting creates a sense of threat and anxiety, since it is not a natural place for a child to be. The fact that most of Ramona's adventures and misadventures take place in school makes us believe that, for this character, school is the most important part of her life.

One of the most interesting ways of using setting to enhance characterization is to be found in *The Secret Garden*. Mary is transposed from India, where she was sickly and profoundly unhappy, to the Yorkshire moors, which she at first hates, but later learns to appreciate. More important, her discovery of the secret garden and her careful tending of it parallel her psychological development and maturation. The setting is thus a powerful device to support the plot itself. The final blooming of the garden coincides with the budding of Mary's personality. The descriptions of setting are in this novel extensive and are repeated alongside the changes happening in nature. The outdoor settings are further contrasted with the dark, gloomy, closed interiors of the mansion in which Colin feels buried alive. The wealthy interiors of Misselthwaite also communicate the social status of the character, without it's being specifically mentioned in the text. Similarly, the interiors of the March household in *Little Women* make us interpret the girls' complaints of poverty with some skepticism.

A character's room can contribute to characterization; for instance, on her first night at Green Gables, Anne's room is described as follows:

> The whitewashed walls were so painfully bare and staring that she thought they must ache over their own bareness. The floor was bare too. . . . The whole apartment was of a rigidity not to be described by words, but which sent a shiver to the very marrow of Anne's bones. (28)

When allowed to stay at Green Gables, Anne tries to "imagine things into this room so that they'll always stay imagined" (61). Her imagination fills the empty room with velvet carpets, pink silk curtains, gold and silver brocade tapestry, and mahogany furniture—she has never seen such things, but read about them in books. Four years later in the plot, the room is described again, and now it bears the traces of Anne's personality; the description carries words such as "pretty matting," curtains "of pale green art muslin," "dainty apple blossom paper" (266f), and instead of mahogany furniture, we see a white-painted bookcase. The text says explicitly that Anne likes her room and enjoys living in it.

Setting is frequently used to symbolize the character's moods and also power position. The bright sunny morning at the beginning of *Anne of Green Gables* corresponds to her hopeful expectations. A change of setting can parallel the change in the character's frame of mind. A storm can symbolize the turmoil in the character's psyche. The close interdependence of character and setting in *The Secret Garden* has already been discussed. Mary's mental and spiritual awakening echoes the garden's starting to bloom again after ten years of lying fallow. Colin's coming out from his voluntary isolation in his bedroom signifies his physical and mental healing. The outdoor settings in *The Secret Garden* emphasize the change of seasons and thus the flow of time. This can be yet another function of setting. In many other books, the change of seasons marks the character's evolution. On the most primitive level, winter symbolizes death; spring, resurrection; summer, heyday; fall, decay. Hundreds of children's books taking place in summer emphasize childhood as a happy, but also static, unchanging period. There is an interesting change in weather conditions in the sequel to *Winnie-the-Pooh*. Although in the first book we have witnessed a flood, the season has constantly been summer. In *The House at Pooh Corner*, the seasons alternate between winter, summer, and fall, with a severe storm. The change of seasons emphasizes the flow of time and the imminent changes in the protagonist's life situation. The fog in which Rabbit tries to lose Tigger in order to "unbounce" him may symbolize the character's confused mind. The storm marks the first radical change in the hierarchy of the Forest: Owl's house is blown down, Piglet is coaxed into ceding his house to Owl, Pooh generously invites Piglet to live with him—some profound changes in the previously static characters are initiated.

Setting can also create a special mood in a story, for instance the feeling of lack and loneliness, threat, nostalgia, joy, and so on. Finally, setting can be perceived as a symbol, like the Hundred Acre Wood in *Winnie-the-Pooh* representing a happy childhood. In many fantasy novels and picture books, the change between the ordinary and the magical setting symbolizes the inner landscape of the child. *Where the Wild Things Are* is one of the best examples of this, as we see how Max creates his own imaginary world where he can play with his feelings and aggressions.

We should further distinguish between the physical environment and the human environment, for instance family or class. Although it may not be of any importance, we can find some additional information in the fact that the character comes from a Catholic, Jewish, Muslim, or atheist family; is a newly arrived immigrant or lives in the same place his ancestors have lived for many generations; and so on.

All these elements of setting are based on conventions, and they are culturally dependent. Rain as a symbol for the character's state of mind will be interpreted differently in a Northern country, where it prevents the children from playing outside, and in an African country or in Southern California, where it is welcome after a period of drought.

EXERCISE

Examine the function of setting in a children's novel of your choice. Consider all the options discussed above. Which function is the most essential? How does the author draw our attention to the importance of the setting?

TIMESPACE

Normally, we view time and space in literature as two separate categories. Contemporary physics, however, beginning with Einstein, has shown than time is merely another dimension of space, alongside length, width, and height. In literary criticism, this daring idea has been developed into the concept of the *chronotope*, first introduced by the Russian scholar Mikhail Bakhtin. Bakhtin defines the chronotope as "the intrinsic connectedness of temporal and spatial relationships that are artistically expressed in literature." In other words, and in what is probably a more correct translation from the Russian, it means "a unity of time and space" presented in a literary work. Bakhtin acknowledges that he has borrowed the term from the natural sciences. The word itself comes from Greek *chronos*—time—and *topos*—place. In Bakhtin's literary theory the term acquires a specific meaning, denoting the unity of fictional time and place, or, in his owns words, "a formal category," an abstract literary concept used to describe spatiotemporal conditions of a literary work.

Unlike the conventional concept of setting, which refers to the combination of place and time, the chronotope denotes the *indivisible* unity of time and space, which according to Bakhtin are mutually dependent. The most important aspect of Bakhtin's concept of the chronotope and what makes it useful in children's literature research is that in Bakhtin's view it is a generic category; that is, specific forms of chronotope are unique for particular genres and text types. Bakhtin discusses the chronotope in both the broad (the medieval chronotope) and narrow meaning of the word (Dante chronotope): every literary mode, epoch, genre, and even writer can be defined on the basis of the way in which they organize time and space. Thus Bakhtin identifies the folktale chronotope, the romance chronotope, the picaresque chronotope, the mystery chronotope, the idyllic chronotope, and so on.

This gives us completely different tools for treating space and time and enables us to make some generalizations about the way time and space work in children's fiction. We can use the chronotope as a generic, thematic, and compositional category, thus complementing some of the approaches introduced in the previous chapters.

LET US EXPLORE

Make a mental inventory of a number of children's novels and try to identify the common denominator in their construction of time and space. What is the universal "children's literature chronotope"?

The Felicitous Space

Many critics who have studied classic children's literature, including such texts as *The Secret Garden*, *Little Women*, Beatrix Potter's stories, *Anne of Green Gables*, and *Winnie-the-Pooh*, have found certain recurrent patterns that qualify the novels as idyll or pastoral. These may include the following:

- the importance of a particular setting, most often rural;
- autonomy from the rest of the world;
- a general sense of harmony;
- the special significance of home;
- the absence of the repressive aspects of civilization such as money, labor, law, or government;
- the absence of death and sexuality;
- indeterminable, cyclical, mythic time (*kairos*), often expressed by iterative frequency;
- and finally, as a result, a general sense of innocence.

The setting of many classic children's novels is indeed rural, and the characters' closeness to nature is accentuated. This is as often as not a reflection of the Romantic view of childhood as natural and innocent. Most of the texts take place in summer; the weather is always fine, unless an occasional storm is used to symbolize a character's state of mind. The imagery is frequently focused on nature. Further, the setting evoked is often vanished or vanishing, thus reflecting the nostalgia of the adult writer and perhaps creating a sense of nostalgia for an adult coreader.

The world of classic children's books is also completely autonomous. In many texts, the secluded kind of setting is emphasized, which is especially felt in the many books featuring a garden (*The Secret Garden* is merely one example). The garden walls or fences are boundaries to the surrounding—

adult—world, boundaries both protecting and restricting. The seclusion enables children to experience the world on their own, since the world is safe. It is also completely balanced and harmonious, joyful and playful. Children and animals live close together; to understand animal language is a privilege given to the most innocent and childlike. Although Dickon, in *The Secret Garden*, does not actually speak animal language, he seems to have a special affinity with them; and Mary's transcendental communication with the robin is also emphasized.

The special significance of home in children's fiction has been pointed out repeatedly. Home is the epitome of security. Home is where the protagonists belong and where they return to after any exploration of the outside world. Home is the inexhaustible source of food, warmth, and love. A young child never asks the question of where food comes from; home is a cornucopia, and food is there simply because it belongs there, as we see clearly in the miraculous appearance of honey jars in *Winnie-the-Pooh*. In other texts, like *Little Women*, home and security are also associated with the mother, the Progenitrix who supplies not only food, but love and care. Similarly, the question of money rarely troubles the child in classic novels. The March sisters may believe themselves poor, but they are not really. Not being able to buy fancy Christmas presents is not exactly being penniless. Money may be a source of moral questions, but actually the March girls have little understanding of real poverty. Mary in *The Secret Garden* is well-off, and for most child characters basic life necessities are not an issue. The adult world with its laws and rules is conveniently detached.

Finally, two most important aspects of adult literature, death and sexuality, are totally absent from classic children's fiction. They are closely interconnected. The characters, whether they are humans or animals, are depicted at the prepubescent stage, the stage of innocence, where their sexual identity has not yet been discovered. Moreover, they are forever conserved in this stage and have neither wish nor possibility of evolving. Therefore, there is no growing up, no maturation, no aging, and subsequently no death. The characters exist in a kind of eternal mythic time, or rather timelessness, described by the Greek word *kairos*, as opposed to *chronos*, the linear, measurable time. In classic children's fiction, time is cyclical: either there is no linear progress whatsoever, or the linear development rounds back into the circular pattern, as in *The Secret Garden*.

As a result, the chronotope of classic children's novels is a safe, secure, and happy place beyond time. Gaston Bachelard's study *The Poetics of Space* suggests the concept of the felicitous space for certain types of fiction. It can be successfully applied to children's novels. However, contemporary children's literature shows considerable deviations from most of these patterns. For instance, the urban settings of *Slake's Limbo* and even *Harriet the Spy* are far from idyllic, strongly interrogating the very idea of childhood's being a happy and secure place. Moreover, even when the setting is rural, its harmony can still be questioned, as in *Bridge to Terabithia*. The horizons of contemporary children's literature are much wider, and the world of childhood is no longer secluded and protected. Home does not necessarily offer a sense of security; rather its restrictive aspects are brought forward. Not least, the long duration, slow pace, and temporal indeterminacy of classic children's literature has given way to intense description of short dramatic moments and turning points in a child's life. We can thus state that the chronotope of contemporary children's fiction is radically different from the chronotope of the literature of the Golden Age. There are, of course, other aspects marking this difference, but the spatiotemporal conditions provide an excellent starting point.

Chronotope as Genre Category

The next question is how the concept of the chronotope can assist us in assessing genres. We have already seen how settings are determined by the premises of such genres as the historical novel or the futuristic novel. For adventure stories, exotic, outdoor settings are common. Time references are vague, perhaps to avoid the books' becoming outdated. Thus, the adventure chronotope is characterized by an exciting, unfamiliar outdoor space (far away from the felicitous space of the idyllic novel), indeterminable time, and disjunctive duration with ellipses between separate episodes. Some concrete examples of adventure chronotopes are islands as the usual settings for Robinsonnades, or caves for treasure hunting. Time is frequently a threatening factor, as the characters are faced with imminent dangers. Setting in domestic novels is usually indoors, at home. Time is continuous and often slow paced. The difference between adventure and domestic novels illustrates very well the interrelationship between genre and setting. While home is a prison for the adventurous hero, the domestic novel inherits the classical chronotope's sense of security at home.

Fantasy novels present a variety of alternative worlds that often have magical creatures, events, and objects. Exactly where these magical countries are situated is often impossible to say. The Neverland in *Peter Pan* is "second to the right, and straight on till morning." In *The Magician's Nephew* the location of fantasy worlds is described as follows:

> another world—I don't mean another planet, planets are part of our world and you could reach them if you went far enough—but a really Other World— another nature—another universe—somewhere you could never reach even if you travelled through space for ever and ever—a world that could be reached only by magic.

The spatiotemporal relations of fantasy are indeed unique. At least two chronotopes are involved, one primary (our own, recognizable world) and at least one secondary, magical world with a time of its own, that may not go at the same pace as time in the primary world. While the protagonist is away in the secondary chronotope, time normally stands still in the primary world. Contemporary fantasy often involves a multitude of secondary worlds, *heterotopia*. The "hetero" of this recent literary term emphasizes dissimilarity, dissonance, and ambiguity of the worlds. Heterotopia denotes a multitude of discordant universes, the ambivalent and unstable spatial and temporal conditions in fiction. The concept itself comes from quantum physics. Heterotopia interrogates the conventional definitions of children's fiction based on simplicity, stability, and optimism. By definition, heterotopic space is neither simple nor stable. On the contrary, it is intricate and convoluted, ever changing, ever shape-shifting. This uncertainty and ambiguity underscores the optimism, since the outcome of heterotopic evolution cannot be predicted. The *His Dark Materials* trilogy is a very good example of this tendency.

The chronotope of the adolescent novel often combines short duration and contemporary time with an urban setting. The city symbolizes a threat, the dangerous world of adults, with all its temptations, enticing and frightening. We could go on investigating other genres in the same manner; however, the examples provided should be sufficient to illustrate the method. The difference between examining the various chronotopes and analyzing concrete settings in particular novels is that the chronotope theory allows generalizations as well as the connection of setting to the other elements of the narrative, such as genre, theme, and plot.

EXERCISE

Analyze the chronotope of some children's books, for instance *The Wonderful Wizard of Oz, The Tale of Peter Rabbit, Winnie-the-Pooh, Charlotte's Web, Ramona the Pest, The Outsiders, Homecoming, Hatchet, The Great Gilly Hopkins*, or *Harry Potter*. Pay attention to the unity of time and space, that is, their mutual dependence: a specific spatial form necessarily demands a specific temporal form to produce the particular genre. Try to determine whether the application of the chronotope theory has given you a different understanding of the novels as compared to the concepts of time and place of action.

The Significance of Home

As already observed, most children's novels are based on two contrasting settings, which, irrespective of their concrete and superficial description, support the basic plot of children's fiction: the home → away → home pattern. The chronotope of home has been thoroughly investigated by scholars, although without necessarily leaning on the chronotope theory. It has been pointed out that children's fiction presents home as a privileged place, a timeless sanctuary where the protagonists are encouraged to stay. Whenever home is presented as problematic, a source of trouble from which the protagonist is trying to escape, we are more likely dealing with adolescent or adult fiction. Further, three main patterns for description of home in children's fiction have been identified:

1. The "Odyssean" pattern, where home is an anchor and a refuge, a place to return to after trials and adventures in the wild world. The pattern refers to Odysseus who returns home after many years of travels. Both *Tom Sawyer* and most of the fantasy novels would fit this pattern.
2. The "Oedipal" pattern is to be found in domestic stories, such as the *Little House* series or *Little Women*; it refers to the power structure in the Oedipus myth;
3. The "Promethean" pattern, where there is no home at the beginning of the story, and the protagonist creates one as a part of his or her maturation. The pattern refers to Prometheus, the cultural hero of Greek mythology who brings fire to people and teaches them more civilized ways of life. *The Secret Garden* would be a good example of this pattern.

The chronotope of home thus shifts its significance depending on the plot in which it appears. The setting of children's novels appears to be much more firmly connected to their themes than could be assumed from the notion of setting as merely describing the time and place of action.

EXERCISE

Consider the function of home in some children's novels, for instance *Little Women*, *The Adventures of Tom Sawyer*, *The Wizard of Oz*, *The Tale of Peter Rabbit*, *Anne of Green Gables*, *Winnie-the-Pooh*, *Little House in the Big Woods*, *Ramona* books, *Where the Wild Things Are*, *Jacob Have I Loved*, *Homecoming*, or *Walk Two Moons*. Which of the three patterns suits each novel best? How does the temporal aspect (home as a permanent or temporary space) fit into the patterns? How does the concept of the chronotope enhance your understanding of the novels?

HOW TO GO FURTHER

Chronotope theory has not been applied to the studies of children's literature on a larger scale, but it seems promising since it proposes new ways of approaching not only settings, but also genres and themes. We could, for instance, from the chronotope of home proceed to discuss the journey chronotope (one of the central concepts in Bakhtin's model), closely connected with the encounter chronotope where two travelers meet. These patterns are universal in literature, but like many other elements, they acquire a special significance in children's fiction. By contrast, the dislocation chronotope (temporary displacement of the protagonist in an unfamiliar place) is considerably more prominent in children's fiction than in the mainstream.

A further possibility is to examine the particular use of time and space by individual writers. The chronotope is a significant part of an author's poetics, and by investigating it, we contribute to the understanding of the author's oeuvre. Naturally, this is an infinitely more sophisticated task than merely stating that the time and place of action is this or that.

Finally, a more detailed discussion of the chronotope of children's literature, or broader still, the chronotope of childhood, brings us closer to the understanding of the essence of children's fiction as such.

REFERENCES

Aers, Lesley. "The Treatment of Time in Four Children's Books." *Children's Literature in Education* 2 (1970): 69–81.

Bachelard, Gaston. *The Poetics of Space.* New York: Orion, 1964.

Bakhtin, Mikhail. "The Forms of Time and Chronotope in the Novel." Pp. 84–258 in his *The Dialogic Imagination.* Austin: University of Texas Press, 1981.

Bal, Mieke. *Narratology: Introduction to the Theory of Narrative.* 2nd ed. Toronto: University of Toronto Press, 1997. Part 2, chap. 6, "From Place to Space."

Carpenter, Humphrey. *Secret Gardens: The Golden Age of Children's Literature.* London: Unwin Hyman, 1985.

Carr, David. *Time, Narrative and History.* Bloomington: Indiana University Press, 1986.

Clausen, Christopher. "Home and Away in Children's Fiction." *Children's Literature* 10 (1982): 141–152.

Empson, William. *Some Versions of Pastoral: A Study of the Pastoral Form in Literature* (1935). London: Chatto & Windus, 1968. Includes a chapter on *Alice in Wonderland.*

Evans, Gwyneth. "The Girl in the Garden: Variations in a Feminine Pastoral." *Children's Literature Association Quarterly* 19, no. 1 (1984): 20–24.

Francis, Elizabeth. "Feminist Versions of Pastoral." *Children's Literature Association Quarterly* 7, no. 4 (1982): 7–9.

Hunt, Peter. "Arthur Ransome's Swallows and Amazons: Escape to a Lost Paradise." Pp. 221–231 in *Touchstones: Reflections of the Best in Children's Literature*, edited by Perry Nodelman. Vol. 1. West Lafayette, IN: Children's Literature Association, 1985.

Inglis, Fred. *The Promise of Happiness: The Value and Meaning in Children's Fiction*. Cambridge: Cambridge University Press, 1981.

Johnston, Rosemary. "Childhood: A Narrative Chronotope." Pp. 137–158 in *Children's Literature as Communication*, edited by Roger D. Sell. Amsterdam: John Benjamins, 2002.

Krips, Valerie. *The Presence of the Past: Memory, Heritage and Childhood in Postwar Britain*. New York: Garland, 2000.

Kumar, Krishan. *Utopia and Anti-Utopia in Modern Times*. London: Blackwell, 1987.

Kuznets, Lois. "The Fresh-Air Kids, or Some Contemporary Versions of Pastoral." *Children's Literature* 11 (1983): 156–168.

Lukens, Rebecca J. *A Critical Handbook of Children's Literature*. 4th ed. New York: HarperCollins, 1990. Chap. 6, "Setting."

Mackey, Margaret. "Growing with Laura: Time, Space and the 'Little House' Books. *Children's Literature in Education* 23, no. 2 (1992): 59–74.

Nikolajeva, Maria. *The Magic Code: The Use of Magical Patterns in Fantasy for Children*. Stockholm: Almqvist & Wiksell International, 1988. In this book the concept of chronotope is used to investigate the construction of time and space in fantasy novels.

———. *Children's Literature Comes of Age: Towards a New Aesthetic*. New York: Garland, 1996. Chap. 5, "Chronotope in Children's Literature."

———. *From Mythic to Linear: Time in Children's Literature*. Lanham, MD: Scarecrow, 2000.

Smedman, M. Sarah. "Springs of Hope: Recovery of Primordeal Time in 'Mythic' Novels for Young Readers." *Children's Literature* 16 (1988): 91–107.

Stephens, John. "Representation of Place in Australian Children's Picture Books." Pp. 97–118 in *Voices From Far Away: Current Trends in International Children's Literature Research*, edited by Maria Nikolajeva. Stockholm: Centre for the Study of Childhood Culture, 1995.

Waddey, Lucy E. "Home in Children's Fiction: Three Patterns." *Children's Literature Association Quarterly* 8, no. 1 (1983): 13–15.

Watkins, Tony. "Reconstructing the Homeland: Loss and Hope in the English Landscape." Pp. 165–172 in *Aspects and Issues in the History of Children's Literature*, edited by Maria Nikolajeva. Westport, CT: Greenwood, 1995.

———. "The Setting of Children's Literature: History and Culture." Pp. 30–38 in *Understanding Children's Literature*, edited by Peter Hunt. London: Routledge, 1998.

Williams, Raymond. *The Country and the City*. London: The Hogarth Press, 1993.

7

The Aesthetic of Character

Characters are the agents performing actions in a story: persons, personified animals, or objects. Character and characterization are such an obvious part of fiction that they are very seldom discussed in critical works or in textbooks on children's literature. If mentioned at all, the questions concerning characters will most likely be who they are, what they do, or what they represent. We may find phrases in children's book reviews about "powerful characterization," but what exactly do critics mean by this? What is the function of characters in the narrative, and what is characterization, that is, the set of artistic devices used by writers to reveal characters for their readers? Despite the postmodern and poststructural denigration of characters, they are still central in fiction; basically, we read fiction because we are interested in human nature and human relationships as revealed through fictive characters.

LET US EXPLORE

Choose a children's novel and try to pose as many questions as you can think of concerning characters. Here are some suggestions for you to develop:

- Are the characters important in themselves, or are they merely instrumental for the plot? Do they represent something? In this case what?
- Is there one clearly identifiable protagonist, or are there several characters who can be considered as main characters?
- What is the relationship between the main character and other characters?
- What kinds of characters are they—good, bad, neutral? Are we as

readers supposed to like them, admire them, empathize with them, or on the contrary, condemn them?

- Are most of the characters clearly divided into good and bad ones, or are they more complex, with contradictory psychological traits?
- How do we as readers get to know the characters? Does the narrator state explicitly what they are like, or are we allowed to draw our own conclusions?

People of Flesh and Blood or Merely Words?

One of the most profound problems in dealing with literary characters is their ontological status (ontology = issue of reality): are we to treat them as real people, with psychologically credible traits, or merely as textual constructions? Literary theory from Aristotle to our day has given a variety of answers to this question. On the one hand, we can view literary characters as real people and ascribe them a background and psychological features that may not have any support in the text. This approach is called mimetic. We have already discussed mimetic approaches to literature in general (chapter 4). Mimesis means imitation, so from this approach we would say that literary characters imitate real people in real life. On the other hand, we can perceive characters merely as a number of words, without any psychological substance. This approach is called semiotic, and semiotics, as we remember, is the theory about signs. With this approach, characters are merely signs or signifiers; they do not have to behave logically or even plausibly; they do not have to be whole, coherent, and believable. These two approaches are extremes; a reasonable attitude is somewhere in between.

The ontological question, that is, the question of the difference between literary characters and real people, is highly relevant for children's literature research. There is a much stronger tendency to treat and judge characters in children's books as if they were real people, as compared to the mainstream.

CHARACTERS AS ACTORS

We have touched upon characters from a formalist and structuralist viewpoint when we were discussing composition (chapter 5): characters as role figures in the plot. Interestingly enough, this approach goes back to classic poetics. For Aristotle, characters are subordinate to the plot, and their function in a literary work is merely to perform actions. Aristotle distinguishes between *pratton* (actor or agent) and *ethos* (psychological figure, personality), maintaining that agents are indispensable in a literary work, while psychological characters are optional. Moreover, the only psychological traits allowed are "noble" or "base"; no other human features are essential for the plot. This theory, primitive as it may seem to us today, has obviously been used as the underlying principle for traditional children's fiction, in which characters' actions are more important than their psychological features.

Within formalist and structuralist theory, developed 2,300 years after Aristotle, characters are also treated merely as agents who perform certain actions and therefore have no psychological features whatsoever. All structural models describe characters in relation to plot and only superficially as to how they relate to each other. This does not allow a deeper analysis of the characters' traits and still less any "inner life." Therefore such models have been successfully applied to plot-oriented children's stories. It would be meaningless to analyze Dorothy in *The Wizard of Oz* in psychological terms, since she only has one feature: she is good. She does not present any complexity inherent to human beings in real life, and she hardly shows any psychological development. She is, by contrast, highly motivated in her behavior by the objective of the plot: to return home. The functional or actantial model would be more than adequate to describe the characters in *The Wizard of Oz*. This does not mean, however, that Dorothy is a deficient character as compared to a protagonist from a modern psychological novel. Dorothy is simply a different kind of character, an actor rather than a personality.

Today we expect psychological dimension in literary characters. We also expect an ethical dimension, of Aristotle's *ethos*, character as a psychological entity. While the majority of children's books are still action oriented, that is, focused more on actions and events than on character and characterization, there has been a notable shift in Western children's fiction toward a more profound interest in character, toward psychological, character-oriented children's novels. Until recently, most children's books did not portray characters with personality traits other than good or evil. Harold Bloom claims in his recent book on Shakespeare that the psychological dimension in literary characters was Shakespeare's invention. Since children's literature is a relatively recent phenomenon in the history of literature, the psychological aspect of literary character in children's fiction does not emerge on a larger scale until the 1970s in the Western countries. A psychological literary character in children's literature is a collective "invention" of several major authors of the last twenty to twenty-five years.

EXERCISE

Consider a number of children's novels in terms of plot orientation or character orientation. Contemplate whether the characters have any psychological or ethical dimensions. See whether you can observe any historical development toward psychological characters.

CHARACTERS AS PEOPLE

With a mimetic approach to literary characters, we are interested in what they are and how they relate to real people as we know them from the real world. In children's literature, main characters are most often children or animals (occasionally inanimate objects) representing children. Mimetically oriented studies of children's literature focus on the kinds of characters that we meet in children's novels, such as boys and girls, men and women, parents, stepparents, grandparents, siblings, teachers, ethnic minorities, immigrants, gay and lesbian characters, animal and toy characters, witches, wizards, dragons, ghosts, and other supernatural creatures.

We can also analyze concrete characters, such as Jo March, Anne Shirley, Ramona, or Harry Potter. We have a variety of tools for such analyses. We can treat characters from a sociohistorical viewpoint, as representatives of their time and social group, or even as representatives of nationhood (for instance, is the Cat in the Hat a truly American hero?). We can treat them from a psychological viewpoint, as bearers of certain psychological features. Many interesting studies of particular characters are based on modern child psychology, for instance, works by Erik Erikson, Melanie Klein, and D. W. Winnicott. We can further treat characters from a biographical viewpoint, as reflections of their authors' lives and opinions. We can also see characters as bearers of ideas, as mouthpieces for ideologies and beliefs, or as models for young readers in their socialization. All these methods are closely connected to mimetic approaches to literature as such, already discussed in chapter 4.

A Typical Children's Literature Character

Another way of looking at characters from a mimetic point of view is trying to identify the most typical traits of all characters in children's fiction. There are two main types of characters we meet in children's books: the underdog and the trickster, both originating from myth and folklore. The most common hero in a folktale is an underprivileged child, the youngest son or youngest daughter, often a child of unknown origin. At the end, the hero finds his fortune, "the princess and half the kingdom," and triumphs over those who seemed cleverer and stronger in the beginning. The abandoned orphan is also the most typical character in children's fiction. The degree of abandonment can vary from the parents' going off for work to their being away traveling or even dead; as shown before, they may be also absent emotionally. We can call children whose parents are alive but do not care about them, "functional orphans."

Another typical character in children's fiction, originating in folklore, is the trickster. Tom Sawyer is a trickster. Peter Rabbit is a trickster. A "tomboy girl," like Jo March and Anne Shirley, alludes to the trickster figure as well, while in *Pippi Longstocking* a girl is put into a typical male-trickster role. While the trickster is more common in entertainment literature, the first character type, the underprivileged child, is the most widespread in contemporary psychological children's novels. Both the underdog and the trickster are characters who, as the plot progresses, change their power position from low to high or at least higher. They are comic heroes, appearing in a comic plot (see chapter 5). This is what we often refer to as the intrinsic hope and optimism of children's literature. As we have discussed before, downward movement and thus tragic heroes are unlikely in children's fiction, although they have recently started to appear in young adult novels.

EXERCISE

Choose two children's novels, one plot oriented, the other character oriented. Compare the characters in terms of their psychological qualities. Is it fruitful at all to consider characters in plot-oriented novels in psychological terms? Is it fruitful to apply structuralist models to character-oriented texts?

FROM GENDER ROLES TO
GENDER PERFORMANCE

The interest in the gender aspect of children's literature emerged in the 1960s and '70s, as part of the general interest in a sociohistorical approach to literature. The early studies of children's books from the gender point of view focused on gender roles: the way boys and girls, or men and women, were portrayed, as well as how these portrayals reflected the actual situation in society. Gender stereotyping was the key concept of these studies. A *stereotype* is a character who behaves in exactly the way he or she is supposed to, according to the prevailing conventions. Since male and female stereotypical traits are opposed to each other, it is easy to present a schematic abstract pattern of "masculinity" and "femininity":

Men/boys	Women/girls
strong	beautiful
violent	nonviolent

unemotional, tough   emotional, soft
aggressive   submissive
competitive   sharing
protective   vulnerable
independent   dependent
active   passive

and so on.

EXERCISE

Apply the schema to a number of male and female characters in children's novels. Do you find that male characters fit into it more often than female ones?

While not all male and female literary characters follow this schema, it can help us evaluate gender stereotypes. In our culture, "male" features are implicitly superior; feminist critics refer to this fact as "phallocentrism." Yet, female characters who show at least some male traits and thus break away from the stereotype, such as Jo March or Anne Shirley, are frequently forced back into female patterns. As one critic has put it, in literature boys grow, while girls shrink. If we tried to apply the schema to Anne, she would match most of the male traits in the beginning of the novel and most of the female ones in the end. That is, rather than showing the character's development toward strength and independence, as would be the case with a male character, the novel instead demonstrates how women were compelled by the patriarchal (= male-oriented) society to adjust to the female stereotype. When Pippi Longstocking, a character genuinely inspired by Anne Shirley, is allowed to be everything that Anne must give up in order to be accepted, she is operating within a different genre. It is in fact only fantasy and science fiction that can, with certain reservations, portray female characters free from stereotyping.

One of the general problems in assessing gender is that the opposition male-female, or masculine-feminine, is more complex than it may seem at first sight. Thus, in examining female characters in children's fiction, we must remember that the plots of children's novels usually follow the patterns of male myths and, generally, "masculine" (or gender-neutral) narratives, oriented toward tangible achievements. "Feminine" narratives are different and can be hard to discern since they are not as pronounced as the rigid beginning-middle-end structures we are used to and the heroic male character associated with it.

Female Archetypes

One clearly feminine pattern that has been identified is the green-world archetype, a girl who lives close to nature. Wendy in *Peter Pan* is one of these heroines, escaping into her green world away from both urban civilization and her parents' oppression, and returning to it in her recuperating memories as an adult. The protagonists of Johanna Spyri's *Heidi* and Burnett's *The Secret Garden* are further examples of the green-world heroines.

The growing-up-grotesque archetype implies meeting the incompatibility of personal freedom and societal demands by going into depression or seclusion. This process has also been described in terms of abjection, a girl's feeling of aversion toward her own body as it develops into a young woman's. Consider this quote from *Lyddie*:

> She hadn't had a new dress since they sold the sheep four years ago. Since then, her body had begun to make those strange changes to womanhood that exasperated her. Why couldn't she be as thin and straight as a boy? Why couldn't she have been a boy? Perhaps, then, her father would not have had to leave. With an older son to help, maybe he could have made a living for them on the hill farm. (22)

The tomboy figure in children's fiction is an excellent example of abjection. Rather than accepting their own femininity, heroines such as Jo March and Anne Shirley suppress it by manifesting nonfeminine behavior. Both characters have to subdue hot tempers incompatible with feminine norms. Anne is literally silenced as she abandons her imaginative, poetic language. Cross-dressing and androgyny are two more ways of denying one's body and gender. In contemporary novels, the grotesque archetype can be stretched quite far, since today's young women's unwomanly manners are slightly more tolerated than in Jo March's day. Louise in *Jacob Have I Loved* suppresses her femininity to distance herself from her pretty and talented twin sister. She is also trying to fulfill her father's secret desire for a son. Louise dresses carelessly; has a male occupation, fishing; and seemingly makes no attempts to grow up as a "normal" woman. Portraying this survival strategy, the author explicitly describes her as unattractive (among other things, with an ugly scar from chicken pox), the way she perceives herself. A much younger heroine, Gilly Hopkins, employs a similar survival strategy by being deliberately nasty.

In children's fiction, girls are doubly oppressed: as women and as children. Such oppression implies that in a children's novel, a female character's development is more universal than that in mainstream fiction, where femininity is overt and explicit. Not least because girls' fiction is historically a relatively recent genre, masculine patterns, as in many other fields, hold a default value in children's fiction. Paradoxically enough, the contemporary character of children's fiction has inherited significantly more traits from the female archetypes than from those of the traditional male hero.

Changing Approaches to Gender

Of course, our ideas about typical male and female traits change with time. Our assessment of "masculine" and "feminine" behavior is also based on our preconceived opinions. Jo March's unladylike behavior was perceived differently when the novel was published than we perceive it today. Contemporary juvenile novels contain much stronger language than Jo's "Christopher Columbus." Female characters especially have changed radically since *Little Women*; and boys in contemporary novels are allowed to be soft and caring. Hermione in the *Harry Potter* books has recently become a favorite object for gender analysis. There are several ways of assessing this character. We can view her as a strong-minded, intelligent, independent female who is her male companions' equal and in some ways even superior (for instance, she is smart and more successful academically). On the other hand, Hermione is a stereotypical "strong and independent" female, who is only allowed to be brilliant in traditionally female areas and is constantly eclipsed by Harry and even Ron when it comes to bravery and action. In one episode she is literally "petrified" and thereby denied agency. Thus in the *Harry Potter* books, masculine characteristics are repeatedly given priority.

For obvious reasons, gender aspects are more prominent in fiction for slightly older readers, especially in young adult fiction, since gender identity is an essential part of the identity quest during adolescence. It many cases, characters in children's novels are "gender neutral" in the sense that their biological gender is not crucial for the plot. For instance, there is nothing precluding a male protagonist in *The Wizard of Oz*. Often the whole issue of gender is simply circumvented by having a group of characters, boys and girls, in the main role, as we see in *The Lion, the Witch and the Wardrobe*. Yet because boys and girls in our society are in fact expected to behave differently, the character's gender is still not an accident. We could not possibly have a girl in the main role in *The Adventures of Tom Sawyer*, simply because it would not be plausible for a girl to go to a graveyard in the middle of the night or to run away to have fun on an island. On the other hand, Jo's revolt against societal norms would not be as radical if she were a boy.

While the strong influence of feminist criticism during the last twenty years has drawn our attention to the portrayal of girls in children's and juvenile novels, the most recent trend has also focused on boys and masculinity. This is a welcome development, since male characters should by no means be overshadowed by girls and women, in a kind of positive discrimination.

EXERCISE

Choose a children's novel with a number of male and female characters. Study carefully the way these characters are portrayed. Here are some questions to help you in your assessment:

- Is the character's gender decisive for the plot? Try to perform a mental gender permutation on the character and see whether the character will still function in the plot.
- Is there a gender balance in the text? Do boys or girls have all the leading parts? Why? Is the gender balance dictated by the plot?
- Who is active and who is acted upon?
- Do boys get away with, and perhaps even get praised for, behavior that girls get punished for? Are boys allowed to speak while girls are silenced?
- Are boys and girls, men and women stereotypically portrayed? Do they behave, speak, and think according to the society's prescribed norms? If there are any deviations from the norms, how do other characters react to those? Where is the author's sympathy?

Gender Performance

A more subtle approach to characters' gender aspects is to examine it in terms of social construction and societal expectations. The concept of *performative gender*, as opposed to the biological gender, draws our attention to the characters' behavior along the prescribed norms, called in feminist criticism a gender *script*. If the character is depicted as female, but behaves like a male, we may say that she is performing according to the prewritten male gender script, or matrix. It is fully possible to put a female character in an adventure plot, but this will be a simple gender permutation, creating a "hero in drag." Quite a few contemporary fantasy novels portray strong, masculine heroines slaying dragons and meeting male opponents in open combat. This is a typical example of tokenism. These seemingly female characters are tokens, a female body set in a male role. Superficial female attributes (most often, long hair) do not create a female identity; the character could have been male without the plot changing significantly, since the plot itself is unmistakably male. By contrast, some of the female characters already mentioned above, such as Jo, Anne, and Louise, deviate from the prescribed gender norms while retaining their feminine identity. In doing so, they in fact interrogate the norms that force women into secondary and submissive roles.

Contemporary feminist and queer theory have given us powerful analytical tools to examine gender patterns in literature, and we have gone much further than merely stating the occurrence of gender stereotyping. While very little of queer theory can be directly applied to literature, the idea of gender as performance rather than an inherent feature is certainly worth pursuing.

EXERCISE

Choose a children's or a young adult novel with a female protagonist and examine whether she is in fact depicted as female in her gender performance. Draft a gender script for the character—it must take into consideration the genre, setting, and plot within which she is performing. Does she comply with the script or deviate from it? What happens if she does deviate, what is the reaction of her surroundings, what is the implied author's position? Has the performative analysis changed your initial assessment of the character?

THE PATRICIDAL CHILD

In chapter 1, we took a brief look at the ways author-oriented psychoanalysis works. In applying psychoanalytical models to literary characters, we must once again remember that they are not real people and do not have to appear in accordance with the actual course of mental disturbances. We will use patterns described by Freud and his followers to examine certain recurrent psychological patterns in literature, which may, but need not be, the consequence of the author's familiarity with Freud. After all, the Oedipus complex, Freud's most famous concept, appears in literary texts thousands of years before Freud described it.

The Oedipus Complex in the Nursery

The essence of Freudian theory can be summarized by stating that all human problems originate in early childhood traumatic experience, most often connected with sexuality. One example is the so-called "primal scene," a young child's accidental witnessing of the parents' sexual intercourse, which causes a disturbing realization of being sexually inadequate. According to Freud, a boy always feels subconscious hate and rivalry toward his father, who possesses the person most dear to the child: the mother. Thus the boy instinctively wishes to get rid of the father so that he can have the mother all for himself. Since hate toward the father and a secret sexual desire for the mother are forbidden sentiments in a civilized society, the boy suppresses them, which may lead to psychic disturbance and in any case becomes manifest in dreams and fancies. A normal psychological process is, by contrast, the child's successive emotional liberation from the parents, in order to be able to develop healthy sexual relations in adulthood. Although Freud's patterns were male oriented, they can also be applied to girls, who ostensibly are secretly in love with their fathers and therefore wish to get rid of their mothers: the Electra complex.

In stories, we meet four types of parent/child relationships that can be examined in terms of Freudian psychoanalysis: mother—daughter, mother—son, father—son, and father—daughter. All these relationships are widely described in myths and fairy tales, as well as in literature. They are the most basic human relationships, which, as already discussed before, acquire a special significance in children's fiction. Let us start with a brief glance at some well-known fairy tales, the importance of which has been especially emphasized in the works of the famous psychoanalytical critic Bruno Bettelheim. In *Puss in Boots*, for instance, the hero, assisted by his trickster friend, kills the ogre and takes over all its riches. In psychoanalytical terms, the ogre represents the young boy's image of his father who must be eliminated before the boy can go on with his own life. The main conflict in *Snow White* is rivalry between an aging mother and the daughter approaching puberty. Although the evil queen is not portrayed as Snow White's biological mother, we know that most figures of evil stepparents in fairy tales are late euphemisms of real parents, since it is less offensive in our society to feel hate toward a stepparent than toward a biological parent. Snow White's biological mother dies, remaining forever benevolent in her daughter's memory. In her stead, an evil mother figure appears, wishing to eliminate the daughter who is a threat to her sexual power over men. *Rapunzel* is a variant of *Snow White*, also centered round mother/daughter relationship. The witch is Rapunzel's foster mother—as in *Snow White*, a less offensive substitute for biological mother. By keeping Rapunzel locked in a tower, the "mother" denies her daughter maturity and sexuality, since she sees her as a future rival. The young heroine's triumph over the witch is, as in *Snow White* or *Cinderella*, a symbolic depiction of a young female adolescent's liberation from her mother's dominance. Yet another version of *Cinderella* and *Snow White*, sometimes called *All-Fir*, *Catskin*, or *Donkeyskin*, depicts a daughter fleeing from her father's incestuous attention. Thus in many fairy tales we see descriptions of relationships and feelings that are highly tabooed in our society but that nevertheless exist in our subconscious and can cause traumas: mothers' rivalry with their daughters, mothers desiring their sons, sons desiring their mothers and therefore hating their fathers, fathers scared of sons as rivals and potential murderers, fathers' desire for their daughters, and so on.

One would presume that these issues are irrelevant for children's litera ture. Freud maintains, however, that we are born with sexuality which stays latent inside us until puberty, and also that all these processes occur at the subconscious levels of our minds. In stories, they are exposed and amplified. One of the children's stories frequently used in Freudian approaches is *Peter Pan*, and the focus of attention is Peter's oedipal confrontation with Hook. Peter, we learn, has once managed to cut off Hook's hand—in Freudian terms, he has symbolically castrated his father, inhibiting his procreation ability—and he is throughout the story trying to kill him, while Hook is after Peter for revenge. At the same time, Peter has a traumatic relationship with his mother, who has rejected him, closing the nursery window on him and getting another baby son. Peter invites Wendy to Neverland to be his mother, and he and Hook clearly compete for Wendy's attention. By getting rid of Hook, Peter is liberated from the patricidal obsession, yet his problems with the mother remain unresolved.

We could easily provide a similar Freudian reading of *The Wizard of Oz*, where Dorothy must kill the witches, representing the evil side of her mother (of whom we actually do not know anything from the novel), so that she can feel free from her oppression. We can interpret Edmund's falling for the White Witch's charms in *The Lion, the Witch and the Wardrobe* as an indication of his dependence on his mother, and his immediate dislike of Aslan as a prime case of Oedipus complex. A Freudian interpretation of the *Harry Potter* novels would naturally revolve around the relationship between Harry and the male parental figures: his biological father; his foster father, Mr. Dursley; the good parent substitutes Dumbledore and Sirius; and the evil parent image Voldemort. There is in the books a recurrent reminder of some obscure connection between Harry and Voldemort, and Harry is just as much fascinated by the evil wizard as he is scared of him. The complex imagery of the novels provides gratifying material for psychoanalytical interpretations. It would, however, be wrong to assume that Freudian readings can be performed only on fantasy. *The Adventures of Huckleberry Finn* offers an excellent ground for Freudian interpretation, with Huck's palpably murderous conflict with his father and with Jim supplying a complex and controversial parent substitute.

Peter Pan Complex

How fruitful one finds such interpretations is a matter of personal preference. Some might find them too speculative and far-fetched. It is important not to apply the psychoanalytical tools mechanically, but to see whether they can indeed open some new dimensions of the text, inaccessible with other methods. While the Oedipus complex is a concept equally applicable to all kinds of literature, in children's fiction we could perhaps distinguish the specific Peter Pan complex: a child character's reluctance to grow up, which, in Freudian terms, is a manifestation of the subconscious fear of sexuality. Peter plays the roles of Wendy's partner and the Lost Boys' father in Neverland, yet when Wendy asks him about his true feelings for her, he answers innocently, "Those of a devoted son." Even though Peter says at one point, "I don't want ever to be a man . . . I want always to be a little boy and have fun," what he is in fact expressing is a fear of growing into a sexual being. Given a chance to stay in London and grow up together with Wendy, he promptly rejects it.

The Peter Pan complex is manifest in many ways in children's and adolescent fiction. In some books, the issue of growing up is simply irrelevant, because the time span is too short (*The Cat in the Hat*) or because the character is never allowed to become aware of the significance of growth and change (*Ramona* books). In other books, such as *Winnie-the-Pooh*, growing up is touched upon, but never fully developed as a theme; instead, the author comes with somewhat false promises that the childhood idyll will go on forever. In *The Catcher in the Rye*, Holden feels envious of his brother Allie, who died young and will therefore stay young forever, without having to go through the painful process of maturation, including the introduction into sexuality. Holden has by many critics been compared to Peter Pan, on the basis of his reluctance to grow up. Although Holden also has social reasons for this (he does not want to grow up to be like his father and most other adults he sees around him), the immature desire to avoid or delay the inevitable step into adulthood is reminiscent of Peter Pan's escape into Neverland. Pippi Longstocking invites her friends to take a magical pill that will make them remain children forever. This can be interpreted in two ways. If the author candidly suggests that growing up is undesirable, her characters are indeed suffering from a Peter Pan complex, giving a bad example to their readers. More likely, Pippi's magical pill is used ironically, to underscore the impossibility of eternal childhood. Pippi herself, one-of-a-kind, may remain unchanged, but her companions, ordinary children, are made aware, together with the readers, that growing up is inevitable and not a reason for fear. The Peter Pan complex as typical pattern of children's fiction draws our attention to the way characters are presented in their psychological development from the innocence of childhood toward sexual awareness and maturity.

EXERCISE

Choose a children's novel or picture book you find suitable for a psychoanalytical interpretation. Examine the child/parent relationship in it in Freudian terms and compare your results with those achieved in a mimetic reading. Do you find that the psychoanalytical tools have provided you with a deeper understanding of the characters?

CHARACTERS AS DESIGN

In narrative theory, we are not so much interested in what the characters are, but in how they are constructed and revealed to us. We also consider their importance for the plot, for instance, distinguish between main characters, or protagonists, and secondary characters, who can be divided into several categories according to their significance: supporting characters, peripheral characters, or backdrop characters.

EXERCISE

Choose a children's novel with a large number of characters. *Anne of Green Gables* or *Harry Potter and the Sorcerer's Stone* would be perfect. Discuss each character in terms of their importance for the plot. Contemplate why the writers needed the different secondary characters.

Static and Dynamic, Flat and Round

Both main characters and secondary characters can be dynamic or static. Dynamic characters change throughout the story, while static characters do not change. Tom Sawyer does not change, and there is not much room for him to change. For one thing, the duration of the story is too short for radical change. For another thing, it is not part of the writer's intention. The book ends by stating that since this is a story of a boy it must stop; otherwise it becomes a story of a man. Changes imply, among other things, growth and maturation. The story about Anne of Green Gables takes several years, and Anne does not only grow up, but changes inside. This is typical of girls' fiction. We should, however, distinguish between chronological dynamism, caused merely by the flow of time in the novel (Anne gets older) and ethical dynamism, manifest in the profound changes in the character's personality.

Old didactic children's fiction often has static characters. Since the foremost goal of the contemporary psychological children's novel is to depict inner growth, such novels presuppose at least one dynamic character, whom we always perceive as the protagonist. Formulaic fiction most often contains static characters. But even quality fiction may have static characters, and they are in no way a sign of lower artistic merit.

Yet another binarity concerning character construction is the concepts of flat and round characters. Flat means that the characters are two-dimensional, not fully developed. They are usually depicted as having one typical trait, or none at all. They can, for instance, be ascribed features such as good or evil. Their actions may be easily predicted. Characters in formulaic fiction are often flat. Characters representing parts of a collective actant can also be flat. Round (multidimensional) characters possess a number of traits, both positive and negative; they are fully developed; we really get to know them well as the story progresses, but we cannot predict their behavior. Protagonists are not necessarily round characters, and secondary characters need not be flat. Many secondary characters of *Tom Sawyer* or *Harry Potter* are more round than the rather flat protagonist. Nor are protagonists always dynamic. Round characters can be both dynamic and static. Pippi Longstocking is undoubtedly a round character, with many exciting traits, but she is static and does not change. Flat characters who possess but few traits have little chance to be dynamic. If a flat character suddenly changes from evil to good, his change is not very plausible. In a round character, who from the beginning possesses both good and bad traits, a change is more convincing. Of the four children in *The Lion, the Witch and the Wardrobe* only Edmund is somewhat round and dynamic. His feelings are contradictory. He knows that he is behaving wrongly, but does it anyway. He is of course under a spell, but all the time he knows that he is doing wrong. On seeing the White Witch transform animals into stone, he feels the first signs of remorse. Edmund's test and transformation are thus the most essential events of the book.

There are, however, certain genres and kinds of children's fiction that presuppose a total change of a flat character to the other extreme, most often from evil to good, from lazy to diligent, and so on. Many nineteenth-century didactic children's books describe such a change. Formulaic fiction also sometimes provides this pattern. There is, however, no assumption of quality in the notions of flat or round, dynamic or static character. A flat character is not necessarily artistically "worse" than a round one, it is merely a matter of constructing characters and giving them a function in the plot. Further, like all binarities, flat/round and static/dynamic are abstract concepts, while actual literary characters lie in a continuum between these extreme poles. That is, every concrete character is delineated with more complexity than being merely flat or merely round. (See fig. 7-1.)

To these basic binarities, we can add some others. For instance, is the character whole or fragmentary; that is, are more or less all character traits presented in the story or merely some odd bits and pieces? Is the character opaque or transparent; that is, do we only get to know them through external events and behavior or are we allowed access to their thoughts and feelings? Is the character coherent or incoherent, consistent or inconsistent, and so on. There are of course many other nuances we can employ while discussing characters, yet we come a good way with the static/dynamic and flat/round orientation.

EXERCISE

Analyze characters in some of the children's novels, for instance *The Cat in the Cat*; *Curious George*; *Where the Wild Things Are*; *Roll of*

Complexity ╲ Dynamism	Flat	Round
Static	Tom Sawyer	Pippi Longstocking
Dynamic	Mary Lennox	Anne Shirley

Fig. 7-1   Complexity and dynamism.

Thunder, Hear My Cry; and *Harry Potter and the Sorcerer's Stone*, in terms of complexity and dynamism. Do you find these concepts somewhat sufficient to describe characters? What other features do you find essential to take into consideration?

Getting to Know a Literary Character

The next question within narrative theory is how we as readers can get to know and understand characters we meet in books. For many critics, the appeal of literature is exactly the fact that we can more easily understand literary figures than we can ever learn to understand real people. As readers, we get to know literary characters successively, from a number of incidents. One may assume that this is similar to our getting to know real people; there is, however, a profound difference. Since literary characters are created by writers, these may employ different strategies in revealing characters. A character's features may be conveyed to the reader through repetition; through comparison to other, well-known literary characters or real figures; through contrast between different features (most often good and evil); or implicitly, when the readers must make conclusions themselves. Writers can give us contradictory information through different characterization devices. For instance, a character's self-evaluation may contradict the other people's opinion or the narrator's overt comments. Writers may even omit essential information or withhold it until later. The amount of information we demand is highly dependent on the kind of text we are dealing with: we expect a character in a psychological novel to have more traits than a fairy-tale hero. In fact, we are rarely interested in all properties of a character. Instead, we should ask what is sufficient in order to understand a character in a particular text type. In children's literature, the question is especially relevant, since young readers may misjudge characters or fail to assemble a number of traits into a whole.

LET US EXPLORE

Choose a children's novel and examine how the main character is presented. Are all the character traits revealed at once, or do we as readers have to assemble a somewhat full and coherent portrait from bits and pieces scattered throughout the story? Are the characterization devices primarily external or internal? Is the character coherent, or is there ambivalent or contradictory information that impedes our understanding of the character? How much of this information is explicit and how much are we as readers supposed to assemble ourselves from the bits and pieces we receive?

Here are the principal characterization devices that can be used by writers to present characters:

- Description
- Narrator's comments
- Other characters' comments and attitudes
- Actions and reactions
- Relationships with other characters
- Direct speech
- Indirect, or reported speech
- Internal representation

External Representation

External representation, including description, comments, actions, and speech, is the least complex way of revealing characters. We get acquainted with them more or less in the same manner we get acquainted with real people: by their appearance and by their behavior. In external representation, characters are opaque, and we do not know any more about them than other characters would. External representation is seldom the only means of characterization in a novel; more often it is combined with other devices. However, we can speak about external orientation in characterization, meaning

that most facts that we learn about a particular character are conveyed
through external means.

External orientation in children's fiction is closely connected to several
literary factors. First, it occurs in older rather than in modern texts. Second,
for obvious reasons it is typical for plot-oriented narratives where it is more
important what characters do than how they feel about it. Third, it is more
likely to be used in formulaic fiction than in psychological narratives.
Fourth, it is more likely to be used in texts addressed to younger children.
Last but not least, external orientation more or less presupposes an omniscient perspective.

Let us agree that external orientation does not imply deficient characterization. While we today attribute higher aesthetic quality to psychological
portrayal, it is wrong to assume that external characterization is artistically
inferior; it is merely a different device. Moreover, external characterization
is part of the overall didactic adaptation of children's fiction to the cognitive
level of its implied readers. Young readers can more easily understand and
judge characters' actions, external description, or the narrator's direct statements than subtle psychological changes and motivations. Since literature is
dependent on language to describe emotional life, it demands a rich and mul-
tifaceted vocabulary to convey the nuances of meaning, which young readers
may not master yet. There is a clear tendency in fiction for younger children
toward external characterization, while young adult fiction frequently employs internal means.

EXERCISE 1

Find and examine passages describing characters in, for instance, *The
Adventures of Tom Sawyer, The Wizard of Oz, Anne of Green Gables,
The Secret Garden,* or *Harry Potter and the Sorcerer's Stone.* Is the description extensive? Is it important, and in this case why? Are looks
more important in girls' books than in boys' books? If yes, why? Are
characters described only once? Do their looks change? Is the change
credible? Is the character interested in his or her looks? How does the
external description contribute to our assessment of character?

EXERCISE 2

Examine the characters' behavior in some of the following novels: *Tom
Sawyer, Anne of Green Gables, The Secret Garden, Ramona the Brave,*
or *Harriet the Spy.* How do characters' actions characterize them? Is
Tom Sawyer clever or naughty when he cheats other boys into white-
washing the fence for him? How does coming to his own funeral char-

acterize him: is he clever, cynical, silly, thoughtless? Is Anne Shirley stupid when she gives Diana wine to drink, or does she simply not know better? Is Mary wicked and insensitive or clever and insightful when she yells at Colin? Is Ramona immature in her behavior? Is Harriet selfish or even solipsistic in her attitude toward other people? How does her final apology to her classmates characterize her? Do characters have intentions behind their actions, do they act on impulse, or do things merely "happen" to them?

Exercise 3

Analyze the use of direct and indirect speech in a children's novel of your choice. First of all, decide whether direct speech is used primarily for carrying on the plot or whether it also contributes to characterization. How is direct speech used to help us distinguish between characters (e.g., do characters have any particular speech idiosyncrasies)? Pay attention to the ratio of direct and indirect speech. Examine how the narrator's discourse governs our interpretation of the characters' utterances.

Internal Representation

Internal, or mental, representation is the most sophisticated characterization device. It allows us to penetrate the characters' minds, to take part in their innermost thoughts and mental states. Characters become fully transparent, in a way that real people can never be. The fact that mental representation is uncommon in children's literature depends on its implied readers. We need certain life experience to be able to interpret characters' thoughts, and still more their unarticulated emotions, such as fear, anxiety, longing, or joy. Of course, a writer can simply state, "He was anxious" or, "She was scared." But the words "anxious" or "scared" are very simple labels for complex and contradictory mental states. Not even a long description can necessarily convey all the shades of a person's feelings.

Narratology discerns a number of artistic devices to depict inner life or consciousness, such as quoted monologue, interior monologue (or free direct discourse), narrated monologue (or free indirect discourse), and psychonarration, a blend of character discourse and narrator's discourse. The latter is the most indirect and ambiguous way to convey consciousness. In children's literature it is often used to manipulate readers, to create an illusion that the text reflects a character's mind, while it is in fact a narrator's comments about a character's mind. As any mixed form, psychonarration can be more or less harmonious. Since the writer and thus most often the narrative agency is an adult, while the character is a child, there is a discrepancy in the cognitive level: the narrator knows and understands more than the child does and can either convey the child character's thoughts from a superior position (dissonant psychonarration) or try to ignore his adult experience and narrate totally from the child's perspective (consonant psychonarration). Close readings of psychonarration in children's novels can often reveal a narrator that pretends to stand on the child's side, but in actual fact comes with statements and judgments that contradict the child's consciousness. We will take a closer look at this problem in chapter 8, devoted to narration.

EXERCISE

Find and analyze passages describing the characters' inner life in some children's novels, for instance *Harriet the Spy*, *Bridge to Terabithia*, *The Great Gilly Hopkins*, *The Planet of Junior Brown*, or *Holes*. Pay attention to the blending of character's and narrator's discourse and examine whether the internal representation is consonant or dissonant. What indication do you find in the text to support your judgment?

HOW TO GO FURTHER

All the various approaches to characters in children's literature must in some way or other address the question of fictionality. Even within mimetic theory, we are still dealing not with real children, but with the authors' image of the child, a fictional child. This image can be affected by a number of factors: the societal norms, the educational intentions, the aesthetic conventions, and also the authors' individual choices. The central question to pose in this connection, prompted by feminist, queer, and postcolonial theories, is whether children's authors inevitably construct the child as "the Other," from what they know—or think they know—about children and childhood, from what they want children to be, or from what they think society wants or needs children to be. The problem of the fictional child, raised in Jacqueline Rose's influential book *The Case of Peter Pan, or The Impossibility of Children's Literature*, and developed in a number of more recent studies, must necessarily become central in any further serious discussions of children's fiction. Irrespective of what approach to literary characters we adopt—mimetic, gender-related, psychoanalytical, or narrative—we must be aware that what we are analyzing is always a social and cultural construct and must be treated accordingly.

REFERENCES

General

Bloom, Harold. *Shakespeare: The Invention of the Human*. New York: Riverhead Books, 1998. Harold Bloom claims that the psychological dimension of literary characters first appears in Shakespeare's plays.

Bradley, A. C. *Shakespearean Tragedy* (1904). 3rd ed. London: Macmillan, 1993. This study has served as a model for all investigations of literary characters treating them as living people.

Docherty, Thomas. *Reading (Absent) Character: Toward a Theory of Characterization in Fiction*. Oxford: Clarendon, 1983. This study questions the mimetic approach to character in favor of the nonmimetic, or semiotic.

Forster, E. M. *Aspects of the Novel* (1927). San Diego: Harcourt, Brace, 1985. Forster introduced the concepts of flat and round characters.

Harvey, W. J. *Character and the Novel*. Ithaca, NY: Cornell University Press, 1965. Primarily a mimetic study.

Hochman, Baruch. *Character in Literature*. Ithaca, NY: Cornell University Press, 1985.

Hourihan, Margery. *Deconstructing the Hero: Literary Theory and Children's Literature*. London: Routledge, 1997. A radical reevaluation of the heroic figure in children's literature.

Lukens, Rebecca J. *A Critical Handbook of Children's Literature*. 4th ed. New York: HarperCollins, 1990. Chap. 3, "Character."

Miller, Dean A. *The Epic Hero*. Baltimore: The Johns Hopkins University Press, 2000.

Nikolajeva, Maria. "The Changing Aesthetics of Character in Children's Fiction." *Style* 35, no. 3 (2001): 430–453.

———. *The Rhetoric of Character in Children's Literature*. Lanham, MD: Scarecrow, 2002.

Petruso, Thomas F. *Life Made Real: Characterization in the Novel since Proust and Joyce*. Ann Arbor, MI: University of Michigan Press, 1991.

Price, Martin. *Forms of Life: Character and Moral Imagination in the Novel*. New Haven: Yale University Press, 1983.

Roser, Nancy, ed. *What a Character!* Austin: International Reading Association, 2004.

Torrance, Robert M. *The Comic Hero*. Cambridge, MA: Harvard University Press, 1978.

Dictionaries of Literary Characters

Fisher, Margery. *Who's Who in Children's Fiction: A Treasury of Familiar Characters of Childhood*. New York: Holt, Rinehart and Winston, 1975.

Jones, Raymond E. *Characters in Children's Literature*. Detroit: Gale Research, 1997.

Mortimore, Artur D. *Index to Characters in Children's Literature*. Bristol: D. Mortimore, 1977.

Snodgrass, Mary Ellen. *Characters from Young Adult Literature*. Englewood, CO: Libraries Unlimited, 1991.

There are also dictionaries of fictional characters in specific texts, such as the Narnia Chronicles, the Prydain Chronicles, Tolkien's novels, and so on.

Structural Approaches

Campbell, Joseph. *The Hero with a Thousand Faces*. New York: Pantheon, 1949.
Cawelti, John G. *Adventure, Mystery and Romance: Formula Stories as Art and Popular Culture*. Chicago: University of Chicago Press, 1976.
Propp, Vladimir. *Morphology of the Folktale*. Austin: University of Texas Press, 1968.
———. *Theory and History of Folklore*. Manchester: Manchester University Press, 1984.

Mimetic Approaches (A Selection)

Avery, Gillian. *Nineteenth-Century Children: Heroes and Heroines in English Children's Stories 1780–1900*. London: Hodder & Stoughton, 1965.
———. *Childhood's Pattern: A Study of the Heroes and Heroines of Children's Fiction 1770–1950*. London: Hodder & Stoughton, 1975.
Blount, Margaret J. *Animal Land: The Creatures of Children's Fiction*. New York: Morrow 1974.
Cunningham, Hugh. *The Children of the Poor: Representation of Childhood since the Seventeenth Century*. Oxford: Blackwell, 1991.
Cuseo, Allan A. *Homosexual Characters in YA Novels: A Literary Analysis, 1969–1982*. Metuchen, NJ: Scarecrow, 1992.
Escarpit, Denise, ed. *The Portrayal of the Child in Children's Literature*. München: Saur, 1985.
Jones, Dudley, and Tony Watkins, eds. *A Necessary Fantasy? The Heroic Figure in Children's Popular Culture*. New York: Garland, 2000.
Jurich, Marilyn. *Scheherazade's Sisters: Trickster Heroines and Their Stories in World Literature*. Westport, CT: Greenwood, 1998.
Kern, Edmund M. *The Wisdom of Harry Potter: What Our Favorite Hero Teaches Us about Moral Choices*. Amherst, NY: Prometheus, 2003.
Kuznets, Lois. *When Toys Come Alive: Narratives of Animation, Metamorphosis and Development*. New Haven: Yale University Press, 1994.
MacCann, Donnarae. *White Supremacy in Children's Literature: Characterizations of African Americans, 1830–1900*. New York: Garland, 1998.
McCoy Lowery, Ruth. *Immigrants in Children's Literature*. New York: Peter Lang, 2000.
Stewart, Susan. *On Longing: Narratives of the Miniature, the Gigantic, the Souvenirs, the Collection*. Baltimore: Johns Hopkins University Press, 1984.
Storey, Dee. *Twins in Children's and Adolescent Literature: An Annotated Bibliography*. Metuchen, NJ: Scarecrow, 1993.

Gender-Related Approaches

Many gender-focused studies also make use of psychoanalytical theories. For the sake of convenience, they are only listed once, in this subsection.

Åhmansson, Gabriella. *A Life and its Mirrors: A Feminist Reading of L. M. Montgomery's Fiction.* Uppsala: Acta Universitatis Upsaliensis, 1991.

Alberghene, Janice M., and Beverly Lyon Clark, eds. *Little Women and the Feminist Imagination: Criticism, Controversy, Personal Essays.* New York: Garland, 1998.

Billone, Amy. "The Boy Who Lived: From Carroll's Alice and Barrie's Peter Pan to Rowling's Harry Potter." *Children's Literature* 32 (2004): 178–202.

Butler, Judith. *Gender Trouble: Feminism and the Subversion of Identity.* 2nd ed. New York: Routledge, 1999. The groundbreaking work on gender performance.

Canadian Children's Literature 76 (1994): a special issue on masculinity.

Chodorow, Nancy. *The Reproduction of Mothering: Psychoanalysis and the Sociology of Gender.* Berkeley, CA: University of California Press, 1978.

———. *Feminism and Psychoanalytical Theory.* New Haven: Yale Univeristy Press, 1989.

Clark, Beverly Lyon. *Regendering the School Story: Sassy Sissies and Tattling Tomboys.* New York: Garland, 1996.

Clark, Beverly Lyon, and Margaret R. Higonnet, eds. *Girls, Boys, Books, Toys: Gender in Children's Literature and Culture.* Baltimore: The Johns Hopkins University Press, 1999.

Crew, Hilary S. *Is It Really "Mommie Dearest"? Daughter-Mother Narratives in Young Adult Fiction.* Lanham, MD: Scarecrow, 2000.

Dresang, Eliza T. "Hermione Granger and the Heritage of Gender." Pp. 211–242 in *The Ivory Tower and Harry Potter: Perspectives on a Literary Phenomenon*, edited by Lana A. Whited. Columbia: University of Missouri Press, 2002.

Flanagan, Victoria. "Cross-dressing as Transvestism in Children's Literature: An Analysis of 'Gender-performative' Model." *Papers* 9, no. 3 (1999): 5–14.

Foster, Shirley, and Judy Simons. *What Katy Read: Feminist Re-readings of "Classic" Stories for Girls.* London: Macmillan, 1995.

Hirsch, Marianne. *The Mother/Daughter Plot: Narrative, Psychoanalysis, Feminism.* Bloomington: Indiana University Press, 1989.

Kristeva, Julia. *Powers of Horror: An Essay on Abjection.* New York: Columbia University Press, 1982.

Lehr, Susan, ed. *Beauty, Brains and Brawn: The Construction of Gender in Children's Literature.* Portsmouth, NH: Heinemann, 2000.

The Lion and the Unicorn 15, no. 2 (1991): a special issue on gender.

Nelson, Claudia. *Boys Will be Girls: The Feminine Ethic and British Children's Fiction, 1857–1917.* New Brunswick, NJ: Rutgers University Press, 1991.

Paul, Lissa. "Enigma Variations: What Feminist Criticism Knows about Children's Literature." Pp. 148–166 in *Children's Literature: The Development of Criticism*, edited by Peter Hunt. London: Rutledge & Kegan Paul, 1990. Apart from an interesting reevaluation of some female characters in children's novels, Paul questions the use of "the hero in drag."

———. "Feminist Criticism: From Sex-Role Stereotyping to Subjectivity." Pp. 101–

112 in *International Companion Encyclopedia of Children's Literature*, edited by Peter Hunt. London: Routledge, 1996. Also pp. 112–123 in *Understanding Children's Literature*, edited by Peter Hunt. London: Routledge, 1999.

———. *Reading Otherways*. Stroud, UK: Thimble Press, 1998. Offers valuable tools for assessing literary characters from the gender perspective.

Pratt, Annis, with Barbara White, Andrea Loewenstein, and Mary Wyer. *Archetypal Patterns in Women's Fiction*. Bloomington: Indiana University Press, 1981.

Reynolds, Kimberley. *Girls Only? Gender and Popular Children's Fiction in Britain 1880–1910*. Hemel Hempstead: Harvester, 1990.

Rollin, Lucy. "The Reproduction of Mothering in Charlotte's Web." *Children's Literature* 18 (1990): 42–52.

Showalter, Elaine, ed. *Speaking of Gender*. New York: Routledge, 1989.

Stanger, Carol A. "Winnie the Pooh Through a Feminist Lens." *The Lion and the Unicorn* 11, no. 2 (1987): 34–50.

Stephens, John. "Gender, Genre and Children's Literature." *Signal* 79 (1996): 17–30.

Stephens, John, ed. *Ways of Being Male: Representing Masculinities in Children's Literature and Film*. New York: Routledge, 2002.

Trites, Roberta Seelinger. *Waking Sleeping Beauty: Feminist Voices in Children's Novels*. Iowa City: University of Iowa Press, 1997.

Warner, Marina. *No Go the Bogeyman: Scaring, Lulling, and Making Mock*. New York: Farrar, Straus and Giroux, 1998. A comprehensive study of masculinity in fiction.

Psychoanalytical Approaches

Bettelheim, Bruno. *The Uses of Enchantment: The Meaning and Importance of Fairy Tales*. New York: Knopf, 1976.

Birkhäuser-Oeri, Sibylle. *The Mother: Archetypal Image in Fairy Tales*. Toronto: Inner City Books, 1988.

Bosmajian, Hamida. "Charlie and the Chocolate Factory and Other Excremental Visions." *The Lion and the Unicorn* 9 (1985): 36–49.

———. "Psychoanalytical Criticism." Pp. 89–100 in *International Companion Encyclopedia of Children's Literature*, edited by Peter Hunt. London: Routledge, 1996. Also pp. 100–111 in *Understanding Children's Literature*, edited by Peter Hunt. London: Routledge, 1999.

Byrnes, Alice. *The Child: An Archetypal Symbol in Literature for Children and Adults*. New York: Peter Lang, 1995.

Canadian Children's Literature 72 (1993): a special issue on psychoanalytical approaches to children's literature.

Egan, Michael. "The Neverland of Id: Barrie, Peter Pan and Freud." *Children's Literature* 10 (1982): 37–55.

Haviland, Erwin Miller. "In Memoriam: Allie Caulfield." Pp. 132–143 in *Holden Caulfield*, edited by Harold Bloom. New York: Chelsea, 1990.

Kidd, Kenneth. "Psychoanalysis and Children's Literature: The Case for Complementarity." *The Lion and the Unicorn* 28, no. 1 (2004): 109–130.

Lundell, Torborg. *Fairy Tale Mothers*. New York: Peter Lang, 1990.

Reed, Michael D. "The Female Oedipal Complex in Maurice Sendak's *Outside Over There.*" *Children's Literature Association Quarterly* 11, no. 4 (1986–87): 176–180.

Rollin, Lucy, and Mark I. West, eds. *Psychoanalytical Responses to Children's Literature.* Jefferson, NC: McFarland, 1999.

Rustin, Margaret, and Michael Rustin. *Narratives of Love and Loss: Studies in Modern Children's Fiction.* London: Verso, 1987. Freudian readings of a number of children's novels.

Smith, Joseph H., and William Kerrigan, eds. *Opening Texts: Psychoanalysis and the Culture of the Child.* Baltimore: The Johns Hopkins University Press, 1985.

Narrative Theory

Bal, Mieke. *Narratology: Introduction to the Theory of Narrative.* 2nd ed. Toronto: University of Toronto Press, 1997. Part 2, chap. 5, "From Actors to Characters"; part 3, chap. 3, "Actors."

Chatman, Seymour. *Story and Discourse: Narrative Structure in Fiction and Film.* Ithaca, NY: Cornell University Press, 1978. Chap. 3, "Story: Existents."

Cohn, Dorrit. *Transparent Minds: Narrative Modes for Presenting Consciousness in Fiction.* Princeton, NJ: Princeton University Press, 1978. The terms for mental representation come from this source.

Golden, Joanne M. *The Narrative Symbol in Childhood Literature: Exploration in the Construction of Text.* Berlin: Mouton, 1990. Chap. 3, "Act: Characterization."

Nikolajeva, Maria. "Imprints of the Mind: The Depiction of Consciousness in Children's Literature." *Children's Literature Association Quarterly* 26, no. 4 (2001–2002): 173–187.

———. "Harry Potter—Return to the Romantic Hero." Pp. 125–140 in *Harry Potter's World: Multidisciplinary Critical Perspectives*, edited by Elizabeth Heilman. New York: Routledge, 2002.

———. "Picturebook Characterization: Text/Image Interaction." Pp. 37–49 in *Art, Narrative and Childhood*, edited by Morag Styles. London: Trentham, 2003.

Rimmon-Kenan, Shlomith. *Narrative Fiction: Contemporary Poetics.* London: Routledge, 1983. Chap. 3, "Story: Characters"; chap. 5, "Text: Characterization."

8

The Aesthetic of Narration

Narration refers to the way a story is told, as distinct from the story itself, or what is told. Of all the literary theories, only narrative theory has seriously investigated the art of narration and the various questions arising out of the relationship between writers, narrators, characters, and readers. In this chapter, therefore, we will concentrate on narrative theory.

EXERCISE

In order to understand why narrative perspective is indeed decisive for our perception of a story, try to retell some famous stories from a different point of view. Such mental exercises are called commutation tests. For instance, tell the story of Snow White from the evil queen's point of view, or one of the dwarfs, or the hunter who takes Snow White to the woods to be killed. Tell the story of Cinderella from the point of view of one of her stepsisters, or the prince, or the fairy godmother, or the rat who got turned into a coach driver (some of these retellings really exist!). You will notice that the story becomes totally different when told from a different perspective.

Narrative Agencies

It is natural to assume that every narrative must be told by somebody, by a narrative agency, a *narrator*. This is, however, not a universal agreement. Some critics claim that we can only speak about a story's having a narrator if we clearly hear this narrator's voice, or even more strictly, if the narrator also appears as a character in the story (that is, a first-person narrator). Other narratives, according to this view, either "narrate themselves," which seems unlikely, or are narrated "by the author." The latter opinion is of course legitimate, but then we are confronted with the need to explain the relationship between the flesh-and-blood author and the ideas, beliefs, and judgments expressed by the text. It is problematic to hold authors responsible for what might be deliberately provoking statements in the text. Therefore most scholars of contemporary narrative theory agree that all narratives are narrated, have a narrator, even though the narrator can be covert. The narration, the narrative act, implies a number of agents, and the relationship between them needs some clarification. Let us consider figure 8-1.

The real author and the real reader are in this schema placed outside the text, while all the other agencies are inside the text. We have agreed that real, flesh-and-blood authors are only important insofar as they affect the creation of the text, through facts of their lives, and their beliefs and ideologies (chapter 1). When we are dealing with the text as such, the real author, male or female, dead or alive, is of less significance. Instead, readers may have an image of the author *inscribed in the text*, for instance an author who is preaching morals or, on the contrary, takes the child's part, who sympathizes with the poor and the oppressed or speaks from a position of power. Such an image of an author that readers reconstruct from the text itself is called the implied author. Unlike a narrator, the implied author does not have a voice in the narrative and thus cannot directly tell us anything. That is, while the implied author's ideology might affect the reader's relationship to the reading experience, the narrator is the only one who actually speaks.

CONTEMPLATE

Think of a dozen books where you do not know anything about the author. What kind of author images do you get from the books themselves? Are they old or young, nice or nasty? A young child, asked a similar question, replied, "This book is written by an old lady in a blue dress." This response is an excellent illustration of the concept of the implied author: the reader's image of the author deduced from the book. When contemplating your selection of books, try to see whether

Narrative text

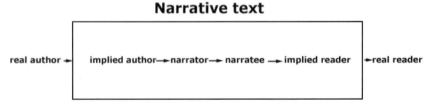

Fig. 8-1   Communication chain.

there are indeed any indications in them that govern your image of the author.

Of course, different readers may construct different implied authors from the same book. Unlike the flesh-and-blood author, the implied author is an abstract notion, and we cannot say that the implied author constructed by a particular real reader is right or wrong. Yet, we can judge what features of the implied author are prompted by the text. Ideology, that is, beliefs and opinions, expressed by the text, come from the implied author, and we assume that they are shared by the real author. In contrast, the views expressed by a narrator do not necessarily have to coincide with those of either the real or the implied author, especially, as happens in children's fiction, when the narrator is a child.

We will embark on a closer examination of readers, real and implied, in chapter 11. So far let us simply state that just as the implied author is an abstract image of the author inscribed in the text, the implied reader is an abstract image of the audience that can be extracted from the text.

The concept of the narratee has been introduced into the communicative model for the sake of symmetry. In figure 8-1, the narratee on the receiver side corresponds to the narrator on the sender side, just as the implied reader corresponds to the implied author. The narratee is an agency within the text that is the recipient of the narrator's story. Just as a narrator can be covert or overt in a particular text, so can a narratee. The fact is that the majority of children's books (as well as mainstream novels) have covert narratees. It does not mean that there are no narratees in a text. There is often some inscribed audience, as in Kipling's *Just-So Stories*, addressed as "O My Best Beloved." The narratee in *The Lion, the Witch and the Wardrobe* is more or less covert. Holden in *The Catcher in the Rye* may be telling his story to a psychiatrist in the clinic where he is treated, but this narratee is never revealed in the text. In contrast, Jerusha in *Daddy-Long-Legs* is addressing her unknown benefactor, who eventually turns up as a character. A good example of an overt narratee is *Winnie-the-Pooh* where Christopher Robin is listening to bedtime stories his father—the overt narrator—is telling him. The narratee can even occasionally interrupt the narrator with questions. In *Walk Two Moons*, Sal is telling the story of Phoebe Winterbottom to her grandparents as they travel by car from Ohio to Idaho. The grandparents are overt narratees of this story. But at the same time Sal is telling the story of the travels with the grandparents to another, covert narratee, maybe to her father, maybe even to herself. The concept of the narratee is seldom decisive for our interpretation of the story, but in some very complex narratives it helps us to see the narrative situation more clearly.

WHO IS TELLING THE STORY?

Most textbooks in literary analysis suggest two types of narrators: first-person (referring to one of the characters as "I") and third-person (referring to all characters as "he" or "she"). It is often stated that second-person narrators (referring to one of the *characters* as "you," not to be confused with addressing the reader or narratee) are theoretically possible, but seldom occur outside purely experimental prose. This is true, but in children's fiction there is at least one well-known example of a story told in second person: the initial chapter of *Winnie-the-Pooh* in which the narratee, who is also a character, Christopher Robin, is consistently referred to as "you": "Well, it just happened that you had been to a party the day before at the house of your friend Piglet, and you had balloons at the party." There are other marginal forms, such as first-person plural (referring to a group of characters as "we," whereupon the exact source of narration is unclear). Yet, most of children's fiction is written either in the first person or in the third person. We will henceforth refer to first-person narration as personal and to third-person narration as impersonal.

It has been generally believed that children prefer impersonal narrators. There are several reasons for this assumption. A personal narrative is naturally more engaging and can be perceived as too frightening and emotionally involving, especially for a younger child. Besides, young children have not yet developed a clear notion of an "I," at least not separate from themselves. They have problems sharing the subjectivity with the strange "I" of the text. Since early children's literature was written mostly for educational purposes, didactic impersonal narrators were considered a suitable mode. We see it very clearly in the fact that adaptations of adult novels into children's books have involved, among other things, a transposition from first to third person (*Robinson Crusoe, Gulliver's Travels*, and many others). In older literature, personal narration could be viewed as the indication of the intended audience. *The Adventures of Huckleberry Finn*, which unlike *Tom Sawyer* was originally published as an adult novel, uses the first person, while *Tom Sawyer* is told in the third person. In contemporary children's and especially young adult fiction, personal narration has become very common.

EXERCISE 1

Compare some children's novels with similar themes and plots, one of which uses impersonal and the other personal narration (e.g., *The Lion, the Witch and Wardrobe* and *Mio My Son*; *Little Women* and *Jacob Have I Loved*; *Ramona the Pest* and *Dear Mr. Henshaw*; *Where the Wild Things Are* and *And To Think That I Saw It on Mulberry Street*). What are the implications? Why do you think the authors have chosen the particular manner of narration? What are the advantages and disadvantages of the two narrative modes?

EXERCISE 2

Another commutation test: take a short passage from a story written in the first person (for instance, *Roll of Thunder, Hear My Cry*) and rewrite it using the third-person perspective. Analyze the two passages. How has the impersonal narration changed our perception of the described events?

Now try the opposite: transpose impersonal narration into personal. Choose two different books, one in which only the external flow of events is rendered (*The Wizard of Oz, Ramona the Pest*), and another focused on the character's inner life (*Bridge to Terabithia, The Great Gilly Hopkins, Slake's Limbo*). You will probably notice that the two kinds of story demand a different approach. A young narrator may not be able to express the scope of emotions going on inside him. You will have to adapt the language and the cognitive level of the narrative to that of the child narrator.

Impersonal Narration

Impersonal narrators may be of four different types:

- *omniscient*: a narrator who literally "knows everything," can enter people's minds and follow them even when they are on their own; who is also omnipresent, that is, knows what is going on at several places simultaneously;
- *limited omniscient*: a narrator who knows more than any of the characters, but not everything; for instance, follows some of the central characters in the story or even just one of them;
- *objective*, or *dramatic*: a narrator who knows more than any character and who can be omnipresent, but who cannot enter the characters' minds—"dramatic" refers to the way events are revealed in drama: only externally;
- *introspective*: a narrator who knows only what one particular character knows, thinks, and feels.

LET US EXPLORE

Examine the kind of narrator in some of the following stories: *Cinderella; Puss in Boots; The Adventures of Tom Sawyer; Little Women; The*

Wizard of Oz; *Anne of Green Gables*; *The Lion, the Witch and the Wardrobe*; *Pippi Longstocking*; *Bridge to Terabithia*; *The Great Gilly Hopkins*; or *Harry Potter*.

Folktales always have omniscient and omnipresent narrators, and early children's fiction took over this device. The narrator of *Little Women* is omniscient as he (I am using the masculine pronoun for the sake of convenience, without any further implications) follows each of the four sisters in their actions and thoughts. The narrator of *The Lion, the Witch and the Wardrobe* is also omniscient; he can switch between Edmund and the other three children when they have parted, bringing the readers' attention to this fact: "And now of course you want to know what had happened to Edmund" (82); "Now we must go back to Mr. and Mrs. Beaver and the three other children" (93); "Edmund meanwhile . . ." (102); "While the dwarf and the White Witch were saying this, miles away the beavers and the children were walking . . ." (113); and so on. The narrator can render all the four children's thoughts and feelings, contrasting them:

> At the name of Aslan each of the children felt something jump in its inside. Edmund felt a sensation of mysterious horror. Peter felt suddenly brave and adventurous. Susan felt as if some delicious smell or some delightful strain of music has just floated by her. And Lucy got the feeling you have when you wake up in the morning and realize that it is the beginning of the holidays or the beginning of summer. (65)

The narrator can even enter the mind of the evil White Witch, their enemy. This destroys some of the suspense of the story; it would have been a more powerful story if the readers were to discover the effect of the evil forces by themselves, together with Edmund or maybe before him. Omniscience is of course a relative quality: no narrator in a story actually tells us everything about every single character and event of the story. Moreover, a narrator can pretend that he does not know everything. For instance, when Aslan has a man-to-man talk with Edmund, the narrator says, "There is no need to tell you (and no one ever heard) what Aslan was saying . . ." (126).

The narrator of *The Adventures of Tom Sawyer* is limited omniscient, as he mostly follows Tom, but he can also enter the mind of Aunt Polly, and toward the end he switches between Tom and Huck. The narrator of *The Wizard of Oz* primarily follows Dorothy; yet occasionally the perspective may switch to another character, for instance the Witch of the West. The narrator of *Anne of Green Gables* follows Anne, but in the beginning of the novel we see the events through Mrs. Lynde's, Matthew's, and Marilla's eyes, and every now and then the narration returns to them. For instance, when Anne goes to a concert, the narrator seems to stay with Marilla, so that Anne has to tell her about it later. The narrator of the *Harry Potter* books is limited omniscient, mostly following Harry. Yet, in the very beginning of the first novel, we see the events through the Dursley family, and in the beginning of book four, we are allowed a glimpse of Voldemort himself. This gives the reader superiority over the characters who are unaware of the villain's plans.

The narrator of *Pippi Longstocking* is objective, simply registering the superficial events ("showing" rather than "telling"), without going into the characters' thoughts or feelings. He never enters Pippi's mind, and the only reflections about her possible feelings are to be found in dialogues between Tommy and Annika. The narrators of *Bridge to Terabithia* and *The Great Gilly Hopkins* are introspective, more or less entering the mind of one character and showing us the events through the character's eyes, without actually involving personal narration. This is the narrative mode most often found in contemporary psychological novels for children.

EXERCISE

Illustrate each type of impersonal narrator with a children's novel of your own choice. Based on the text, discuss advantages and disadvantages of each narrative mode.

Personal Narration

LET US EXPLORE

Examine the narrators in some of the following novels: *Treasure Island*; *The Cat in the Hat*; *The Catcher in the Rye*; *Roll of Thunder, Hear My Cry*; *Jacob Have I Loved*; and *Walk Two Moons*. Are they all alike? If not, what is the difference? What is the main attraction of personal narration? What, if anything, do you find problematic with personal narration?

Personal narrators have the advantage of a deeper penetration into thoughts and feelings, but the disadvantage is a restricted access to knowledge. A personal narrator can only be in one place at a time. For instance, Doctor Livesey in *Treasure Island* takes over the story to tell about the events that happened in Jim's absence. Further, a personal narrator cannot enter other people's minds. Finally, we get only one subjective rendition of events. In the case of a child narrator, an additional disadvantage is limited life experience, capacity of self-reflection, and vocabulary. This is only true if the narrator is simultaneous, telling the story as it unfolds, as in *Roll of Thunder*. This narrator lacks adult experience, which compels the writer to use simple language and an unsophisticated worldview. Let us not, however, see this as a fault, but on the contrary, a daring attempt to render a young child's perspective, a child living and telling her story "here and now." Cassie Logan is a character in her own story, yet she mainly tells us about the external flow of events rather than reflecting on her own reactions to them. Such personal narrators, not focused on their own internal life, are called witness narrators. In adult literature, the often-quoted example of witness narrator is Doctor Watson in Sherlock Holmes stories, which allows the writers to withhold essential knowledge from the readers and let them follow the investigation together with Watson, without access to the detective's sharp mind. In children's literature, witness narration does not call for self-reflection, which a young narrator may not be capable of. The narrator of *The Cat in the Hat* is also merely rendering the events rather than reflecting on them.

Another way of circumventing the problem is to use retrospection: an adult character telling the story of when he was young, as in *Treasure Island*. Retrospective personal narration is widely used in children's literature. In *Jacob Have I Loved*, the adult Louise is rendering the events of several years earlier. Louise's narrative is also very much focused on herself and her feelings at the time of the events rather than on the events themselves: the narrator is self-reflexive, or introspective. The narrator of *The Catcher in the Rye* is also retrospective, even though his story does not lie so far away in the past.

Ironic and Nonironic, Reliable and Unreliable

Irony as a rhetorical figure implies that words have meanings different from their dictionary definitions. An ironic narrator says one thing, but means something else. He sees through the actions, intentions, mistakes, and fallacies of the characters. An ironic personal narrator sees his own faults and can comment on them. A nonironic, or naive, narrator is unable to judge the events around him, the actions and utterances of the other characters, or his own behavior and emotions. Basically, a child narrator is always nonironic, and therefore it is an extremely difficult narrative mode, since authors must pretend to abandon their adult experience and way of thinking and adjust them to the level of a child. As we have seen, some children's novels avoid the problem by letting adult characters tell about their childhood, thus allowing reflections and judgments.

Many contemporary children's novels involve unreliable narrators, especially personal narrators, whose narrative strategy is to conceal rather than tell the true story. Personal narration is unreliable by definition. A character can only convey his or her subjective perception of the events and other characters. Yet for some reason we trust some narrators more than others. We assume that Huck Finn is giving us a true account of his adventures on the Mississippi River, while we have our doubts about Holden Caulfield's account of his roaming around in New York. In fact, Holden, a model for the modern narrative voice in children's fiction, says himself that he is the worst liar in the world, and we have no proof of how much of what he tells us has really happened. Even if it has happened, Holden's perception of what has happened is highly subjective. An unreliable narrator can conceal even information that is absolutely indispensable in order to interpret the story. For instance, Holden never tells us explicitly that he has had a nervous breakdown. Sal in *Walk Two Moons* is until the very end of the story deliberately suppressing the fact that her mother is dead. Such omission of information is called *paralipsis*. Since it puts higher demands on the reader, paralipsis is used more often in adolescent fiction than in novels for younger readers.

A child narrator is naturally unable to evaluate events and people around him and instead relates them from his naive, inexperienced perspective. But even impersonal narration can by means of introspection create an illusion of a naive perspective, for instance in *The Planet of Junior Brown*. The narrator in this novel does not comment on the faults and failures of the character, and the events seem as though they were presented by the protagonist himself. Thus children's literature has met the primary challenge of narratology: a totally unreliable narrator, approximated in *The Sound and the Fury* or *Forrest Gump*. A young narrator is unreliable by default, due to his lack of experience. This effect is amplified if the narrator also is mentally disturbed, mute, or autistic. We have so far few examples of such narrators in children's fiction.

EXERCISE

Examine the narrators in some of the following texts: *And to Think That I Saw it on Mulberry Street*, *Roll of Thunder*, *Daddy-Long-Legs*, *Dance on My Grave*, *Jacob Have I Loved*, and *Walk Two Moons*, in terms of their reliability. What factors affect your judgment?

Besides the young narrators' inexperience, some reasons to doubt their reliability can be, for instance, the nature of the story. The narrator of *Mulberry Street* is most likely making up the whole adventure, while Jerusha is conscientiously rendering what is happening to her. Another factor is the agitated state at the moment of narration. Both Hal in *Dance on My Grave* and Sal in *Walk Two Moons* are grieving for the loss of their loved ones, and grief can distort their objectivity. Louise in *Jacob Have I Loved* renders the events of the past, but she may remember them wrong, and her memory may be affected by the strong emotions she once felt and still feels toward her sister.

THE VOICE AND THE VIEW

Narrative theory has given us considerably more precise instruments to analyze perspective. Already from the examples discussed above, it should be clear that the simple distinction between personal and impersonal narrators is insufficient to describe the wide variety of narrative perspective we encounter in children's fiction. Let us therefore examine the different aspects of narration more systematically.

Narrator's Presence in the Text

Narrative theory makes a distinction between mimesis ("showing") and diegesis ("telling"), which naturally goes back to the difference between drama and epic. Aristotelian poetics claims that narrators should be as inconspicuous as possible, that showing is preferable. Shakespeare has been universally praised for not interfering in the events of his plays, letting the events and the characters "speak for themselves." With the rise of the novel in the eighteenth century, a shift toward telling rather than showing became evident, while contemporary prose has primarily gone back to figural discourse, thus to showing. Discussing which mode is best is fruitless; yet we can observe that conventional children's literature, with its openly didactic tone, tends to have a clear narrative voice, moreover, an authoritarian adult voice which can manipulate young readers toward a correct understanding of the depicted events and characters.

LET US EXPLORE

Contemplate the narrators' presence in some of the following children's books: *The Adventures of Tom Sawyer; The Wizard of Oz; Winnie-the-Pooh; The Lion, the Witch and the Wardrobe;* and *The Cat in the Hat.* Consider the following: Is the narrator a character in the story? How does the narrator have access to the information he conveys? Do we actually hear the narrator referring to himself? Does the narrator comment on the events and characters; does he come with judgments and opinions? How do these comments and judgments affect the reader?

Your first reaction to the assignment was probably, "That's easy." In *The Cat in the Hat* we have a narrator who is also a character in the story, so he is overtly present in the text, we hear his voice, and we hear him referring to himself in the first person, as "I." In all the other books, the narrators are covert, that is, not manifest in the texts. On closer examination, we see that in these other texts, the narrators are also highly perceptible. Consider the following sentence from *Tom Sawyer*: "If [Tom] had been a great and wise philosopher, like the writer of this book . . ." (19). This comment draws our attention to the fact that the story is indeed narrated, that is does not "narrate itself," that there is an agency behind the narration that can comment on the events, judge the characters, and even decide what to narrate and what to omit. When Tom makes a blunder in Sunday school, saying that the first apostles' names were David and Goliath, the narrator says, "Let us draw the curtain of charity over the rest of the scene" (36). He thus has the power to skip over the embarrassing episode, leaving it to the reader's imagination.

In the first chapter of *Winnie-the-Pooh* we meet an overt narrator telling a bedtime story for his son, who is also a character in this bedtime story. In the following chapters, this overt adult narrator takes a step back and in the sequel, *The House at Pooh Corner*, disappears completely. In *The Lion, the Witch and the Wardrobe*, the narrator, who mostly stays in the background, steps forward every now and then with comments such as, "And now we come to one of the nastiest things in this story" (44), or revealing himself, "How long this really lasted I don't know" (86). In contrast, in *The Wizard of Oz* we will hardly find any traces of the narrator's overt presence in the form of comments, judgments, or self-references. This form of covert narrator leads some critics to claim that the story "narrates itself."

Yet, narrative theory suggests other indicators of the narrator's presence besides direct comments: descriptions of settings, descriptions of characters, invocation of the reader or narratee, narrative summaries, reported speech or thought, and comments on story and discourse. The first two features are self-explanatory. Somebody must be describing the scenery or interiors and the characters' looks, unless the description is figural; that is, the setting or a character's exterior are presented through another character's eyes. When a reader (or narratee) is directly invoked by the narrator, it naturally draws our attention to the narrator's presence. In *The Lion, the Witch and the Wardrobe*, the narrator addresses the reader, "Have you ever had a gallop on a horse? Think of that; and then take away the heavy noise of the hoofs. . . . And then imagine you are going about twice as fast as the fastest racehorse" (149). A narrative summary implies that events taking place for some time are rendered in a more compact form (see chapter 5 on temporality). An extreme form of summary is a sentence such as, "Three years passed." Since this is naturally a case of telling rather than showing, some narrative agency must be involved.

Reported speech or thought implies that what the characters say or think is not rendered directly, but is mediated through a narrative agency. Dealing with direct speech, we assume that we hear the character's exact words, perceiving them as "non-narrated." In reported speech, we hear the narrator's words. We cannot be sure whether the character's exact words are used, or whether the narrator only mediates a short version of what the character has actually said, or whether the narrator has manipulated or even distorted the character's original utterance.

Comments on story, that is, events, happenings, and characters, also come from a narrator. They may include interpretations, judgments, or generalizations. Moreover, a narrator can comment on his own narration, thus destroying the fictional illusion. A much-quoted example from the mainstream is chapter 13 in *The French Lieutenant's Woman*, in which the narrator reflects on his own plot and characters. Although such openly metafictive comments in children's fiction are rare, they do occur. The narrator in *Dance on My Grave* constantly complains about his problems in narrating the story properly.

EXERCISE

Read a children's novel of your own choice carefully and note all the occurrences of the narrator's presence in the text. You may be amazed to discover how conspicuous the narrator is, although normally we do not pay much attention to it. Try to find at least one example of each indicator. Which are dominant? How does the narrator's presence affect you as a reader? Are the narrator's comments helpful or annoying? How do you think a young reader responds to them? Using a commutation test, try to make the narrator more or less perceptible and see how this affects the narrative.

In children's fiction, narrators are not seldom intrusive, meddling in the story with their comments and direct address to the reader. This interference makes many narrators didactic or authoritative: they explain every reason for the characters' behavior, condemning their faults and mistakes, and thus leaving very little room for the readers' own reflections. A didactic narrator addresses the reader in comments, explanations, and exhortations, allowing no ambiguity. Such a narrator has more knowledge and experience than both the young readers and the characters, which means that he acts in a superior manner. When the narrator is covert, such comments are likely to escape our attention, resulting in our failing to recognize the didactic tone of the text.

From all these observations, we may come to the conclusion that the narrative voice in children's fiction most often belongs to an adult. This fact demonstrates yet another inevitable dilemma of children's fiction, as well as its aesthetic characteristic: there is a discrepancy between the cognitive and emotional level of the narrator and that of both the young character and the young reader. The many successful attempts by contemporary writers to circumvent this discrepancy by using either a first-person child narrator or an introspective impersonal narrator do not eliminate the dilemma as such.

Narrative Levels and the Narrator's Relation to the Story

LET US EXPLORE

Contemplate the narrator's relationship to the narrated story in some of the following texts: *Little Women*; *The Adventures of Tom Sawyer*; *Treasure Island*; *Winnie-the-Pooh*; *The Catcher in the Rye*; *Ramona the Pest*; *Bridge to Terabithia*; and *Roll of Thunder, Hear My Cry*. Is the narrator inside or outside the story he is telling? Is he telling the story as it unfolds or from a distance?

Contemporary narrative theory has given us many useful tools to describe and analyze the narrator's relation to what is narrated. Some of the concepts are derived from the levels of the narrative. The level where the story takes place is called *diegetic* (from "diegesis"—telling, that is, the fictional level). All events and characters featured on this level are part of the story. Let us call it level zero. Normally, it is the only narrative level in a text. There may, however, be other levels, both above and below the zero level. The level above the zero level is called *metadiegetic* ("meta" = over, above), and the level below is called *hypodiegetic* ("hypo" = below). The question of which level should be considered zero, the diegetic level, is a matter of interpretation. If the adventures in the Hundred Acre Wood are perceived as the diegetic level, then the frame in which the father is telling his son bedtime stories is metadiegetic. If the level in which father and son are sitting in the study is the diegetic level, then all narratives concerning Pooh and his friends are hypodiegetic. (See fig. 8-2.)

Theoretically, there may be narratives with a considerably larger number

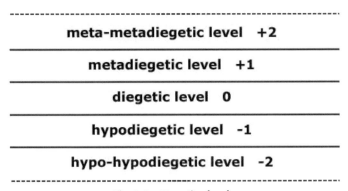

meta-metadiegetic level   +2

metadiegetic level   +1

diegetic level   0

hypodiegetic level   -1

hypo-hypodiegetic level   -2

Fig. 8-2   Narrative levels.

of levels. They abound in mainstream literature (*The Canterbury Tales, Decameron*) and in folklore (*Arabian Nights*), where character A tells a story about a character B who tells a story about a character C—and so on. If the level on which character A appears is diegetic, and the level on which character B appears is hypodiegetic, then the level on which character C appears must be called hypo-hypodiegetic, and so on. Such structures are rare in children's literature, but it is useful to be aware of the possibility. The recognition of the interconnection between levels and the relationship between the narrators at different levels is essential in order to assess the story and to understand how we as readers make meaning of the information we receive from the narrative. (See fig. 8-3.)

Let us go further in examining the various possibilities of narrators' involvement. First: how is the narrator connected to the narrative level? A narrator appearing on the same level as the story he is telling is called *homodiegetic* ("identical with fiction"). He is, in other words, one of the characters in his own story. If he also is the protagonist in his own story, he is *autodiegetic*. A narrator appearing on another level is called *heterodiegetic* ("nonidentical with fiction"). He is not a character in the story he is telling.

Second: what is the narrator's distance from the narrative? A narrator telling the story as it is happening, without distance, is called *intradiegetic* ("inside fiction"). A narrator who is telling from a distance, for instance in retrospect, is called *extradiegetic* ("outside fiction"). Observe that in this classification, we do not make any difference between personal and impersonal narration. A personal narrator telling about his childhood and an impersonal narrator telling about a character's childhood are both extradiegetic.

The two binaries give us four combinations regarding the narrator's involvement in the text, as shown in figure 8-4.

An extradiegetic-heterodiegetic narrator is outside the narrative at the time of narration, and is not a character in the story. This is the narrator whom we most often call omniscient and omnipresent, as in *Little Women* or *Tom Sawyer*. We assume that this narrator is an adult person. This means that in children's fiction there is always a great discrepancy between an extra-

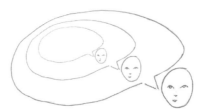

Fig. 8-3   Multilevel narrators.

Presence / Distance	Heterodiegetic	Homodiegetic
Extradiegetic	Extradiegetic-heterodiegetic	Extradiegetic-homodiegetic
Intradiegetic	Intradiegetic-heterodiegetic	Intradiegetic-homodiegetic

Fig. 8-4 Types of narrator.

diegetic-heterodiegetic narrator and the character, a more noticeable discrepancy than in adult literature.

An extradiegetic-homodiegetic narrator is outside the story during the narrative act, but is a character in this story. The conventional term for such a narrator would be personal retrospective, for instance in *Treasure Island* and *The Catcher in the Rye*. In the first book, the narrator is an adult man telling the story of his youth, and the temporal gap between the narrative act and the story is many years. In the second book, the temporal gap is one year, and the narrator is still a young person. This of course makes the narrative quite different than it would be if a sophisticated adult were telling the story.

If an extradiegetic narrator appears on a different level than the story as a character and not merely a voice, we can call such a narrator *metadiegetic* or *hypodiegetic* respectively. The father in *Winnie-the-Pooh* is a metadiegetic narrator. Anne telling Marilla about her visit to the concert is a hypodiegetic narrator. Theoretically, we can also find meta-metadiegetic as well as hypo-hypodiegetic narrators, and so on. In modern experimental prose, extradiegetic narrators sometimes enter their own stories and thus become intradiegetic. So far this is a very rare, but not totally nonexistent phenomenon in children's fiction.

An intradiegetic-heterodiegetic narrator means that the narrator is telling the story without a distance, but is not a character. This is what we have earlier called impersonal introspection. In some contemporary novels for children, narrative present tense is used, which amplifies the sense of immediacy. But even in a past-tense narrative, an illusion may be created that the narrator is just behind the character and possesses no greater knowledge than the character. *Ramona* books and *Bridge to Terabithia* are examples of such narrators. Although we still assume that the narrator is an adult, especially if the vocabulary is more advanced than that which a child would use, this adult does not talk down to his readers.

An intradiegetic-homodiegetic narrator is narrating the story as it unfolds and is also a character in it. Cassie in *Roll of Thunder, Hear My Cry* is a good example. The gap between the narrative act and the story is minimal; it seems "as if" the narrator is telling the story just as it is happening. Fictitious diaries, a popular form in both classical and contemporary children's literature, also involves this type of narrator, for instance in *Daddy-Long-Legs* and in *The Secret Diary of Adrian Mole, Aged 13 3/4*. Intradiegetic-homodiegetic narrators in children's fiction are most often children, which means that only through this form can we hear something that we perceive as a "genuine" child voice, sometimes an inner voice. Adult narrators who participate in the events are not very common, but not altogether impossible. In Lloyd Alexander's Vesper series, the narrator is the protagonist's guardian, an adult man. This narrative mode creates a distance between the character and the reader.

A homodiegetic narrator who is also the protagonist is autodiegetic, he is telling his own story. It may seem that this is always the case, but as already shown, Cassie Logan is not telling about herself, but rather about other people and events. In contrast, Holden is telling us exclusively about himself, his feelings, and thoughts. He is an autodiegetic narrator. Sal in *Walk Two Moons* is an interesting case. Seemingly, she is telling about her friend Phoebe, Phoebe's mother, and Phoebe's "lunatic." On closer examination, Sal is revealing her own story, in a kind of self-therapy; she is then of course an autodiegetic narrator.

Similar terms can be applied to narratees: a homodiegetic narratee is a character in the story, an intradiegetic narratee appears on the same level as the story, and so on. If we assume that the narrator is telling the story to himself (for instance, recalling memories of the past), the narratee is autodiegetic.

EXERCISE

Find examples of children's novels illustrating the four main types of narrators. On the basis of the text, discuss the advantages and disadvantages of each type. Try some commutations to support your argument.

Point of View

Besides the different narrative voices, writers can vary narrative technique by using different points of view. The narrative voice refers to the agency that speaks in the text. Point of view refers to the agency through whose eyes and mind we experience the events. Although it might seem that these agencies always coincide, in practice they seldom do, except in the case of intra-diegetic-homodiegetic narrators.

Further, the concept of point of view can be used in three senses:

1. Literal, or perceptual, point of view implies that the reader sees the described events from a certain vantage point, which may be an impersonal narrator's (we see the events in *Tom Sawyer* from outside), a personal narrator's (we see the events in *Roll of Thunder* through Cassie's eyes), or a character's (we see the events in *Bridge to Terabithia* through Jess's eyes).

2. Figurative, conceptual, or ideological point of view implies that the reader is presented with certain thoughts, beliefs, and opinions—again either a narrator's or a character's. For instance, *Roll of Thunder* is clearly told from the position that ethnic discrimination is unacceptable.

3. Transferred, or interest, point of view implies that the story is told from someone's interest vantage, for a certain purpose, for instance in defense (Louise is trying to justify her attitude toward her sister) or, as in Sal's case, as self-therapy.

In concrete texts the three types of point of view do not necessarily coincide. In *The Lion, the Witch and the Wardrobe* the perceptual point of view is the children's. But when Father Christmas says that women should not participate in battle, an adult, ideological point of view is imposed on the reader (cf. the argument on the implied author above). When Anne Shirley wakes up on her first morning and sees the beautiful landscape from the window, we read, "She has seen so few attractive places in her life, poor child." Without the comment, "poor child," we as readers would share Anne's perceptual point of view, seeing the cherry tree and the flowers through her eyes. The statement "poor child" is the narrator's and has a clear ideological tone: the narrator feels sorry for children who grow up in a poor environment. The interaction of points of view allows an endless variety of narrative perspective, but at the same time it also implies authorial manipulation, since adult values can be imposed on young readers, although they may share the child characters' perceptual point of view, as in examples above.

Point of view in a text can be fixed or variable. In a personal narrative, point of view is of course always fixed. In an impersonal narrative, it can stay consistently with one and the same character throughout the story (*Bridge to Terabithia*) or alternate between characters (*The Lion, the Witch and the Wardrobe*) or just occasionally shift onto a secondary character to provide an additional standpoint (*Tom Sawyer*). Thus while the narrative voice is unchanged, the alternating point of view can add to the variation of narrative technique.

EXERCISE

Find examples of novels illustrating the different points of view. Pay special attention to the discrepancy between the narrative voice and the point of view.

Focalization

Focalization is an additional concept that allows us more precise examination of narrative perspective. Focalization denotes a limitation of the information that the narrator allows to reach the reader through the focalizing character (or focalizer). Focalization thus implies manipulation with point of view, resulting in our perceiving the narrative as if it were told by the focalizing character. This "as-if" narration deceives the reader and pushes the actual narrator into the background. In children's fiction, an adult narrator is most often combined with a focalizing child character, which creates an illusion that the events are rendered through the child's eyes and mind.

The concept of focalization thus helps us to separate the narrator from the character whose point of view is imposed on us, since it is connected to both the narrator's presence in the text and the character's point of view. Being connected to the point of view, focalization can also be fixed or variable. Further, there are three focalization patterns that can be used in a narrative (see fig. 8-5):

- *Zero focalization*: narrator sees and knows more than the focalized character (for instance, what other characters think).
- *External focalization*: narrator sees and knows less than the focalized character (for instance, does not know what the character thinks).
- *Internal focalization*: narrator sees and knows as much as the focalized character.

One of the most revolutionary discoveries in contemporary narrative theory is that there is no radical difference between personal and impersonal narra-

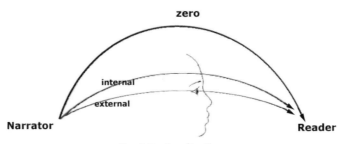

Fig. 8-5   Focalization.

tors if we apply the concept of focalization. The only difference is that impersonal narrators focalize characters, and such focalization can be variable, while personal narrators focalize themselves, either simultaneously or in retrospect, externally or internally, and this focalization is always fixed. The pattern of focalization proves to be more important than the difference between the personal and the impersonal voice. We have already seen that impersonal narrators often have very distinct voices and refer to themselves as "I"; in other cases this omniscient "I" is simply hidden, covert, imperceptible.

The concept of focalization gives us more precise tools to analyze narrative perspective. We have earlier classified *The Lion, the Witch and the Wardrobe* as having an omniscient narrator. This is still true, yet this omniscience is combined with a variety of focalization patterns, external as well as internal. We are usually trained to share the subjectivity with focalizing characters (or do this by intuition), assuming that they also are the main characters. In *The Lion, the Witch and the Wardrobe*, of the four children, Lucy is most often used as a focalizer, which prompts us to view her as the protagonist. She is not only the focalizer in the chapters where she is on her own, but also when she is part of the group. Edmund is naturally the focalizer, internal and external, in the chapters where he is on his own, but also in other situations. Peter is very seldom used as a focalizing character, and Susan hardly ever. Aslan, the central figure of the book, but definitely not its protagonist, is never a focalizer. Instead, Lucy is allowed to guess his feelings. Since Aslan is not even an external focalizer, the dramatic episode of his sacrificial death must be told from some other's point of view, so Lucy and Susan are allowed to follow him unseen—a very common narrative device, when the narrator or the focalizer "happens" to be present to witness an important event which they otherwise would never learn about.

Focalization in *The Lion, the Witch and the Wardrobe* is variable, which may seem natural with a collective character. In *Homecoming*, also featuring a group of children, only Dicey is focalized. She is therefore perceived as the sole protagonist of the novel.

EXERCISE

Analyze focalization in some of the following texts: *The Wizard of Oz, Little House in the Big Woods, Charlotte's Web, Ramona the Pest, Homecoming, The Great Gilly Hopkins, The Giver,* and *Holes.* By way of commutation test, try to change focalizers as well as focalization patterns (zero, external, internal) and see how it affects the narrative. Contemplate why the author's choice of focalization pattern is the most effective (or maybe why it is not).

Narrative Voice and Point of View

The difference between narrative voice (who is speaking) and point of view (who is seeing) is crucial in a children's book. The narrator's point of view does not have to coincide with the character's, and indeed, in traditional children's literature, it most often does not, because the narrator is an authoritarian, educating adult. Further, the reader may also have a different point of view, which most often is imposed on the reader by the point of view of the narratee, whether the narratee is overt or covert. The discrepancy between the point of view of the narrator and the narratee is called *slant*. The slant in a text can be fixed or variable. If the slant changes throughout the text it may move in different directions as well as back and forth. Most often, however, authors try to create an illusion that there is no slant in the text, that is, that the reader knows as much as the narrator. A very simple example is that the narrator may know all along that the silver shoes can take Dorothy back to Kansas, but withholds this information. Slant makes narrators unreliable, but in a slanted narrative there may be "cracks" which hint that the narrator, consciously or not, omits important information, distorts it, or adds details. When the narrator in *The Lion, the Witch and the Wardrobe* tells us that Turkish Delight is enchanted, we become aware that the narrator obviously knows more than he chooses to reveal.

The discrepancy between the narratee's and the focalizing character's point of view is called *filter*. In a filtered narrative the reader knows and understands more than the character, and an ironic effect is achieved. Even small children apparently realize what happens when Pooh tries to catch a Woozle and follows his own footprints, although it is not mentioned explicitly in the text until later. In some respects, filter is similar to the device called *estrangement*: describing familiar things as if they were unfamiliar. Sometimes, this will only work for the adult co-reader. For instance, when

Lucy meets a strange creature in Narnia, adult readers may understand from the description what the creature was, but apparently neither Lucy nor the reader are expected to know this, so the writer hurries to add, "It was a faun."

A filtered narrative tells us more about the protagonists and their perception of the events than about the events themselves. In a way, the narrator and the narratee are communicating over the protagonist's head, and the reader, sharing the narratee's point of view, is allowed to make inferences beyond the protagonist's grasp. In children's literature, this may appear as a sign of the author's trust in the reader, since adult authors address young readers on equal terms. On the other hand, as already suggested, young readers are trained to adopt the characters' subjectivity, most often by sharing their point of view. When this reading strategy is deliberately impeded, young readers may feel frustrated, or on the contrary, they may find satisfaction in their superiority over the character. The delicate balance between having confidence in the young readers' ability to disengage themselves from characters and evoking enough empathy to involve the reader is one of the many dilemmas of contemporary children's writers.

If a narrator is also a character in his own story, the narrative can be both slanted and filtered. This is the case of Holden's narration in *The Catcher in the Rye* or Louise's narration in *Jacob Have I Loved*. In a filtered personal narrative, the narratee, and thus the reader, know and understand more than both the narrator and the character. (See fig. 8-6.)

Both slant and filter denote shifts in point of view between the central agents of the narrative act: the narrator, the character, and the narratee. In children's fiction, slant and filter will probably work differently for sophisticated and unsophisticated readers. Sophisticated readers may decode a filtered narrative better than naive readers because of greater life experience. A writer can deliberately use slant and filter so that children and adult co-readers will enjoy the different aspects of texts. In many modern picture books, the text tells the story from a child's point of view, while pictures reflect an adult's point of view, and occasionally the other way round.

Multiple and Mixed Narration

Contemporary children's and especially young adult fiction has successfully experimented with narrative perspective, resulting in stories with extremely complex narrative structure. In a multiple-plot narrative (see chapter 5), there may naturally be different narrators. In *Holes*, one narrative is focalized through Stanley, while the other narrative is zero focalized. But a single plot may also involve more than one narrator. *Harriet the Spy* combines impersonal narration with Harriet's notes. *Dance on My Grave* has two personal narrators, Hal and the female social worker investigating his case. The

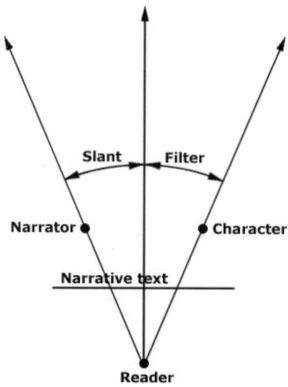

Fig. 8-6   Slant and filter.

two narratives reflect and complement each other, since the social worker does not have access to the information that Hal possesses. Further, at one point, Hal chooses to render a difficult episode in third person, referring to himself as "he." This is a good illustration of our sense of impersonal narration's being more detached. Finally, two newspaper clippings add a seemingly objective picture of the events, which of course from Hal's point of view is highly erroneous. In *Breaktime*, Ditto also switches between personal and impersonal narration, and some excerpts from a travel guide as well as Benjamin Spock's parenting manual are inserted in the narrative—an example of "non-narrated" texts. *I Am the Cheese* alternates between personal narration and transcripts of tape-recorded conversations. We can ask ourselves why contemporary authors choose multiple and heterogeneous narrators; one possible answer is that they attempt to reflect a modern adolescent's ambivalent and fragmented worldview. This trend is also found in the postmodern aesthetics.

Some Concluding Remarks

It looks as though in their narrative strategy, children's authors are inevitably torn between two incompatible desires: to educate and socialize the child, or to take the child's part. If the nineteenth-century authors tended to be overdidactic, we may perhaps state that contemporary authors have gone to the other extreme. When children's writers choose to let their narrators take a definite step back, readers are left without any guidance as to the characters and events depicted. Readers must themselves decide whether characters are morally acceptable, whether their openly expressed feelings are sincere, and whether they act on impulse or by conviction. To foist such decisions on the readers is demanding of them, for the adult author is addressing young readers on equal terms. We may applaud the effort but doubt the results.

Sophisticated readers may be expected to be able to liberate themselves from the subjectivity imposed by the text. Unsophisticated, or naive, readers, children and adults alike, often automatically adopt the subjectivity set by the text. A naive reader is unable to recognize the irony created by the discrepancy between the voice and the point of view and, at best, will be confused if these pose attitudes and opinions that are too far apart. From their inferior power position, young readers are more likely to listen to an adult narrative voice, while they at the same time are persuaded, by the age of the child characters, to share their subjectivity. While the split and fluctuating subjectivity has become a token and a conscious narrative strategy in postmodern literature, it is perhaps less desirable in literature geared toward readers whose sense of self is not quite established yet. On the other hand, it is exactly those books in which the didactic narrative agency has taken a step back that scholars of children's literature value highest, such as *Bridge to Terabithia* or *Walk Two Moons*. It would be undesirable to call for a return to didactic writing for children. Yet, another danger of naive reading is that readers may fail to recognize covert ideologies, whether they are expressed by the narrator or by the character. As we know, covert ideologies are more effective than explicit ones.

The contemporary children's and adolescent novel tends to put its implied readers into active subject positions. While as critics we undoubtedly welcome such narrative strategies, they do present a number of problems. If we want to train children to be critical readers, we must first ourselves learn to identify the ways children's writers, consciously or subconsciously, manipulate their texts and thus their readers in the construction of subjectivity. Narrative theory has provided us with adequate tools for this task.

HOW TO GO FURTHER

Some more advanced studies of narrative perspective are based on speech act theory and the modes of mental representation, briefly discussed in chapter 7. Such books as *Transparent Minds*, by Dorrit Cohn; *Unspeakable Sentences*, by Ann Banfield; and *The Fictions of Language and the Languages of Fiction*, by Monika Fludernik, offer a number of sophisticated analytical tools and elaborate terminology for the various modes for depicting consciousness. The narrative techniques in which the narrator's discourse is blended with the character's discourse hold the focus of attention in these studies. Generally speaking, the narrative perspective has perhaps received more critical attention than any other formal aspect of literature. Modernistic experimental fiction offers new challenging material for such studies, but it is also amazing how many "daring" and "innovative" techniques can be discovered in classic nineteenth-century novels.

In the field of children's literature, the study of narrative perspective is a relatively new direction. The subtleties of personal and impersonal narration and their implications specifically for children's literature have recently occupied a number of scholars, but no full-scale examination has appeared as yet. Here lies a vast area for future investigations.

REFERENCES

Aristotle. "Poetics." In *Classical Literary Criticism*. Harmondsworth: Penguin, 1965.

Austin, J. L. *How to Do Things with Words*. New York: Oxford University Press, 1962. The fundamental work of speech act theory.

Bakhtin, Mikhail. "Author and Hero in Aesthetic Activity." Pp. 4–256 in his *Art and Answerability: Early Philosophical Essays*. Austin: University of Texas Press, 1990. Bakhtin discusses the relationship between the voice of the narrator and the consciousness of the character, resulting in "dual-voice discourse," which later narratologists have labeled free indirect discourse.

Bal, Mieke. *Narratology: Introduction to the Theory of Narrative*. 2nd ed. Toronto: University of Toronto Press, 1997. Part 1, "Text: Words."

Banfield, Ann. *Unspeakable Sentences: Narration and Representation in the Language of Fiction*. Boston: Routledge and Kegan Paul, 1982.

Booth, Wayne C. *The Rhetoric of Fiction*. Chicago: University of Chicago Press, 1961. The groundbreaking work on narration.

Cadden, Mike. "The Irony of Narration in the Young Adult Novel." *Children's Literature Association Quarterly* 25, no. 3 (2000): 146–154.

Chatman, Seymour. *Story and Discourse: Narrative Structure in Fiction and Film*. Ithaca, NY: Cornell University Press, 1978. Chap. 4, "Nonnarrated Stories"; chap. 5, "Covert Versus Overt Narrators."

———. *Coming to Terms*. Ithaca, NY: Cornell University Press, 1990. In this study, Chatman introduces the concepts of slant and filter.

Cohn, Dorrit. *Transparent Minds: Narrative Modes for Presenting Consciousness in Fiction*. Princeton, NJ: Princeton University Press, 1978.

Fludernik, Monika. *The Fictions of Language and the Languages of Fiction: The Linguistic Representation of Speech and Consciousness.* London: Routledge, 1993.

Genette, Gérard. *Narrative Discourse: An Essay in Method.* Ithaca, NY: Cornell University Press, 1980.

———. *Narrative Discourse Revisited.* Ithaca, NY: Cornell University Press, 1988.

Golden, Joanne M. *The Narrative Symbol in Childhood Literature: Exploration in the Construction of Text.* Berlin: Mouton, 1990. Chap. 4, "Act: Narration."

Goodenough, Elizabeth, et al., eds. *Infant Tongues: The Voices of the Child in Literature.* Detroit: Wayne State University Press, 1994.

Hamburger, Käte. *The Logic of Literature.* 2nd revised edition. Bloomington, Indiana University Press, 1973.

Lanser, Susan Sniader. *The Narrative Act: Point of View in Prose Fiction.* Princeton, NJ: Princeton University Press, 1981.

Lukens, Rebecca J. *A Critical Handbook of Children's Literature.* 4th ed. New York: HarperCollins, 1990. Chap. 7, "Point of View."

McCallum, Robyn. *Ideologies of Identity in Adolescent Fiction: The Dialogic Construction of Subjectivity.* New York: Garland, 1999.

McGillis, Roderick. "The Embrace: Narrative Voice and Children's Books." *Canadian Children's Literature* 63 (1991): 24–40.

Nikolajeva, Maria. "The Child as Self-Deceiver: Narrative Strategies in Katherine Paterson's and Patricia MacLachlan's Novels." *Papers* 7, no. 1 (1997): 5–15.

———. "Imprints of the Mind: The Depiction of Consciousness in Children's Literature." *Children's Literature Association Quarterly* 26, no. 4 (2001): 173–187.

———. *The Rhetoric of Character in Children's Fiction.* Lanham, MD: Scarecrow, 2002. Chap. 12, "Internal Representation."

———. "The Art of Self-deceit: Narrative Strategies in Katherine Paterson's Novels." Pp. 10–33 in *Bridges for the Young: The Fiction of Katherine Paterson*, edited by Joel Chaston and Sarah Smedman. Lanham, MD: Scarecrow, 2002.

———. "Beyond the Grammar of Story, or How Can Children's Literature Criticism Benefit from Narrative Theory." *Children's Literature Association Quarterly* 28, no. 1 (2003): 5–16.

———. "Toward a Genuine Narrative Voice." *Bookbird* 42, no. 1 (2004): 13–18.

Nikolajeva, Maria, and Carole Scott. *How Picturebooks Work.* New York: Garland, 2001. Chap. 4, "Narrative Perspective."

Otten, Charlotte von, and Gary D. Smith, eds. *The Voice of the Narrator in Children's Literature: Insights from Writers and Critics.* New York: Greenwood, 1989.

Pratt, Mary Louise. *Toward a Speech Act Theory of Literary Discourse.* Bloomington: Indiana University Press, 1977.

Rimmon-Kenan, Shlomith. *Narrative Fiction: Contemporary Poetics.* London: Routledge, 1983. Chap. 6, "Focalization"; chap. 7, "Narration: Levels and Voices."

Searle, John R. *Speech Acts: An Essay in the Philosophy of Language.* Cambridge: Cambridge University Press, 1969.

Wall, Barbara. *The Narrator's Voice: The Dilemma of Children's Fiction.* London: Macmillan, 1991.

Wyile, Andrea Schwenke. "Expanding the View of First-Person Narration." *Children's Literature in Education* 30, no. 4 (1999): 185–202.

———. "The Value of Singularity in First- and Restricted Third-person Engaging Narration." *Children's Literature* 31 (2003): 116–141.

9

The Aesthetic of Language

One of the most common prejudices about children's fiction is that it utilizes simple and meager language as compared to general fiction. The immediate reaction to such a statement is to ask what exactly is meant by simple and meager. It is true that children's fiction normally does not employ sentences expanding to whole paragraphs or even pages, but not all kinds and genres of fiction geared toward an adult audience do so either. It is also true that children's writers tend to avoid uncommon words that are unlikely to be familiar to their readers, or words denoting abstract notions beyond the scope of their readers' experience. The simplicity of language may, however, be a deliberate artistic device, comparable to the sparseness of certain kinds of poetry, such as haiku. The repetitive nature of some children's stories is also a conscious device, well-known from the oral tradition, used as a support for memory. Verbal repetition in children's fiction, besides structuring the story itself, can be a means to enrich and train the readers' vocabulary, that is, to serve for the overall didactic purpose of children's literature. Many children's writers are well aware of the educational potentials of language acquisition through literature and make a point of it in their texts.

A certain direction of children's literature studies focused on language has developed an elaborate system for determining the quality of texts by calculating a readability index, involving the length of words and sentences, the number of words per sentence, and other external criteria (an approach to literature marvelously ridiculed in the film *Dead Poets Society*). Some of these studies have shown that books by renowned children's writers, such as Astrid Lindgren, are, by these criteria, significantly less reader friendly than an average mainstream novel text. Obviously, the simplicity or complexity of language lies in something other than the length of sentences.

Linguistic Adaptations

Unfortunately, the presumption about simple language often leads to ferocious interference in children's classics. Several critics have pointed out the injudicious treatment of language in modern retellings of *The Tale of Peter Rabbit*. Compare the original,

> Once upon a time there were four little Rabbits, and their names were—
> > Flopsy,
> > > Mopsy,
> > Cottontail,
> and Peter.
> They lived with their Mother in a sand-bank, underneath the root of a very big fir-tree.
> "Now, my dears," said Old Mother Rabbit one morning, "you may go into the fields or down the lane, but don't go into Mr. McGregor's garden: your father had an accident there; he was put in a pie by Mrs. McGregor."

with a modern retelling,

> Once upon a time there were four little rabbits. Their names were Flopsy, Mopsy, Cottontail, and Peter. They lived in a burrow under the root of a big tree. One day they were allowed to play outside. "Stay near home," said their mother. "Please don't go to Mr. McGregor's garden."
> "Why not?" asked Peter.
> "Because he doesn't like rabbits," answered Mrs. Rabbit. "He will try to catch you."

The scope of alterations is enormous, from the personal style and sentence structure to a complete change in characterization, from the elimination of irony to text layout. This is, however, far from unique. Here follows the beginning of a retelling of *The Wizard of Oz*:

> Dorothy lived with her Aunt Em and Uncle Henry. She had a small dog called Toto.
> One day there was a whirlwind. Dorothy and Toto were alone in the house. The whirlwind lifted them high up into the sky.
> The house came to rest in the Land of the Munchkins. It fell on top of the Wicked Witch of the East and killed her.
> The Munchkins were very pleased. They gave Dorothy the Wicked Witch of the East's magic shoes. (*Eric Kincaid's Book of Fairy Tales*, 76–77)

Weighed against the original, this plot summary—for this boiled-down text is nothing else—has lost the richness of detail, every aspect of characterization, and, not least, the sense of wonder as Dorothy finds herself in an unfamiliar realm. It has also completely lost the individual style of the original. Compare:

> Dorothy lived in the midst of the great Kansas prairies, with Uncle Henry, who was a farmer, and Aunt Em, who was the farmer's wife. Their house was small, for the lumber to build it had to be carried by wagon many miles. There were four walls, a floor and a roof, which made one room; and this room contained a rusty looking cooking stove, a cupboard for the dishes, a table, three or four chairs, and the beds. Uncle Henry and Aunt Em had a big bed in one corner, and Dorothy a little bed in another corner. (7)

And so on, for two more pages before the cyclone comes along. In the plot, this establishing scene is necessary as a contrast to the imminent adventures in the land of Oz. In terms of style, it is a vivid description that triggers the reader's imagination. It has a soft and slow, fairy-tale-like rhythm, totally broken in the short, choppy sentences of the retelling. It uses juxtaposition in the imagery (great prairies—small house, big bed—little bed), parallelism ("who was . . . who was . . ."), enumeration, and in general does not avoid complex sentence structure. Since one of the many purposes of children's literature is to develop the child's linguistic proficiency, we may only wonder what purpose retellings like the one cited may serve. Critics who have looked into the matter claim that simplification is the result of ignorance about the extensive research into children's literature and into the young readers' appreciation of literary texts. We could add that it is a token of disrespect for young readers and their mental capacity.

EXERCISE

Find a retelling of a well-known children's book (there are retellings and "condensations" of *The Wizard of Oz* other than the one discussed above; some other suggestions are *Alice in Wonderland*, *Pinocchio*, or Andersen's fairy tales) and compare it to the original in terms of language. Pay special attention to the following aspects:

- Have compound sentences with subordinate clauses, participle constructions, and other multipart structures been consistently replaced by short, simple ones?
- Have polysyllabic and less common words been deleted?
- Has the language been "updated" to modern usages?
- Have descriptions been eliminated?
- Has direct speech been replaced by summaries?
- Have complex imagery and figurative language been replaced by simple substitutes or been eliminated?

- Have irony and ambiguity been eliminated (such as the "accident" of Mr. Rabbit's in the above-mentioned retelling)?

How does this simplification affect our understanding of the text? How does it affect our aesthetic appreciation? What do you think the reteller's incentive was in tampering with the original?

Educational Aspects of Language

Many children's writers seem to use difficult words as a conscious device to arouse the reader's curiosity and enrich their vocabulary. Falling through the rabbit hole, Alice wonders, "'what Latitude or Longitude I've got to?' (Alice had not the slightest idea what Latitude was, or Longitude either, but she thought they were grand words to say)" (17). Apart from characterizing the protagonist, the passage hopefully encourages the readers to find out the meaning of the words. Occasionally, we may wonder whether writers overestimate their audience's vocabulary. Continuing the fall, Alice goes on with her soliloquy: "'I wonder if I shall fall right *through* the earth! How funny it'll seem to come out among the people that walk with their heads downwards! The antipathies, I think—' (she was rather glad there *was* no one listening, this time, as it didn't sound at all the right word)" (17; italics in the original). Sure enough, it is not, but Carroll does not provide his readers with the correct word—antipodes—apparently assuming that they, unlike Alice, know it. It is, however, doubtful that young readers will indeed know both words and the difference between them, so Carroll's play on words is more geared toward adults. He is quite aware of it, though, when he lets one of his characters comment on the use of obscure language:

> "In that case," said the Dodo solemnly, rising to his feet, "I move that the meeting adjourn, for the immediate adoption of more energetic remedies—"
> "Speak English!" said the Eaglet. "I don't know the meaning of half those long words, and, what's more, I don't believe you do either!" (33)

In *Winnie-the-Pooh*, Owl especially is characterized by using bizarre words: "Owl was telling Kanga an Interesting Anecdote full of long words like Encyclopaedia and Rhododendron" (110). For adults, the two words are rather incompatible, while for a young reader they probably make no sense at all. However, the writer frequently helps his readers by translating Owl's convoluted speech into a more everyday idiom:

> "The atmospheric conditions have been very unfavourable lately," said Owl.
> "The what?"
> "It has been raining," explained Owl.

"Yes," said Christopher Robin. "It has."
"The flood-level has reached an unprecedented height."
"The who?"
"There is a lot of water around," explained Owl. (127)

In the following sections, we will look at some approaches to the meaning and function of language in children's fiction. This is a vast area of research, so we can only touch upon a few aspects.

ELEMENTS OF STYLE

The language of fiction is different from the language of nonfiction in several respects. First, it is different in the communicative purpose. The purpose of a nonfiction text is to convey information. The language has to be precise and unambiguous—nonfiction does not allow a variety of interpretations. The purpose of a literary text may include conveying information, but in the first place it has an aesthetic function, to create an aesthetic experience. The language in a literary text is deliberately polysemantic and ambivalent; it not only allows but demands interpretation. It appeals to all our senses in its imagery, evoking sights, sounds, smells, tastes, and touch. It stimulates intellectual and emotional response.

Stylistic Devices

One of the foremost tokens of literary language is figurative speech, which is a collective label for the different uses of language other than its direct dictionary meaning. Figurative speech creates a dimension in a literary text that is absent from nonfiction. Once again, it is common prejudice about children's literature that figurative language should be used sparsely, since young readers have not yet developed an understanding of words having a meaning other than literal (cf. Ramona and the "present" in chapter 2). There is, in fact, some empirical research showing that young children have difficulties with such elements as metaphors, symbols, or irony. Yet, as has already been pointed out, one of the purposes of children's literature is to train and stimulate language acquisition, and many writers make it a special issue in their writing. In fact, while some common figures of speech are indeed used sparingly in children's literature, others acquire quite a different significance as compared to the mainstream. The following is not an exhaustive catalogue of stylistic devices, but some examples of the variety of their usage in children's stories.

A *simile* is one of the simplest stylistic devices, implying a stated comparison between two things and most often using the adverbs "like" or "as":

"away went Alice like the wind" (18). Anne Shirley tends to imagine that her hair is "a glorious black, black as a raven's wing" (17). Flying in her house, carried by the cyclone, Dorothy is "rocked gently, like a baby in a cradle" (10). When the Cowardly Lion has jumped over a ditch, with Dorothy on his back, he is panting "like a big dog that has been running too long" (58). Similes are normally easy to understand and are widely used in children's novels. Yet similes can also be quite complex and demanding, such as this one, describing Jess trying to grasp that his friend Leslie is dead: "the words turned over uneasily in his mind like leaves stirred up by a cold wind" (106).

Unlike simile, a *metaphor* is an implied comparison, for instance when Anne says, once again creating an ideal image of herself, "My hair is of midnight darkness and my skin is a clear ivory pallor" (a simile would be "my hair is as dark as midnight"). By the end of the novel, Anne uses more elaborate imagery, such as, "I'm not a bit changed—not really. I'm only just pruned down and branched out" (277). The metaphor is lucid, but very vivid and expressive. A slightly more complex metaphor is, "Water was the wild, untamed kingdom of our men" (*Jacob Have I Loved*, 43). Paterson lets her narrator Louise use metaphors frequently, for instance when comparing herself to an oyster, with its shell tightly closed: "I was a good oyster in those days. Not even the presence . . . of a radiant, grown-up Caroline could get under my shell" (190). Naturally, the phrase "I was an oyster" demands a more sophisticated interpretation than the simile "I was like a oyster," since it cannot be treated literally. The meaning of the metaphor "I was an oyster" is "I was closed tight inside myself."

Symbols are images (people, objects, or situations) working on two levels, the literal and the transferred. Some symbols are universal; for instance, the rose is the symbol of love. When a rose is used as a character in *The Little Prince*, it is natural to interpret it as denoting love. Another symbol used in the same book is the lamb, a frequent image connected with the pastoral. When the Little Prince wants a lamb to take home to his planet, we can interpret this as his desire to recreate the pastoral, a childhood idyll. Another type of symbols are those specific to a particular story. Anne Shirley's clothes, ugly and stiffening in the beginning of the novel, pretty and tasteful toward the end, can naturally be merely viewed for what they are; yet they are also a powerful symbol of Anne's development and emancipation. Jo March's cutting off her hair has a practical purpose in *Little Women*: she sells it to earn money. At the same time, hair is a token of femininity, and, by cutting it off, Jo is liberated from the gender stereotyping imposed on her by the patriarchal society. Cutting off hair is a recurrent symbol in feminine writing, thus becoming universal rather than specific.

An *epithet* is an adjective or adjectival phrase denoting a special quality of a person or thing. Epithets were widely used in ancient and medieval literature (fleet-footed Achilles, Roland the Furious) and in folktales (Vasilisa the Beautiful), while they almost never occur in contemporary adult fiction, except in an ironic sense, such as the Great Gatsby. In children's books, epithets are frequently used, apparently for didactic purposes, to emphasize the most prominent feature of the character, such as Curious George or Ramona the Brave. The four children in *The Lion, the Witch and the Wardrobe* are awarded the titles Peter the Magnificent, Susan the Gentle, Edmund the Just, and Lucy the Valiant. In *The Wizard of Oz*, the wizard calls himself Oz the Great and Terrible, and after he is exposed, Dorothy calls him "The Great and Terrible Humbug." If a noun rather than an adjective is used for a similar purpose, the device is called *appellation*, for instance Ramona the Pest. Apart from characterization, epithets and appellations are perhaps used to stimulate language acquisition. However, they can also be used on transferred sense. Gilly Hopkins has pronounced herself "the Great," which is of course ironic, since she is in reality vulnerable and insecure. The epithet may in fact allude to the Great Gatsby, although the character is unlikely to be aware of this.

Personification is a device that hardly ever occurs in contemporary mainstream literature, but belongs among the most popular devices in children's fiction. Personification implies bestowing nonhuman beings and inanimate objects with human qualities. Further, the sun and the moon, the four seasons, day and night, the wind, the rain, and so on, are frequently ascribed anthropomorphic features, not least in picture books, where visual images support personification. But personification can also imply something other than making animals and inanimate objects tangible characters in a story. It can be used as a natural part of the story's imagery. In *The Wizard of Oz*, the cyclone is personified: "From the far North they heard a low wail of the wind" (9); "There now came a sharp whistling" (9); "there came a great shriek from the wind" (10); and "the wind howled horribly around her" (10). In the land of Oz, Dorothy hears a brook "murmuring in a voice very grateful to a little girl" (14). Reading the book, we may not pay attention to these details, but they contribute to our appreciation of the story.

Hyperbole means exaggeration and is vastly used in children's fiction, not least in direct speech. For instance, Anne Shirley often resorts to hyperbolic statements for emphasis, such as, "children should be seen and not heard. I've had that said to me a million times" (16). *Understatement* is the opposite of hyperbole. In *Alice in Wonderland*, Alice finds a bottle with a label saying, "Drink me." Being a sensible girl, she checks whether the bottle is marked "poison," because she knows that "if you drink much from a bottle marked 'poison,' it is almost certain to disagree with you, sooner or later" (20). Of course, both "almost certain" and "disagree," referring to a lethal end, is putting things too mildly. The understatement is used for comic effect, as an absurdity. Yet if the young reader does not know about the impact of poison, the understatement is lost. In *The Tale of Peter Rabbit*, the mother, warning the little bunnies against going into Mr. McGregor's house, explains, "your father had an accident there; he was put in a pie by Mrs. McGregor." Referring to violent death as "an accident" is a typical understatement; but only a mature reader will probably appreciate it.

Irony as a rhetorical figure implies that a word or statement is used to mean exactly the opposite of its literal meaning. For instance, Alice remembers "nice little stories about children who had got burnt, and eaten up by wild beasts" (20). The word "nice" in this quote is used ironically; it is the author's comment on the kind of didactic stories children in his time were usually given to read. If we perceive the word in its literal meaning, the implication is lost, and we may wonder why the author calls these horrible cautionary tales "nice." It is widely believed, and supported by empirical research, that young readers generally do not understand irony, at least not until the age of ten or twelve. In spite of this, irony is frequently used in children's fiction. In some cases, irony may be deliberately addressed to the adult co-reader; in other cases writers may have misjudged the audience.

While normally *repetition* is considered poor style, in many cases it is a deliberate and very effective device, for instance, in *Where the Wild Things Are*: "And when he came to the place where the wild things are they roared their terrible roars and gnashed their terrible teeth and rolled their terrible eyes and showed their terrible claws. . . ." The repetition works as amplification, and the whole sentence is also repeated once more when Max is leaving. *Polysyndeton* (repetition of the conjunction "and") further underscores the structure. *Distant repetition* is a powerful stylistic device, which implies that a key word or phrase is spread over the text echoing itself in significant moments. For instance, the protagonist's favorite expression, "There is scope for imagination," is repeated about a dozen times throughout *Anne of Green Gables*. *Parallel constructions* are used to emphasize actions as well as character traits:

> At the mention of Aslan each one of the children *felt* something jump in its inside. Edmund *felt* a sensation of mysterious horror. Peter *felt* suddenly brave and adventurous. Susan *felt* as if some delicious smell or some delightful strain of music has just floated by her. And Lucy *got the feeling* you have when you wake up in the morning and realize that it is the beginning of the holidays or the beginning of summer. (*The Lion, the Witch and the Wardrobe* 65; italics added)

Enumeration can be used for a variety of purposes. It can simply be used for a more vivid description, like this from *Charlotte's Web*: "The barn . . . was full of all sorts of things you find in barns: ladders, grindstones, pitch forks, monkey wrenches, scythes, lawn mowers, snow shovels, ax handles, milk pails, water buckets, empty grain sacks, and rusty rat traps" (13–14). The author was very much aware of the effect of such a device, providing detail and, especially for an urban child, introducing a variety of unfamiliar objects. Yet enumerations can also have other functions. Several critics have pointed out the use of enumeration as a conspicuous stylistic device in *Charlotte's Web*, not least the lavish menus of the various characters: Wilbur's, Charlotte's, and Templeton's. The focus on food supports the central theme of the novel: eating or being eaten. Finally, enumeration is, like many other stylistic devices, a learning tool. For variation, writers can use polysyndeton or asyndeton (omission of conjunctions), group the words in pairs, emphasize the structure rhythmically, employ alliteration (repetition of initial consonants) and assonance (repetition of vowels), and so on, which among other things, is a demonstration of complex syntax.

Onomatopoeia, or sound imitation, is one of the favorite stylistic devices in children's literature, especially books for younger children, while it is not at all prominent in general fiction. Obviously, writers believe that children appreciate sounds; surely children at play frequently imitate the sounds around them. Here are some examples:

> After a time [Peter] began to wander about, going lippity—lippity—not very fast . . . but suddenly, quite close to him, he heard the noise of a hoe—scr-r-ritch, scratch, scratch, scritch. (*The Tale of Peter Rabbit*)

> And then something went BUMP! . . .
> We saw those two Things
> Bump their kites in the wall!
> Bump! Thump! Thump! Bump!
> Down the wall in the hall. . . .
> Then I let down my net.
> It came down with a PLOP!
> (*The Cat in the Hat*)

> DING-A-LING-A-LING! GEORGE HAD TELEPHONED THE FIRE STATION! (*Curious George*; capitals in the original)

Yet it would be wrong to state that onomatopoeia is only or predominantly used in books for very young readers. Alice has been falling down the rabbit hole for quite a long time "when suddenly, thump! thump! down she came upon a heap of sticks and dry leaves, and the fall was over." Later in the story, "in another moment, splash! she was to her chin in salt-water" (27). Let us remember that *Alice* was first told orally, and in oral storytelling sound imitation is a natural ingredient. Carroll may have employed onomatopoetic phrases in his book to preserve the immediate storytelling effect.

Similarly, *Winnie-the-Pooh* emulates in its style an oral story, thus an abundance of onomatopoetic elements: "[Pooh] was nearly there now, and if he just stood on that branch . . . *Crack!* (6; italics in the original). Books such as *The Cat in the Hat* or *Curious George* are likely to be read aloud to young children, and sound imitation can be emphasized by voice modulations. Also in stories not intended for oral performance, onomatopoeia is frequently used. *Bridge to Terabithia* begins as follows: "*Ba-room, ba-room, ba-room, baripity, baripity, baripity, baripity*—Good. His dad had the pickup going" (1; italics in the original). The sound of the truck sets the scene; we feel ourselves immediately drawn into the story, and our senses get alerted to perceive the world together with the protagonist.

Nonce words (not to be confused with nonsense) are words coined by writers for a particular occasion: "Piglet said that Tigger *was* very bouncy, and that if they could think of a way to unbounce him it would be a Very Good Idea" (106; italics in the original). "Unbounce" is not a standard English word, but its meaning is quite clear from the context and creates a comic effect.

From the many examples above it can be seen than children's writers often use purely graphic stylistic devices for emphasis, such as italics or capitals, either capitalizing the first letter in a word ("a Very Good Idea") or a word or phrase throughout. In *Where the Wild Things Are*, the mother's careless charge "WILD THING!" is capitalized, as well as Max's retort "I'LL EAT YOU UP!" which indicates that the characters are shouting (a practice recently adopted in netiquette). Dr. Seuss's books are filled with caps and italics for various purposes, for instance to emphasize important words and onomatopoeia. *Alice in Wonderland* and *Winnie-the-Pooh* also use graphic devices to bring essential words and phrases to the readers' attention.

Wordplay and Nonsense

Puns and *wordplay* are devices frequently associated with children's literature. Two classic children's novels excel in linguistic acrobatics by consistently employing wordplay as their most conspicuous stylistic device: *Alice in Wonderland* and *Winnie-the-Pooh*. We have already discussed the intricate exercises with language and the shifting of the signifiers and signifieds in both books (chapter 2). Some further examples of the use of language are puns and other wordplay. Puns are based on homonyms (words that have two different meanings), homophones (words that are spelled differently, but pronounced similarly), and homographs (words that are spelled the same, but pronounced differently and have different meanings). A good example of homonyms comes from *Winnie-the-Pooh*, namely the chapter in which the characters go searching for the North Pole. Christopher Robin consults Rabbit,

"What does the North Pole *look* like? . . . I suppose it's just a pole stuck in the ground?"
"Sure to be a pole," said Rabbit, "because of calling it a pole . . ." (109–110; italics in the original)

It is typical that a child chooses a more concrete meaning of a homonym. A clear example of a pun based on homophones is to be found in *Alice in Wonderland*:

"Mine is a long and sad tale!" said the Mouse, turning to Alice, and sighing.
"It *is* a long tail, certainly," said Alice, looking down with wonder at the Mouse's tail; "but why do you call it sad?" (34; italics in the original)

The words "tail" and "tale" are homophones. There are dozens of similar puns in *Alice*, some of them more elaborate, such as, "We called him Tortoise because he taught us" (93). By contrast, the chapter title, "The Rabbit sends in a little bill," is based on the homonymous meaning of the word "bill" (invoice, statement, receipt) and the name of a character, Bill. Some of the puns in *Alice* get quite complicated, alternating back and forth between the two meanings, which demands the reader's full attention to be appreciated. Since puns are often based on one concrete and one more abstract meaning of a homonym, some of them might be beyond a young reader's comprehension. Slightly more complex plays on words occur in Mock Turtle's story about his school days, with subjects such as "Reeling and Writhing . . . the different branches of Arithmetic—Ambition, Distraction, Uglification, and Derision. . . . Mystery, ancient and modern, with Seaography: then Drawling—the Drawling-master was an old conger-eel, that used to come once a week: he taught us Drawling, Stretching, and Fainting in Coils" as well as classics "Laughing and Grief" (94–95). These are not exactly puns, but comic distortions of existing words. The comic effect is amplified by the connection of subjects to characters, such as an eel teaching drawling and stretching.

In some cases wordplay occurs when a set phrase is misinterpreted by a character. For instance, when Alice says, "I beg your pardon," the King replies, "It isn't respectable to beg" (205). Similarly, in *Winnie-the-Pooh*, when the narrator says, "Winnie-the-Pooh lived in a forest all by himself under the name of Sanders," the listening child interrupts the story by inquiring, "*What does 'under the name' mean?*" receiving the explanation, "*It means he had the name over the door in gold letter and lived under it*" (2; italics in the original). *Pooh* books also have numerous examples of play with the difference between two meanings or shades of meaning of a word. Finding Eeyore's lost tail, Pooh says that Eeyore used to be very fond of it, in fact "[a]ttached to it" (47). The literal and the transferred meaning of the word "attached" are combined. A good example of a pun, showing a character's misinterpretation, comes from the final chapter in *The House at Pooh Corner*, when Christopher Robin tells Pooh about all kinds of things he has learned from his lessons, including "when Knights were Knighted." Confused, Pooh asks, "Is it a very Grand thing to be an Afternoon?" Not being literate, Pooh goes after the sound rather than spelling of the word, and chooses the most familiar one to him, "night" rather than "knight," further supplanting it with "afternoon."

If the *Alice* books and the *Pooh* books utilize puns and wordplay as their foremost stylistic device, quite a few other children's novels only use this artistic means occasionally and sparsely. For instance, when the Wizard has filled the Scarecrow's head with a mixture of bran, pins, and needles, he says that he has given him "a lot of bran-new brains" (148). In *Jacob Have I Loved*, Louise likes to tease her friend Call by telling him jokes she knows he does not appreciate, for instance, "Do you know why radio announcers have tiny hands? . . . Wee paws for station identification." While Louise herself can hardly refrain from laughing at the homophonic pair "wee paws"— "we pause," Call starts asking her whether she has seen any radio announcer and how she knows what kind of hands they have. At the same time, Louise shows considerable linguistic deficiency by confusing "fiancée" and "finance," or "consumption" and "consummation." As in the cases of Alice's "antipathies," the writer does not provide the readers with the correct word, apparently trusting them to recognize Louise's mistakes.

Puns and wordplay are often associated with nonsense. As discussed in chapter 3, nonsense is sometimes treated as a genre; however, since it is present in a variety of genres, it is preferable to consider it a stylistic device. We can define nonsense as any stylistic feature based on deviation from logic, including the discrepancy between the literal meaning of a word and its metaphorical meaning, or between its true meaning and the way the characters interpret it. Note that nonsense is something different from slapstick, or merely from humor based on absurd and comic situations and events. When Alice keeps growing and shrinking, or when Pooh gets stuck in Rabbit's hole, we may find it funny, but it is not nonsense as such.

We may wonder why children's authors are so fond of puns and wordplay—definitely more fond than their mainstream colleagues. One answer can certainly be that it is a didactic implement to teach children the use of language. Wordplay is seldom used for its own sake, but to accentuate that words have different meanings and shades of meaning, that language has certain rules of grammar and syntax, and so on. Young readers have not yet mastered language to perfection (of course, some adults never do); therefore by drawing the readers' attention to the functioning of language, writers pursue an educational task. On the other hand, wordplay is usually funny, provided it is comprehensible for young readers; and if one of the features of children's literature is being entertaining, wordplay and nonsense definitely contribute to this effect.

EXERCISE

Choose a children's book and study the use of language in it. Pay attention to imagery, figurative language, wordplay, and other stylistic devices. Contemplate the function of style: does it contribute to the sense of setting and atmosphere, to characterization, and so on, or is it perhaps a purpose in itself, for instance to create a comic effect or to stimulate language acquisition? Are all elements of style accessible for young readers? If some of them are geared more toward an adult audience, do you think it is the author's intention or a miscalculation?

LANGUAGE AS POWER

A particular direction of language studies, called sociolinguistics, investigates how language works in society, or more specifically, examines the use of language and access to language by the different social and ethnic groups, by men and women, and not least by adults and children. Although sociolinguistics is not directly connected with literature, we can make use of some ideas from this discipline to discuss the way language is presented as a social factor in children's novels.

Some contemporary children's novels draw the readers' attention to the manipulative power of language. *The Giver* describes a futuristic society where language has been purged of all words referring to phenomena undesirable in the eyes of authorities, and where "language precision" is used as a means of oppression. First, there are no words to describe human emotions and relationships. When Jonas asks his parents whether they love him, they reply, "you used a very generalized word, so meaningless that it's become almost obsolete" (127). Instead, they suggest that he ask whether they take pride in his accomplishments. Jonas has learned the word "love" from the Giver; but it has long been eliminated from the common vocabulary. When there are no words to describe feelings, the feelings themselves disappear from human mentality. Halfway through the novel we realize that in Jonas's world, there are no colors. When Jonas, in his training to be a Receiver, experiences color for the first time, he lacks the language to describe what he sees. This is another example of manipulation by language: if you take away from people words to describe their sensations, it is then easy to take away the sensations as such. Jonas has been trained to express himself accurately. The novel in fact begins with him trying to sort out his feelings and discarding

the word "frightened" for the more appropriate "apprehensive." It is important in this society to put correct labels on feelings, therefore every family
goes through a round of "confessions" every evening, telling each other
about the improper emotions they have experienced during the day. The understanding is of course that whatever cannot be described by words does
not exist. Toward the end of the novel, Jonas wonders whether the people
around him have actually experienced any feelings at all or whether they
merely use empty words.

Many words in the novel are used euphemistically. A *euphemism* is a word
or phrase used instead of another word or phrase that may be perceived as
offensive, such as "go to the bathroom" instead of "urinate." In the society
of *The Giver*, euphemisms are practiced to conceal less attractive sides of
existence. For instance, family units denote people brought together by the
authorities' will: spouses carefully matched and two children per family, a
male and a female, received on application. Profession is called Assignment
and is imposed on every citizen, once and for all. Volunteer hours stand for
forced labor. Sexual desire is referred to as "stirrings" and gets treated like a
serious illness. The most striking example, however, is "release," the euphemism for execution. Release is practiced on old citizens who have become a
burden to society, on babies born too weak, and not least on political dissidents. Yet it takes the reader some time, together with Jonas, to come to this
realization. First, Jonas believes, as he has been brainwashed to believe, that
"releasing" an erring citizen means that the offender is sent Elsewhere. It
becomes clear later on that Elsewhere is just another euphemism. Release of
the elderly is presented as a "a time of celebration for a life well and fully
lived" (7), and again it takes Jonas a long time to understand that his friend
Fiona, who is assigned the job in The House of the Old, will soon be introduced into "the fine art of release" (153), that is, giving the old men and
women the lethal injection. The worst revelation comes to Jonas when he
realizes that his father practices killing infants.

Even ordinary words are used to denote something else. Jonas calls his
parents mother and father, but they have no biological bonds whatsoever.
Nobody in the community knows what an animal is, but the word is used
"to describe someone uneducated or clumsy, someone who didn't fit in" (5).
Figurative language is banished as imprecise. When Jonas says, "I am starving," he is immediately corrected by his teacher. The phrase "I am starving"
is a hyperbole, and Jonas is using it in the figurative meaning, implying that
he is very hungry. But the authorities want no misunderstandings: "No one
in the community was starving, had never been starving, would ever be
starving. To say 'starving' was to speak a lie" (70). The correct language is
important, because it assures that no unpleasant memories of starvation will
ever disturb the community.

The riches of the natural language, including synonyms, are also eliminated to manipulate the citizens. When everybody wears the same clothes, there is no need for a variety of words for the various garments. When all the food is the same, no words are necessary to refer to the various dishes. When there is no difference between individual houses or apartments, it is easiest to use the word "dwelling." Or as Jonas himself puts it, "If everything's the same, then there aren't any choices" (97). The conformity of language emphasizes the conformity of society itself.

As Jonas is trained to become a Receiver and gets access to the collective memory of generation upon generation of his forefathers, he becomes aware of the multitude of objects and concepts banned from his community and therefore lacking words to describe them. On the other hand, when the Giver says, "It's like going downhill through deep snow on a sled," Jonas does not understand the words "downhill," "snow," or "sled," and the reader is brought to realize that the world Jonas lives in not only lacks colors and emotions, but also weather, seasons, and landscape. By and by, Jonas learns to put words to his new experiences, joyous as well as painful. Together with the protagonist, the reader realizes how meager his life has been without the richness of language. With the language comes the richness of emotional life.

It may seem that the language situation in *The Giver* is grotesque and far from anything we know; however, it is only an extreme case of political correctness, when by replacing or eliminating an offensive word the authorities pretend that the problem itself has been solved. In George Orwell's famous novel *1984*, a manipulated, simplified language is presented, "newspeak," used to brainwash the population. Orwell's novel is, however, a political dystopia geared toward an adult audience. The implicit interrogation of language in a children's novel, such as *The Giver*, is daring; yet it has a clear educational purpose and is, the way it appears and is developed in the text, not beyond the grasp of a young reader.

The use of language in *The Devil's Arithmetic* is not as prominent as in *The Giver* and pursues a different purpose; yet we can notice similar euphemistic expressions. Food, clothes, and other necessities in the concentration camp are not stolen, but "organized." The euphemism is employed to eliminate the ethical question of stealing, even though the stealing in this case is the matter of life and death. And of course "choosing" as a euphemism for sending people to ovens and gas chambers is a tragically ironic illustration of language manipulation. As Rivka explains, "A person is not killed here, but *chosen*. They are not cremated in the ovens, they are *processed*. . . . Because what is not recorded cannot be blamed" (128–129; italics in the original).

The two novels discussed here are unusual, but not unique in their use of language. It can be quite a challenge to see how language is used for manipulation, as not all genres and modes of writing offer a good opportunity for writers to draw the readers' attention to language. Fantasy, science fiction, and historical fiction are among genres that make this possible.

EXERCISE

The *Harry Potter* books and *His Dark Materials* trilogy contain many words and concepts used euphemistically or otherwise describing phenomena we do not know from our existing reality. Contemplate the use of language in these books and investigate whether the authors employ any special devices to draw the readers' attention to language. For instance, do the characters ever contemplate the matter?

IMAGINARY AND SYMBOLIC LANGUAGE

Some extremely fruitful ideas about the function and significance of language in human life have been developed on the crossroads of linguistics and psychoanalysis. Especially the works of the French scholar Jacques Lacan have thrown some new light on the uses of language. Of the many aspects of Lacan's quite dense theories we will here discuss one, the connection between language and psychological development, since it is of utmost importance for children's literature.

Language and Growth

Lacan was a follower of Freud, but while Freud saw the origins of psychological disturbances in our frustrated sexual desires, Lacan sought them in the inadequacy of human language or, to be more precise, in the discrepancy between the structure of language and the chaos of the unconscious. An individual's psychological development is, in Lacan's model, tightly connected with language acquisition and includes three stages: the Imaginary, the Symbolic, and the Real.

The Imaginary comes from "image," which is in practice the same as icon (see chapter 2), that is, a communicative sign in which the signifier and the signified are connected by similarity. No special training is needed to decode imaginary language, for this is how young children communicate before they have been introduced to symbolic language. At this stage, according to Lacan, an infant lives in symbiosis with the mother and expresses its feelings preverbally, for instance by crying, smiling, or gestures. Thus the Imaginary stage in Lacanian psychology implies communication by preverbal signs, before the child has mastered the verbal language, or, in adult life, deliberately rejecting verbal language as a means of communication. Imaginary communication is nonlinear and nonstructured.

The Symbolic refers to the semiotic concept of "symbol" (not in the ordinary meaning, but the same as a conventional sign; see chapter 2). The Symbolic stage, or Symbolic Order, according to Lacan, is verbal, because language is based on conventional signs. The signifiers of Symbolic language—for instance, letters and words—are incomprehensible to outsiders. Unlike the Imaginary, Symbolic language, especially written language, is linear and structured. To have a better command of these quite complicated concepts, let us simplify them by noting that the Imaginary is preverbal, or nonverbal, while the Symbolic is verbal. Further, since the Imaginary is defined by the infant's assumed oneness with the mother, and since the Symbolic Order is linked to what Lacan calls Father's Law (or Name-of-the-Father, which is a matter of translation), we may by inference conclude that in Lacanian terms, Imaginary language is feminine while Symbolic language is masculine (or, if we adapt it to children's literature, the Imaginary is of the child, and the Symbolic is of the adult). The third, Real stage is an attempt—according to Lacan, often failed—to reconcile the two previous ones.

In Lacan's and his followers' psychological model, the transition from the Imaginary to the language of the Symbolic Order is presented as a traumatic experience during which the child's natural mastery of preverbal language is irrevocably lost. Since Lacan connects the Imaginary stage with the mother, the child must inevitably reject the mother in order to transfer into the Symbolic stage (Father's Law). A passage from the preverbal to the verbal stage thus implies, for one thing, an infant's awareness of not being a whole with the mother, and for another thing, giving up the "natural," preverbal language and acquiring verbal language. In Lacan's model, this happens around the age of eighteen months and is called "the mirror stage," as it is connected with the infant's affiliation to its own mirror reflection. The key concept is misrecognition, that is, the child's failure to recognize itself as a separate individual and to distinguish between itself and the image in the mirror. The magical mirror Erised in *Harry Potter and the Sorcerer's Stone* is a perfect illustration of this, since it does not reflect things as they are, but the individual's futile desires. Typically enough, Harry—and the reader with him—must employ literacy to acknowledge the mirror for what it is, that is, read its name backward. Before that, Harry is, in Lacanian terms, stuck at the mirror stage and cannot go further.

The process of transition from the Imaginary to the Symbolic is gender specific, since the individual proceeds from being a genderless "infant" to becoming either a boy or a girl. This must imply—although the adepts of the theory never admit it—that the process is less painful for boys, because they supposedly acquire their "natural" verbality, while girls must give up their "natural" image-based language and forcibly acquire the "unnatural," male language. Drawing this to the extreme, we would conclude that all women are more or less mentally disturbed because they are forced into an unnatural state. Contemporary feminist criticism, deriving from Lacan, shows, however, how female writers have circumvented this dilemma by incorporating the imaginary language into their writing, for instance, through using fragmented, nonlinear language rich in visual and sensual images. Among others, Julia Kristeva has further developed Lacan's ideas to show how female creativity is based on the restoration of the Imaginary. Applying this standpoint to children's literature, we can examine whether children's writers present their characters' transition from the Imaginary (childhood) to the Symbolic (adulthood) as positive, desirable, inevitable, or agonizing, and whether the Imaginary is given a value at all.

LET US EXPLORE

Contemplate how the Imaginary and the Symbolic are presented in some of the following books: *Anne of Green Gables, The Secret Garden, Winnie-the-Pooh, Pippi Longstocking, Charlotte's Web, Ramona the Brave*, and the *Harry Potter* books. Consider the following:

- At what stage is the character initially presented? Is this stage portrayed as positive and appealing?
- What, if anything, instigates the transition into the next stage? How does the transition affect the character?
- Is the transition presented as painless and natural, or does it imply anxiety and maybe even trauma?
- Are there any subversive elements in the text suggesting that the transition is unnecessary and oppressive?

Transition from Imaginary to Symbolic

Young children are always "preverbal" in the sense that they are unable to articulate their emotions to an adult's satisfaction and also in the sense that they have no access to written language. Wilbur in *Charlotte's Web* is a good example, while Charlotte, a wise and insightful adult, is able to restructure the Imaginary (the web) into the Symbolic (the words she weaves into the web), which has an immediate effect. On the most elementary level it implies that the solution to all problems goes through literacy, that is, the ability to articulate oneself in writing.

Many children's books depict children who must be socialized, who must adjust to adults' demands and rules, in order to become integrated into the Symbolic. As they do so, they lose their ability to experience the Lacanian

Imaginary. One aspect of socialization is learning to read. Thus the use of Lacan's concepts of the Imaginary and the Symbolic can be modified to demonstrate a frequent contradiction in children's fiction, that between the desire to keep the fictional child in the state of natural innocence and ignorance and the societal pressure for education. Anne Shirley must give up her vivid imagination and her exalted, poetic language in order to adjust to the norms of formal (read, male and adult-imposed) education. While her choice is certainly positive in some sense, since her only way to material and spiritual independence and integrity is through education, she is undoubtedly suppressed and silenced by society and is obliged to yield an essential part of her personality to be accepted by it.

The Secret Garden appears to be one of few children's novel in which the child is taken from order back to nature, from the Symbolic back to the Imaginary. Burnett's characters are magically liberated from the constraints of civilization; displaced in a Gothic faraway manor, they do not have to learn to read and write. The only books they read are "about gardens and . . . full of pictures" (161). Although Mary's ability to write proves useful in communication with Dickon, he can easily make himself understood by iconic, Imaginary language:

> There were some roughly printed letters on it and a sort of picture. At first she could not tell what it was. Then she saw it was meant for a nest with a bird sitting on it. Underneath were the printed letters and they said: "I will cum bak." (115)

In his capacity as the child of nature, Dickon proves to be superior to both Mary and Colin, and they have to learn his skills (among other things, talking to the robin in its—obviously nonverbal—language) in order to find their paradise. The novel ends with the characters dissolving into the kind of mythical existence that goes beyond all realistic dimensions. Obviously, the ability to read and write is superfluous in the magical garden that communicates by a richness of smells, colors, sounds, and tactile contact.

This is, however, a rare exception in the canon of Western children's literature. The dramatic clash between the Imaginary and the Symbolic in *Winnie-the-Pooh* is much more typical. As already shown in the section above, language is extremely important in *Pooh* books, reflecting the young child's gradual mastery of language, testing of rules by breaking them, and exploration of the boundaries and possibilities of language. Pooh represents oral culture in which language is not restricted by rules, in which grammar can be incorrect, spelling does not matter (Pooh writes "HUNNY" on his jars and knows exactly what it means), and new words can be easily invented. By contrast, the education that Christopher Robin receives in the outside (read, civilized) world is written, ordered, and strictly regulated; it does not have room for Spotted and Herbaceous Backsons.

In Lacanian terms, Pooh's poetry is Imaginary, based on sound play rather than meaning. Moreover, the language of the narrative as such is often visual, or iconic, for instance when Pooh climbs the tree,

He
climbed
and
he
climbed
and
he
climbed
and
as
he
climbed
he
sang
a
little
song
to
himself.
(5)

The visual image of the text looks like a tree Pooh is climbing. Similarly, when Piglet is carried by Kanga in her pocket, the text follows Kanga's jumps:

```
      this                              take
"If         is            shall    really       to
          flying I                never              it." (93)
```

Both Christopher Robin and his toys (who are projections of his persona, in the Jungian sense; see chapter 4) are in the preverbal stage as the book opens, but throughout the story we repeatedly witness how Christopher Robin is trained in Symbolic, verbal language. Writing the signs on Owl's door, he still makes a direct connection between the name of letters and their pronunciation, thus spelling "please" as "PLES" and "answer" as "RNSER;" yet he is recognized as "the only one in the forest who could spell." Owl is "able to read and write and spell his own name WOL, yet somehow went all

to pieces over delicate words like MEASLES and BUTTEREDTOAST."
(43). The author cleverly shifts the boy's ineptitude onto his animal friends,
which is especially tangible in the chapter about Eeyore's birthday. Quite
apparently, Owl cannot read and write, but is reluctant to admit it (it is made
clear later, when he is unable to read Christopher Robin's message and
coaxes Rabbit to read it to him). He asks Pooh whether he can read the signs
on his door, and Pooh explains that Christopher Robin has told him what
the signs said, and then he could. Relieved, Owl says that he will tell Pooh
what he has written, and then Pooh will be able to read it. So he writes:
"HIPY PAPY BTHUTHDTH THUTHDA BTHYTHDY." From the
point of view of the Symbolic Order, this is gibberish. Within the Imaginary,
it can just as well mean "Happy birthday," if this is what it is intended to
mean.

The most lucid illustration of the discrepancy between the Imaginary and
the Symbolic is, however, to be found in the chapter "What Christopher
Robin Does in the Mornings," in *The House at Pooh Corner*. Piglet comes
to visit Eeyore who is fully engrossed in contemplating three sticks on the
ground in front of him. "Two of the sticks were touching at one end, but not
at the other, and the third was laid across them" (84). In case the reader has
any doubts, there is a picture to assist. But Piglet, who is illiterate without
being concerned about it, "thought that perhaps it was a Trap of some kind."
That is, Piglet sees the Imaginary, iconic value of the sign rather than its
symbolic value. Eeyore enlightens Piglet, acting as a mouthpiece for a wise
adult, "Do you know what A means, little Piglet? . . . It means Learning, it
means Education, it means all the things that you and Pooh haven't got"
(85). In this chapter, Christopher Robin writes his first correct message, thus
taking a definite step away from the innocence of childhood, from the Imaginary into the Symbolic. The author's message seems to be that however plea-
surable, the Imaginary has to be left behind.

Yet another example of a child's problematic introduction into the Symbolic order can be gathered from *Ramona the Pest*. Ramona's last name is
Quimby, therefore she is especially keen on learning the letter *Q*. Her
teacher tells her that the best way to make a *Q* is to start with an *O* and add
"a little tail like a cat." Ramona still cannot see letters for what they are, that
is, abstract signs, and is encouraged by her teacher to perceive them as pictures: "Miss Binney said A was pointed like a witch's hat. . . . O was easy. It
was a round balloon" (73); and Ramona is glad that she "had one balloon
and two Halloween hats in her first name and a cat in her last name." Practicing to print her *Q*s, Ramona adds two ears and whiskers "so that her *Q*
looked the way the cat looked when crouched on a rug in front of the fire-
place" (77) (see fig. 9-1). She also tells her classmate Davy who is struggling
with his *D*, which is supposed to look like a robin, "That D doesn't look
like a robin. . . . It doesn't have any feathers" (78). Davy obediently draws a

Fig. 9-1 Ramona's Q.

D that "did not look like Miss Binney's D, but it did look, in Ramona's opinion, more like the front of a robin with feathers mussed by the wind, which was what Miss Binney wanted, wasn't it? A D like a robin redbreast" (78). As happens to her repeatedly, Ramona gets deeply disappointed when the teacher does not appreciate her ways of seeing things. Obviously at this stage Ramona is not ready to enter the Symbolic Order, as she is consistently perceiving letters imaginarily, as pictures.

In all these examples, the child's ability to use and appreciate the Imaginary language is presented as a deficiency, while the passage into the Symbolic order is hailed as the desirable goal. There are very few children's books in which the value of the Symbolic order is openly interrogated. One of them is *Pippi Longstocking*. Pippi has never attended school, she can barely read, and her spelling leaves much to be desired. In the chapter "Pippi goes to school," the teacher shows her a picture of an ibex and the letter *i* (in the Swedish original it is a hedgehog, an image more likely to be familiar to a child than an ibex), while Pippi says, quite reasonably, that she sees a little stick with a fly speck above it (54f). Pippi employs imaginary reading, interpreting the icon and ignoring the conventional aspect of the sign, which is of course what the other children are taught in school. Yet because Pippi is what she is, she not only gets away with it, but can insist on her right to remain at the Imaginary stage. At the question-and-answer bee, Pippi says, "S-e-e-s-i-k is the way I have always spelled it, and it seems to have worked out just fine" (*Pippi in the South Seas*, 45). Pippi's deconstruction of language in her inadequate spelling skills gives the young readers a confirmation of their own language proficiency. At the same time, the arbitrariness of the spelling rules imposed by adults is interrogated. Pippi is, however, as has already been pointed out, one of a kind, and her breaking the rules only emphasizes the existence of rules.

Yet, while *Pippi* books are explicitly subversive in their attitude toward the Symbolic, we might argue that all children's books that in some way or other touch upon this matter are subversive, as they bring to our attention one of the central dilemmas in writing for children.

EXERCISE

Choose a children's novel dealing, even briefly, with education and literacy. Some suggestions are *Little Women, The Adventures of Tom Sawyer, Heidi, Daddy-Long-Legs, Anne of Green Gables, Harriet the*

Spy, *Ramona the Pest*, *Dear Mr. Henshaw*, or *Lyddie*. Consider the way writers present the Imaginary and the Symbolic and how they deal with the reconciliation of the two orders. Contemplate why the issue is so often avoided in children's books.

HOW TO GO FURTHER

Some of the more versatile models for studying the language of fiction can be found at the crossroads of linguistics, philosophy, and psychoanalysis, not least in the Lacan-inspired French feminist criticism (Julia Kristeva, Hélène Cixous), since they operate with the connection between power and access to language by marginalized groups. Desire is one of the central concepts of these theories that can be successfully applied to children's texts. In a broader sense, communication theory and literary pragmatics focus on language as a means of mediation between text and its recipients.

The vast area commonly referred to as metafiction includes the investigation of the role of language in achieving metafictive effects, since it is primarily through language that metafictive devices can be employed. Metafiction is defined as self-conscious literature, that is, texts that deliberately and consistently draw the readers' attention to their existence as artistic constructs. Framing and frame breaking are the most prominent features of metafiction, implying the combination and transgression of different diegetic levels in a literary text. This can obviously only be achieved through language. While the term itself has only been in circulation for about thirty years, the phenomenon occurs in children's literature long before, yet it has not been studied sufficiently.

Finally, all poststructural theories of literature in some way or other investigate the function of language in literary activity. Postmodern aesthetics has strongly interrogated the inadequacy of language in depicting human experience. Since the premise of traditional children's literature has been, among other things, the simplicity of language, including an unproblematic connection between language and portrayed reality, the emergence of more complex children's novels calls for our attention in this respect. Deconstruction theory provides some fruitful directions to pursue.

REFERENCES

Anderson, Celia Catlett, and Marilyn Fain Apseloff. *Nonsense Literature for Children: Aesop to Seuss*. Hamden, CT: Library Professional Publications, 1989.

Barthes, Roland. *S/Z*. New York: Hill & Wang, 1974.

Chukovsky, Kornei. *From Two to Five* (1925). Berkeley: University of California Press, 1963. A comprehensive study of children's language acquisition through imagination and nonsense.

Cixous, Hélène. *The Hélène Cixous Reader*. Edited by Susan Sellers. New York: Routledge, 1994.

Coats, Karen. "Lacan with Runt Pigs." *Children's Literature* 27 (1999): 105–128.

———. *Looking Glasses and Neverlands: Lacan, Desire, and Subjectivity in Children's Literature*. Iowa City, University of Iowa Press, 2004.

Culler, Jonathan. *On Deconstruction: Theory and Criticism after Structuralism*. Ithaca, NY: Cornell University Press, 1982.

Derrida, Jacques. *Of Grammatology*. Baltimore: Johns Hopkins University Press, 1976.

———. *Writing and Difference*. London: Routledge, 1978.

Fordyce, Rachel, and Carla Marello, eds. *Semiotics and Linguistics in Alice's Worlds*. Berlin: de Gruyter, 1994.

Hunt, Peter. "Dialogue and Dialectic: Language and Class in The Wind in the Willows." *Children's Literature* 16 (1988): 159–168.

———. *Criticism, Theory and Children's Literature*. London: Blackwell, 1991. Chap. 6, "Style and Stylistics."

Kristeva, Julia. *Desire in Language: A Semiotic Approach to Literature and Art*. Oxford: Blackwell, 1980.

———. *Revolution in Poetic Language*. New York: Columbia University Press, 1984.

Lacan, Jacques. *Ecrits: A Selection*. New York: Norton, 1977.

———. *The Four Fundamental Concepts of Psychoanalysis*. Harmondsworth: Penguin, 1979.

———. "The Insistence of Letter in the Unconscious." Pp. 79–109 in *Modern Criticism and Theory: A Reader*, edited by David Lodge. London: Longman, 1988.

Lecercle, Jean-Jacques. *Philosophy of Nonsense: The Intuitions of Victorian Nonsense Literature*. London: Routledge, 1994.

Leech, Geoffrey, and Michael H. Short. *Style in Fiction: A Linguistic Introduction to English Fictional Prose*. London: Longman, 1981. A good general introduction to literary stylistics.

Lukens, Rebecca J. *A Critical Handbook of Children's Literature*. 4th ed. New York: HarperCollins, 1990. Chap. 8, "Style"; chap. 9, "Tone" (includes a section on humor).

May, Jill P. *Children's Literature and Critical Theory*. New York: Oxford University Press, 1995. Chap. 7, "Poetic Language and Literary Style."

McGillis, Roderick. "Another Kick at La/can: 'I Am a Picture,'" *Children's Literature Association Quarterly* 20, no. 1 (1995): 42–46.

———. *The Nimble Reader: Literary Theory and Children's Literature*. New York: Twayne, 1996. Chap. 7, "Criticism at Work and at Play: Poststructuralism."

Nikolajeva, Maria. *Children's Literature Comes of Age: Towards a New Aesthetic*. New York: Garland, 1996. Chap. 7, "Metafiction in Children's Literature."

———. "Tamed Imagination: A Rereading of Heidi." *Children's Literature Association Quarterly* 25, no. 2 (2000): 68–75. The essay offers a Lacanian reading of

Heidi, by Johanna Spyri, using the concepts of the imaginary and the symbolic language.

Sewell, Elizabeth. *The Field of Nonsense*. London: Chatto & Windus, 1952.

Stanger, Carol A. "Winnie the Pooh Through a Feminist Lens." *The Lion and the Unicorn* 11, no. 2 (1987): 34–50. Contains some consideration on the imaginary and the semiotic language in the *Pooh* books.

Stephens, John. *Language and Ideology in Children's Fiction*. London: Longman, 1992. Chap. 3, "Not by Words Alone: Language, Intertextuality, Society."

———. "Linguistics and Stylistics." Pp. 58–70 in *International Companion Encyclopedia of Children's Literature*, edited by Peter Hunt. London: Routledge, 1996. Also pp. 56–68 in *Understanding Children's Literature*, edited by Peter Hunt. London: Routledge, 1999.

Stewart. Susan. *Nonsense: Aspects of Intertextuality in Folklore and Literature*. Baltimore: Johns Hopkins University Press, 1979.

Waugh, Patricia. *Metafiction: The Theory and Practice of Self-Conscious Fiction*. London: Methuen, 1984.

10

The Aesthetic of the Medium

Today children's literature exists very much on the crossroads of different media: film, theater, television, video, music, computer games, and so on. The spin-off products, including merchandise (toys, clothes, office supplies, and the like), often play a more important role in the promotion of a book than the book itself. The area is much too broad to be covered in merely one chapter; besides, many questions will take us away from the field of children's literature into culture and media studies. We will therefore be content with three aspects of multimediality that are most immediately connected with children's literature: illustration, transmediation (transformation from one medium into another), and translation.

WHAT CAN PICTURES DO?

Although the term "multimedia" is a recent invention, the multimedial concept—conveying information by at least two different media, for instance the verbal and the visual—has existed ever since the beginning of literacy, and in children's literature it has been manifest in the practice of illustrations. As stated in chapter 3, picturebooks are not a separate genre, but a special art form in which the meaning is created by the interaction of information conveyed through the two media, words and pictures. In this, picturebooks are a synthetic medium, like theater or film, where the overall meaning is assembled by the receiver in the interaction between the different communicative means. Unlike theater or film, picturebooks are discontinuous and have no fixed duration. Unlike theater, but similar to film, picturebooks are two-dimensional. Unlike both theater and film, picturebooks do not require acoustic communication, although they may be—and often are—read aloud. Unlike art, picturebooks are sequential; they only have meaning through a

223

sequence of images. It is therefore pointless to study separate pictures in picturebooks: they must always be studied as a whole and always in their interaction with words.

Iconic and Conventional Signs in Picturebooks

Making use of semiotic terminology we can say that picturebooks communicate by means of two separate sets of signs, the iconic and the conventional. In chapter 2 we discussed the difference between iconic and
conventional signs, stating that we usually do not need special knowledge to
understand icons, but we must be part of the convention in order to understand conventional signs. Pictures in picturebooks are complex iconic signs,
and words in picturebooks are complex conventional signs; however, the
basic relation between the two levels is the same. The function of pictures,
iconic signs, is to describe or represent. The function of words, conventional
signs, is primarily to narrate. Conventional signs are often linear (in our culture, for instance, we read left to right), while iconic signs are nonlinear. The
tension between the two functions creates unlimited possibilities for interaction between word and image in a picturebook. The two extremes of such a
tension are a book without pictures and a book with only pictures in it,
without words.

In wordless picturebooks, images carry the whole load of storytelling.
They may contain a sequence of individual panels on every page, more or
less reminiscent of comic strips, or they may use the whole doublespread
and employ page turning for plot development; they may be simple and action oriented or very complex in imagery and symbolism. Yet since there are
no words to accompany the pictures, the readers have to construct their own
narrative from the pictures. Usually the title of the book offers at least some
guidelines for interpretation.

A verbal text, for instance a fairy tale or a short story, can be illustrated
by one or several pictures; however, this does not necessarily make a picturebook as such, since pictures will often remain subordinated to the words.
A number of very significant children's stories (Bible stories; folktales; and
Charles Perrault's, the Grimm Brothers', or Hans Christian Andersen's
tales) have been illustrated by different artists, who impart different, and
even on occasion inappropriate, interpretations to the text. Still the story remains basically the same and can still be read without looking at the pictures.
Even if we have preferences for certain illustrations, perhaps because we have
grown up with them, the text is not dependent on illustrations to convey its
essential message.

LET US EXPLORE

Visit your library and find several illustrated versions of the same
story, for instance, *Little Red Riding Hood*, *Cinderella*, *Snow White*,

or *Hansel and Gretel*. Study the books carefully and contemplate how illustrations enhance your interpretation of the story. Here are some aspects you may consider:

- How many pictures are there in the book? Which episodes of the story are illustrated? Which are not? Why?
- What does the layout look like and how does it affect our perception of the story? For instance, are illustrations placed on separate pages, facing the text, or do they feel like an integrated part of the narrative?
- How do the pictures interact with the text? Do they add anything substantial to the story? Do they offer new interpretations beyond the text itself? Is there anything in the pictures that creates a totally new dimension?
- Is the visual setting time bound or anachronistic, realistic or fairy-tale-like, rich in detail or almost nonexistent? How does this affect our understanding of the story?
- Is characterization a significant part of the visual solution? Are the characters presented as children, adolescents, or adults; as human beings, animals, or fairy-tale creatures? Is the protagonist portrayed in every picture? Is the protagonist placed in the center of every picture? Are there any close-ups of the protagonist or any other character? What is the effect of these?
- Which picture is chosen for the cover, and how does it affect our interpretation?

The overall question is of course whether the pictures are merely decorative or whether they indeed affect and enhance our perception of the story, and in this case, how.

Text/Image Interaction

In illustrating an existing text, for instance a fairy tale, artists have a number of choices. They can merely provide a visual counterpart of what the text says, without adding anything essential. They can, however, also use the text as a point of departure for a new interpretation, thus creating a new literary work, based on text/image interaction. They can supply settings that the words do not mention explicitly. For instance, in the various illustrated versions of famous fairy tales, the pictures set the story in an indeterminable fairy-tale time, in the Middle Ages, in the Baroque epoch, or even in our own time, with anachronistic details such as cars and television sets. The number of illustrations may vary considerably. In his illustrations to the

Grimm Brothers' fairy tales, Maurice Sendak has managed to capture the whole story in one single dynamic and powerful picture for each tale. Generally, the larger the number of illustrations, the more they work as mere decorations instead of taking over some of the storytelling. The choice of illustrated episodes naturally emphasizes their significance. An illustrator may play down the scary part of the story by choosing not to illustrate the most dramatic episodes or the negative characters. The nature of the individual illustrations may amplify the dynamic development of the story or slow it down. Visual characterization can take the stories in various directions. In some versions of *Hansel and Gretel*, the witch looks very much like the (step)mother, which naturally prompts a certain interpretation. Sendak's illustrations for *Dear Mili* have caused much debate since they introduce images of the Holocaust in this fairy tale written in the beginning of the nineteenth century.

All these considerations demonstrate what choices artists also have when they create original picturebooks, in which neither words nor images can be given priority: they are an inseparable whole and cannot exist without one another. In between illustrated texts and wordless picture narratives, however, a variety of relationships between words and images can be discovered. Here are the most essential types of interaction:

- Symmetrical: words and pictures basically tell the same story repeating what is essentially the same information in different forms of communication.
- Complementary: words and pictures complement each other's stories and compensate for each other's insufficiencies.
- Enhancing: pictures significantly enhance (amplify, reinforce) the verbal story, or occasionally the words expand the picture so that different information in the two modes of communication produces a more complex meaning.
- Counterpointing: words and pictures tell two different stories, cooperating to create a new meaning; both are indispensable for decoding the message.
- Contradictory: the tension between words and pictures becomes too strong, they take the story in different directions; the story becomes ambiguous, less understandable.

Let us consider a few examples. In *Goodnight, Moon*, the pictures meticulously illustrate what the words say. Of course, the large panoramic pictures have more details than those mentioned in words, so the interaction is not fully symmetrical, but the concept of the book is using words to guide the reader's attention to the pictures. The text is substantially more poetic than in a picture dictionary, yet the relationship between words and images is almost the same.

Curious George begins with an introduction of the main character, verbal as well as visual. The picture shows us a little monkey swinging from a tree and eating a banana. The text says, "This is George. He lived in Africa. He was happy. But he had one fault. He was too curious." Seemingly, the words and the picture are symmetrical. Let us, however, consider the text sentence by sentence. "This is George" is not the same kind of statement that we would find in a picture dictionary: "This is a monkey." The text does not inform us that the animal we see is a monkey; we are supposed to know it. On the other hand, from the picture we have no possibility of knowing that the monkey's name is George. We can guess that the action takes place in some faraway country, but the words give us a concrete location: Africa. Furthermore, the verbal text uses two different tenses: "This *is* George," but, "He *lived* in Africa." While the first sentence makes the reader an immediate beholder of the situation, the past tense distances us by suggesting that the story in fact happened long ago. The words prepare us for a change in the character's situation occurring later in the book: George used to live in Africa, but he does not live there anymore. The sentence "He was very happy" seems symmetrical to the happy countenance of the character in the picture. Yet it is an evaluative statement. Does it convey an internal focalization of the protagonist (= "George considered himself happy"), an omniscient narrator's statement (= "I know that George was happy"), or an objective narrator's inference (= "I believe that George was happy")? The next two sentences are indisputably a didactic narrator's judgment, and they have no correspondence whatsoever in the picture, since visual signs cannot convey judgments and opinions. The words and the picture thus compensate for each other's limitations; the interaction is complementary. On the next double spread, the text says, "One day George saw a man." The picture, however, does not show the scene from George's point of view, but the man's, corresponding more to the sentence "The man saw George, too." The picture reinforces the change of perspective from the child character to the adult man. Moreover, we are also immediately allowed to share the man's internal point of view, his thoughts: " 'What a nice little monkey,' he thought." By sharing the man's thoughts, expressed in words, we are also involved in his plan to capture George; thus, as readers/viewers, we are on the adult's side. This obvious contradiction in narrative perspective between words and images is easy to overlook, but it is decisive for our interpretation of the story.

Later in the book, the words say, "oh, what happened! First this—and then this!" But for the pictures, we would not be able to know what happened to George, while the pictures show his actions immediately, without having to describe them. Although throughout the book the dominant relationship between words and pictures is indeed symmetrical, there are some interesting deviations revealed by close reading. We can therefore hardly maintain that a picturebook is wholly symmetrical or wholly counterpointing. The tension can vary from spread to spread, and it can be different for the various aspects of the narrative.

In *Sylvester and the Magic Pebble*, we can also observe that the verbal text does not initially mention that Sylvester is a donkey. The text merely states that Sylvester Duncan lived with his mother and father, and collected pebbles as a hobby. Without the pictures, we would assume that Sylvester was a boy. The pictures provide information that the text omits, while they show us exactly what Sylvester and the other characters look like. Apart from these complementary elements, the pictures do not add much to the narrative. Moreover, the text is richer than the pictures: there are several episodes in the verbal text that are not illustrated. For instance, when Sylvester realizes that the pebble can grant wishes, the text conveys his joy at being able to have anything he wants and to give his family and friends anything they want. Here a great chance to visualize the phrase "anything they want" is lost. Another missed pictorial opportunity occurs when the didactic narrator elaborates on what Sylvester could have done when confronted with a lion: could have made the lion disappear, could have wished himself safe at home, could have wished the lion would turn into a butterfly. And Sylvester's thoughts and feelings when he is transformed into a rock are not visualized.

In *Where the Wild Things Are*, the text is substantially enhanced by the pictures. Although the basic storyline can be gathered from the words alone, it is the pictures that create the tone and the message of the narrative. The pictures emphasize the child/adult conflict by portraying Max, but excluding his mother; they convey the change in Max's feelings, both in his posture and facial expression and in the imagery around him; they visualize his aggressions, presenting them as monsters; they express the dynamic nature of the narrative, showing the transformation of Max's room and first his outward journey from left to right and then the homeward journey from right to left; they provide details suggesting the temporal duration of the narrative, that contradict the verbal statement about Max's supper being hot. Especially the three wordless double spreads, corresponding to the words "let the wild rumpus start," expand the verbal story.

John Burningham's *Come Away from the Water, Shirley* is based on the ironic counterpoint between the information conveyed by words and by pictures. While the words and one set of pictures describe a boring day on the beach, the other visual sequence takes the protagonist on breathtaking adventures on high seas. Words and pictures actually tell two different stories, from two different points of view. The stories are, among other things, conflicting in their genres: one is realistic, the other a fantasy.

Note that the terms describing the verbal/visual interaction are in themselves not evaluative: a symmetrical book is not aesthetically inferior to a counterpointing one; it is just a different concept of using the medium. Yet it is obvious that picturebooks that employ counterpoint are especially stimulating because they elicit many possible interpretations and involve the reader's imagination. Quite a number of contemporary picturebook creators deliberately and consistently employ counterpoint in their works.

EXERCISE

Choose a number of picturebooks and analyze carefully the text/image interaction in them. Observe that the various types of interaction may work differently at the various narrative levels. For instance, words and pictures may be symmetrical in plot, enhancing in characterization, and counterpointing in perspective.

FROM BOOK TO SCREEN

The process of the transformation of a text into another media is called transmediation (or sometimes transmodalization). Another widely used term is adaptation, but it also includes all kinds of transformations performed on texts within the same medium, for instance abridgements and censorial interference, as well as the general adjustment of texts to the presumed audience. The concept of transmediation emphasizes the crossing from one medium to another.

Some of the earliest examples of transmediation in children's literature involve stage versions of stories. Normally, a story would exist as a novel before it was staged, but occasionally it is the other way round. *Peter Pan* was first written as a play, and later turned by the author into a novel (novelization). A comparison of the two versions provides interesting insights into the difference between theater and literature, between showing and telling, that are vital for our understanding the essence of literature. Not least in the field of characterization, the difference is striking. Other types of transmediation include radio plays, musicals, operas, ballets, films, television series, and computer games based on written stories. Some stories are in fact better known in transmediated form, for instance the ballet *The Nutcracker*, based on a story by the German writer E. T. A. Hoffmann. Occasionally the direction of transmediation is the opposite. For instance, Sergey Prokofiev's famous musical piece *Peter and the Wolf* has been published as a storybook, as have the ballet *Swan Lake* and the movie *E.T.*

In analyzing transmediated stories, we examine how the choice of the medium affects the form and the content, what changes are dictated by the necessity to adapt to the new medium and the new presumed audience, which of those are justified and which are not, and so on. The most illuminating examples can be gathered from film versions of children's stories; therefore we will confine ourselves to discussing those.

LET US EXPLORE

Choose a children's book or a fairy tale and compare it to a film version, for instance an animated Disney movie: *Cinderella, Snow White, Beauty and the Beast, The Little Mermaid, Pinocchio,* or *Peter Pan.* Pay close attention to all the changes made in the movie. If you have seen the movie before you read the book, you may be struck by the scope of changes. Remember that the book existed first, and the film version was changed to adapt it to what the filmmakers believe are the needs and interests of a contemporary Western young audience. Try to identify the principles guiding the filmmakers.

"Disneyfication"

Much has been written about "Disneyfication" of classical stories. Many studies have complained about gender stereotyping; others focus on commercialism and unscrupulous marketing; still others mainly note the profound changes the stories undergo in the process of transmediation. From the aesthetic point of view, the observations made by various critics can be summarized as follows:

- The most "child-friendly" version of the story is chosen, for instance Perrault's rather than Grimm's version of *Cinderella,* in which the sisters cut off their toes and heels to be able to put on the slipper, and finally get punished by the birds' picking out their eyes. Generally, all graphic and offensive details from original versions are toned down in the movies, making the stories more suitable for family entertainment.
- Conflict and action are amplified; a tangible antagonist is added, for instance the Sea Witch in *The Little Mermaid.* Hence a simple person-against-person conflict is substituted for a complex person-against-self one. In *Peter Pan,* Peter's combat against Hook totally eclipses the tragic dilemma of the child who is unable to grow up. In *Beauty and the Beast,* the psychological dilemma of the heroine is somewhat diminished by the attempts of the Beast's human rival, Gaston, to kill him.
- A happy ending is provided instead of an unhappy or ambivalent one. For instance, in the original version of *The Little Mermaid,* the heroine dies when the prince marries another girl, while in the film version she gets back her voice and lives happily ever after.

- Human characters are changed into animals, for instance in *Robin Hood* or *Oliver Twist*. Apparently, this is based on the assumption that children prefer animal characters to human. The result is that some people may go through their lives believing that Robin Hood was a fox and Oliver Twist a kitten.
- Additional characters, often comic, and not seldom talking animals and animated objects, are introduced, for instance the mice in *Cinderella*; the fish, the crab, and the seagull in *The Little Mermaid*; or the enchanted servants in *Beauty and the Beast*.
- A character is added or changed to be an authoritative narrative agency, supplying comments and judgments, for instance the cricket in *Pinocchio*.

All these aspects give us a good starting point for a more general discussion of what happens when a book is transmediated into a motion picture. The filmmakers naturally strive to make the most of the medium they are working with, which includes visual and acoustic aspects; yet in the process some sacrifices are inevitably made.

Let us start with considering the choice of episodes. Depending on the length of the original, the film version can either follow the plot faithfully or adapt the length, by either cutting episodes or adding new ones. The *Harry Potter* movies are good examples of transmediated versions that are maximally true to the books; according to the filmmakers, this was their working concept (whether aesthetic or commercial is another question). In the film version of *The Wizard of Oz*, the very last journey is cut, presumably because it would feel too long and repetitive. In Disney's *Alice in Wonderland*, both the episode in the Duchess's kitchen and the encounter with Mock Turtle are omitted. By contrast, in many films based on short fairy tales, fill-ins are necessary to extend the duration to full length; new episodes are often comic musical numbers (e.g., in *The Little Mermaid, Beauty and the Beast*, or *Aladdin*). By means of adding or cutting episodes, the plot can be either simplified or complicated. In *The Grinch*, to compensate for the meager plot of the book, the filmmakers have supplied a story of the Grinch being abandoned as a baby, which ostensibly has made him mean and grumpy. Apart from expanding the story, the addition provides a background to explain the character's behavior. Naturally, this makes the Grinch a much more mimetic, that is, psychologically plausible, character than he is in the original.

Another typical fill-in in a film version is the setting. While a long verbal description of a the character's journey through an ever-so-exciting setting would be unbearable in a children's novel, in films we often meet both establishing sequences in the beginning and prolonged episodes of spatial transportation, for instance Snow White in the woods or Aladdin's flight on the flying carpet. Dynamic visual details, especially accompanied by music or song, make such descriptions enjoyable, which is a good example of adaptation to the specific medium. Some film versions change the original settings altogether; for instance, Tom Davenport's film versions of famous fairy tales are set in various historical environments in North America. Naturally, such a version cannot but interrogate the ideology of the original, adding its own critical standpoints.

Transmediated Plots

The many Disney movies of *Winnie-the-Pooh* provide a good example of how an intervention into the original plot also radically affects the message and the impact on the audience. Although the plots of Milne's two books are primarily episodic, with a separate and self-contained adventure in every chapter, we have in an earlier chapter observed some peculiarities in the composition of the *Pooh* stories. First, the story has a cumulative nature, introducing one character at a time and adding conflict (especially with the arrival of Kanga and Tigger) to the initial harmony. The ten-minute movies have no special order; they are purely episodic and have a fixed set of characters. In the novels, there is a vague progressive plot, leading toward the ending in which Christopher Robin has to leave his childhood idyll. This tragic end is prepared by some profound changes in the forest, for instance the storm during which Owl's home is destroyed. The arbitrary order of the movies naturally precludes any progressive development or, still less, a closure. On the contrary, it allows an endless row of new adventures, no longer based on the original stories. The Pooh characters are thus used in the same manner as Mickey Mouse or Donald Duck. The outer frame of the original stories is seemingly preserved in the movies as each of them starts and ends in the nursery. Yet the implication of the frame—the inner story being the projection of the young boy's psychological development and conflict—is definitely gone, as is the question of power and authority. The movies emphasize action and ignore the psychological and philosophical dimensions of the original.

Also in some full-length films, the endings are changed to allow for a sequel. The novel *Stuart Little* has an open ending in which the protagonist leaves home to seek his fortune. The ending emphasizes his transition from the security of childhood to the uncertain world of adolescence. In the film version, Stuart is more or less left to live happily ever after, with *Stuart Little 2* continuing a ceaseless chain of adventures.

Transmediated Genre

Adaptation of the genre is a frequent change in film versions. The transformation of human characters into animals has been mentioned, which naturally makes the story more fairy-tale-like. A similar amplification of the fairy-tale atmosphere occurs when animals are allowed to talk. For instance, in an animated version of Hector Malot's *The Foundling*, both the dogs and the monkey can talk. This presumably makes the story more exciting, creates more intense bonds between the protagonist and his companions, and takes away the sense of loneliness and abandonment as the protagonist wanders along without human company.

However, an opposite tendency can also be traced, when the transmediated version is more rationalized than the written text. In *Stuart Little*, the little mouse's origin is a textual mystery: he is somehow born to completely ordinary parents. In the recent film version, a mimetic interpretation is applied: Stuart is not the natural son, but an adopted one. The change illustrates the difference between the mimetic and the semiotic treatment of plot and character. In a semiotic approach, the question of Stuart's origin is irrelevant. The filmmakers apparently felt obliged to adapt the story to what they believed to be the mimetic demands of their audience. It is, however, conceivable that the young readers and viewers are more open to semiotic interpretations than many adults, accepting Stuart's background without further contemplation. The adaptation is thus made for the sake of adults (critics, parents, teachers) rather than the primary target group.

Focus on the Plot

Changing or amplifying the central conflict of the plot, as has been done in *The Little Mermaid*, leads, among other things, to the transformation of the narrative from character oriented to plot oriented. Even when a change is not as pronounced, certain elements can be underscored, affecting the overall impact. In the recent film version of *Little Women*, the romance between Jo and Laurie is given an unproportionally large space as compared to the novel.

The Disney version of *The Little Mermaid* is an excellent illustration of its creators' drive to supply the protagonist with a set of supporting characters in order to clarify (and oversimplify) the plot. In the original version, the little mermaid's chief enemy is herself, and as she leaves the sea, there is no one to assist or comfort her on land. In the Disney version, the witch—originally the agent of magical transformation, a helper—is turned into an antagonist, and three helpers—the crab, the fish, and the seagull—accompany Ariel during her adventures. The conflict becomes more tangible and concrete, while the philosophical implications of Andersen's tale are gone. The victory over the antagonist reestablishes the protagonist's power position. The Disney plot is thus substantially closer to the traditional folktale plot. Yet the most essential change concerns the little mermaid's motivation for becoming human and the conditions for her transformation. In

Andersen's story, the mermaid's desire for the prince is connected with her desire for an immortal soul, which she can only obtain through marriage with a human. The desire for an immortal soul is, in its turn, an indication of her fear of death. In the movie, her motives are entirely romantic. In the original the little mermaid has to make a great sacrifice to achieve her goal. The loss of voice is irreversible, and her acquisition of legs instead of a tail causes enormous physical suffering: she feels as if she were all the time walking on sharp knives. And of course, as already noted, the ending has been changed to exactly the opposite. Finally, the mermaid has in the film version been given a name, Ariel, which makes her more human and offers a clearer subjectivity. Also the anonymous prince of the original has been given a name, which creates a sense of intimacy between the character and the audience.

While some characters have been added in *The Little Mermaid* and *Beauty and the Beast*, other characters have been removed, notably, the sisters in both stories and the little mermaid's grandmother. The grandmother's role in the original is that of the sender: she tells the mermaid about the world of humans and about the immortal soul. She is also the bearer of the feminine heritage and wisdom in the mermaid family. Since this dimension of the story is eliminated in the film, the figure of the grandmother becomes superfluous. The absence of sisters brings the protagonist still more to the foreground, but it does not allow the contrast between the sisters and the mermaid, who in the original is presented as unusually thoughtful and strange. In the original version of *Beauty and the Beast*, the sisters are used for several purposes. First, they refuse to sacrifice themselves to save the father, while the protagonist does so. Second, on hearing how happy the protagonist is with her beastly bridegroom, they encourage her to stay at home and thus break his heart (in some other versions of the tale, they induce the protagonist to burn her bridegroom's animal attire, with fatal results). In the Disney movie, the role of the evil and envious sisters is partially transferred to Gaston; thus the rivalry is shifted from the sisters onto the successful and the unsuccessful male. Furthermore, an additional factor has to be introduced to provide suspense and compensate for the absence of the sisters' plot: the countdown of the rose losing petals. Again, an external conflict is substituted for an internal one.

The change in the protagonist is a frequent intervention in the original story. The convention of film media generally demands that positive characters are good-looking. Film versions of *Anne of Green Gables* present Anne as pretty from the beginning, totally downplaying the profound evolution of the character in the novel. Still more amazing is the choice of the actor for the leading part in *The Neverending Story*. The protagonist, Bastian, is presented in the novel as fat and almost disgusting physically, which is a substantial part of his identity crisis. In the film, he is slim and attractive. Apart from the exterior, the protagonist's inner qualities can also be tampered with. In the film version of *Pippi Longstocking*, Pippi is repeatedly presented as a typical slapstick hero, pie throwing and destructive. The original Pippi has in fact deep respect for food and in one episode makes the local hooligan pick up and pay for the sausage he has thrown on the ground. Furthermore, the film-version Pippi obediently allows the authorities to put her into an orphanage, which the original Pippi would of course never consent to. The tragic aspect of Pippi, the child unable to grow up, is in the film lost, just as it is in the Disney version of *Peter Pan*.

The shift in the importance of secondary characters can substantially change the ideology of the film. In *The Little Mermaid*, the father is given a strongly authoritative role, and the whole story is much more focused on the parent-child relationship than the original. This is presumably better suited to the idea of socialization and the patriarchal social order.

A change in narrative perspective can manipulate the interpretation of the story. In the recent film version of *Little Women* a first-person narration is added, emphasizing not only Jo's role as the sole protagonist, but also her subjective point of view. The shift may seem insignificant, yet it radically affects our perception of the events and characters. The *Little Women* film also presents an anachronistic feminist ideology, expressed by the mother with explicitness unheard of at the time of action. Presenting different messages in film versions has been one of the major issues in the study of transmediation.

Simplification

Not least, film versions have been notorious for imposing specific interpretations on stories that in the original allow for ambivalence. The classic film version of *The Wizard of Oz* clearly presents Dorothy's adventures as a dream. For instance, the realistic frame is shot in black-and-white, while the dream sequences introduce color; and all the figures in the land of Oz are projected from Dorothy's reality. Such a straightforward interpretation certainly deprives the original story of some of its charm.

Many of the changes discussed above may seem insignificant and even irrelevant since films naturally can exist irrespective of their literary models and be evaluated for what they are rather than in comparison with the books. However, since film versions, not least the Disney ones, often become the best-known version of the story, they feed back into our appreciation of the original. When Disney movies are transmediated back into printed stories, the narrative has to be adapted to the existing pictures, and a new text is written to match the illustrations. Since such books are normally very short, there is no dialogue, and the events are rendered in a flat and meager language (you will hardly find the text author's name on the cover). The text/

image relationship is symmetrical, and all deeper dimensions of the original story are eliminated. With the aggressive marketing of the Disney merchandise, these oversimplified versions often become better known than the originals.

EXERCISE 1

Compare an original children's novel or story (*The Little Mermaid, Beauty and the Beast, Pinocchio, Alice in Wonderland, Winnie-the-Pooh, Peter Pan*) and a book based on the Disney version of the story. Consider the difference in plot structure, character gallery, characterization, language, and ideology.

EXERCISE 2

Watch two or more film versions of the same story. Most of the fairy tales animated by Disney also exist in other versions, as live-action films. There are also several film versions of *Little Women*; *The Lion, the Witch and the Wardrobe*; *Lord of the Rings*; and many other famous children's novels. Study the versions, paying attention to all the aspects discussed above, and consider how the various filmmakers' decisions affect our understanding of the story.

While studies of children's films naturally have a value of their own, the comparison between books and film versions is illuminating for our understanding of some preconceived opinions about the needs and interests of the young audience.

CROSSING THE BORDERS

Children's literature is an international phenomenon in the sense that the most outstanding and successful children's books usually get translated into other languages. The *Harry Potter* books are a recent and convincing example, as they have already been translated into more than thirty languages. *Alice in Wonderland*, universally considered a major children's classic, has been translated into many languages, as has *Winnie-the-Pooh* (including Latin and Esperanto), and Astrid Lindgren's books are available in more than eighty languages, including Frisian, Catalonian, Kymrian, Swahili, and Zulu.

The art of translation is perhaps as old as literature itself, and the most important translations in the Western world have been the translations of the

Bible. Because the Bible is supposed to be the true words of God, great importance has always been attributed to the "correct" translation, and the debates of what exactly is the most correct translation have occupied learned men throughout the centuries. Since words in any language are polysemantic (have several different meanings or shades of meaning), the process of translation does not simply imply substitution of one word for another. A translator is faced with the necessity of choosing between several meanings of a word in the source language (the language of the original text) and finding the adequate word in the target language (the language of the translated text). Further, translation implies not only conveying denotation (the literal, dictionary meaning of words), but also connotation, that is, contextual meaning that may change from text to text.

Faithful to the Text or the Reader?

One of the two radically different approaches to translation propagates equivalence, that is, a maximal approximation of the target text to the source text. A translation, in this view, should be "faithful" to the original, and no liberties are to be taken. The opposite view suggests that the translator should take into consideration the target audience, whereupon changes may not only be legitimate, but imperative, if the translated text in its specific context is to function somewhat similarly to the way in which the original functions in its initial situation. This view can be called dialogical, since it presupposes an active dialogue, or interaction, between the target text and its readers. The key question in dialogical translation is "For whom?" unlike the question "What?" in the equivalence theory.

These two views, elaborated in general translation theory, acquire special significance in connection with children's fiction, and both have been ardently defended by their respective advocates. This has in the first place to do with the practice of translating children's books, which in some essential ways differs from the practice of translating general literature. First of all, children's books have to a considerably higher extent been subjected to adaptation rather than translation. Adaptation means that a text is adjusted to what the translator believes to be the needs of the target audience, and it can include deletions, additions, explanations, purification, simplification, modernization, and a number of other interventions. Let us consider some of them.

Common Practices

Robinson Crusoe, the text perhaps most often subjected to adaptation, which is about five hundred pages in the original, has in some adaptations been cut down to twenty-four pages. The incentive has naturally been to make the book more accessible to young readers. The nature of the cuts has varied; most frequently, the self-reflexive and religious passages have been removed from this particular book. In the shortest versions, of course, only the very gist of the storyline remains. Quite a few classics, including *Alice in Wonderland*, have been subjected to similar surgery. A frequent interference implies periphrasis (retelling), abridgment, and text compressions. Rather than merely cutting out pieces of text, the translator retells the story, often turning direct speech into summaries, focusing on the central episodes, omitting characterization and other more complex dimensions of the original.

The practice of additions would seem to contradict the drive to make the story shorter and thus more suitable for children, but in some cases, translators have added passages explaining the characters' actions and other aspects of the source text. In one of the most famous adaptations of *Robinson Crusoe*, made by the German pedagogue Joachim Heinrich Campe, a frame story is added, in which a father is telling Robinson's story to his children. This enables the narrator to explain, comment, and pass judgment, in accordance with the didactic purpose of the adaptation.

Alterations can include such instances as changing the ending to suit the target audience. The ending of Andersen's *The Little Match Girl* has been in many translations changed from the character's death to her finding a good and loving family. Omissions and alterations for political, cultural, or religious reasons are called purification: the text is purified from passages that are perceived as offensive (another term is bowdlerization, after the nineteenth-century British clergyman Thomas Bowdler who produced *Family Shakespeare*, fit to be read in the presence of ladies). It may be the matter of abusive language, the mention of bodily functions viewed as inappropriate in a children's book, or an expression of ideology unacceptable by the target culture. While in the original of the Swedish children's classic *The Wonderful Adventures of Nils*, the protagonist's parents go to a church, in the Russian translation they go to a market. Churches and religion were not supposed to appear in children's books published in the Soviet Union. Most translations (as well as English-language abridgements) of *Gulliver's Travels* omit the episode in which Gulliver extinguishes the fire in the royal palace of Lilliput by passing water.

Simplification implies that a foreign notion is supplanted by something less specific, for instance when a particular dish is simply translated as "food" or the title of a newspaper is changed into the general "newspaper." *Rewording* means that a metaphor or some other figure of speech, nonexistent in the target language, is rendered by a circumscription. *Modernization* means bringing everyday details, objects, and concepts up to date in translation, including changing or deleting what may be perceived as offensive, such as racism and sexism. Also purely linguistic modernization is frequent, when, for instance, nineteenth-century fiction is translated into more modern idiom. *Harmonization* may include, for instance, changes in children's behavior, if considered improper in the target culture, or changes in adults' attitudes. For instance, in many cultures adults in children's fiction are supposed to be impeccable, thus any mention of drunkards and the like are eliminated. *Embellishment* means any form of beautification, from using more high-flown language than the original to adding longish descriptions.

In many theoretical discussions of children's literature, all these practices are unconditionally condemned, since they are perceived as censorship. While we may indeed interrogate the intentions, the practice itself is merely an extreme form of the dialogical approach to translation mentioned above, the one that takes into consideration the target audience. In fact, the use of foul language can be less offensive in some cultures than in others, and the attitude toward nakedness varies substantially between countries and epochs. The practice of adaptation of target texts is then in no way radically different from adapting originals to what authors (or publishers) believe to be the needs and interests of the young audience, which in its turn depends on the views on childhood and education.

Justified?

Let us consider some cases where various alterations have been made in translations and argue whether the changes are reasonable and justified. Two possible ways of dealing with elements of source texts that may hamper the target audience's understanding are *domestication* and *foreignization*. In domesticating a translated text, the translator substitutes familiar phenomena and concepts for what may be perceived as strange and hard to understand. It is not uncommon in translations of children's books to change foreign food, weights and measures, currency, flora and fauna, customs, and traditions to something that the target readers will more easily understand. *Localization* implies a form of domestication through changing the setting of a book to a more familiar one. For instance, the German translations of Enid Blyton's adventure novels are set in Germany. In assessing domestication and localization (universally condemned by the adherents of the equivalence theory), we should ask ourselves what the translator's motivation might have been. When a novel for adults is translated, the target audience may be expected to understand that certain objects and concepts are different in a foreign culture. Young readers have less knowledge of foreign countries and cultures. Children are seldom aware that the book they are reading is a translation, and as several empirical studies show, tolerance for strangeness is usually lower in children's texts as compared to literature for adults. While transposing the setting of a British novel to Germany may be an unnecessary interference, some other changes may be fully justified, to make the text more accessible to the target audience.

If a translated text is foreignized, the translator may decide to keep some words untranslated, in order to preserve the foreign flavor. The proponents of this approach maintain that it is essential that young readers become aware of cultural differences as they read translated books. Admirable as it is, the approach may sometimes be stretched too far. In the English translation of *Pippi Longstocking*, Pippi is shown "busy making *pepparkakor*—a kind of Swedish cookie" (25; italics in English translation). The motivation behind this translation is apparently to show the American readers that Sweden is a different country with different sorts of cookies. The cookies are, however, nothing more exotic than the universally known gingerbread. By using a foreign word in the English text, the translator focuses the readers' attention on the cookies, thus creating a different effect than is the case with source-text readers. Further, the phrase "a kind of Swedish cookie" is of course an addition, the translator's explanation of the foreign word, which is unnecessary in the source text, and which would have been superfluous if the word had been translated as "gingerbread." On the other hand, if Pippi were indeed making a cookie that completely lacked a correspondence in the target language (which is more likely with a translation into Chinese or Swahili), would it be motivated to supplant the exotic *pepparkakor* with something more familiar? After all, Swedish readers do not experience a sense of foreignness and exoticism while meeting this word in a text. The question in each individual case is whether the cultural detail is indeed significant.

In a dialogic translation, the goal is to approximate the response of the source-text readers, and substituting a familiar notion for a foreign one would be considered more adequate. A famous example can be gathered in the Bible translations: in translating the phrase "God's lamb" into Inuit, the translator changed it into "God's seal cub," since a lamb is an animal unknown to the Inuit. In fact, in a Swahili translation of Astrid Lindgren's *Noisy Village*, spring is changed to the rainy season, because spring is an unknown concept for the target audience, and the Noisy Village children's joyful anticipation of spring has to be translated into a similar experience.

How to Deal with Names

Personal and geographic names in translation present a special dilemma. The equivalent theory prescribes that names should always be retained as they are in the original. There may, however, be several reasons why names are changed. First, the sound of the name may give undesirable associations in the target language. The name Pippi, for instance, in a number of languages suggests urinating. The character is therefore renamed Fifi in French, Pippa in Spanish, and Peppi in Russian. In the translation of Astrid Lindgren's *Mio, My Son*, the protagonist's name was changed from Bo Wilhelm Olsson to Karl Andrew Nilsson, seemingly without reason. However, the last name "Olsson" carries comic connotations for English-speaking readers, which is highly objectionable in Lindgren's text. Another reason may be that the name in the target language is already firmly connected with a famous literary character. The hero of Astrid Lindgren's *Emil's Pranks* has been renamed Mickel in the German translation, since the name Emil is associated with the protagonist of the German classic *Emil and the Detectives*. By contrast, when the name of the title character in Lindgren's *Ronia, the Robber's Daughter* is changed to Kersti, the only motivation seems to be foreignization, since Ronia is just as much a nonexisting name in Swedish as in English, or was, before the novel was written. Yet another problem may arise if a name has a specific sound in the source language that gives some associations for the source-text readers. Many names in the *Harry Potter* books carry associations that critics have tried to interpret: Dumbledore, Malfoy, Lupin, and especially Voldemort. The translators around the world have either retained the names, thus losing the association (equivalent solution), or invented new names with similar associations in the target language (dialogic solution). Some translators have even considered—and rejected—changing Harry's last name, to stress its plainness, into a corresponding last name in the target language, meaning "the maker of ceramic vessels."

Finally, names may refer to a phenomenon in the source language known by a different name in the target language. The name of Andersen's figure Ole Lukøje, which means literally "Ole-close-your-eyes" (Ole is a personal name), has in some translations been changed into Willie Winkie. It seems a very sensible solution, since it connects the name with an English folklore character similar to that in the Danish tradition to which Andersen refers. The target readers are thus offered the same association as the source readers. From the point of view of the equivalent theory, such changes are unacceptable.

Translating Cultural Context

Some examples of foreignization of culturally dependent phenomena are also connected to the practice of explanatory additions, strongly questioned by the equivalent theory. For instance, for a Swedish reader, the connotation of "the blue and yellow flag" is as clear as "stars and stripes" for an American reader. In translation, two strategies have been employed. The equivalent translator has chosen to write "the blue and yellow flag," providing a footnote with the explanation that the colors of the Swedish flag are blue and yellow. While the solution may seem fortunate, using footnotes in fiction, especially children's fiction, is definitely undesirable. Another translator has circumvented the problem by adding one single word: "the blue and yellow Swedish flag."

As we have seen in chapter 2, discussing intertextuality, many children's novels contain allusions and other literary and extraliterary references. In translation, it is of course pointless to retain the allusion to a text that is completely unknown to the target readers. Dialogic translators may choose to delete the reference or, if it works, to provide another reference that will create a similar effect. Naturally, if the text alludes to another text widely known in the target language, this available translation should preferably be used, even if the translator judges it to be poor. For instance, the title of Philip Pullman's trilogy *His Dark Materials* is translated literally into Swedish, ignoring the fact that the Milton quotation to which the title alludes is in Swedish rendered as "the dark element." The readers of the target text have no chance to make the connection between the title and the poem it alludes to.

Some more fundamental alterations, motivated as well as unmotivated, include the shift from personal to impersonal narration (such as the many abridged versions of *Robinson Crusoe* retold in the third person); the change of tense, sometimes resulting in a more distanced narration or occasionally depriving the readers of guidelines when complex temporal switches are involved; and forced changes of the characters' gender (usually only possible with animal and inanimate-object characters), resulting in distorted gender relationships between the characters in the story.

There are, of course, many other difficulties that translators may meet. One is how to deal with puns and other linguistic games often found in children's books. Some critics claim that certain texts are "untranslatable." It is indeed a challenge to translate a title such as *War and Peas* into any language in which the pun will not be possible. Yet a skillful translator can resort to something called compensatory translation, which implies adding a different pun or wordplay to compensate for the lost one. The American translator of *Pippi Longstocking* has basically lost all puns and Pippi's witty comments, either because of incompetence or because dialogical translation, including compensatory, was believed to be disadvantageous.

In many cases, the difference between the two approaches becomes clearly manifest. In *Alice in Wonderland*, the Duchess says to Alice, among the many platitudes, "Take care of the sense, and the sounds will take care of themselves." For a source reader, the statement alludes to the existing English proverb, "Take care of the pence, and the pounds will take care of themselves." If translated literally, as has been done in many languages, the allusion and thus the humor is lost. All the nonsensical verses in *Alice in Wonderland* are parodies on children's anthology pieces from Carroll's time. For instance, the song that the Duchess sings to the baby is a parody on a sentimental children's verse by David Bates:

> Speak gently to the little child!
> Its love be sure to gain;

Teach it in accents soft and mild;
It may not long remain.

In Carroll's version, the poem goes:

Speak roughly to your little boy,
And beat him when he sneezes:
He only does it to annoy,
Because he knows it teases.

The translators of *Alice* into different languages have chosen two opposite strategies. Some have translated the verses literally, which certainly has kept their nonsensical character, but lost the allusion to existing verses. The translations are thus superficially "faithful," yet they are devoid of a deeper equivalence based on the allusion. The adherents of the dialogical theory have chosen to write their own parodies of verses from their own culture. These verses have nothing to do with the source text, yet they evoke the same response in the target-text readers as the original verses evoke in the source-text readers. Such translation strategies may be less faithful to the source text, but instead more loyal toward the target audience. What is a "good" translation is thus a matter closely connected with the general views on what is "good" children's literature.

EXERCISE

There are many cases of several existing translations of international children's classics into English: Grimms' and Andersen's fairy tales, *The Nutcracker, Pinocchio, Heidi, The Foundling, The Little Prince,* and more. *Pippi Longstocking* has been published in different translations in the United States and in Britain. Even if you do not know the source language, a comparison of the two versions can be illuminating. You may find whole chapters and lengthy passages omitted, explanatory sentences added, names changed, offensive or merely complicated passages purged, and so on. Consider in each case which of the translators have chosen an equivalent or a dialogic solution (some translations may naturally be in between). Contemplate which translation you prefer and why. If you have grown up with a certain translation, do not let this fact affect your evaluation.

HOW TO GO FURTHER

One of the most exciting theoretical studies of textual transformations is Gérard Genette's *Palimpsests: Literature in the Second Degree,* already mentioned in connection with intertextuality in chapter 2. Genette examines all kinds of alterations and transpositions of literary texts: sequels and continuations (some of which he regards as "unfaithful" and even "murderous"), versification and prosaization, transstylization, different types of quantitative transformations, transmotivation, transvaluation, and many more. Apart from the useful terminology, many of these interferences are especially relevant for children's literature. Versification (rendering an originally prosaic work in verse) and especially prosaization (retelling an originally versified work in prose) are common practices in children's literature. Both can occur within the same language or in translation. The "ethnic" musical *The Wiz* is an excellent example of transmediation that at the same time presents transmotivation (new intentions) and transvaluation (new ideology) as compared to the original. It is also an obvious example of a text that shifts its primary audience in the process. Not least, Genette's plentiful examples offer insight in method and point out the textual elements to look for in such types of studies. Here the field for research is unlimited.

REFERENCES

General

Children Literature 9 (1981): special issue on children's literature and the media.
Kinder, Marcia. *Playing with Power in Movies, Television and Video Games*. Berkeley: University of California Press, 1991.
Mackey, Margaret. *The Case of Peter Rabbit: Changing Conditions of Literature for Children*. New York: Garland, 1998.
Maynard, Sally, Cliff McKnight, and Melanie Keady. "Children's Classics in the Electronic Medium." *The Lion and the Unicorn* 23, no. 2 (1999): 184–201.

Illustrations and Picturebooks

Bader, Barbara. *American Picturebooks: From Noah's Ark to the Beast Within*. New York: Macmillan, 1976.
Doonan, Jane. *Looking at Pictures in Picture Books*. Stroud: Thimble Press, 1993.
Feaver, William. *When We Were Young: Two Centuries of Children's Book Illustrations*. London: Thames and Hudson, 1977.
Freudenburg, Rachel. "Illustrating Childhood—'Hansel and Gretel.'" *Marvels & Tales* 12, no. 2 (1998): 263–318.
Hendrickson, Linnea. "The View from Rapunzel's Tower." *Children's Literature in Education* 31, no. 4 (2000): 209–23.
Hürlimann, Bettina. *Picture-Book World*. Translated and edited by Brian W. Alderson. London: Oxford University Press, 1968.

Kiefer, Barbara. *The Potential of Picturebooks: From Visual Literacy to Aesthetic Understanding*. Englewood Cliffs, NJ: Prentice Hall, 1995.

Klemin, Diana. *The Art of Art for Children's Books*. New York: Clarkson N. Potter, 1966.

Lewis, David. *Reading Contemporary Picturebooks: Picturing Text*. London: Routledge, 2001.

Nikolajeva, Maria, and Carole Scott. *How Picturebooks Work*. New York: Garland, 2001.

Nodelman, Perry. *Words About Pictures: The Narrative Art of Children's Picture Books*. Athens, GA: The University of Georgia Press, 1988.

Schwarcz, Joseph H. *Ways of the Illustrator: Visual Communication in Children's Literature*. Chicago: American Library Association, 1982.

Schwarcz, Joseph, and Chava Schwarcz. *The Picture Book Comes of Age*. Chicago: American Library Association, 1991.

Stewig, John Warren. *Looking at Picture Books*. Fort Atkinson, WI: Highsmith Press, 1995.

Whalley, Joyce Irene, and Tessa Rose Chester. *A History of Children's Book Illustration*. London: John Murray, 1988.

Transmediation

Cummins, June. "Romancing the Plot: The Real Beast of Disney's Beauty and the Beast." *Children's Literature Association Quarterly* 20, no. 1 (1995): 23–28.

Haase, Donald. "Gold into Straw: Fairy-Tale Movies for Children and the Culture Industry." *The Lion and the Unicorn* 12, no. 2 (1988): 193–207.

Hastings, Waller. "Moral Simplification in Disney's The Little Mermaid." *The Lion and the Unicorn* 17, no. 1 (1993): 82–92.

Hollindale, Peter. "Peter Pan, Captain Hook and the Book of the Video." *Signal* 72 (1993): 152–175.

Rahn, Suzanne. "Snow White's Dark Ride: Narrative Strategies at Disneyland." *Bookbird* 38, no. 1 (2000): 19–24.

Rollin, Lucy. "Fear of Faerie: Disney and the Elitist Critics." *Children's Literature Association Quarterly* 12, no. 2 (1987): 90–93.

Russell Thorn, Joan. "Children's Literature: Reading, Seeing, Watching." *Children's Literature in Education* 22, no. 1 (1991): 51–58.

Street, Douglas, ed. *Children's Novels and the Movies*. New York: Ungar, 1983.

Zipes, Jack. *Happily Ever After: Fairy Tales, Children and the Culture Industry*. New York: Routledge, 1997. Chap. 3, "Toward a Theory of the Fairy-Tale Film"; chap. 4, "Once Upon a Time Beyond Disney"; chap. 5, "Lion Kings and the Culture Industry."

———. *When Dreams Came True: Classical Fairy Tales and Their Tradition*. New York: Routledge, 1999.

Translation Theory and Translating for Children

Baker, Mona. *In Other Words: A Coursebook on Translation*. London: Routledge, 1992.

Bassnet, Susan. *Translation Studies*. London: Methuen, 1980.

Bell, Anthea. "Children's Books in Translation." *Signal* 28 (1979): 47–53.

———. "Children's Literature and International Identity? A Translator's Viewpoint." Pp. 23–30 in *Children's Literature and National Identity*, edited by Margaret Meek. Stoke-on-Trent: Trentham Books, 2001.

Desmet, Mieke K. T. "Intertextuality/Intervisuality in Translation: The Jolly Postman's Intercultural Journey from Britain to the Netherlands." *Children's Literature in Education* 32, no. 1 (2001): 31–43.

Fernández Lopez, Marisa. "Translation Studies in Contemporary Children's Literature: A Comparison of Intercultural Ideological Factors." *Children's Literature Association Quarterly* 25, no. 1 (2000): 29–37.

Klingberg, Göte. *Children's Fiction in the Hands of the Translators*. Lund: Gleerup, 1986.

Klingberg, Göte, et al., eds. *Children's Books in Translation: The Situation and the Problems*. Stockholm: Almqvist & Wiksell International, 1978.

Malarté-Feldman, Claire-Lise. "The Challenges of Translating Perrault's Contes into English." *Marvels & Tales* 13, no. 2 (1999): 184–197.

Netley, Noriko Shimoda. "The Difficulty of Translation: Decoding Cultural Signs on Other Languages." *Children's Literature in Education* 23, no. 4 (1992): 195–202. Discusses the translation of Roald Dahl into Japanese.

Nikolajeva, Maria. *Children's Literature Comes of Age: Towards a New Aesthetic*. New York: Garland, 1996. Pp. 27–34, "Cultural Context and Translatability."

Nikolajeva, Maria, and Carole Scott. *How Picturebooks Work*. New York: Garland, 2001. Chap. 1, "Whose Book is It."

Oittinen, Riitta. *Translating for Children*. New York: Garland, 2000.

O'Sullivan, Emer. "Translating Pictures." *Signal* 90 (1999): 167–175.

———. "Alice in Different Wonderlands: Varying Approaches in the German Translations of an English Children's Classic." Pp. 11–21 in *Children's Literature and National Identity*, edited by Margaret Meek. Stoke-on-Trent: Trentham Books, 2001.

Tomlinson, Carl M. *Children's Books from Other Countries*. Lanham, MD: Scarecrow, 1998.

Weaver, Warren. *Alice in Many Tongues: The Translations of Alice in Wonderland*. Madison, WI: The University of Wisconsin Press, 1964.

11

The Aesthetic of the Reader

We have now come to the recipients of children's fiction. In this chapter we will investigate the various categories of readers, real and implied. Let us first take another look at the communication chain: real author → implied author → narrator → narratee → implied reader → real reader. We have earlier distinguished between real flesh-and-blood authors and implied authors, that is, images of authors that can be constructed from the text. Similarly, we distinguish between real readers and implied readers. One and the same flesh-and-blood reader can read books presupposing different audiences, while several real readers may have different perceptions of the same text. The implied reader is the authors' idea about their audience, the idea found in the text itself. It is, however, doubtful whether we can rely on writers' statements such as, "I write for boys between 11 and 14." The author's statement and the implied reader found in the text are not necessarily identical. Nor can we rely on the publishers' recommendations: "For girls 10 years and up." The implied readership may also be subject to change as time passes: books that were originally intended for adults are now more suitable for children (and, occasionally, the other way round). The construction of the implied reader is a more complicated process than merely putting a label on the book.

WHAT DO CHILDREN REALLY READ?

Let us, however, start with real readers. Empirical research of children's reading is perhaps one of the oldest approaches to children's literature. It includes a vast number of methods and tools, such as quantitative analysis, longitudinal studies, response protocols, interviews, and individual observation. Since this research lies within the field of reading and literacy rather than children's literature, we will consider just a few brief examples. Empirical research may embrace broad surveys, including nationwide, of children's reading habits as well as small-scale surveys, for instance of reading habits in a particular area. Such surveys are often conducted through detailed questionnaires distributed in schools, whereupon collected data are analyzed statistically. Results are presented in the form of staple diagrams. Some of the questions common in such surveys involve the readers' preferences for genres and kinds of books, the frequency and intensity of reading at school and at leisure, favorite and most recently read books, comparison of reading to other pastimes, especially television, and so on. Various information about respondents is taken into consideration, such as age, gender, or the parents' occupation. A representative selection of respondents is a prerequisite, and control groups are used. Often two or more categories of respondents are compared, for instance, from different social circumstances or from different states or even countries. A survey may also be devoted to evaluation of a number of specific books, for instance the top ten in library loans or the top ten on booksellers' lists. Small-scale surveys have been done concerning the popularity of a particular author. All such surveys, mapping readers, help scholars as well as mediators to understand how children's literature functions in society, what makes certain books popular, and what can be done to promote reading. (See fig. 11-1.)

Quantitative survey methods are very elaborate, and scholars working with questionnaires know how to formulate questions to ensure a somewhat reliable response. One device is to put the same question twice, worded in a different way. For instance, one question may ask, "Do you like the Sweet Valley books?" while another, appearing twenty lines further down, is "How many Sweet Valley books have you read during the past year?" If a respondent has answered "No" to the first question and "25" to the second, there is reason to mistrust the candor of the first response.

Individual interviews with children can reveal more than broad field studies, but they are naturally more laborious. In deep interviews, both those concerning reading habits and those focused on understanding and interpretation, scholars talk to children, recording conversations and then analyzing the transcripts. There is also some interesting research following one particular child from birth to a certain age, logging her encounters with books and every response to them. For obvious reasons, such studies are very rare, since they demand continued observation of a child over a period of several years. Usually, scholars conduct such research with their own children.

Some important discoveries made by recent empirical studies include the following:

- that children who read much also watch television and play computer games a lot, while children who do not read normally do not engage in

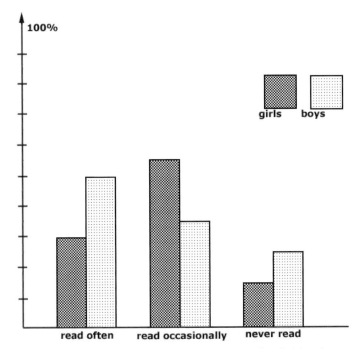

Fig. 11-1   Mock staple diagram showing reading habits of
third-graders in Paradise Elementary, somewhere.

other activities either. The common claim that television "steals" time
from reading is not quite true;
- that, contrary to common belief, boys do not prefer nonfiction;
- that the most common ways of getting information about books is from
  friends and classmates, while recommendations from adults, including
  teachers, parents, and librarians, play a negligible role. This should be
  an eye-opener for adult reading promoters;
- that young children (under seven) understand temporality, but not causality in narratives;
- that young children have problems understanding first-person narratives. This should be a serious warning to writers who use personal narration even in picture books for very young readers;
- that children up to ten to twelve years do not understand irony. Thus
  writers who use ironic narration miss their primary audience and at
  best create confusion.

Like all other areas of inquiry, empirical reader research has its problems.
Very often, reader surveys are conducted with preconceived opinions. The

answers received are naturally highly governed by the way questions are worded. For instance, the question, "What did the writer want to say by his story?" presupposes that the writer indeed wanted to say something, which is far from self-evident, especially for a child. The question, "What have you learned from this story?" presupposes that there was something to learn. In an empirical study of children's understanding of Shel Silverstein's *The Giving Tree*, some respondents thought the question concerned their reading skills, while others replied that they learned that apples come from apple trees, or that one could build houses and boats from wood, which was definitely not what the researcher had anticipated. On the other hand, schoolchildren know very well that teachers value reading and also what kind of books adults tend to value highest; therefore they may supply answers that they think the teachers expect them to give. Unless many control questions are provided, the validity of such studies is dubious. As repeatedly stated, children seldom remember the authors of the books they read. If questions contain authors' names rather than titles (or better still, main characters), children may fail to respond even though they have read the books. The statistical method, in other words, contains many pitfalls.

Predictability of results is another frequent weakness. For instance, surveys from many countries repeatedly state that girls read more than boys, or that children from educated families read more than children from families with lower levels of education, or that teenagers understand complex stories better than younger readers. Since field studies are time-consuming, they are often conducted by a team of researchers, while the analysis and evaluation is performed by someone who may not even be familiar with the conditions of the surveys. Often statistics are assumed to be self-sufficient, and evaluation as such is absent. The risk of individual interviews is that researchers affect respondents by their own reaction to responses, even as minute as nodding or voice modulation. An interviewer can be easily influenced by the outcome of the previous interview. In assessing children's understanding of stories, researchers often use themselves as models, viewing their own interpretations as the only possible ones. As a result, children who present unusual and original interpretations get lower scores than those who come with expected and conventional answers.

ACTIVITY

To test the method, conduct a small-scale reader survey of your classmates or friends. Here are some things you should think about:

- Formulate your objective clearly. What exactly do you want to know about your respondents?

- What parameters are relevant for your survey? Age, gender, social background, marital status, smoking habits? Why are they relevant?
- Word your questions carefully and do not forget control questions.
- Remember that collecting data and compiling diagrams is merely the initial stage of the job. You have to evaluate your results and draw conclusions matching your initial objective.

THE READER IN THE TEXT

The various reader-response theories do not deal with real flesh-and-blood readers, but with implied readers, the images of readers that can be extracted from the text. The aesthetics of reader response is a vast and firmly established field of inquiry, and children's literature research has begun to borrow methods and ideas from it. The objective of theoretical reader-response studies (the original term, introduced in Germany, is reception theory) is not to map the actual audience, but to theorize how readers decode and understand what they read. It is therefore oriented toward readers as abstract textual constructions rather than concrete recipients outside the text.

The Reader as Co-creator

The joint and most essential premise of all the various directions of reader-response theory is that the literary text as such is not created by the author, but rather by the reader. A book, some critics argue, is merely an artifact, sheets of paper bound together, with some printing ink on the pages. A book that is not read remains a material object, until a reader extracts the meaning from it, decants the text from the book, just as you might decant wine from a bottle. The difference between a work and a text is decisive in reader-response theory. (There are other terms used to describe this distinction, but to avoid confusion we will not plunge into unnecessary terminology.) A work is something an author has left behind, a dead, static object. A text is a living, dynamic process, created anew at the crossroads of the readers' different experiences. A text in this meaning is rather an interpretation of a work. Some critics say that literary texts are realized by readers through their participation. This is an interesting and daring idea, but it has its problems. If each reader creates his own text out of a work, does it mean that every book has thousands and maybe millions of versions? We will see how reader-response theory deals with this question.

The theoretical points of departure for reader-response analytical models are phenomenology (examining what happens in our minds when we read) and hermeneutics (examining how we make things mean). We have already discussed some aspects of hermeneutics in chapter 2. Some of the central ideas of phenomenology, relevant for our argument here, are that external objects and phenomena are not what we think they are, that art is only a reflection of reality, and that writing means creating an illusion. Our ability to understand art and literature is therefore based on our experience, literary as well as extraliterary, with which we compare what we read. Hermeneutics emphasizes that texts cannot be understood without the process of decoding, or interpretation.

There may, however, be two radically different approaches to the question of how this decoding happens. One view can be summarized by the question, what does the text do to the reader? It is based on the assumption that there are intrinsic qualities in a text forcing the reader to interpret the text in a certain way. Hence, a book as an artifact has a number of unrealized possibilities, and it is up to the reader to "realize" them, that is, to extract a meaning from something that is already encoded and merely waiting to be uncovered.

The opposite question is, what does the reader do with the text? This approach emphasizes the reader's active role in decoding. Rather than extracting intrinsically existing and a once-and-for-all established meaning from the work, the reader becomes a co-creator, contributing to the establishment of meaning with his experience and understanding. This direction, connected in the first place with the German scholar Wolfgang Iser, views reading as an active dialogue between the text and the reader. Iser argues that readers relate the information they get from the text partly to their experience of real life, partly to their previous reading; in this respect, each individual reader's previous experience is decisive for the interpretation.

The Reader's Expectations and the Text's Premises

The meaning of a text is, according to Iser, revealed through interaction of anticipation and retrospection. For instance, when we start to read *The Wizard of Oz*, we have certain expectations, based on our earlier experience of stories. We know that something must happen to Dorothy, and when she is carried away, our expectations are confirmed. We expect that her good deeds toward the Scarecrow, the Tin Woodman, and the Lion will be rewarded, and in retrospect we see the connection between her behavior and her friends' gratitude. Thus we do not simply retrieve the preset meaning from the book, but the meaning is created from our reactions and responses to what we read, including emotional responses, such as empathy, sympathy, and antipathy, and cognitive responses, that is, understanding the deeper meaning of the text. In this process, we are governed by the position (or subjectivity) of the implied reader, the reader in the text. Other terms in use include inscribed, encoded, ideal, hypothetical, model, and virtual readers.

The scholars who proposed these terms have argued for a subtle difference between them, which are of little significance for our argument here.

As already suggested, the implied reader is roughly defined as the real authors' idea of their audience as inscribed in the texts. In other words, the implied reader is an abstract receiver assumed to have the capacity to assess the text. In the mainstream, we can clearly see that the implied reader of Joyce's *Ulysses* is different from that of a supermarket novel, or historically, the implied reader of *Gulliver's Travels* was assumed to have certain knowledge of Swift's contemporary England which present-day real readers may lack. The implied readers of *Ulysses* are supposed to be able to penetrate the complexity of the novel; the implied readers of a supermarket novel are supposed to be satisfied by its plot and its superficial and stereotypical characterization. The contemporary implied readers of *Gulliver's Travels* were supposed to recognize the real events and the real people whom Swift depicts in a satirical manner. Similarly, in a children's novel, the text is deliberately constructed so that it can be understood by the implied readers. For instance, settings should be recognizable or at least conceivable; events should be somewhat relevant for the readers' experience; characters should think, behave, and speak the way the implied readers are assumed to think, behave, and speak; and the vocabulary should not be significantly above the average level of the targeted group. Implied readers of children's fiction have a particular age, gender, ethnicity, religion, politics, level of education, cultural background, and so on, which all affect the construction of the texts. As already mentioned, it is not uncommon for writers to misjudge their audience. Writers may declare that they write for boys and girls between ten and twelve, while the implied readers of the novels may have to be slightly older and more mature to understand the story, or the character's experiences will only appeal to girls, or the settings and events will feel alien or even offensive to ethnic readers or members of a particular religious confession, or the events presuppose a certain knowledge of American nineteenth-century history, or the intertextual links address a reader with substantial reading habits. All this does not necessarily prevent real readers from enjoying a text that postulates a different implied reader.

In our discussion of the narrator's presence in the text (chapter 8), we considered a quote from *The Lion, the Witch and the Wardrobe*: "Have you ever had a gallop on a horse? Think of that. . . . And then imagine you are going about twice as fast as the fastest racehorse" (149). This sentence presupposes an implied reader who has indeed had experience of horseback riding, presumably an English middle-class child who has attended a privileged private school. Far from all real readers of the novel will actually have this experience. A more implicit aspect would be that the reader is supposed to be familiar with European or more precisely British history, since readers are presumed to understand why the children were sent away from London.

Naturally, the implied reader of the Narnia Chronicles is expected to be a
Christian with good knowledge of the Bible. The reader is also expected to
know about the British school system, since it is mentioned that Edmund
had attended a "wrong" school. Another very subtle detail involves the description of Lucy's tea with the faun, where it is pointed out that they got a
boiled egg each. This fact is wasted on a reader who does not know that
during the Second World War, eggs in Britain were rationed to one per person every other week. The original implied reader was supposed to be awed
by the luxury of the meal. Yet none of these facts would inhibit the reading
and understanding of the book.

CONTEMPLATE

Choose a book that you enjoyed as a child and remember well. Reread
it, noting carefully the differences between your original responses and
your present reading. You are now a different reader from what you
once were; as an adult reader, especially as a scholar of children's literature, you have a different life experience than the implied reader. This
does not mean that you automatically have become a better reader,
merely that you are different. You may have lost some of your earlier
spontaneous perception of what you read.

Horizon of Expectations

Real readers may differ from the implied audience due to a number of extraliterary factors. When we today read books written two hundred or a
hundred or fifty or even ten years ago, we do not necessarily interpret them
in the same way contemporary readers did. Reader-response theory refers to
this phenomenon as *horizon of expectations*. Nineteenth-century readers had
certain views on society, politics, race, gender, or education that we do not
share today. Their reference frames concerning literature were also different.
They did not have our current knowledge of, for instance, world wars and
genocides of the twentieth century, and they had not been exposed to modernistic and postmodernistic literature. In other words, the readers' horizon
of expectations has changed during the past hundred years. Mark Twain's or
Louisa M. Alcott's contemporaries understood their books differently than
we do today. Some radical contemporary reevaluations of classic children's
novels are based on changes in expectations and values, not least reevaluations of gender and race. But even much closer events can affect our horizon
of expectations. After the attack on the World Trade Center on September
11, 2001, our perception of movies such as *Towering Inferno* or *Independence Day* will be forever changed. We must thus distinguish between syn-

chronic and diachronic readers. Diachronic real readers are always detached from the implied readers of the text. (It is of course conceivable that an author deliberately addresses a future audience, but the case is marginal.)

Similarly, speaking of located versus dislocated readers, we acknowledge that a Swedish or Bulgarian or Chinese reader will each have a slightly—or sometimes substantially—different understanding of an American novel as compared to an American reader. Nationhood, school system, family values, and everyday life, that the implied reader is not even supposed to pay any attention to, may seem strange and therefore more prominent to a dislocated reader.

In order to avoid dealing with an infinite number of individual readers, reader-response criticism has also proposed the concept of *interpretative community*. It describes an implied audience that is supposed to have a somewhat common background concerning age, education, life experience, reading habits, and so on. A college class of children's literature is a different interpretative community than a group of third-graders, even though they may read the same books. An EFL class in France or Sweden is a different interpretative community than an English class in the United States. A class with a dedicated English teacher is a different interpretative community than a class that has had seven substitute teachers during one semester. An interpretative community has certain common points of departure and common reference frames in making meaning of a literary text. For instance, a class that has read *The Lion, the Witch and the Wardrobe* will be more prepared to interpret *Bridge to Terabithia* than a class that has not.

Real and Implied Audience

LET US EXPLORE

Try to construct the implied audience of the *Harry Potter* books. In doing this, you have to pretend that you do not know anything about their actual audience and their tremendous success. Just see what the text presupposes. Pay attention to the readers' age, gender, education, cultural background, and so on.

Unlike many famous children's writers, J. K. Rowling did not tell her story to a particular child; her daughter was much too young at the time the first book was written. Although we can never know exactly what kind of readers she had in mind (whatever she may say afterward, we should not trust it too much), we can from the text itself see what features are inherent to its implied reader. First, we must look at the protagonist's age. Harry is eleven in the first book and gets one year older in each sequel. Empirical research shows that, unlike adults, children prefer to read about characters who are their age or slightly older. The implied reader of *Harry Potter* is thus between ten and twelve. Considerably younger readers would find the books too long and complicated, while for older readers, the tribulations of an eleven- or even fifteen-year-old may seem too childish.

Second, the protagonist is a boy. We would perhaps assume that the implied reader is male. However, empirical research shows that female readers generally have no preference as to the protagonist's gender (while male readers do). Furthermore, in his function in the plot, Harry is "gender-neutral"; that is, most of his adventures could have involved a female protagonist. Finally, there is a female character, Hermione, by Harry's side, providing a subject position for female readers who for some reasons have problems adopting a male subjectivity.

Harry Potter books are generically eclectic and play with many genres: a sentimental Victorian poor-orphan story, boarding-school story, and of course fantasy. In order to understand the parody and the author's ironic games with genres, the implied reader must be well-read in these kinds of literature, not least fantasy novels by Tolkien and C. S. Lewis. Since the boarding-school story is a typical British middle-class phenomenon, the implied reader of the books is a British white middle-class child, most likely a child with some form of Christian upbringing. The vocabulary of the books is rather advanced, and to appreciate the sound of certain names (e.g., Professor Lupin, from Latin "lupus," wolf) and the magical incantations, some knowledge of Latin is necessary, which is required of British privileged-school students. The rich intertextual layers of the books presuppose a certain level of encyclopedic knowledge.

Having thus constructed the image of the implied reader of the *Harry Potter* books, we can immediately state that their real audience does not match this image at all. The *Harry Potter* novels are read by children and adults alike, and they are appealing to much younger children than ten-year-olds. They have conquered audiences all over the world, including such countries as China, where the system of British private schools would certainly feel alien. Most important, perhaps, the books have for many children become the first encounter with reading, the first gateway into the world of literature, their complexity notwithstanding. So much for the implied audience then? Yet we can readjust the implied reader from what we know about real readers, noting exactly what features of the book appeal to a considerably broader implied readership than we have constructed.

EXERCISE

Construct the implied audience of some of the following stories: *Cinderella*; *The Little Mermaid*; *Little Women*; *The Adventures of Tom Saw-*

yer; *Little House in the Big Woods*; *Pippi Longstocking*; *The Outsiders*; and *Roll of Thunder, Hear My Cry*. Take into consideration all the factors we have discussed. Make a distinction between the original implied reader and an average contemporary North American elementary-school interpretative community.

Filling the Gaps

Another extremely valuable concept proposed by reader-response theory is textual gaps. To illustrate the idea, let us remember that the word "text" originally comes from the Latin "textus," meaning fabric, derived from "texere," to weave (the word "textile" has the same root). A woven fabric consists of horizontal and vertical threads, warp and weft, while in between, there are empty spaces, gaps. (See fig. 11-2.)

The warp and weft of a literary text are what is explicitly present in a book. In between, the authors leave gaps that the readers fill according to their previous experience and imagination. This, again, ascribes readers a much more active role than do many traditional views on reading, and also presupposes that individual readers will fill the gaps differently. It does not

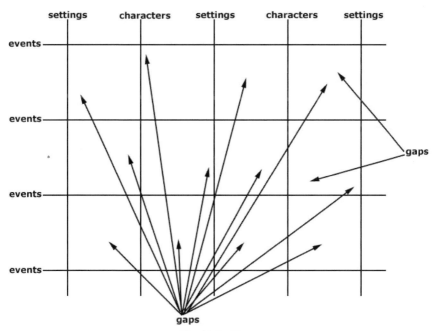

Fig. 11-2   Text.

necessarily mean, however, that an infinite number of interpretations are possible. Gaps prove to be a powerful device to steer the reader toward a certain interpretation.

The gaps may be of at least three different kinds. First, there are gaps that we fill based on our experience of real life. For instance, writers seldom if ever tell us that their characters have two eyes, two ears, a nose and a mouth, two arms, and two legs. We do not need this information to have a general portrait of a human being. But if there is something deviant in a character's appearance, we must be told so, for instance that the character has only one leg (John Silver in *Treasure Island*) or red hair (Anne Shirley or Pippi Long-stocking). Unless we are given these specific details, we fill the gap left by the writer from the most common repertory of human features. Similarly, we do not have to be told that people go to bed in the evening and wake up in the morning, nor that they eat and drink and go to the bathroom. We assume that children go to school while adults have a job. We assume that every child has had parents even though they may not be mentioned in the text. We assume that the sun rises in the east. Unless any of these events become, for some reason or other, significant in the story, we fill such gaps automatically.

Activating the Reader

Another kind of gaps are those left by the authors in order to stimulate the readers' active participation in text decoding. It is these gaps that are connected to the concept of the implied reader. A writer expects his implied audience to be able to fill the gaps properly. For instance, the implied reader of *Roll of Thunder, Hear My Cry* is expected to know about ethnic segregation in the Southern states. The very mention of the South and the 1930s encourages readers to fill in the facts that the writer has left as a deliberate gap. A dislocated reader (for instance, if the book is translated into German or French or Italian) may not have the necessary knowledge of U.S. history to fill the gap. Therefore, translated books are often furnished with forewords explaining the facts that the initial implied audience is expected to be familiar with. Deliberate gaps are thus culturally dependent. Still the implied readers of *Roll of Thunder* are displaced from the described events, since the book was published in 1976. The writer must therefore explain at least some things for her readers that would be self-evident for the characters, for instance that black children had to stay away from school up to late October to help with cotton picking. In this case, the writer has carefully filled a gap that the implied reader may not be able to fill.

As mentioned above, the implied readers of *The Lion, the Witch and the Wardrobe* are supposed to understand that the action takes place during the Second World War, although it is never mentioned explicitly. The prompt is the reference to air raids over London. For a reader who does not know about the air raids, the gap will remain unfilled, and as a result, the reader will not draw the parallel between the events in Narnia and the events in the real world outside the text. This does not necessarily impede the understanding of the text, but at least one additional dimension is lost.

The inability to fill a cultural gap can cause various reactions from a reader. If the gap is small, and the missing information is not significant for understanding the basic flow of events, readers may just skip the gap. For instance, if readers do not know what exactly Turkish Delight is in *The Lion, the Witch and the Wardrobe*, it will not prevent them from reading on, and they will most probably make the correct inference that Turkish Delight is a sort of candy. By contrast, a gap may be filled wrongly, which may lead to a serious misunderstanding. In *That Was Then, This Is Now*, it is mentioned that one of the characters receives a draft. In an empirical study of EFL readers in Finland, high school students misinterpreted the word "draft," believing that it was a bill, a parking or speeding ticket, a tax-return receipt, or an IOU. This naturally affected their understanding of the story and the character's situation. Today's young readers in the United States, diachronic as compared to the initial implied readers of *That Was Then, This Is Now*, published in 1971, may understand the literal meaning of the word "draft" but still fail to recognize its significance out of the context of the Vietnam war. In the previously discussed example of *Ramona the Pest* (chapter 3), the implied reader is supposed to recognize the U.S. national anthem, which Ramona misinterprets ("Oh say can you see in the dawnzer lee light"). If the book is read by British or Australian young readers, they will probably get as frustrated as Ramona, because the information needed in order to fill the gap is beyond their knowledge. The author helps the audience several chapters later, when Ramona learns about her mistake. This is a good example of filling a gap in retrospect, when the reader will look back at the previous events in view of newly gained information. Such gap is called temporary, as opposed to the permanent gap that remains unfilled through the end.

Finally, readers may totally reject a book that contains too many cultural gaps for them to fill so that the process becomes painful and frustrating. We sometimes say that a young reader has chosen a book beyond her or his capacity. This can refer to age as well as to cultural competence. As mediators, we should be able to assist young children in filling gaps, so we should start by being aware of the existence of gaps and the various strategies for filling them.

Creative Gaps

The third kind of gaps can be called creative or imaginative. These are the gaps that authors leave to stimulate the readers' imagination and active involvement with the text. Some scholars of children's literature have suggested that the literary quality of children's books depends highly on the scope of gaps in them. If the text is so tight that it has no gaps the readers can fill with their imagination, we perceive such a text as overtly didactic. The author explains everything, leaving no questions unanswered, and the book does not stimulate the reader's further contemplation. In *The Lion, the Witch and the Wardrobe*, we constantly come across explicit comments both on the characters' permanent traits and their state of mind: "Lucy was a very truthful girl" (29); "Edmund could be spiteful" (29); "For the next few days [Lucy] was very miserable" (28); "Lucy . . . was happy and excited" (41); "They were pretty tired by now" (114). Such narrative statements are examples of the author filling textual gaps for the readers. Rather than allowing the reader to assemble the characters' portraits from their behavior, the author serves up a complete portrait, with clear and unambiguous labels. In *The Secret Garden*, it seems that the author does not trust the readers to recognize and account for the profound physical and mental changes in the characters. Not only does she promptly spell out all the changes, but she also sums them up toward the end of the novel in a most didactic manner.

Some scholars claim that children prefer didactic texts and dislike books that leave problems unresolved. There is, however, no empirical research to support this view, so it may be one of the many prejudices about children's literature. By contrast, texts with many gaps where the readers can enter with their own questions and ponderings are called creative, or interrogative. They stimulate the imagination and allow the readers to make their own inferences and conclusions. An open ending, or aperture, discussed in connection with composition (chapter 5), is a good example of a creative gap. The difference between didactic and creative texts cannot of course be applied as a definite criterion of the aesthetic quality of a text; however, we can state that most children's books which we by intuition regard as "good" are of the creative type. Also the general tendency in contemporary children's literature is toward more creative texts.

EXERCISE

Read a novel of your choice carefully and note every occurrence of textual gaps. Make a distinction between gaps that you fill automatically and gaps that stimulate your active participation, cultural as well as imaginative. Have you encountered any gaps that you were unable to fill? What was your strategy in dealing with them: skip them, look up facts in an encyclopedia (today, lots of facts can be found on the Internet; you can actually find a recipe for Turkish Delight), or try to figure them out from the context? Did you feel frustrated faced with any of the gaps? Do you think a young reader would encounter more gaps than you have? How would you help a young reader to fill these gaps?

Literary Competence

While some reader-response theories maintain that any reader can interpret any text, others emphasize that the understanding of literary texts is an acquired rather than a natural ability and can be trained. If literary texts are coded messages, as we have considered in our discussion of semiotics (chapter 2), we have to possess the code in order to interpret them. To master the code, the reader has to be trained, or socialized, to gain something that in this direction of reader-response studies is called literary competence. It does not only pertain to children's literature; but in childhood we have the best prerequisites to develop into competent readers. As adult mediators we teach children to recognize genres and patterns, to analyze plots and characters, even though children may lack the means to articulate their understanding, and of course they do not need labels on the analytical tools they are using. In order to become a competent reader—a key notion of this model—children must be taught various reading strategies. These include the following:

- placing books in relevant social, cultural, and literary contexts
- recognizing literary conventions, not least fictionality and the ontological status of fictive characters
- understanding temporality and causality as the necessary components of a narrative
- distinguishing between story and discourse
- understanding figurative speech, irony, and other advanced usages of language
- understanding explicit and implicit ideology
- identifying intertextual connections

This is a more restricted view of implied readers. It presupposes some inherent features of the text itself that guide (or manipulate) the reader to adopt a certain interpretation. In children's fiction, such guidance or manipulation is generally stronger than in the mainstream. A children's author will probably be more explicit about generic features, events, and characters, as well as about the choice of themes and vocabulary. The author's construction of the implied reader is more conscious and deliberate. This makes reader-response theory in some respects more pertinent to children's fiction.

Literary competence does not necessarily give adult readers superiority over young ones. It is therefore preferable to speak about sophisticated and unsophisticated readers (other frequently used terms are competent and in-competent, or informed and uninformed), since these terms do not judge the readers' literary competence on the basis of their age.

EXERCISE

Choose a children's novel and examine what aspects of literary compe-tence are required to understand it properly. Pay attention to genre, theme, composition, creation or destruction of fictionality, language and style, and intertextuality. Do you find that the necessary literary competence matches the recommended reading level you may see ei-ther on the book itself or in handbooks, publishers' catalogues, and library lists? Do mediators have a tendency to overestimate or underes-timate young readers' capacity?

DOUBLE ADDRESS, DUAL ADDRESS, AND CROSS-WRITING

Let us once again return to our communication chain: real author → implied author → narrator → narratee → implied reader → real reader.

Since, as repeatedly stated, authors of children's books are adult while the recipients are children, the balance is unequal. An adult author has more ex-perience than the child recipient; an adult's vocabulary is normally larger and their cognitive level higher. Authors can hardly help addressing the adult co-reader alongside the child, which means that the right-hand part of the chain is in fact duplicated:

child narratee→implied child reader→real child reader

real author→implied author→narrator→

adult narratee→implied adult reader→real adult reader

There are scholars who claim that *single address* in children's literature is possible; that is, adult authors can address the child reader alone, adapting their texts to what they believe suits children's needs and interests. This pos-sibility is dubious. Adult authors can no more address the child alone than members of an ethnic majority can address an ethic minority group without in some way co-addressing their own group. Moreover, in the case of chil-dren's literature, it is not only written but always mediated through an adult (editor, bookseller, critic, librarian, teacher, parent), and authors simply can-not avoid having these adult co-readers in mind, consciously or subconsciously. The ambivalence of address, based on asymmetrical power position, is inevitable. It can, however, be dealt with in two ways. The adult author can speak to the adult co-reader over the child's head, sharing experience at the expense of the child. This is what we find in traditional, especially nineteenth-century children's literature, where authors sometimes make fun of the child protagonist's inexperience and lack of insight. This type of writing is called *double address*, comparable to double morals, and is of course contemptuous toward child readers. Another way is a *dual* (or *equal*) address where the child and the adult co-reader are addressed on the same level, each in their own right. *Winnie-the-Pooh* and many other favorite children's books offer the adult reader much joy, without taking anything away from the child. Many contemporary picture books contain irony and intertextual (or interpictorial) elements that are beyond the comprehension of a young reader. Since picture books, more than any other kind of children's literature, are indeed perused by children and adults together, picture book creators deliberately include levels that would provide the adult co-reader with a source of enjoyment.

A recent concept of *cross-writing* is another way of dealing with duplicate addressees. It was initially only applied to writers who have written for both children and adults. The French author Michel Tournier has rewritten some of his adult novels, adjusting them to what he believed to be the needs, interests, and cognitive capacity of a young audience. In doing so, Tournier discovered that addressing children put much higher demands on him as a writer, including linguistic precision and elaboration of plot and character. Roald Dahl turned a short story, written for an adult audience, into a children's book, *Danny the Champion of the World*. In doing so, he both elaborated and simplified the original text, adapting it to a new audience.

Nowadays cross-writing has become a concept covering many various aspects of ambivalent address. It includes all kinds of duplicate reader appeal that can be found in texts, even such texts that have seldom been questioned as children's, such as Edith Nesbit's novels. Thus the concept of cross-writing has brought us back to the question we started this book with: what exactly is children's literature?

HOW TO GO FURTHER

Reader-oriented semiotics opens vast possibilities for studies of children's literature. One model that has so far been applied to children's novels on only a very modest scale is presented in Roland Barthes's *S/Z*. Barthes treats literary texts as multilayered structures and therefore proposes a number of codes that readers use in their interpretation:

- The proairetic code controls the reader's understanding of the plot.

- The hermeneutic code involves the questions of interpretation, especially on the plot level.
- The semic code governs the understanding of literary characters.
- The symbolic code assists the reader in understanding the symbolic meaning of the text.
- The referential code points to the cultural context.

The reader-oriented examination of a work will thus proceed along this hierarchy, from the most elementary code (proairetic) to the most complex (referential). Other types of codes are conceivable, as Barthes and his followers indicate: metalinguistic, social or socioethnic, and so on. In combination with the analytical tools offered above, this concept may prove extremely fruitful, not least with regard to double audience.

Another useful paradigm originating from the same source is the distinction between readerly and writerly texts. Readerly texts are those consciously based on the conventions common to the writer and the reader and therefore open to a plurality of interpretation. Writerly texts deliberately break conventions and thus defy the reader's interpretations. Obviously, the majority of children's novels would fall under the first category, while some texts that have been interrogated as suitable for children or, in more recent terms, cross-writing child and adult, could be understood as writerly. Writerly texts demand that the reader be creative—a function traditionally ascribed to the writer. Yet we have seen how contemporary writers successfully involve the readers in the interpretation of complex, norm-breaking texts. This approach could also bring us closer to some aspects in the specific nature of children's literature.

REFERENCES

Overviews of the Field

Benton, Michael. "Reader-Response Criticism." Pp. 71–88 in *International Companion Encyclopedia of Children's Literature*, edited by Peter Hunt. London: Routledge, 1996. Also pp. 81–99 in *Understanding Children's Literature*, edited by Peter Hunt. London: Routledge, 1999.

Rimmon-Kenan, Shlomith. *Narrative Fiction: Contemporary Poetics*. London: Routledge, 1983. Chap. 9, "The Text and its Reading."

Empirical Reader Studies (A Selection)

Applebee, Arthur N. *The Child's Concept of Story: Age Two to Seventeen*. Chicago: University of Chicago Press, 1978.

Appleyard, J. A. *Becoming a Reader: The Experience of Fiction from Childhood to Adulthood.* Cambridge, Cambridge University Press, 1990.

Benton, Michael, et al. *Young Readers Responding to Poems.* London: Routledge, 1985.

Butler, Dorothy. *Cushla and Her Books.* London: Hodder & Stoughton, 1975.

Cherland, Meredith Rogers. *Private Practices: Girls Reading Fiction and Constructing Identity.* London: Taylor & Francis, 1994.

Cochran-Smith, Marylin. *The Making of a Reader.* Norwood: Ablex, 1984.

Crago, Hugh, and Margot Crago. *Prelude to Literacy: A Preschool Child's Encounter with Picture and Story.* Carbondale, IL: Southern Illinois University Press, 1983.

Fry, Donald. *Children Talk About Books: Seeing Themselves as Readers.* Milton Keynes: Open University Press, 1985.

May, Jill P. *Children's Literature and Critical Theory.* New York: Oxford University Press, 1995. Chap. 8, "Reader Response in Children's Literature: Listening to Determine Audience."

Naidoo, Beverley. *Through Whose Eyes? Exploring Racism: Reader, Text and Context.* London: Trentham, 1992.

Pinsent, Pat, ed. *The Power of the Page: Children's Books and Their Readers.* London: Fulton, 1993.

Sarland, Charles. *Young People Reading: Culture and Response.* Milton Keynes: Open University Press, 1991.

White, Dorothy Neal. *Books Before Five.* New York: Oxford University Press, 1954.

Wolf, Anne Shelby, and Shirley Brice Heath. *The Braid of Literature: Children's Worlds of Reading.* Cambridge, MA: Harvard University Press, 1992.

Reader-Response Criticism

Barthes, Roland. *S/Z.* New York: Hill & Wang, 1974.

———. "From Work to Text." Pp. 155–164 in his *Image—Music—Text.* London: Fontana, 1977.

———. "Theory of the Text." Pp. 31–47 in *Untying the Text: A Post-structuralist Reader,* edited by Robert Young. London: Routledge, 1980.

Booth, Wayne C. *The Rhetoric of Fiction.* Chicago: University of Chicago Press, 1961.

Chambers, Aidan. "The Reader in the Book." Pp. 34–58 in his *Booktalk: Occasional Writing on Literature and Children.* London: Bodley Head, 1985.

Culler, Jonathan. *Structuralist Poetics: Structuralism, Linguistics and the Study of Literature.* London: Routledge, 1975.

Eco, Umberto. *The Role of the Reader.* Bloomington: Indiana University Press, 1979.

———. *Six Walks in the Fictional Woods.* Cambridge, MA: Harvard University Press, 1995.

Fish, Stanley. *Is There a Text in This Class? The Authority of Interpretive Communities.* Cambridge, MA: Harvard University Press, 1982.

Holland, Norman. *The Dynamics of Literary Response.* New York: Norton, 1968.

Holub, Robert C. *Reception Theory: A Critical Introduction.* London: Methuen, 1984.

Hunt, Peter. *Criticism, Theory and Children's Literature*. London: Blackwell, 1991. Chap. 4, "Approaching the Text"; chap. 5, "The Text and the Reader"; chap. 7, "Narrative."

Ingarden, Roman. *The Literary Work of Art: An Investigation on the Borderline of Ontology, Logic, and Theory of Literature*. Evanstone, IL: Northwestern University Press, 1973.

Iser, Wolfgang. *The Implied Reader: Patterns of Communication in Prose Fiction from Bunyan to Beckett*. Baltimore: The Johns Hopkins University Press, 1974.

———. *The Act of Reading: A Theory of Aesthetic Response*. Baltimore: The Johns Hopkins University Press, 1974.

Jauss, Hans Robert. *Toward an Aesthetic of Reception*. Minneapolis: University of Minnesota Press, 1982.

McGillis, Roderick. *The Nimble Reader: Literary Theory and Children's Literature*. New York: Twayne, 1996. Chap. 8, "Investigating the Reading Subject: Response Criticism."

Meek, Margaret. *How Texts Teach What Readers Learn*. South Woodchester: Thimble Press, 1988.

Richards, I. A. *Principles of Literary Criticism*. London: Routledge and Kegan Paul, 1924.

Rosenblatt, Louise. *The Reader, the Text, the Poem: The Transactional Theory of the Literary Work* (1938). Carbondale, IL: Southern Illinois University Press, 1978.

Steig, Michael. *Stories of Reading: Subjectivity and Literary Understanding*. Baltimore: The Johns Hopkins University Press, 1989.

Stephens, John. *Language and Ideology in Children's Fiction*. London: Longman, 1992. Chap. 2, "Readers and Subject Positions in Children's Fiction."

Suleiman, Susan, and Inge Crossman, eds. *The Reader in the Text: Essays on Audience and Participation*. Princeton, NJ: Princeton University Press, 1980.

Tabbert, Reinbert. "The Impact of Children's Books—Cases and Concepts." Pp. 34–58 in *Responses to Children's Literature*, edited by Geoff Fox and Graham Hammond. München: Saur, 1980.

Tompkins, Jane P., ed. *Reader-Response Criticism: From Formalism to Post-Structuralism*. Baltimore: The Johns Hopkins University Press, 1980.

Tucker, Nicholas. *The Child and the Book*. Cambridge: Cambridge University Press, 1980.

Vandergrift, Kay, ed. *Ways of Knowing: Literature and the Intellectual Life of Children*. Lanham, MD: Scarecrow, 1996.

Dual Readership and Cross-writing

Beckett, Sandra L. "From Re-writing for Children to Crosswriting Child and Adult: The Secret of Michel Tournier's Dual Readership." Pp. 9–31 in *Voices from Far Away: Current Trends in International Children's Literature Research*, edited by Maria Nikolajeva. Stockholm: Centre for the Study of Childhood Culture, 1995.

Beckett, Sandra L., ed. *Transcending Boundaries: Writing for a Dual Audience of Children and Adults*. New York: Garland, 1999.

Cadden, Mike. "Speaking to Both Children and Genre: Le Guin's Ethics of Audience." *The Lion and theUnicorn* 24, no. 1 (2000): 128–139.

Children's Literature 25 (1997): special issue on crosswriting child and adult.

Wall, Barbara. *The Narrator's Voice: The Dilemma of Children's Fiction*. London: Macmillan, 1991.

12
Conclusion: Which Tool Shall I Choose?

In this book, you have been introduced to a large number of theories and analytical methods. When faced with a concrete assignment, whether a book, an essay, a dissertation, or a conference paper, you will need to decide which theory and method to choose, since you cannot possibly use all of them at once. There are several considerations that should govern your choice.

First of all, no theory or method is universal. When the advocates of feminist criticism try to present their theory in opposition to all other directions of criticism, they subscribe to a serious fallacy. Feminist criticism is merely one way to approach literature, among others, and it provides neither better nor more profound answers; it just opens new dimensions of texts, inaccessible by other methods. Moreover, feminist criticism is closely connected to and gets inspiration from a number of other areas of inquiry, such as psychoanalysis, history, social anthropology, and linguistics. Similarly, psychoanalytically inspired literary criticism is just one theoretical approach among many, not a universal theory opposed to "general criticism." Narrative theory is just one way to treat one specific aspect of literary texts. And so on. We cannot therefore pose the question of which theory or method is best: all of them have their advantages and disadvantages. Each provides insight into some aspects of literary texts, but may prove worthless while addressing the rest.

Second, it is essential to distinguish between theory and method. Theory implies a general attitude toward literary texts. We have seen, for instance, that some theories view literature as a reflection of reality, while others prefer to treat it as a depiction of an individual's mind. Some theories attach more importance to authors, while others focus on the readers. No theory, however, can be directly applied to a literary text. In fact, it is quite possible to conduct theoretical discussions of literature without ever mentioning one concrete text. One can of course argue whether such abstract negotiations are of any use, and a reasonable answer will be "no," unless they can be further elaborated into workable analytical methods. A theory that cannot be applied for practical purposes is like a bicycle with square wheels: a daring idea, but not of much use. Hence, in order to analyze texts, we have to move from the theoretical abstraction onto a more concrete level of thought and develop a toolkit, based on the theory, but applicable in practical work. In natural sciences, this corresponds to creating a theoretical equation and building adequate equipment to conduct an experiment.

Further, in assessing the suitability of the method you are about to choose, the following prerequisites should be taken into consideration:

- Is the method appropriate from the point of view of your material?
- Is the method appropriate from the point of view of your purpose?
- Is the method appropriate from the point of view of your results?
- Is the method appropriate from the point of view of the general lines of criticism?

In this book, we have used different methods and tools, depending on what aspect of the text was under scrutiny. We agreed that it is pointless to apply formalist models to contemporary psychological novels because they do not follow the straightforward narrative patterns of the stories for which the formal method was originally developed. It would be equally pointless to apply complex psychological or psychoanalytical methods to characters who are obviously flat and static. It is not very fruitful to examine gender stereotyping in formulaic fiction, since gender stereotyping is by definition part of its aesthetics. It is next to impossible to pursue biographical studies unless there is at least some biographical material available.

This does not mean, however, that we necessarily choose a model that would neatly match our text. The famous Russian semiotician Yuri Lotman used to say that there must be something wrong with a model that fits all texts. It is, on the contrary, a greater challenge to adapt a method to something else than it was originally proposed for.

In choosing our analytical tools, we naturally also should ask ourselves what the purpose of examination is. What do we want to do with our material? If we want to dig out a hole to build a house, we will use a bulldozer; if we are engaged in archeological excavations, we will use a tiny blade; and if we are looking for water, we will need a divining rod. Similarly, if we are interested in the general build-up of the text, we will choose structuralism or narratology; if we want to analyze gender patterns, feminist criticism will be suitable. From this general attitude we will proceed toward more precise tools. What elements in the build-up of the text are we going to investigate:

plot, characterization, temporality, or style? What aspect of gender are we setting out to examine: the relationship between the author's and the protagonist's gender, stereotyping, power structures, or reader appeal? Before we have decided what the purpose of our work will be, we cannot pick the necessary instrument.

The result of our examination will of course depend on the tool. Nobody wants predictable results, so if we from the start know what will happen if we use a particular analytical method, why bother? Further, a large-scale, time-consuming investigation that ends up with a handful of banalities suggests that the method was perhaps wrongly chosen.

Finally, although we have stated that no theory is better than any other, it is clever to choose your tools in accordance with current directions in research. Some aspects of children's fiction have been investigated thoroughly, while others are still waiting for their scholars. You do not want to spend a lot of time merely repeating what has already been examined by other scholars—that is not what true scholarship is about. This book has pointed toward some hot spots in children's literature research in the concluding sections of every chapter, "How to go further." Some of the theories and methods that seem to be expanding rapidly, judging by conference themes and special issues of professional journals, are cross-writing, fictionality, some advanced variants of gender theory, and multimediality.

Every new theoretical direction is only legitimate if it allows us to disclose such dimensions in literary texts that we would not be able to discover with other methods. We have recently seen how children's literature research has reached new depths as it has borrowed analytical tools from two separate, but in some respects similar, areas: feminist and postcolonial criticism. Both directions have taught us to read literary texts from the point of view of a marginalized social group. Children in our society are also marginalized and oppressed. With tools from feminist and postcolonial theories, we have learned to discern between conservative and subversive elements in children's books, classic as well as modern.

Narrative theory has given us tools to analyze in detail how texts are constructed and to understand why certain devices work well in children's books while others do not. It has also facilitated historical comparison, which not only pinpoints changes in themes and values, but the profound changes in the aesthetic form of children's literature.

Now, the crucial question: why do we need theories and methods at all? All we want is to read and enjoy books, or if we are children's literature scholars, help children enjoy books. Hopefully, this book has persuaded you that the aesthetic enjoyment of literature is not hampered, but on the contrary, enhanced, by our understanding of its various mechanisms. Good luck in your further work!

Bibliography

Primary Sources

Aiken, Joan. *The Wolves of Willoughby Chase*. London: Cape, 1962.

Alcott, Louisa May. *Little Women* (1868). Harmondsworth: Penguin, 1994.

Alexander, Lloyd. *The Book of Three*. New York: Holt, 1964—The first of the five chronicles of Prydain.

———. *The Illyrian Adventure*. New York: Dutton, 1986—The first book in the Vesper series.

———. *Westmark*. New York: Dutton, 1981—The first of the three books in the Westmark series.

Andersen, Hans Christian. *The Complete Fairy Tales and Stories*. New York: Doubleday, 1974.

Applegate, K. A. *The Invasion*. Jefferson City: Scholastic, 1996—The first of over forty books in the Animorphs series.

Avi. *The True Confessions of Charlotte Doyle* (1990). New York: Avon, 1992.

Barrie, James M. *Peter Pan and Wendy* (1911). In *Peter Pan in Kensington Gardens; Peter and Wendy*. Oxford: Oxford University Press, 1999.

Baum, L. Frank. *The Wonderful Wizard of Oz* (1900). New York: HarperCollins, 2000.

Brown, Margery Wise, and Clement Hurd. *Goodnight, Moon* (1947). New York: Harper, 2002.

Brunhoff, Babar. *The Story of Babar, The Little Elephant* (1931). *The Travels of Babar* (1932). *King Babar* (1933). In *Bonjour, Babar!* New York: Random House, 2000.

Burnett, Frances Hodgson. *Little Lord Fauntleroy* (1886). London: Penguin, 1995.

———. *A Little Princess* (1905). New York: Signet, 1990.

———. *The Secret Garden* (1911). London: Penguin, 1995.

Burningham, John. *Come Away from the Water, Shirley*. New York: Crowell, 1977.

Burton, Virginia Lee. *Mike Mulligan and His Steam Shovel*. Boston: Houghton Mifflin, 1939.

Carle, Eric. *The Very Hungry Caterpillar*. New York: World Publishing, 1969.

Carroll, Lewis. *Alice's Adventures in Wonderland* (1865). In *The Penguin Complete Lewis Carroll*. Harmondsworth: Penguin, 1982.

——. *Through the Looking Glass* (1872). In *The Penguin Complete Lewis Carroll*. Harmondsworth: Penguin, 1982.

Chambers, Aidan. *Breaktime* (1978). London: Random House, 1995.

——. *Dance on My Grave* (1982). London: Random House, 1995.

Cleary, Beverly. *Dear Mr. Henshaw* (1983). Harmondsworth: Penguin, 1985.

——. *Ramona the Brave* (1975). New York: Avon, 1995.

——. *Ramona the Pest* (1968). New York: Avon, 1992.

Collodi, Carlo. *The Adventures of Pinocchio* (1881). Oxford: Oxford University Press, 1996.

Cormier, Robert. *The Chocolate War*. New York: Pantheon, 1974.

——. *I Am the Cheese* (1977). New York: Dell, 1997.

Creech, Sharon. *Walk Two Moons*. London: Macmillan, 1994.

Dahl, Roald. *Charlie and the Chocolate Factory* (1964). Harmondsworth: Penguin, 1973.

——. *Danny, the Champion of the World* (1975). New York: Knopf, 2002.

Dixon, Franklin W. *The Missing Chums* (1928). Bedford, MA: Applewood Books, 1996—The first of the Hardy Boys novels.

Ende, Michael. *The Neverending Story* (1979). New York: Penguin, 1984.

Fitzhugh, Louise. *Harriet the Spy*. New York: Harper, 1964.

Foreman, Michael. *War and Peas*. London: Hamish Hamilton, 1974.

Gág, Wanda. *Millions of Cats*. New York: Coward, 1928.

Grimm, Jacob, and Wilhelm Grimm. *The Complete Fairy Tales of the Brothers Grimm*. Vols. w–2. New York: Bantam Books, 1988.

Hamilton, Virginia. *The Planet of Junior Brown*. New York: Macmillan, 1971.

Hinton, S. E. *The Outsiders* (1967). Harmondsworth: Penguin, 1997.

——. *That Was Then, This Is Now* (1971). Harmondsworth: Penguin, 1998.

Hoban, Russell, and Lillian Hoban. *Bread and Jam for Frances*. New York: Harper, 1964.

Hoffman, E.T.A. *The Nutcracker*. New York: Ariel Books, 1987.

Holman, Felice. *Slake's Limbo*. New York: Scribner, 1974.

Hughes, Thomas. *Tom Brown's Schooldays* (1856). Harmondsworth: Penguin, 1994.

Jones, Diana Wynne. *A Tale of Time City* (1987). London: HarperCollins, 2000.

Keene, Carolyn. *The Secret of the Old Clock* (1930). Bedford, MA: Applewood Books, 1991—The first book in the Nancy Drew series.

Kincaid, Eric. *Eric Kincaid's Book of Fairy Tales*. Adapted by Lucy Kincaid. Newmarket: Brimax Books, 1987.

Kipling, Rudyard. *The Jungle Book* (1894). New York: Viking, 1996.

——. *Just So Stories* (1902). In *The Complete Just So Stories*. New York: Viking, 1993.

Lagerlöf, Selma. *The Wonderful Adventures of Nils* (1906–07). New York: Dover, 1995.

Lewis, C. S. *The Last Battle*. New York: Macmillan, 1956.

——. *The Lion, the Witch and the Wardrobe* (1950). Harmondsworth: Penguin, 1959.

————. *The Magician's Nephew*. New York: Macmillan, 1955.

Lindgren, Astrid. *The Children of Noisy Village* (1947). New York: Viking, 1962.

————. *Emil's Pranks* (1963). Chicago: Folett, 1971.

————. *Mio, My Son* (1954). New York: Viking, 1956.

————. *Pippi Goes Aboard* (1947). New York: Viking, 1957.

————. *Pippi in the South Seas* (1948). New York: Viking, 1959.

————. *Pippi Longstocking* (1945). New York: Viking, 1950.

————. *Ronia, the Robber's Daughter* (1981). New York: Viking, 1983.

Lionni, Leo. *Little Blue and Little Yellow*. New York: McDowell, 1959.

Lowry, Lois. *The Giver*. New York: Doubleday, 1993.

MacLachlan, Patricia. *Unclaimed Treasures*. New York: Harper, 1984.

Malot, Hector. *The Foundling* (1878). New York: Harmony Books, 1986.

Milne, A. A. *The House At Pooh Corner* (1928). London: Methuen, 1965.

————. *Winnie-the-Pooh* (1926). London: Methuen, 1965.

Montgomery, L. M. *Anne of Green Gables* (1908). New York: Bantam, 1992.

Munsch, Robert N., and Michael Martchenko. *The Paper Bag Princess*. Toronto: Annick Press, 1980.

O'Dell, Scott. *The Island of the Blue Dolphins* (1960). New York: Bantam, 1987.

Opie, Iona, and Peter Opie. *The Classic Fairy Tales*. London: Oxford University Press, 1974.

Pascal, Francine. *Best Friends*. New York: Bantam, 1986—The first book in the Sweet Valley Twins series.

Paterson, Katherine. *Bridge to Terabithia* (1977). New York: HarperCollins, 1987.

————. *The Great Gilly Hopkins* (1978). New York: HarperCollins, 1987.

————. *Jacob Have I Loved* (1980). New York: HarperCollins, 1990.

————. *Lyddie*. New York: Dutton, 1991.

————. *Park's Quest*. New York: Dutton, 1988.

Paulsen, Gary. *Hatchet*. Scarsdale, NY: Bradbury, 1987.

Perrault, Charles. *The Fairy Tales*. New York: Avon, 1977.

Potter, Beatrix. *The Tale of Peter Rabbit*. London: Warne, 1902.

Pullman, Philip. *The Amber Spyglass*. New York: Knopf, 2000.

————. *The Golden Compass* (1995). New York: Knopf, 1996.

————. *The Subtle Knife*. New York: Knopf, 1997.

Rey, H. A. *Curious George*. Boston: Houghton Mifflin, 1941. Revised edition 1969.

Rey, Margret, and H. A. Rey. *Spotty*. New York: Harper, 1945.

Rowling, J. K. *Harry Potter and the Sorcerer's Stone* (1997). New York: A. A. Levine Books, 1998—The first of the Harry Potter series.

Sachar, Louis. *Holes* (1998). New York: Dell Yearling, 2000.

Saint-Exupéry, Antoine de. *The Little Prince* (1943). Harmondsworth: Penguin, 1962.

Salinger, Jerome D. *The Catcher in the Rye* (1951). Philadelphia: Chelsea House, 2000.

Sendak, Maurice. *Dear Mili*. New York: Farrar, Straus, Giroux, 1980.

————. *In the Night Kitchen*. New York: Harper, 1970.

————. *Outside Over There*. New York: Harper & Row, 1981.

————. *Where the Wild Things Are*. New York: Harper, 1963.

Seuss, Dr. *ABC*. New York: Random House, 1963.
———. *And To Think That I Saw It on Mulberry Street*. New York: Vanguard, 1937.
———. *The Cat in the Hat*. New York: Random House, 1957.
———. *Green Eggs and Ham*. New York: Random House, 1960.
———. *Horton Hears a Who*. New York: Random House, 1954.
———. *How the Grinch Stole Christmas*. New York: Random House, 1957.
———. *Marvin K. Mooney, Will You Please Go Now?* New York: Random House, 1972.
Silverstein, Shel. *The Giving Tree*. New York: Harper & Row, 1964.
Spyri, Johanna. *Heidi* (1881). Ware: Wordsworth, 1993.
Steig, William. *Sylvester and the Magic Pebble*. New York: Windmill Books, 1969.
Stevenson, Robert Louis. *Treasure Island* (1883). New York: Signet, 1998.
Tatar, Maria, ed. *The Classic Fairy Tales*. New York: Norton, 1999.
Taylor, Mildred D. *Roll of Thunder, Hear My Cry* (1976). New York: Penguin, 1991.
Tolkien, J. R. R. *The Hobbit* (1937). Boston: Houghton Mifflin, 1997.
———. *Lord of the Rings* (1954–55). Philadelphia: Chelsea House, 1999.
Tournier, Michel. *Friday and Robinson* (1971). New York: Knopf, 1972.
Townsend, Sue. *The Secret Diary of Adrian Mole, Aged 13 3/4* (1982). London: Mandarin, 1989.
Twain, Mark. *The Adventures of Huckleberry Finn* (1884). New York: Penguin, 1995.
———. *The Adventures of Tom Sawyer* (1876). Harmondsworth: Penguin, 1985.
Voigt, Cynthia. *Homecoming*. New York: Atheneum, 1981.
Webster, Jean. *Daddy-Long-Legs* (1912). Harmondsworth: Penguin, 1995.
White, E. B. *Charlotte's Web* (1952). New York: HarperCollins, 1999.
———. *Stuart Little* (1945). New York: HarperCollins, 1999.
Wilder, Laura Ingalls. *Little House in the Big Woods* (1932). New York: HarperCollins, 1971—The first book in the series.
Yolen, Jane. *The Devil's Arithmetic* (1988). New York: Penguin, 1990.
Zipes, Jack, ed. *The Great Fairy Tale Tradition: From Straparola and Basile to the Brothers Grimm*. New York: Norton, 2001.

Secondary Sources

The bibliography contains all the sources mentioned in the individual chapters and a selection of general sources on children's literature, including author biographies and studies of the children's novels excessively discussed in the book, such as *Anne of Green Gables*; *The Lion, the Witch and the Wardrobe*; *Winnie-the-Pooh*; *The Adventures of Tom Sawyer*, and so on. Journal articles are normally only included if they are uniquely important in introducing or developing a particular concept, or if they are explicitly mentioned in the book. Articles focused on a specific text are included if they also offer an interesting theoretical dimension.

Abrams, M. H. *The Mirror and the Lamp: Romantic Theory and Critical Tradition*. Oxford: Oxford University Press, 1953.
Adams, Gillian. "The First Children's Literature: The Case of Sumer." *Children's Literature* 14 (1986): 1–30.

———. "Medieval Children's Literature: Its Possibility and Actuality." *Children's Literature* 26 (1998): 1–24.

Aers, Lesley. "The Treatment of Time in Four Children's Books." *Children's Literature in Education* 2 (1970): 69–81.

Agnew, Kate, and Geoff Fox. *Children at War: From the First War to the Gulf.* London: Continuum, 2001.

Åhmansson, Gabriella. *A Life and its Mirrors: A Feminist Reading of L. M. Montgomery's Fiction.* Uppsala: Acta Universitatis Upsaliensis, 1991.

Alberghene, Janice M., and Beverly Lyon Clark, eds. *Little Women and the Feminist Imagination: Criticism, Controversy, Personal Essays.* New York: Garland, 1998.

Allen, Graham. *Intertextuality.* London: Routledge, 2000.

Anatol, Goselle Liza, ed. *Reading Harry Potter: Critical Essays.* London: Praeger, 2003.

Anderson, Celia Catlett, and Marilyn Fain Apseloff. *Nonsense Literature for Children: Aesop to Seuss.* Hamden, CT: Library Professional Publications, 1989.

Anderson, William. *Laura Ingalls Wilder: A Biography.* New York: HarperCollins, 1992.

Andronik, Catherine M. *Kindred Spirit: A Biography of L. M. Montgomery, Creator of Anne of Green Gables.* New York: Atheneum, 1996.

Applebee, Arthur N. *The Child's Concept of Story: Age Two to Seventeen.* Chicago: University of Chicago Press, 1978.

Appleyard, J. A. *Becoming a Reader: The Experience of Fiction from Childhood to Adulthood.* Cambridge: Cambridge University Press, 1990.

Ariès, Philippe. *Centuries of Childhood: A Social History of Family Life.* New York: Vintage-Random House, 1962.

Aristotle. "Poetics." In *Classical Literary Criticism.* Harmondsworth: Penguin, 1965.

Attebery, Brian. *The Fantasy Tradition in American Literature: From Irving to Le Guin.* Bloomington: Indiana University Press, 1980.

———. *Strategies of Fantasy.* Bloomington: Indiana University Press, 1992.

Auerbach, Erich. *Mimesis: The Representation of Reality in Western Literature.* 4th ed. Princeton, NJ: Princeton University Press, 1974.

Austin, J. L. *How to Do Things with Words.* New York: Oxford University Press, 1962.

Avery, Gillian. *Nineteenth-Century Children: Heroes and Heroines in English Children's Stories 1780–1900.* London: Hodder & Stoughton, 1965.

———. *Childhood's Pattern: A Study of the Heroes and Heroines of Children's Fiction 1770–1950.* London: Hodder & Stoughton, 1975.

Avery, Gillian, and Kimberley Reynolds, eds. *Representations of Childhood Death.* New York: St. Martin's Press, 2000.

Bachelard, Gaston. *The Poetics of Space.* New York: Orion, 1964.

Bader, Barbara. *American Picturebooks: From Noah's Ark to the Beast Within.* New York: Macmillan, 1976.

Baker, Mona. *In Other Words: A Coursebook on Translation.* London: Routledge, 1992.

Bakhtin, Mikhail. *Rabelais and His World.* Cambridge, MA: MIT Press, 1968.

———. *The Dialogic Imagination.* Austin: University of Texas Press, 1981.

———. *Problems of Dostoyevsky's Poetics.* Minneapolis: University of Minnesota Press, 1984.

———. *Speech Genres and Other Late Essays.* Austin: University of Texas Press, 1986.

———. *Art and Answerability: Early Philosophical Essays.* Austin: University of Texas Press, 1990.

Bal, Mieke. *Narratology: Introduction to the Theory of Narrative.* 2nd ed. Toronto: University of Toronto Press, 1997.

Banfield, Ann. *Unspeakable Sentences: Narration and Representation in the Language of Fiction.* Boston: Routledge and Kegan Paul, 1982.

Barthes, Roland. *Elements of Semiology.* London: Cape, 1967.

———. *S/Z.* New York: Hill & Wang, 1974.

———. *Image—Music—Text.* London: Fontana, 1977.

Bassnet, Susan. *Translation Studies.* London: Methuen, 1980.

Bator, Robert, ed. *Signposts to Criticism of Children's Literature.* Chicago: American Library Association, 1988.

Baum, L. Frank. *The Annotated Wizard of Oz.* With an introduction, notes, and bibliography by Michael Patrick Hearn. New York: Clarkson N. Potter, 1973.

Beckett, Sandra, ed. *Reflections of Change: Children's Literature Since 1945.* Westport: Greenwood, 1997.

———. *Transcending Boundaries: Writing for a Dual Audience of Children and Adults.* New York: Garland, 1999.

Bedell, Madelon. *The Alcotts: Biography of a Family.* New York: Clarkson N. Potter, 1980.

Bell, Anthea. "Children's Books in Translation." *Signal* 28 (1979): 47–53.

Benton, Michael, et al. *Young Readers Responding to Poems.* London: Routledge, 1985.

Bergsten, Staffan. *Mary Poppins and Myth.* Stockholm: Almqvist & Wiksell International, 1978.

Bettelheim, Bruno. *The Uses of Enchantment: The Meaning and Importance of Fairy Tales.* New York: Knopf, 1976.

Billone, Amy. "The Boy Who Lived: From Carroll's Alice and Barrie's Peter Pan to Rowling's Harry Potter." *Children's Literature* 32 (2004): 178–202.

Birkhäuser-Oeri, Sibylle. *The Mother: Archetypal Image in Fairy Tales.* Toronto: Inner City Books, 1988.

Birkin, Andrew. *J. M. Barrie and The Lost Boys.* London: Constable, 1979.

Bixler, Phyllis. *Frances Hodgson Burnett.* Boston: Twayne, 1984.

———. *The Secret Garden: Nature's Magic.* New York: Twayne, 1996.

Bloom, Harold. *The Anxiety of Influence: A Theory of Poetry.* New York: Oxford University Press, 1973.

———. *A Map of Misreading.* Oxford: Oxford University Press, 1975.

———. *Shakespeare: The Invention of the Human.* New York: Riverhead Books, 1998.

Bloom, Harold, ed. *J. D. Salinger.* New York: Chelsea House, 1987.

———. *Holden Caulfield.* New York: Chelsea House, 1990.

Blount, Margaret J. *Animal Land: The Creatures of Children's Fiction.* New York: Morrow, 1974.

Booth, Wayne C. *The Rhetoric of Fiction.* Chicago: University of Chicago Press, 1961.

———. *The Company We Keep: An Ethics of Fiction.* Berkeley: University of California Press, 1988.

Bosmajian, Hamida. "Charlie and the Chocolate Factory and Other Excremental Visions." *The Lion and the Unicorn* 9 (1985): 36–49.

———. *Sparing the Child: Children's Literature About Nazism and the Holocaust.* New York: Garland, 2001.

Bottigheimer, Ruth. *Grimm's Bad Girls and Bold Boys: The Moral and Social Vision of the Tales.* New Haven: Yale University Press, 1987.

Bradley, A. C. *Shakespearean Tragedy.* 3rd ed. London: Macmillan, 1993.

Brannigan, John. *New Historicism and Cultural Materialism.* New York: St. Martin's Press, 1998.

Brooks, Peter. *Reading for the Plot: Design and Intention in Narrative.* Cambridge, MA: Harvard University Press, 1984.

Burke, Sean, ed. *Authorship: From Plato to the Postmodern.* Edinburgh: Edinburgh University Press, 1995.

Burnett, Vivian. *The Romantic Lady (Frances Hodgson Burnett): The Life Story of an Imagination.* New York: Scribner, 1927.

Butler, Dorothy. *Cushla and Her Books.* London: Hodder & Stoughton, 1975.

Butler, Francelia, and Richard Rotert, eds. *Reflections on Literature for Children.* Hamden, CT: Library Professional Publications, 1984.

———. *Triumphs of the Spirit in Children's Literature.* Hamden, CT: Library Professional Publications, 1986.

Butler, Judith. *Gender Trouble: Feminism and the Subversion of Identity.* 2nd ed. New York: Routledge, 1999.

Butts, Dennis. *Good Writers for Young Readers.* St. Albans: Hart-Davis, 1977.

Butts, Dennis, ed. *Stories and Society: Children's Literature in its Social Context.* London: Macmillan, 1992.

Byrnes, Alice. *The Child: An Archetypal Symbol in Literature for Children and Adults.* New York: Peter Lang, 1995.

Cadden, Mike. "Speaking to Both Children and Genre: Le Guin's Ethics of Audience." *The Lion and the Unicorn* 24, no. 1 (2000): 128–139.

———. "The Irony of Narration in the Young Adult Novel." *Children's Literature Association Quarterly* 25, no. 3 (2000): 146–154.

Cadogan, Mary, and Patricia Craig. *You're a Brick, Angela! The Girls' Story 1839–1985.* London: Gollanz, 1986.

Campbell, Joseph. *The Hero with a Thousand Faces.* New York: Pantheon, 1949.

Carpenter, Humphrey. *Secret Gardens: The Golden Age of Children's Literature.* London: Unwin Hyman, 1985.

Carr, David. *Time, Narrative and History.* Bloomington: Indiana University Press, 1986.

Cart, Michael. *From Romance to Realism: 50 Years of Growth and Change in Young Adult Literature.* New York: HarperCollins, 1996.

———. *Gay and Lesbian Fiction for Young Adults.* Lanham, MD: Scarecrow, 2004.

Cawelti, John G. *Adventure, Mystery and Romance: Formula Stories as Art and Popular Culture.* Chicago: University of Chicago Press, 1976.

Chambers, Aidan. *Booktalk: Occasional Writing on Literature and Children.* London: Bodley Head, 1985.

Chaston, Joel D. "The Other Deaths in Bridge to Terabithia." *Children's Literature Association Quarterly* 16, no. 4 (1991–92): 238–241.

———. *Lois Lowry.* New York: Twayne, 1997.

———. "Baum, Bakhtin, and Broadway: A Centennial Look at the Carnival of Oz." *The Lion and the Unicorn* 25, no. 1 (2001): 128–149.

Chaston, Joel D., and Sarah Smedman, eds. *Bridges for the Young: The Fiction of Katherine Paterson.* Lanham, MD: Scarecrow, 2002.

Chatman, Seymour. *Story and Discourse: Narrative Structure in Fiction and Film.* Ithaca, NY: Cornell University Press, 1978.

———. *Coming to Terms.* Ithaca, NY: Cornell University Press, 1990.

Cherland, Meredith Rogers. *Private Practices: Girls Reading Fiction and Constructing Identity.* London: Taylor & Francis, 1994.

Chodorow, Nancy. *The Reproduction of Mothering: Psychoanalysis and the Sociology of Gender.* Berkeley, CA: University of California Press, 1978.

———. *Feminism and Psychoanalytical Theory.* New Haven: Yale University Press, 1989.

———. *Femininities, Masculinities, Sexualities: Freud and Beyond.* Lexington, KY: University of Kentucky Press, 1994.

Chomsky, Noam. *Syntactic Structures.* The Hague: Mouton, 1957.

Christensen, Nina. "Fictive Childhoods: On the Relationship between Childhood Studies and Children's Literature." *Tidsskrift for børne- & ungdomsklultur* 46 (2003): 107–122.

Chukovsky, Kornei. *From Two to Five.* Berkeley, CA: University of California Press, 1963.

Cixous, Hélène. *The Hélène Cixous Reader.* Edited by Susan Sellers. New York: Routledge, 1994.

Clark, Beverly Lyon. *Regendering the School Story: Sassy Sissies and Tattling Tomboys.* New York: Garland, 1996.

———. *Kiddie Lit: The Cultural Construction of Children's Literature in America.* Baltimore: The Johns Hopkins University Press, 2003.

Clark, Beverly Lyon, and Margaret R. Higonnet, eds. *Girls, Boys, Books, Toys: Gender in Children's Literature and Culture.* Baltimore: The Johns Hopkins University Press, 1999.

Clausen, Christopher. "Home and Away in Children's Fiction." *Children's Literature* 10 (1982): 141–152.

Clayton, Jay, and Eric Rothstein. *Influence and Intertextuality in Literary History.* Madison, WI: University of Wisconsin Press, 1991.

Clyde, Laurel A. *Out of the Closet and into the Classroom: Homosexuality in Books for Young People.* Melbourne: ALIA Thorpe, 1992.

Coats, Karen. "Lacan with Runt Pigs." *Children's Literature* 27 (1999): 105–128.

———. "Keepin' It Plural: Children's Studies in the Academy." *Children's Literature Association Quarterly* 26, no. 3 (2001): 140–150.

———. *Looking Glasses and Neverlands: Lacan, Desire, and Subjectivity in Children's Literature.* Iowa City: University of Iowa Press, 2004.

Cobley, Paul. *Narrative*. London: Routledge, 2001.

Cochran-Smith, Marylin. *The Making of a Reader*. Norwood: Ablex, 1984.

Cohen, Morton N. *Lewis Carroll: A Biography*. New York: Knopf, 1995.

Cohn, Dorrit. *Transparent Minds: Narrative Modes for Presenting Consciousness in Fiction*. Princeton, NJ: Princeton University Press, 1978.

Colbert, David. *The Magical Worlds of Harry Potter: A Treasury of Myths, Legends, and Fascinating Facts*. Wrightsville Beach, NC: Lumina Press, 2001.

Collingwood, Stuart Dodgson. *The Life and Letters of Lewis Carroll (Rev. C. L. Dodgson)*. New York: The Century, 1899.

Connolly, Paula. *Winnie-the-Pooh and The House at Pooh Corner: Recovering Arcadia*. New York: Twayne, 1995.

Cooper, J. C. *Fairy Tales: Allegories of Inner Life*. Wellingborough: The Aquarian Press, 1983.

Coren, Michael. *The Man who Created Narnia: The Story of C. S. Lewis*. Grand Rapids, MI: Eerdman, 1996.

Coveney, Peter. *The Image of Childhood: The Individual and Society: A Study of the Theme in English Literature*. Harmondsworth: Penguin, 1967.

Crago, Hugh, and Margot Crago. *Prelude to Literacy: A Preschool Child's Encounter with Picture and Story*. Carbondale, IL: Southern Illinois University Press, 1983.

Crew, Hilary S. *Is It Really "Mommie Dearest"? Daughter-Mother Narratives in Young Adult Fiction*. Lanham, MD: Scarecrow, 2000.

Christopher, Joe R. *C. S. Lewis*. Boston: Twayne, 1987.

Culler, Jonathan. *Structuralist Poetics: Structuralism, Linguistics and the Study of Literature*. London: Routledge, 1975.

———. *On Deconstruction: Theory and Criticism after Structuralism*. Ithaca, NY: Cornell University Press, 1982.

———. *The Pursuit of Signs: Semiotics, Literature, Deconstruction*. Ithaca, NY: Cornell University Press, 1983.

Cullinan, Bernice E. *Literature and the Child*. San Diego: Harcourt Brace Jovanovich, 1981.

Cummins, June. "Romancing the Plot: The Real Beast of Disney's Beauty and the Beast." *Children's Literature Association Quarterly* 20, no. 1 (1995): 23–28.

———. "The Resisting Monkey: 'Curious George,' Slave Captivity, and the Postcolonial Condition." *ARIEL* 28, no. 1 (1997): 69–83.

Cunningham, Hugh. *The Children of the Poor: Representation of Childhood since the Seventeenth Century*. Oxford: Blackwell, 1991.

Cuseo, Allan A. *Homosexual Characters in YA Novels: A Literary Analysis, 1969–1982*. Metuchen, NJ: Scarecrow, 1992.

Daly, Jay. *Presenting S. E. Hinton*. Boston: Twayne, 1989.

Day, Frances Ann. *Lesbian and Gay Voices: An Annotated Bibliography and Guide to Literature for Children and Young Adults*. Westport, CT: Greenwood, 2000.

Derrida, Jacques. *Of Grammatology*. Baltimore: The Johns Hopkins University Press, 1976.

———. *Writing and Difference*. London: Routledge, 1978.

Desmet, Mieke K. T. "Intertextuality/Intervisuality in Translation: The Jolly Postman's Intercultural Journey from Britain to the Netherlands." *Children's Literature in Education* 32, no. 1 (2001): 31–43.

Dixon, Bob. *Catching Them Young*. Vols. 1–2. London: Pluto Press, 1977.

Docherty, Thomas. *Reading (Absent) Character: Toward a Theory of Characterization in Fiction*. Oxford: Clarendon, 1983.

Doonan, Jane. *Looking at Pictures in Picture Books*. Stroud: Thimble Press, 1993.

Dunbar, Janet. *J M Barrie: The Man Behind the Image*. London: Collins, 1970.

Dusinberre, Juliet. *Alice to the Lighthouse: Children's Books and Radical Experiments in Art*. London: Macmillan, 1987.

Dyer, Carolyn Stewart, and Nancy Tillman Romalov, eds. *Rediscovering Nancy Drew*. Iowa City: University of Iowa Press, 1995.

Eagleton, Mary, ed. *Feminist Literary Theory: A Reader*. Oxford: Blackwell, 1986.

Eagleton, Terry. *Literary Theory: An Introduction*. Oxford: Blackwell, 1983.

Eccleshare, Julia. *A Guide to the Harry Potter Novels*. London: Continnum, 2002.

Eco, Umberto. *A Theory of Semiotics*. Bloomington: Indiana University Press, 1976.

———. *The Role of the Reader*. Bloomington: Indiana University Press, 1979.

———. *Six Walks in the Fictional Woods*. Cambridge, MA: Harvard University Press, 1995.

Edström, Vivi. *Astrid Lindgren: A Critical Study*. Stockholm: Rabén & Sjögren, 2000.

Egan, Michael. "The Neverland of Id: Barrie, Peter Pan and Freud." *Children's Literature* 10 (1982): 37–55.

Egoff, Sheila. *Worlds Within: Children's Fantasy from the Middle Ages to Today*. Chicago: American Library Association, 1988.

Egoff, Sheila, et al., eds. *Only Connect: Readings on Children's Literature*. 3rd ed. Toronto: Oxford University Press, 1996.

Elbert, Sarah. *A Hunger for Home: Louisa M. Alcott and Little Women*. Philadelphia: Temple University Press, 1984.

Elick, Catherine L. "Animal Carnivals: A Bakhtinian Reading of C. S. Lewis's *The Magician's Nephew* and P. L. Travers's *Mary Poppins*." *Style* 35, no. 3 (2001): 454–471.

Ellman, Mary. *Thinking about Women*. London: Virago, 1968.

Empson, William (1935). *Some Versions of Pastoral: A Study of the Pastoral Form in Literature*. London: Chatto & Windus, 1968.

Epperly, Elizabeth Rollin. *The Fragrance of Sweet-grass: L.M. Montgomery's Heroines and the Pursuit of Romance*. Toronto: University of Toronto Press, 1992.

Epstein, William, ed. *Considering the Subject: Essays in the Postmodern Theory and Practice of Biography and Biographical Criticism*. West Lafayette, IN: Purdue University Press, 1991.

Escarpit, Denise, ed. *The Portrayal of the Child in Children's Literature*. München: Saur, 1985.

Evans, Gwyneth. "The Girl in the Garden: Variations in a Feminine Pastoral." *Children's Literature Association Quarterly* 19, no. 1 (1984): 20–24.

Feaver, William. *When We Were Young: Two Centuries of Children's Book Illustrations*. London: Thames and Hudson, 1977.

Fensch, Thomas, ed. *Of Sneetches and Whos and the Good Dr. Seuss: Essays on the Writings and Life of Theodore Geisel*. Jefferson, NC: McFarland, 1997.

Fernández Lopez, Marisa. "Translation Studies in Contemporary Children's Literature: A Comparison of Intercultural Ideological Factors." *Children's Literature Association Quarterly* 25, no. 1 (2000): 29–37.

Fish, Stanley. *Is There a Text in This Class? The Authority of Interpretative Communities.* Cambridge, MA: Harvard University Press, 1982.

Fisher, Margery. *Who's Who in Children's Fiction: A Treasury of Familiar Characters of Childhood.* New York: Holt, Rinehart and Winston, 1975.

————. *The Bright Face of Danger: An Exploration of the Adventure Story.* London: Hodder & Stoughton, 1986.

Flanagan, Victoria. "Cross-dressing as Transvestism in Children's Literature: An Analysis of 'Gender-performative' Model." *Papers* 9, no. 3 (1999): 5–14.

Fludernik, Monika. *The Fictions of Language and the Languages of Fiction: The Linguistic Representation of Speech and Consciousness.* London: Routledge, 1993.

Flynn, Richard. "The Intersection of Children's Literature and Childhood Studies." *Children's Literature Association Quarterly* 22, no. 3 (1997): 143–146.

Fordyce, Rachel, and Carla Marello, eds. *Semiotics and Linguistics in Alice's Worlds.* Berlin: de Gruyter, 1994.

Forster, E. M. *Aspects of the Novel* (1927). San Diego: Harcourt, Brace, 1985.

Foster, Shirley, and Judy Simons. *What Katy Read: Feminist Re-readings of "Classic" Stories for Girls.* London: Macmillan, 1995.

Foucault, Michel. *The Archeology of Knowledge.* London: Tavistock, 1972.

————. *Discipline and Punish: The Birth of the Prison.* New York: Random House, 1979.

————. *The Essential Foucault.* Edited by Paul Rabinow and Nicholas Rose. New York: New Press, 2003.

Fowler, Alastair. *Kinds of Literature: An Introduction to the Theory of Genres.* Cambridge, MA, Harvard University Press, 1982.

Fox, Geoff, and Graham Hammond, eds. *Responses to Children's Literature.* München: Saur, 1980.

Francis, Elizabeth. "Feminist Versions of Pastoral." *Children's Literature Association Quarterly* 7, no. 4 (1982): 7–9.

Franson, J. Karl. "From Vanity Fair to Emerald City: Baum's Debt to Bunyan." *Children's Literature* 23 (1995): 91–114.

Franz, Marie-Louise von. *Interpretation of Fairy Tales.* Zürich: Spring, 1970.

————. *Problems of the Feminine in Fairytales.* Zürich: Spring, 1972.

————. *Shadow and Evil in Fairy Tales.* Zürich: Spring, 1974.

————. *Puer Aeternus: A Psychological Study of the Adult Struggle with the Paradise of Childhood.* 2nd ed. Santa Monica: Sigo, 1981.

Fraser, James H., ed. *Society and Children's Literature.* Boston: Godine, 1978.

Freud, Sigmund. *The Freud Reader.* Edited by Peter Gray. New York: Norton, 1989.

Freudenburg, Rachel. "Illustrating Childhood—'Hansel and Gretel,'" *Marvels & Tales* 12, no. 2 (1998): 263–318.

Fry, Donald. *Children Talk About Books: Seeing Themselves as Readers.* Milton Keynes: Open University Press, 1985.

Frye, Northrop. *Anatomy of Criticism: Four Essays.* Princeton, NJ: Princeton University Press, 1957.

————. *Fables of Identity: Studies in Poetic Mythology.* New York: Harcourt, Brace & World, 1963.

————. *The Secular Scripture: A Study of the Structure of Romance.* Cambridge, MA: Harvard University Press, 1976.

Gadamer, Hans-Georg. *Truth and Method*. London: Sheed & Ward, 1989.

Galbraight, Mary. "What Must I Give Up in Order to Grow Up? The Great War and Childhood Survival in Transatlantic Children's Books." *The Lion and the Unicorn* 24, no. 3 (2000): 337–359.

———. "Hear My Cry: A Manifesto for an Emancipatory Childhood Studies Approach to Children's Literature." *The Lion and the Unicorn* 25, no. 2 (2001): 187–208.

Gallagher, Catherine, and Stephen Greenblatt. *Practicing New Historicism*. Chicago: University of Chicago Press, 2000.

Gannon, Susan R., and Ruth Anne Thompson, eds. *Cross-Culturalism in Children's Literature*. West Lafayette, IN: Children's Literature Association, 1989.

Gardner, Martin, and Russel B. Nye. *The Wizard of Oz and Who He Was*. East Lansing, MI, Michigan State University Press, 1957.

Gavin, Adrienne, and Christopher Routledge. *Mystery in Children's Literature: From the Rational to the Supernatural*. Basingstoke: Palgrave, 2001.

Genette, Gérard. *Narrative Discourse: An Essay in Method*. Ithaca, NY: Cornell University Press, 1980.

———. *Narrative Discourse Revisited*. Ithaca, NY: Cornell University Press, 1988.

———. *The Architext: An Introduction*. Berkeley, CA: University of California Press, 1992.

———. *Palimpsests: Literature in the Second Degree*. Lincoln, NE: University of Nebraska Press, 1997.

Gilbert, Sandra M., and Susan Gubar. *The Madwoman in the Attic: The Woman Writer and the Nineteenth-Century Literary Imagination*. New Haven: Yale University Press, 1977.

———. *No Man's Land: The Place of the Woman Writer in the Twentieth Century*. New Haven: Yale University Press, 1988.

Gillen, Mollie. *The Wheel of Things: A Biography of L. M. Montgomery, Author of Anne of Green Gables*. London: Harrap, 1975.

Golden, Joanne M. *The Narrative Symbol in Childhood Literature: Exploration in the Construction of Text*. Berlin: Mouton, 1990.

Goodenough, Elizabeth, et al., eds. *Infant Tongues: The Voices of the Child in Literature*. Detroit: Wayne State University Press, 1994.

Green, Roger Lancelyn. *C. S. Lewis*. London: Bodley Head, 1957.

———. *Tellers of Tales: British Authors of Children's Books from 1800 to 1964*. London: Ward, 1965.

Greimas, Algirdas Julien. *Structural Semantics: An Attempt at a Method*. Lincoln, NE: University of Nebraska Press, 1983.

Griffith, John. *Charlotte's Web: A Pig's Salvation*. New York: Twayne, 1993.

Griswold, Jerry. *The Classic American Children's Story: Novels of the Golden Age*. New York: Penguin, 1996.

Grönbech, Bo. *Hans Christian Andersen*. New York: Twayne, 1980.

Haase, Donald. "Gold into Straw: Fairy-Tale Movies for Children and the Culture Industry." *The Lion and the Unicorn* 12, no. 2 (1988): 193–207.

Hamburger, Käte. *The Logic of Literature*. 2nd revised ed. Bloomington: Indiana University Press, 1973.

Haring-Smith, Tori. *A. A. Milne: A Critical Biography*. New York: Garland, 1982.

Harvey, W. J. *Character and the Novel*. Ithaca, NY: Cornell University Press, 1965.

Hastings, Waller. "Moral Simplification in Disney's The Little Mermaid." *The Lion and the Unicorn* 17, no. 1 (1993): 82–92.

Hawthorn, Jeremy. *Unlocking the Text: Fundamental Issues in Literary Theory*. London: Arnold, 1987.

———. *A Concise Glossary of Contemporary Literary Theory*. 2nd ed. London: Arnold, 1994.

Hearne, Betsy. *Choosing Books for Children: A Commonsense Guide*. 2nd revised ed. New York: Delacorte, 1990.

Heilman, Elizabeth, ed. *Harry Potter's World: Multidsciplinary Critical Perspective*. New York: Routledge, 2002.

Hendrickson, Linnea. "The View from Rapunzel's Tower." *Children's Literature in Education* 31, no. 4 (2000): 209–223.

Hillman, Judith. *Discovering Children's Literature*. 2nd ed. Upper Saddle River, NJ: Merrill, 1999.

Hirsch, E. D. *Validity in Interpretation*. New Haven: Yale University Press, 1967.

———. *The Aims of Interpretation*. Chicago: University of Chicago Press, 1976.

Hirsch, Marianne. *The Mother/Daughter Plot: Narrative, Psychoanalysis, Feminism*. Bloomington: Indiana University Press, 1989.

Hochman, Baruch. *Character in Literature*. Ithaca, NY: Cornell University Press, 1985.

Hohne, Karen, and Helen Wussow, eds. *A Dialogue of Voices: Feminist Literary Theory and Bakhtin*. Minneapolis: University of Minnesota Press, 1994.

Holbrook, David. *The Skeleton in the Wardrobe: C. S. Lewis's Fantasies: A Phenomenological Study*. Lewisburg: Bucknell University Press, 1991.

Holland, Norman. *The Dynamics of Literary Response*. New York: Norton, 1968.

Hollindale, Peter. "Ideology and the Children's Book." *Signal* 55 (1988): 3–22.

———. "Peter Pan, Captain Hook and the Book of the Video." *Signal* 72 (1993), 152–175.

———. *Signs of Childness in Children's Books*. Stroud: Thimble Press, 1997.

Holub, Robert C. *Reception Theory: A Critical Introduction*. London: Methuen, 1984.

Hourihan, Margery. *Deconstructing the Hero: Literary Theory and Children's Literature*. London: Routledge, 1997.

Hoy, David. *The Critical Circle: Literature, History, and Philosophical Hermeneutics*. Berkeley, CA: University of California Press, 1978.

Hume, Kathryn. *Fantasy and Mimesis: Responses to Reality in Western Literature*. New York: Methuen, 1984.

Hunt, Peter. "Childist Criticism: The Subculture of the Child, the Book and the Critic." *Signal* 43 (1984): 42–59.

———. "Questions of Method and Methods of Questioning: Childist Criticism in Action." *Signal* 45 (1984): 180–200.

———. "Narrative Theory and Children's Literature." *Children's Literature Association Quarterly* 9, no. 4 (1984–85): 191–194.

———. "Necessary Misreadings: Directions in Narrative Theory for Children's Literature." *Studies in the Literary Imagination* 18, no. 2 (1985): 107–121.

———. "Dialogue and Dialectic: Language and Class in The Wind in the Willows." *Children's Literature* 16 (1988): 159–168.

———. *Criticism, Theory and Children's Literature*. London: Blackwell, 1991.

———. *An Introduction to Children's Literature*. Oxford: Oxford University Press, 1994.

———. *Children's Literature*. London: Blackwell, 2001.

Hunt, Peter, ed. *Children's Literature: The Development of Criticism*. London: Routledge & Kegan Paul, 1990.

———. *Literature for Children: Contemporary Criticism*. London: Routledge, 1992.

———. *Children's Literature: An Illustrated History*. Oxford: Oxford University Press, 1995.

———. *International Companion Encyclopedia of Children's Literature*. London: Routledge, 1996.

———. *Understanding Children's Literature*. London: Routledge, 1998.

Hunt, Peter, and Millicent Lenz. *Alternative Worlds in Fantasy Fiction*. London: Continuum, 2001.

Hürlimann, Bettina. *Picture-Book World*. Translated and edited by Brian W. Alderson. London: Oxford University Press, 1968.

Hurwitz, Johanna. *Astrid Lindgren: Storyteller to the World*. New York: Viking Penguin, 1989.

Hutcheon, Linda. *A Poetics of Postmodernism: History, Theory, Fiction*. New York: Routledge, 1988.

Ingarden, Roman. *The Literary Work of Art: An Investigation on the Borders of Ontology, Logic, and Theory of Literature*. Evanston, IL: Northwestern University Press, 1973.

Inglis, Fred. *The Promise of Happiness: The Value and Meaning in Children's Fiction*. Cambridge: Cambridge University Press, 1981.

Inness, Sherrie A., ed. *Nancy Drew and Company: Culture, Gender, and Girls' Series*. Bowling Green, OH: Bowling Green State University Popular Press, 1997.

Iser, Wolfgang. *The Implied Reader: Patterns of Communication in Prose Fiction from Bunyan to Beckett*. Baltimore: The Johns Hopkins University Press, 1974.

———. *The Act of Reading: A Theory of Aesthetic Responce*. Baltimore: The Johns Hopkins University Press, 1974.

Jackson, Rosemary. *Fantasy: The Literature of Subversion*. New York: Methuen, 1981.

Jameson, Fredric. *The Political Unconscious: Narrative as a Socially Symbolic Art*. London: Methuen, 1981.

Jauss, Hans Robert. *Toward an Aesthetic of Reception*. Minneapolis: University of Minnesota Press, 1982.

———. *Aesthetic Experience and Literary Hermeneutics*. Minneapolis: University of Minnesota Press, 1982.

Johnson, Dianne. *Telling Tales: The Pedagogy and the Promise of Afro-American Literature for Children*. Westport, CT: Greenwood, 1990.

Jones, Amanda Rogers. "The Narnian Schism: Reading the Christian Subtext as Other in the Children's Stories of C. S. Lewis." *Children's Literature Association Quarterly* 29, nos. 1–2 (2004): 45–61.

Jones, Dudley, and Tony Watkins, eds. *A Necessary Fantasy? The Heroic Figure in Children's Popular Culture.* New York: Garland, 2000.

Jones, Raymond E. *Characters in Children's Literature.* Detroit: Gale Research, 1997.

Juhl, Peter D. *Interpretation: An Essay in the Philosophy of Literary Criticism.* Princeton, NJ: Princeton University Press, 1986.

Jung, C. G., ed. *Man and His Symbols.* London: Aldus, 1964.

Jurich, Marilyn. *Scheherazade's Sisters: Trickster Heroines and Their Stories in World Literature.* Westport, CT: Greenwood, 1998.

Kaplan, Justin. *Mr. Clemens and Mark Twain: A Biography.* New York: Simon & Schuster, 1966.

Keith, Lois. *Take Up Thy Bed and Walk: Death, Disability, and Cure in Classic Fiction for Girls.* New York: Routledge, 2002.

Kelley-Lainé, Kathleen. *Peter Pan: The Story of Lost Childhood.* Shaftesbury: Element, 1997.

Kermode, Frank. *The Sense of an Ending: Studies in the Theory of Fiction.* London: Oxford University Press, 1968.

Kern, Edmund M. *The Wisdom of Harry Potter: What Our Favorite Hero Teaches Us about Moral Choices.* Amherst, NY: Prometheus, 2003.

Keyser, Elizabeth Lennox. *Whispers in the Dark: The Fiction of Louisa May Alcott.* Knoxville: University of Tennessee Press, 1993.

———. *Little Women: A Family Romance.* Athens, GA: University of Georgia Press, 1999.

Khorana, Meena. *Africa in Literature for Children and Young Adults: An Annotated Bibliography of English-language Books.* Westport, CT: Greenwood, 1994.

Khorana, Meena, ed. *Critical Perspectives on Postcolonial African Children's and Young Adult Literature.* Westport, CT: Greenwood, 1998.

Kidd, Kenneth. "Psychoanalysis and Children's Literature: The Case for Complementarity." *The Lion and the Unicorn* 28, no. 1 (2004): 109–130.

Kiefer, Barbara. *The Potential of Picturebooks: From Visual Literacy to Aesthetic Understanding.* Englewood Cliffs, NJ: Prentice Hall, 1995.

Kies, Cosette. *Young Adult Horror Fiction.* New York: Twayne, 1992.

Kincaid, James. *Child-Loving: The Erotic Child and Victorian Culture.* New York: Routledge, 1992.

Kinder, Marcia. *Playing with Power in Movies, Television and Video Games.* Berkeley, CA: University of California Press, 1991.

Klemin, Diana. *The Art of Art for Children's Books.* New York: Clarkson N. Potter, 1966.

Klingberg, Göte. *Children's Fiction in the Hands of the Translators.* Lund: Gleerup, 1986.

Klingberg, Göte, et al., eds. *Children's Books in Translation: The Situation and the Problems.* Stockholm: Almqvist & Wiksell International, 1978.

Kokkola, Lydia. *Representing the Holocaust in Children's Literature.* New York: Routledge, 2003.

Krips, Valerie. *The Presence of the Past: Memory, Heritage and Childhood in Postwar Britain.* New York: Garland, 2000.

Kristeva, Julia. *Desire in Language: A Semiotic Approach to Literature and Art.* Oxford: Blackwell, 1980.

———. *Powers of Horror: An Essay on Abjection.* New York: Columbia University Press, 1982.

———. *Revolution in Poetic Language.* New York: Columbia University Press, 1984.

———. *The Kristeva Reader.* Edited by Toril Moi. London: Blackwell, 1986.

———. *Abjection, Melancholia and Love.* London: Routledge, 1990.

Kumar, Krishan. *Utopia and Anti-Utopia in Modern Times.* London: Blackwell, 1987.

Kutzer, Daphne M. *Empire's Children: Empire and Imperialism in Classic British Children's Books.* New York: Garland, 2000.

Kuznets, Lois. "The Fresh-Air Kids, or Some Contemporary Versions of Pastoral." *Children's Literature* 11 (1983): 156–168.

———. *When Toys Come Alive: Narratives of Animation, Metamorphosis and Development.* New Haven: Yale University Press, 1994.

Lacan, Jacques. *Ecrits: A Selection.* New York: Norton, 1977.

———. *The Four Fundamental Concepts of Psychoanalysis.* Harmondsworth: Penguin, 1979.

Lanser, Susan Sniader. *The Narrative Act: Point of View in Prose Fiction.* Princeton, NJ: Princeton University Press, 1981.

Latham, Don. "Discipline and Its Discontents: A Foucauldian Reading of *The Giver.*" *Children's Literature* 32 (2004): 134–151.

Lathey, Gillian. *The Impossible Legacy: Identity and Purpose in Autobiographical Children's Literature Set in the Third Reich and the Second World War.* Bern: Lang, 1999.

Leach, Karoline. *In the Shadow of the Dreamchild: A New Understanding of Lewis Carroll.* London: Peter Owen, 1999.

Lecercle, Jean-Jacques. *Philosophy of Nonsense: The Intuitions of Victorian Nonsense Literature.* London: Routledge, 1994.

Leech, Geoffrey, and Michael H. Short. *Style in Fiction: A Linguistic Introduction to English Fictional Prose.* London: Longman, 1981.

Leeson, Robert. *Children's Books and Class Society: Past and Present.* London: Writers and Readers Publishing Cooperative, 1977.

Lesnik-Oberstein, Karín. *Children's Literature: Criticism and the Fictional Child.* Oxford: Clarendon, 1994.

Lesnik-Oberstein, Karín, ed. *Children in Culture: Approaches to Childhood.* London: Macmillan, 1998.

———. *Children's Literature: New Approaches.* London: Palgrave Macmillan, 2004.

Lévi-Strauss, Claude. *Structural Anthropology.* Garden City, NY: Doubleday, 1967.

———. *The Raw and the Cooked: Introduction to a Science of Mythology.* Chicago: University of Chicago Press, 1983.

Lewis, David. *Reading Contemporary Picturebooks: Picturing Text.* London: Routledge, 2001.

Lindskoog, Kathryn. *Journey into Narnia.* Pasadena, CA: Hope, 1998.

Lochhead, Marion. *The Renaissance of Wonder in Children's Literature.* Edinburgh: Canongate, 1977.

Lodge, David. *The Modes of Modern Writing: Metaphor, Metonymy, and the Typology of Modern Literature.* London: Arnold, 1977.

Lodge, David, ed. *Modern Criticism and Theory: A Reader.* London: Longman, 1988.

Logan, Mawuena Kossi. *Narrating Africa: George Henty and the Fiction of Empire.* New York: Garland, 1999.

Lotman, Yuri. *Semiotics of Cinema.* Ann Arbor, MI: University of Michigan Press, 1976.

———. *Analysis of the Poetic Text.* Ann Arbor, MI: University of Michigan Press, 1976.

———. *The Structure of the Artistic Text.* Ann Arbor, MI: University of Michigan Press, 1977.

Lowe, Virginia. "'Stop! You Didn't Read Who Wrote It!': The Concept of the Author." *Children's Literature in Education* 22, no. 2 (1991): 79–88.

Lukens, Rebecca J. *A Critical Handbook of Children's Literature.* 4th ed. New York: HarperCollins, 1990.

Lundell, Torborg. *Fairy Tale Mothers.* New York: Peter Lang, 1990.

Lurie, Alison. *Don't Tell the Grownups: Subversive Children's Literature.* Boston: Little, Brown, 1990.

Lüthi, Max. *The Fairytale as Art Form and Portrait of Man.* Bloomington: Indiana University Press, 1984.

Lynch-Brown, Carol, and Carl M. Tomlinson. *Essentials of Children's Literature.* Boston: Allyn and Bacon, 1993.

MacCann, Donnarae. *White Supremacy in Children's Literature: Characterizations of African Americans, 1830–1900.* New York: Garland, 1998.

MacCann, Donnarae, and Gloria Woodard, eds. *The Black American in Books for Children: Readings in Racism.* Metuchen, NJ: Scarecrow, 1972.

MacDonald, Ruth K. *Louisa M. Alcott.* Boston: Twayne, 1983.

———. *Beatrix Potter.* Boston: Twayne, 1986.

Mackey, Margaret. "Ramona the Chronotope: The Young Reader and the Social Theories of Narrative." *Children's Literature in Education* 21, no. 3 (1990): 179–187.

———. "Growing with Laura: Time, Space and the 'Little House' Books." *Children's Literature in Education* 23, no. 2 (1992): 59–74.

———. *The Case of Peter Rabbit: Changing Conditions of Literature for Children.* New York: Garland, 1998.

Mackey, Margaret, ed. *Beatrix Potter's Peter Rabbit: A Children's Classic at 100.* Lanham, MD: Scarecrow, 2002.

MacLeod, Anne Scott. *American Childhood: Essays on Children's Literature of the Nineteenth and Twentieth Century.* Athens, GA: University of Georgia Press, 1994.

Malarté-Feldman, Claire-Lise. "The Challenges of Translating Perrault's Contes into English." *Marvels & Tales* 13, no. 2 (1999): 184–197.

Manlove, C. N. *Modern Fantasy: Five Studies.* Cambridge: Cambridge University Press, 1975.

———. *The Chronicles of Narnia: The Patterning of a Fantastic World.* New York: Twayne, 1993.

Martin, Wallace. *Recent Theories of Narrative.* Ithaca, NY: Cornell University Press, 1986.

Matejka, Ladislav, and Krystyna Pomorska, eds. *Readings in Russian Poetics: Formalist and Structuralist Views*. Cambridge, MA: MIT Press, 1971.
de Mause, Lloyd, ed. *The History of Childhood*. New York: Harper & Row, 1974.
May, Jill P. *Children's Literature and Critical Theory*. New York: Oxford University Press, 1995.
McCallum, Robyn. *Ideologies of Identity in Adolescent Fiction: The Dialogic Construction of Subjectivity*. New York: Garland, 1999.
McCoy Lowery, Ruth. *Immigrants in Children's Literature*. New York: Peter Lang, 2000.
McGavran, James Holt, ed. *Romanticism and Children's Literature in the Nineteenth-Century England*. Athens, GA: University of Georgia Press, 1991.
———. *Literature and the Child: Romantic Continuations, Postmodern Contestations*. Iowa City: University of Iowa Press, 1999.
McGillis, Roderick. "The Embrace: Narrative Voice and Children's Books." *Canadian Children's Literature* 63 (1991): 24–40.
———. "Another Kick at La/can: 'I Am a Picture,'" *Children's Literature Association Quarterly* 20, no. 1 (1995): 42–46.
———. *The Nimble Reader: Literary Theory and Children's Literature*. New York: Twayne, 1996.
———. "Self, Other, and Other Self: Recognizing the Other in Children's Literature," *The Lion and the Unicorn* 21 (1997): 215–229.
McGillis, Roderick, ed. *Voices of the Other: Children's Literature and the Postcolonial Context*. New York: Garland, 1999.
McQuillan, Martin, ed. *The Narrative Reader*. London: Routledge, 2000.
Medvedev, P. N., and Mikhail Bakhtin. *The Formal Method in Literary Scholarship*. Baltimore: The Johns Hopkins University Press, 1978.
Meek, Margaret. *How Texts Teach What Readers Learn*. South Woodchester: Thimble Press, 1988.
Meek, Margaret, ed. *Children's Literature and National Identity*. Stoke-on-Trent: Trentham Books, 2001.
Meigs, Cornelia. *Invincible Louisa: The Story of the Author of Little Women*. Boston: Little, Brown, 1933.
———. *Louisa M. Alcott and the American Family Story*. London: Bodley Head, 1970.
Metcalf, Eva-Maria. *Astrid Lindgren*. New York: Twayne, 1995.
Mikkelsen, Nina. *Virginia Hamilton*. New York: Twayne, 1994.
Miller, Dean A. *The Epic Hero*. Baltimore: The Johns Hopkins University Press, 2000.
Milne, Christopher. *The Enchanted Places*. London: Methuen, 1974.
Mitchell, Juliet. *Psychoanalysis and Feminism*. London: Allen Lane, 1974.
Moi, Toril. *Sexual/textual Politics: Feminist Literary Theory*. London: Methuen, 1985.
Molson, Francis J. *Children's Fantasy*. San Bernardino: Borgo, 1989.
Montgomery, Lucy Maud. *The Annotated Anne of Green Gables*. Edited by Wendy E. Barry, Margaret Anne Doody, and Mary E. Doody Jones. New York: Oxford University Press, 1997.
Morgan, Judith, and Neil Morgan. *Dr. Seuss & Mr. Geisel: A Biography*. New York: Da Capo Press, 1996.

Morris, Charles. *Writings on the General Theory of Signs.* The Hague: Mouton, 1971.

Morris, Pam, ed. *The Bakhtin Reader: Selected Writings of Bakhtin, Medvedev, Voloshinov.* London: Arnold, 1994.

Morson, Gary Saul, and Caryl Emerson. *Mikhail Bakhtin: Creation of a Prosaics.* Stanford: Stanford University Press, 1990.

Mortimore, Artur D. *Index to Characters in Children's Literature.* Bristol: D. Mortimore, 1977.

Myers, Mitzi. "Missed Opportunities and Critical Malpractice: New Historicism and Children's Literature." *Children's Literature Association Quarterly* 13, no. 1 (1988): 41–43.

Naidoo, Beverley. *Through Whose Eyes? Exploring Racism: Reader, Text and Context.* London: Trentham, 1992.

Natov, Roni. *The Poetics of Childhood.* New York: Routledge, 2003.

Nelson, Claudia. *Boys Will be Girls: The Feminine Ethic and British Children's Fiction, 1857–1917.* New Brunswick, NJ: Rutgers University Press, 1991.

Netley, Noriko Shimoda. "The Difficulty of Translation: Decoding Cultural Signs on Other Languages." *Children's Literature in Education* 23, no. 4 (1992): 195–202.

Neumeyer, Peter. "A Structural Approach to the Study of Literature for Children." *Elementary English* 44, no. 8 (1977): 883–887.

Nikolajeva, Maria. *The Magic Code: The Use of Magical Patterns in Fantasy for Children.* Stockholm: Almqvist & Wiksell International, 1988.

———. "How Fantasy is Made: Patterns and Structures in *The Neverending Story* by Michael Ende." *Marvels and Tales* 4, no. 1 (1990): 34–41.

———. "Stages of Transformation: Folklore Elements in Children's Novels." *Canadian Children's Literature* 73 (1994): 48–54.

———. *Children's Literature Comes of Age: Towards a New Aesthetic.* New York: Garland, 1996.

———. "The Child as Self-Deceiver: Narrative Strategies in Katherine Paterson's and Patricia MacLachlan's Novels." *Papers* 7, no. 1 (1997): 5–15.

———. "Exit Children's Literature?" *The Lion and the Unicorn* 22, no. 2 (1998): 221–236.

———. *From Mythic to Linear: Time in Children's Literature.* Lanham, MD: Scarecrow, 2000.

———. "Tamed Imagination: A Rereading of Heidi." *Children's Literature Association Quarterly* 25, no. 2 (2000): 68–75.

———. "The Changing Aesthetics of Character in Children's Fiction." *Style* 35, no. 3 (2001): 430–453.

———. "Imprints of the Mind: The Depiction of Consciousness in Children's Literature." *Children's Literature Association Quarterly* 26, no. 4 (2001): 173–187.

———. "'A Dream of Complete Idleness': The Depiction of Labor in Children's Literature." *The Lion and the Unicorn* 26, no. 3 (2002): 305–321.

———. "Harry Potter—Return to the Romantic Hero." Pp. 125–140 in *Harry Potter's World: Multidisciplinary Critical Perspectives,* edited by Elizabeth Heilman. New York: Routledge, 2002.

———. *The Rhetoric of Character in Children's Literature.* Lanham, MD: Scarecrow, 2002.

———. "Fairy Tales and Fantasy: From Archaic to Postmodern." *Marvels & Tales* 17, no. 1 (2003): 138–156.

———. "Picturebook Characterization: Text/Image Interaction." Pp. 37–49 in *Art, Narrative and Childhood*, edited by Morag Styles. London: Trentham, 2003.

Nikolajeva, Maria, ed. *Voices from Far Away: Current Trends in International Children's Literature Research*. Stockholm: Centre for the Study of Childhood Culture, 1995.

———. *Aspects and Issues in the History of Children's Literature*. Westport, CT: Greenwood, 1995.

Nikolajeva, Maria, and Carole Scott. *How Picturebooks Work*. New York: Garland, 2001.

Nilsen, Alleen Pace, and Kenneth L. Donelson. *Literature for Today's Young Aduts.* 6th ed. New York: Longman, 2001.

Nilsen, Don L. F. "Northrop Frye Meets Tweedledum and Tweedldee: Adolescent Literature as Comedy, Romance, Tragedy, and Irony." *Journal of Evolutionary Psychology* 19, nos. 1–2 (1998): 10–20.

Nodelman, Perry. "Interpretation and the Apparent Sameness of Children's Literature." *Studies in the Literary Imagination* 18, no. 2 (1985): 5–20.

———. "Text as Teacher: The Beginning of Charlotte's Web." *Children's Literature* 13 (1985): 109–127.

———. *Words About Pictures: The Narrative Art of Children's Picture Books*. Athens, GA: University of Georgia Press, 1988.

———. "Children's Literature as Women's Writing." *Children's Literature Association Quarterly* 13, no. 1 (1988): 31–34.

———. *The Pleasures of Children's Literature*. New York: Longman, 1992. 2nd ed. 1996.

———. "The Other: Orientalism, Colonialism, and Children's Literature." *Children's Literature Association Quarterly* 17, no. 1 (1992): 29–35.

———. "Pleasure and Genre: Speculations on the Characteristics of Children's Fiction." *Children's Literature* 28 (2000): 1–14.

Nodelman, Perry, ed. *Touchstones: Reflections on the Best in Children's Literature*. Vols. 1–3. West Lafayette, IN: Children's Literature Association, 1985–89.

Nodelman, Perry, and Mavis Reimer. *The Pleasures of Children's Literature*. 3rd ed. Boston: Allyn and Bacon, 2003.

Norton, Donna E. *Through the Eyes of a Child: An Introduction to Children's Literature*. 5th ed. Upper Saddle River, NJ: Merrill, 1999.

O'Dell, Felicity Ann. *Socialization Through Literature: The Soviet Example*. Cambridge: Cambridge University Press, 1978.

Oittinen, Riitta. *Translating for Children*. New York: Garland, 2000.

Oliver, Kelly. *French Feminist Reader*. Lanham, MD: Rowman & Littlefield, 2000.

Onega, Susana, and José Angel García Landa, eds. *Narratology*. London: Longman, 1996.

Ord, Priscilla A., ed. *Proceedings of the 6th Annual Conference of ChLA*. Villanova, PA: Villanova University Press, 1980.

O'Sullivan, Emer. *Friend or Foe? The Image of Germany and the Germans in British Children's Fiction from 1870 to the Present*. Tübingen: Narr, 1990.

———. "Translating Pictures." *Signal* 90 (1999): 167–175.

Otten, Charlotte von, and Gary D. Smith, eds. *The Voice of the Narrator in Children's Literature: Insights from Writers and Critics.* New York: Greenwood, 1989.

Palmer, Richard E. *Hermeneutics: Interpretation Theory on Schleiermacher, Dilthey, Heidegger, and Gadamer.* Evanson, IL: Northwestern University Press, 1969.

Paul, Lissa. *Reading Otherways.* Stroud: Thimble Press, 1998.

Petruso, Thomas F. *Life Made Real: Characterization in the Novel since Proust and Joyce.* Ann Arbor, MI: University of Michigan Press, 1991.

Pflieger, Pat. *Beverly Cleary.* Boston: Twayne, 1991.

Philips, Robert, ed. *Aspects of Alice.* New York: The Vanguard Press, 1971.

Phillips, Richard. *Mapping Men and Empire: A Geography of Adventure.* London: Routledge, 1997.

Pinsent, Pat, ed. *The Power of the Page: Children's Books and Their Readers.* London: Fulton, 1993.

Powling, Chris. *Roald Dahl.* London: Puffin Books, 1985.

Pratt, Annis, with Barbara White, Andrea Loewenstein, and Mary Wyer. *Archetypal Patterns in Women's Fiction.* Bloomington: Indiana University Press, 1981.

Pratt, Mary Louise. *Toward a Speech Act Theory of Literary Discourse.* Bloomington: Indiana University Press, 1977.

Price, Martin. *Forms of Life: Character and Moral Imagination in the Novel.* New Haven: Yale University Press, 1983.

Prince, Gerald. *A Grammar of Stories.* The Hague: Mouton, 1973.

———. *Narratology: The Form and Functioning of Narrative.* Berlin: Mouton, 1982.

———. *A Dictionary of Narratology.* Lincoln, NE: University of Nebraska Press, 1987.

Propp, Vladimir. *Morphology of the Folktale.* Austin: University of Texas Press, 1968.

———. *Theory and History of Folklore.* Manchester: Manchester University Press, 1984.

Quigly, Isabel. *The Heirs of Tom Brown: The English School Story.* London: Chatto & Windus, 1982.

Rahn, Suzanne. *The Wizard of Oz: Shaping an Imaginary World.* New York: Twayne, 1998.

———. "Snow White's Dark Ride: Narrative Strategies at Disneyland." *Bookbird* 38, no. 1 (2000): 19–24.

Reed, Michael D. "The Female Oedipal Complex in Maurice Sendak's *Outside Over There.*" *Children's Literature Association Quarterly* 11, no. 4 (1986–87): 176–180.

Reid, Suzanne Elizabeth. *Presenting Cynthia Voigt.* New York: Twayne, 1995.

Reimer, Mavis, ed. *Such a Simple Little Tale: Critical Responses to L. M. Montgomery's Anne of Green Gables.* Lanham, MD: Scarecrow, 1992.

Reynolds, Kimberley. *Girls Only? Gender and Popular Children's Fiction in Britain 1880–1910.* Hemel Hempstead: Harvester, 1990.

Reynolds, Kimberley, Geraldine Brennan, and Kevin McCarron. *Frightening Fiction.* London: Continuum, 2001.

Richards, I. A. *Principles of Literary Criticism.* London: Routledge & Kegan Paul, 1924.

Ricoeur, Paul. *The Conflict of Interpretations: Essays in Hermeneutics.* Evanston, IL: Northwestern University Press, 1974.

———. *Interpretation Theory: Discourse and the Surplus of Meaning.* Fort Worth, TX: Texas Christian University Press, 1976.

———. *The Rule of Metaphor: Multi-disciplinary Studies of the Creation of Meaning in Language.* London: Routledge & Kegan Paul, 1978.

———. *Hermeneutics and the Human Sciences: Essays on Language, Action and Interpretation.* Cambridge: Cambridge University Press, 1981.

———. *Time and Narrative.* Vols. 1–3. Chicago: University of Chicago Press, 1984–88.

———. *A Ricoeur Reader: Reflection and Imagination.* Edited by Mario J. Valdés. New York: Harvester Wheatsheaf, 1991.

Riffaterre, Michael. *Semiotics of Poetry.* London: Methuen, 1978.

Rimmon-Kenan, Shlomith. *Narrative Fiction: Contemporary Poetics.* London: Routledge, 1983.

Robinson, Debra. *Portraying Persons with Disabilities: An Annotated Bibliography of Fiction for Children and Teenagers.* New Providence, NJ: Bowker, 1992.

Rodari, Gianni. *The Grammar of Fantasy: An Introduction in the Art of Inventing Stories.* New York: Teachers and Writers Collaborative, 1996.

Rollin, Lucy. "Fear of Faerie: Disney and the Elitist Critics." *Children's Literature Association Quarterly* 12, no. 2 (1987): 90–93.

———. "The Reproduction of Mothering in Charlotte's Web." *Children's Literature* 18 (1990): 42–52.

Rollin, Lucy, and Mark I. West, eds. *Psychoanalytical Responses to Children's Literature.* Jefferson, NC: McFarland, 1999.

Rose, Jacqueline. *The Case of Peter Pan, or The Impossibility of Children's Fiction.* London: Macmillan, 1984.

Roser, Nancy, ed. *What a Character!* Austin: International Reading Association, 2004.

Rosenblatt, Louise. *The Reader, the Text, the Poem: The Transactional Theory of the Literary Work* (1938). Carbondale, IL: Southern Illinois University Press, 1978.

Roxburgh, Stephen D. "'Our First World': Form and Meaning in The Secret Garden." *Children's Literature in Education* 10, no. 3 (1979): 120–130.

Rubio, Mary, ed. *Harvesting Thistles: The Textual Garden of L. M. Montgomery.* Guelph, Ont.: Canadian Children's Press, 1994.

Rubio, Mary, and Elizabeth Waterston. *Writing a Life: L. M. Montgomery.* Toronto: ECW Press, 1995.

Rudd, David. *Enid Blyton and the Mystery of Children's Literature.* New York: St. Martin's Press, 2000.

Rudman, Masha Kabakow. *Children's Literature: An Issues Approach.* 3rd ed. White Plains, NY: Longman, 1995.

Rushdy, Ashraf H. A. "The Miracle of the Web: Community, Desire, and Narrativity in Charlotte's Web." *The Lion and the Unicorn* 15 (1991): 35–60.

Russ, Joanna. *To Write Like a Woman: Essays in Feminism and Science Fiction.* Bloomington: Indiana University Press, 1995.

Russell, David L. *Literature for Children: A Short Introduction.* New York: Longman, 2000.

———. "Pippi Longstocking and the Subversive Affirmation of Comedy." *Children's Literature in Education* 31, no. 3 (2000): 167–177.

Russell Thorn, Joan. "Children's Literature: Reading, Seeing, Watching." *Children's Literature in Education* 22, no. 1 (1991): 51–58.
Rustin, Margaret, and Michael Rustin. *Narratives of Love and Loss: Studies in Modern Children's Fiction.* London: Verso, 1987.
Sale, Roger. *Fairy Tales and After.* Cambridge: Cambridge University Press, 1978.
Sammonds, Martha C. *"A Better Country": The Worlds of Religious Fantasy and Science Fiction.* New York: Greenwood, 1988.
Sarland, Charles. *Young People Reading: Culture and Response.* Milton Keynes: Open University Press, 1991.
Saussure, Ferdinand de. *Course in General Linguistics.* Edited by Charles Bally. New York: McGraw-Hill, 1966.
Saxton, Martha. *Louisa May: A Modern Biography.* New York: Avon, 1978.
Scharnhorst, Gary, ed. *Critical Essays on The Adventures of Tom Sawyer.* New York: Hall, 1993.
Scholes, Robert. *Structuralism in Literature: An Introduction.* New Haven: Yale University Press, 1974.
———. *Semiotics and Interpretation.* New Haven: Yale University Press, 1982.
Scholes, Robert, and Robert Kellogg. *The Nature of Narrative.* London: Oxford University Press, 1966.
Schwarcz, Joseph H. *Ways of the Illustrator: Visual Communication in Children's Literature.* Chicago: American Library Association, 1982.
Schwarcz, Joseph, and Chava Schwarcz. *The Picture Book Comes of Age.* Chicago: American Library Association, 1991.
Searle, John R. *Speech Acts: An Essay in the Philosophy of Language.* Cambridge: Cambridge University Press, 1969.
Segal, Robert A., ed. *Jung on Mythology.* Princeton, NJ: Princeton University Press, 1998.
Selden, Raman, et al. *A Reader's Guide to Contemporary Literary Theory.* 4th ed. London: Harvester, 1997.
Sell, Roger D. *Literature as Communication: The Foundation of Mediating Criticism.* Amsterdam: John Benjamins, 2000.
Sell, Roger D., ed. *Children's Literature as Communication.* Amsterdam: John Benjamins, 2002.
Sewell, Elizabeth. *The Field of Nonsense.* London: Chatto & Windus, 1952.
Shapiro, Marc. *J. K. Rowling: The Wizard behind Harry Potter.* New York: Griffin, 2000.
Shavit, Zohar. "The Ambivalent Status of Texts: The Case of Children's Literature." *Poetics Today* 173 (1980): 75–86.
———. *Poetics of Children's Literature.* Athens, GA: University of Georgia Press, 1986.
Showalter, Elaine. *A Literature of Their Own.* London: Virago, 1982.
———. *Sister's Choice: Tradition and Change in American Women's Writing.* Oxford: Clarendon, 1991.
Showalter, Elaine, ed. *The New Feminist Criticism: Essays on Women, Literature, and Theory.* London: Virago, 1986.
———. *Speaking of Gender.* New York: Routledge, 1989.

Sigman, Joseph. "The Diamond in the Ashes: A Jungian Reading of the 'Princess' Books." Pp. 183–194 in *For the Childlike: George MacDonald's Fantasies for Children*, edited by Roderick McGillis. Metuchen, NJ: Scarecrow, 1992.

Slapin, Beverly, and Dora Seale. *Through Indian Eyes: Native Experience in Books for Children*. Philadelphia: New Society, 1992.

Smedman, M. Sarah. "When Literary Works Meet: Allusion in the Novels of Katherine Paterson." *International Conference of the Children's Literature Association* 16 (1989): 59–66.

———. "Springs of Hope: Recovery of Primordeal Time in 'Mythic' Novels for Young Readers." *Children's Literature* 16 (1988): 91–107.

Smith, Joseph H., and William Kerrigan, eds. *Opening Texts: Psychoanalysis and the Culture of the Child*. Baltimore: The Johns Hopkins University Press, 1985.

Smith, Karen Patricia. *The Fabulous Realm: A Literary-Historical Approach to British Fantasy, 1780–1990*. Metuchen, NJ: Scarecrow, 1993.

Snodgrass, Mary Ellen. *Characters from Young Adult Literature*. Englewood, CO: Libraries Unlimited, 1991.

Sonheim, Amy. *Maurice Sendak*. New York: Twayne, 1991.

Spaet, Janet. *Laura Ingalls Wilder*. Boston: Twayne, 1987.

Spanos, William V., ed. *Martin Heidegger and the Question of Literature: Towards a Postmodern Literary Hermeneutics*. Bloomington: Indiana University Press, 1979.

Spender, Dale. *Man Made Language*. 2nd ed. London: Pandora, 1998.

Spitz, Ellen Handler. *Inside Picture Books*. New Haven: Yale University Press, 1999.

Stanger, Carol A. "Winnie the Pooh Through a Feminist Lens." *The Lion and the Unicorn* 11, no. 2 (1987): 34–50.

Stanzel, F. K. *A Theory of Narrative*. Cambridge: Cambridge University Press, 1984.

Steig, Michael. *Stories of Reading: Subjectivity and Literary Understanding.* Baltimore: The Johns Hopkins University Press, 1989.

———. "Never Going Home: Reflections on Reading, Adulthood and the Possibility of Children's Literature." *Children's Literature Association Quarterly* 18, no. 1 (1993): 36–39.

Stephens, John. *Reading the Signs: Sense and Significance in Written Texts*. Kenthurst: Kangaroo, 1992.

———. *Language and Ideology in Children's Fiction*. London: Longman, 1992.

———. "Gender, Genre and Children's Literature." *Signal* 79 (1996): 17–30.

Stephens, John, ed. *Ways of Being Male: Representing Masculinities in Children's Literature and Film*. New York: Routledge, 2002.

Stephens, John, and Robyn McCallum. *Retelling Stories, Framing Culture: Traditional Story and Metanarratives in Children's Literature*. New York: Garland, 1998.

Stern, Madeleine B. *Louisa May Alcott*. Norman: University of Oklahoma Press, 1950.

Stewart, Susan. *Nonsense: Aspects of Intertextuality in Folklore and Literature*. Baltimore: The Johns Hopkins University Press, 1979.

———. *On Longing: Narratives of the Miniature, the Gigantic, the Souvenirs, the Collection*. Baltimore: The Johns Hopkins University Press, 1984.

Stewig, John Warren. *Looking at Picture Books*. Fort Atkinson, WI: Highsmith Press, 1995.

Stone, Michael, ed. *Children's Literature and Contemporary Theory*. Wollongong: University of Wollongong Press, 1991.

Stoodt-Hill, Barbara D., and Linda B. Amspaugh-Corson. *Children's Literature: Discovery for a Lifetime*. 2nd ed. Upper Saddle River, NJ: Merrill, 2001.

Storey, Dee. *Twins in Children's and Adolescent Literature: An Annotated Bibliogrpahy*. Metuchen, NJ: Scarecrow, 1993.

Street, Douglas, ed. *Children's Novels and the Movies*. New York: Ungar, 1983.

Styles, Morag, Eve Bearne, and Victor Watson, eds. *After Alice: Exploring Children's Literature*. London: Cassell, 1992.

Suleiman, Susan, and Inge Crossman, eds. *The Reader in the Text: Essays on Audience and Participation*. Princeton: Princeton University Press, 1980.

Sutherland, Zena, and May Hill Arbuthnot. *Children and Books*. 8th revised ed. New York: HarperCollins, 1991.

Swinfen, Ann. *In Defence of Fantasy: A Study of the Genre in English and American Literature since 1945*. London: Rutledge & Kegan Paul, 1984.

Tatar, Maria. *Off With Their Heads! Fairy Tales and the Culture of Childhood*. Princeton, NJ: Princeton University Press, 1992.

Taylor, Judy. *Beatrix Potter: Artist, Storyteller and Countrywoman*. London: Warne, 1986.

Thacker, Debora Cogan, and Jean Webb. *Introducing Children's Literature: From Romanticism to Poststructuralism*. London: Routledge: 2002.

Thompson, John B. *Critical Hermeneutics: A Study in the Thought of Paul Ricoeur and Jürgen Habermas*. Cambridge: Cambridge University Press, 1981.

Todorov, Tzvetan. *The Fantastic: A Structural Approach to a Literary Genre*. Cleveland: Press of Case Western Reserve University, 1973.

———. *The Poetics of Prose*. Ithaca, NY: Cornell University Press, 1977.

———. *Mikhail Bakhtin: The Dialogical Principle*. Manchester: Manchester University Press, 1984.

———. *Genres in Discourse*. Cambridge: Cambridge University Press, 1990.

Tomlinson, Carl M. *Children's Books from Other Countries*. Lanham, MD: Scarecrow, 1998.

Tompkins, Jane P., ed. *Reader-Response Criticism: From Formalism to Post-Structuralism*. Baltimore: The Johns Hopkins University Press, 1980.

Torrance, Robert M. *The Comic Hero*. Cambridge, MA: Harvard University Press, 1978.

Townsend, John Rowe. *Written for Children: An Outline of English-Language Children's Literature*. 6th ed. London: Bodley Head, 1990.

Travisano, Thomas. "Of Dialectic and Divided Consciousness: Intersection between Children's Literature and Childhood Studies." *Children's Literature* 28 (2000): 22–29.

Treglown, Jeremy. *Roald Dahl: A Biography*. London: Faber & Faber, 1994.

Trites, Roberta Seelinger. *Waking Sleeping Beauty: Feminist Voices in Children's Novels*. Iowa City: University of Iowa Press, 1997.

———. *Disturbing the Universe: Power and Repression in Adolescent Literature*. Iowa City: University of Iowa Press, 2000.

Tucker, Nicholas. *The Child and the Book: A Psychological and Literary Exploration*. Cambridge: Cambridge University Press, 1981.

Tucker, Nicholas, and Nikki Gamble. *Family Fictions*. London: Continuum, 2001.

Tunnell, Michael O., and James S. Jacobs. *Children's Literature Briefly*. 2nd ed. Upper Saddle River, NJ: Merrill, 2000.

Twaite, Ann. *A. A. Milne: His Life*. London: Faber, 1990.

———. *Waiting for a Party: The Life of Frances Hodgson Burnett*. London: Faber, 1994.

Uspensky, Boris. *A Poetics of Composition: The Structure of the Artistic Text and Typology of a Compositional Form*. Berkeley, CA: University of California Press, 1973.

Vandergrift, Kay, ed. *Ways of Knowing: Literature and the Intellectual Life of Children*. Lanham, MD: Scarecrow, 1996.

Veglahn, Nancy. "Images of Evil: Male and Female Monsters in Heroic Fantasy." *Children's Literature* 15 (1987): 106–119.

Vesser, Aram H., ed. *The New Historicism*. London: Routledge, 1989.

von Wright, Georg Henrik. *Explaining and Understanding*. Ithaca, NY: Cornell University Press, 1971.

Waddey, Lucy E. "Home in Children's Fiction: Three Patterns." *Children's Literature Association Quarterly* 8, no. 1 (1983): 13–15.

Wadsworth, Ginger. *Laura Ingalls Wilder: Storyteller of the Prairie*. Minneapolis: Lerner, 1997.

Wall, Barbara. *The Narrator's Voice: The Dilemma of Children's Fiction*. London: Macmillan, 1991.

Warhol, Robyn R., and Diane Price Herndl, eds. *Feminisms: An Anthology of Literary Theory and Criticism*. New Brunswick, NJ: Rutgers University Press, 1977.

Warner, Marina. *From the Beast to the Blonde: On Fairy Tales and Their Tellers*. New York: Farrar, Straus and Giroux, 1994.

———. *Six Myths of Our Time: Little Angels, Little Monsters, Beautiful Beasts, and More*. New York: Vintage, 1994.

———. *No Go the Bogeyman: Scaring, Lulling, and Making Mock*. New York: Farrar, Straus and Giroux, 1998.

Watson, Victor. *Reading Series Fiction: From Arthur Ransome to Gene Kemp*. London: Routledge, 2000.

Watson, Victor, ed. *The Cambridge Guide to Children's Books in English*. Cambridge: Cambridge University Press, 2001.

Waugh, Patricia. *Metafiction: The Theory and Practice of Self-Conscious Fiction*. London: Methuen, 1984.

Webb, Jean, ed. *Text, Culture and National Identity in Children's Literature*. Helsinki: Nordinfo, 2000.

Weaver, Warren. *Alice in Many Tongues: The Translations of Alice in Wonderland*. Madison: University of Winconsin Press, 1964.

Weinreich, Torben. *Children's Literature: Art or Pedagogy?* Roskilde, Denmark: Roskilde University Press, 2000.

Wellek, René, and Austin Warren. *Theory of Literature* (1949). Harmondsworth: Penguin, 1963.

West, Mark I. *Roald Dahl*. New York: Twayne, 1992.

Westfall, Gary, and George Edgar Slusser. *Nursery Realms: Children in the Worlds of*

Science Fiction, Fantasy, and Horror. Athens, GA: University of Georgia Press, 1999.

Whalley, Joyce Irene, and Tessa Rose Chester. *A History of Children's Book Illustration.* London: John Murray, 1988.

White, Dorothy Neal. *Books Before Five.* New York: Oxford University Press, 1954.

White, E. B. *The Annotated Charlotte's Web.* Edited by Peter Neumeyer. New York: HarperCollins, 1994.

Whited, Lana A., ed. *The Ivory Tower and Harry Potter: Perspectives on a Literary Phenomenon.* Columbia: University of Missouri Press, 2002.

Wiggins, Genevieve. *L. M. Montgomery.* New York: Twayne, 1992.

Wilkie-Stibbs, Christie. *The Feminine Subject in Children's Literature.* New York: Routledge, 2002.

Williams, Raymond. *Marxism and Literature.* Oxford: Oxford University Press, 1977.

————. *The Country and the City.* London: The Hoggarth Press, 1993.

Wilson, Andrew Norman. *C. S. Lewis: A Biography.* London: Collins, 1990.

Wilson, Raymond. "Slake's Limbo: A Myth-Critical Approach." *Children's Literature in Education* 18, no. 4 (1987): 219–226.

Wimsatt, William K. *The Verbal Icon: Studies in the Meaning of Poetry.* Lexington, KY: University of Kentucky Press, 1954.

Wolf, Anne Shelby, and Shirley Brice Heath. *The Braid of Literature: Children's Worlds of Reading.* Cambridge, MA: Harvard University Press, 1992.

Wolf, Virginia L. "Paradise Lost? The Displacement of Myth in Children's Novels." *Studies in the Literary Imagination* 18, no. 2 (1985): 47–64.

————. "The Cycle of Seasons: Without and Within Time." *Children's Literature Association Quarterly* 10, no. 4 (1986): 192–196.

————. *Louise Fitzhugh.* New York: Twayne, 1991.

Woolf, Virginia. *A Room of One's Own* (1929). San Diego: Harcourt Brace Jovanovich, 1989.

Worton, Michael, and Judith Still. *Intertextuality: Theories and Practices.* Manchester: Manchester University Press, 1990.

Wullschläger, Jackie. *Inventing Wonderland: The Lives and Fantasies of Lewis Carroll, Edward Lear, J. M. Barrie, Kenneth Grahame and A. A. Milne.* London: Methuen, 1995.

————. *Hans Christian Andersen: The Life of a Storyteller.* New York: Knopf, 2001.

Wyile, Andrea Schwenke. "Expanding the View of First-Person Narration." *Children's Literature in Education* 30, no. 4 (1999): 185–202.

————. "The Value of Singularity in First- and Restricted Third-person Engaging Narration." *Children's Literature* 31 (2003): 116–141.

Young, Robert, ed. *Untying the Text: A Post-structuralist Reader.* London: Routledge, 1980.

Zipes, Jack. *Breaking the Magic Spell: Radical Theories of Folk and Fairy Tales.* Austin: University of Texas Press, 1979.

————. *Fairy Tales and the Art of Subversion.* New York: Wildman, 1983.

————. *Fairy Tale as Myth, Myth as Fairy Tale.* Lexington, KY: University of Kentucky Press, 1994.

————. *Happily Ever After: Fairy Tales, Children and the Culture Industry*. New York: Routledge, 1997.

————. *When Dreams Came True: Classical Fairy Tales and Their Tradition*. New York: Routledge, 1999.

————. *Sticks and Stones: The Troublesome Success of Children's Literature from Slovenly Peter to Harry Potter*. New York: Routledge, 2001.

Zipes, Jack, ed. *The Oxford Companion to Fairy Tales*. Oxford: Oxford University Press, 2000.

Zornado, John. *Inventing the Child: Culture, Ideology, and the Rise of Childhood*. New York: Garland, 2000.

Subject and Name Index

Title Index

About the Author

Maria Nikolajeva is a professor of comparative literature at Stockholm University (Sweden) and associate professor of comparative literature at Åbo Akademi University (Finland), where she teaches children's literature and literary theory. She is the author and editor of several critical works on children's literature, among them *Children's Literature Comes of Age: Toward the New Aesthetic* (Garland 1996), a ChLA Honor Book, *From Mythic to Linear: Time in Children's Literature* (Scarecrow 2000), and *The Rhetoric of Character in Children's Literature* (Scarecrow 2002). She was the president of the International Research Society for Children's Literature from 1993 to 1997. She is also one of the senior editors of the *Oxford Encyclopedia of Children's Literature*.